AF361258

ERASMUS AND CALVIN ON THE FOOLISHNESS OF GOD

Reason and Emotion in the Christian Philosophy

KIRK ESSARY

Erasmus and Calvin on the Foolishness of God

Reason and Emotion in the Christian Philosophy

UNIVERSITY OF TORONTO PRESS
Toronto Buffalo London

ISBN 978-1-4875-0188-4

♾ Printed on acid-free, 100% post-consumer recycled paper with
vegetable-based inks.

Library and Archives Canada Cataloguing in Publication

Essary, Kirk, 1984–, author
Erasmus and Calvin on the foolishness of God : reason and
emotion in the Christian philosophy / Kirk Essary.

(Erasmus studies)
Includes bibliographical references and index.
ISBN 978-1-4875-0188-4 (cloth)

1. Erasmus, Desiderius, – 1536 – Criticism and interpretation.   2. Erasmus,
Desiderius, – 1536 – Influence.   3. Calvin, Jean, 1509–1564 – Criticism and
interpretation.   4. Christian philosophy – History – 16th century.
5. Theology – History – 16th century.   6. Paul, the Apostle, Saint –
Influence.   7. Bible. Epistles of Paul – Criticism, interpretation, etc.
I. Title.   II. Series: Erasmus studies

BR350.E7 E87 2017   199'.492   C2016-908095-1

University of Toronto Press acknowledges the financial assistance to its
publishing program of the Canada Council for the Arts and the Ontario Arts
Council, an agency of the Government of Ontario.

Funded by the   Financé par le
Government   gouvernement
of Canada   du Canada

Canadä

Contents

Acknowledgments

This book was completed with the help of a number of teachers, colleagues, and friends. I am forever grateful, in the first place, to François Dupuigrenet Desroussilles, who enthusiastically encouraged a project on foolishness and biblical interpretation, in addition to the ostensibly more elusive topic of Calvin's Erasmianism. François' boundless erudition will always serve as a boon and an inspiration. I owe a great deal as well to other faculty members in the Department of Religion at Florida State University, all of whom provided guidance and helpful comments on this work in its first iteration. David Levenson long served as a mentor and became a friend, and his unrelenting emphasis on the importance of close reading heavily informs the approach taken in this book. John Kelsay was a faithful guide through Calvin's *Institutes* and could always be counted on for healthy theological disputation at Tallahassee's Leon Pub. Reinier Leushuis welcomed me into the world of Erasmus studies and has continued to help me find my way through it, and I'm thankful to count him as a colleague.

For the opportunity to put to the finishing touches on the book, I am thoroughly indebted to the Australian Research Council Centre of Excellence for the History of Emotions (Europe, 1100–1800), whose extraordinary name is surpassed in size only by the charity and collegiality of the researchers and administrators who constitute it. In particular, I am grateful to Yasmin Haskell for bringing me on as a postdoctoral research fellow and for her willingness to collaborate on various projects in early modern intellectual history. Many of the ideas in this book, especially those to do with the history of emotions, benefited from the many conversations I've had at the University of Western Australia and at CHE symposia across Australia from the beginning of 2015. I have also taken advantage of the kindness of Calvin scholars outside my institutional settings, and I am especially thankful to Barbara Pitkin for her continuous encouragement over the past few years. Special thanks as well to Ward Holder and Randall Zachman, who were gracious in offering perceptive comments on an early chapter draft despite never (or only briefly in the case of Ward) having met me. Two anonymous reviewers for the University of Toronto Press read the manuscript with keen eyes and offered insightful suggestions for improvement. I hope to have done them all justice, and I bear the responsibility for any shortcomings.

Finally, I must thank my dear partner Dalina, who willingly accompanied me from Brooklyn to the mysterious antipodes of Western Australia. Without her constant support I couldn't have finished this book.

Abbreviations and Early Modern Editions

Note on Texts and Translations

I made use of good modern English translations of sixteenth-century texts where available, occasionally with modifications. Otherwise, translations of primary sources are my own. The Latin or French original is provided in the notes, taken either from reliable modern editions or from sixteenth-century printed editions.

Common Abbreviations for Modern Editions

ASD   *Opera omnia Desiderii Erasmi Roterodami* (Amsterdam, 1969–). Cited by *ordo*, volume, and page number.

LB   *Desiderii Erasmi Roterodami opera omnia* (ed. Jean LeClerc, 10 vols. [Leiden, 1703–6]). Cited by volume, column, and column section number.

CWE   *Collected Works of Erasmus*. 1974–. Ed. Richard J. Schoeck, and Beatrice Corrigan. Toronto: University of Toronto Press.

CO   *Calvini Opera* (*Opera Quae Supersunt Omnia*, ed. Guilielmus Baum, Eduardus Cunitz, Eduardus Reuss); *Corpus Reformatorum* Series II (vols. 29–87).

COR   *Ioannis Calvini opera omnia denuo recognita et adnotatione critica instructa notisque illustrata*. Geneva, Droz, 1992–.

Early Modern Editions Commonly Cited

Erasmus' New Testament *and* Annotations

– *Novum Instrumentum omne: diligenter ab Erasmo Roterodamo recognitum and emendatum ... una cum Annotationibus*. Basel: Johannes Froben, 1516.

- *Novum Testamentum ... cum Annotationibus.* Basel: Johannes Froben, 1539–40.
- *Erasmus' Annotations on the New Testament: Romans, I and II Corinthians: Facsimile of the Final Latin Text with All Earlier Variants* (ed. Anne Reeve and M.A. Screech; Leiden: Brill, 1990).

Erasmus' Paraphrases

- *Paraphrasis in duas epistolas Pauli ad Corinthios.* Basel: Joannes Froben, 1519.
- *Tomus primus Paraphraseon Des. Erasmi Roterodami in Novum Testamentum.* Basel: Johannes Froben, 1541.
- *Tomus secundus continens Paraphrasim in omnes epistolas apostolicas.* Basel: Johannes Froben, 1532. ·

Calvin's New Testament Commentaries

- *Joannis Calvini commentarii, in quatuor Pauli Epistolas: ad Galatas, ad Ephesios, ad Philippenses, ad Colossenses.* Geneva: Jean Girard, 1548.
- *In omnes Pauli apostoli Epistolas, atque etiam in Epistolam ad Hebraeos, item in canonicas Petri, Johannis, Jacobi, et Judae, quae etiam catholicae vocantur, Joh. Calvini Commentarii.* Geneva: Robert Estienne, 1556.
- *Harmonia ex tribus Evangelistis composita, Matthaeo, Marco, et Luca ... cum Johannis Calvini commentariis.* Geneva: Nicolas Barbier & Thomas Courteau, 1563.

Calvin's Institutes of the Christian Religion

- *Institutio christianae religionis.* Geneva: Robert Estienne, 1559.

Heinrich Bullinger

- *In priorem D. Pauli ad Corinthios epistolam.* Zurich: Froschauer, 1534.
- *In D. Apostoli Pauli ad Galatas, Ephesios, Phillipen. et Colossenses epistolas.* Zurich: Froschauer, 1535.
- *In sacrosanctum Iesu Christi domini nostri Evangelium secundum Matthaeum commentariorum libri XII.* Zurich: Froschauer, 1542.

Philip Melanchthon

- *Brevis et utilis commentarius in priorem epistolam Pauli ad Corinthios.* Wittenberg: Johannes Crato, 1561.

Konrad Pellikan

- *In omnes apostolicas epistolas, Pauli, Petri, Iacobi, Ioannis, et Iudae.* Zurich: Froschauer, 1539.

Huldrych Zwingli/Leo Jud

- *Annotatiunculae per Leonem Iudae, ex ore Zvinglij in utranq; Pauli ad Corinthios Epistolam publice exponentis conceptae.* Zurich: Froschauer, 1528.

Preface

The poet only asks to get his head into the heavens. It is the logician who seeks to get the heavens into his head. And it is his head that splits.

– G.K. Chesterton

Nonne infatuavit deus sapientiam mundi huius? Thus Erasmus, and Calvin after him, render Paul's Greek at 1 Corinthians 1:20. "Has God not made foolish the wisdom of this world?" It is a rhetorical question: according to Paul, God had indeed. And alongside his denunciations of human wisdom in his first letter to the Corinthian churches, Paul further writes that he had refrained from using human forms of eloquence in his preaching to the new Christians at Corinth. Though he knew that they had desired solid food, Paul, realizing their shortcomings, fed them only milk. Paul's insistence that the cross of Christ is an offence and stumbling block to those who try to comprehend it through human reason and the mundane philosophies which attend it, or who try to express it with the eloquence of the Greek and Roman orators, led prominent sixteenth-century interpreters to suggest that an alternative religious epistemology, as well as a new method of teaching, is necessary for Christian wisdom to be fully realized. In the dedicatory epistle to Erard de la Marck, Bishop of Liège, appended to the 1519 edition of his *Paraphrase* on 1 and 2 Corinthians, Erasmus describes the situation in first-century Corinth (and, it might be pointed out, in sixteenth-century Europe as well):

> Such a mass of weeds sprang up, which almost overwhelmed Christ's sowing while it was still young and still in the blade; nor was it long before

> worldly philosophy and Jewish superstition, as though they had delib-
> erately joined forces, were conspiring against Christ. Philosophy threw
> doubt on the resurrection and began to some extent to spoil the simplicity
> of the gospel with quibbles of men's making ... Philosophy at that time, led
> by sage fools (*morosophos*) with tongue and pen and even by tyrants with
> the sword, was advancing against Christ's small and innocent flock and
> has left traces which remain to this day.[1]

A student of Erasmus immediately recognizes here the language of the *philosophia Christi* or, perhaps more accurately, the *philosophia Christiana* (a designation he uses vastly more often), which encourages simplicity in teaching and concord in the Church. Not very subtle either is a reference to the contemporary situation, and more specifically to Erasmus' and other biblical humanists' contentions against a form of university theology which they thought brought unnecessary complications (*humanis argutiis*) to what was supposed to have been a simple gospel.

Erasmus had already gestured towards the importance of Pauline folly and its attendant methodology for his conception of the Christian philosophy in the preface to his revolutionary *Novum Instrumentum* – the first-ever published Greek edition of the New Testament accompanied by a fresh Latin translation in parallel columns – a work that would shake the foundations of sixteenth-century biblical studies and theology. One of several prefatory works to Erasmus' new New Testament was, in a later edition, subtitled "an exhortation to the study of the Christian philosophy" (full title: *Paraclesis, id est, adhortatio ad christiane philosophiae studium*). The *Paraclesis* begins with a contrast between Christian and Ciceronian eloquence, and an elaboration on the title: "so long as I exhort all men to the most holy and wholesome study of Christian philosophy and summon them as if with the blast of a trumpet, that an eloquence far different from Cicero's be given me: an eloquence certainly much more efficacious, if less ornate, than his."[2] Wishing that "if Peitho moves any heart" his own exhortation too would persuade all of the wholesome truth, Erasmus then acknowledges that Christ, rather, would "deeply affect and move the minds of all," without need of the proclamations and exclamations of the orators.[3] Several comparisons of Christ with ancient philosophers as well as Christianity with pagan philosophies follow, the purpose being to encourage his readers to study the *Christian* philosophy above all others, and to do so with pious rather than profane curiosity.[4]

"This kind of wisdom," Erasmus continues, "so extraordinary that once for all it renders foolish the entire wisdom of this world, may be drawn from its few books as from the most limpid springs with far less labor than Aristotle's doctrine is extracted from so many obscure volumes."[5] Unlike the unnecessarily obscure nature of other philosophies, "this one accommodates itself equally to all, lowers itself to the little ones, adjusts itself to their measure, nourishing them with milk."[6] Thus, in Erasmus' preface to the New Testament we find outlined his Pauline doctrine of accommodation, infused with themes from 1 Corinthians, together constituting an outline of his attempts to articulate a renewed approach to theological study and discourse. Repeated appeals to the simplicity of the gospel, and arguments for democratic access to it in the form of vernacular versions, run through the economical exhortation. Not just "little women," but Scots and Turks should have access to the biblical text, and a farmer should sing its verses at the plow, all thus becoming the true theologians. "This kind of philosophy," Erasmus writes, "is seated in emotions rather than in syllogisms, is a life rather than a disputation, inspiration rather than erudition, transformation rather than reason."[7] The Christian philosophy is an affective rather than purely intellectual endeavour.

John Calvin, in his commentary on 1 Corinthians, first published in Strasbourg in 1546, writes that the "foolishness of preaching" described by Paul at 1 Cor. 1:21 is not truly foolish, but is only regarded as such "by those sage fools (*morosophoi*), who, drunk on false confidence, hold nothing sacred when it comes to subjecting the inviolable truth of God to their own tasteless censorship."[8] The Greek term *morosophos* used here first appears in Lucian, but Calvin almost certainly borrowed it from Erasmus, who, apart from the instance cited above, uses it multiple times throughout his vast oeuvre.[9] It would be only one of many examples of the positive reception of Erasmus' exegesis to be found in Calvin's commentaries, and the primary purpose of this book is to examine the relationship between these two exegetes from the perspective of their reception of Pauline folly and their conceptions of what they both called a *philosophia Christiana*. Interpretations of Paul's discourse on worldly wisdom and divine folly bore implications not only for abstruse debates among intellectuals over propriety in sixteenth-century academic theology, but also for approaches to Christian preaching, and for conceptions of religious knowing and feeling in the Christian tradition.

The reception of Paul's discourse on the foolishness and wisdom of God is itself a fascinating and seriously neglected topic in the history of biblical interpretation. In the words of L.L. Welborn, from his study on the Greco-Roman context of 1 Corinthians 1–4, "the assumption of self-evidence and the familiarity of the theme have erected an invisible barrier to exploration of one of Paul's most astonishing formulations. Until such an investigation is undertaken, a chapter in the history of Christian theology remains unread, and it is one of the most interesting."[10] What's at stake in taking Paul's condemnations of worldly wisdom seriously is the extent to which the human disciplines of philosophy and rhetoric ought to be explicitly permitted to undergird theological discourse – an issue of perennial import, whether explicit or implicit, in the history of Christian thought. The tension involved in negotiating the contours of Paul's "astonishing formulations" in the intellectual context of sixteenth-century biblical humanism are illustrated in Calvin's comments on 1 Cor. 3:19 ("For the wisdom of the world is folly in the eyes of God"):

> This is an argument from the contrary. The confirmation of the one means the destruction of the other. Therefore since the wisdom of this world is foolishness with God, it follows that the only way we can be wise in God's sight is to be foolish in the world's ... for natural insight is a gift of God. The arts men naturally pursue, and all the disciplines by which wisdom is acquired are also gifts of God. But they have their definite limits, for they do not penetrate into the heavenly Kingdom of God. Accordingly, they ought to be maid-servants, not mistresses. Besides that, they must be looked upon as useless and worthless until they are subordinated completely to the Word and Spirit of God. But if they set themselves up against Christ they must be considered injurious pests. If they maintain that they are capable of anything by themselves, they must be regarded as the worst of hindrances.[11]

Calvin is clear that worldly wisdom is insufficient for understanding the mysteries of God, but he is always careful to avoid an apparent lapse into philistinism. The early chapters of 1 Corinthians serve as a substantial foundational text for the articulation of the methodological underpinnings of a "Christian philosophy" for Erasmus and for Calvin. Exegesis of these chapters lies at the very heart of their approaches to theology at a time when questions about the nature of theology and how it ought to be carried out took on great significance for a quite prominent group of European intellectuals. In the exegetical writings of Erasmus and Calvin on Pauline folly one finds excurses on epistemology, anthropology, Christology, and the role of rhetoric in theological discourse, not to mention exhortations to humility, utility, and efficacy in developing a Pauline approach to Christian learned piety. Moreover, the language of a theology of foolishness makes its way into a number of other works by Erasmus and Calvin, both exegetical and not. This is not surprising, of course, given the importance of Paul and Paulinism in sixteenth-century Christianity. But "Paulinism" is a rather malleable category, as Paul himself was, in the words of Erasmus, a chameleon.[12] While Richard Muller can refer to the "Pauline center of biblical interpretation" in describing Calvin's *Melanchthonian* approach to method, the law/gospel dichotomy that pervades Melanchthon's exegesis is only one aspect of his Paulinism, and Melanchthon is not always the most fitting forerunner for understanding Calvin's reception of Paul. As Bruce Gordon has noted, Calvin's Paul, like Erasmus', is multidimensional: "the educated Jew well versed in the Law; the rhetorician addressing the Greeks and Romans in classical terms; the towering figure of authority; the patient pastor, full of love and humility."[13]

Lutherans did not monopolize Paul in the early sixteenth century, however hard they tried. Erasmus published his *Paraphrase on Romans* in November 1517, just as Wittenberg was first becoming acquainted with Luther's *Ninety-Five Theses*, which he had sent to Albert of Brandenberg, Archbishop of Mainz, on 31 October (a moment whose quincentennial commemoration is already beginning to overshadow celebrations of Erasmus' 1516 *Novum Instrumentum* as this book goes to press at the end of 2016). Erasmus, too, thought of Paul as the "foremost interpreter of our religion," as he puts it in his dedicatory epistle to the *Paraphrases* on 1 and 2 Corinthians. And as Gordon points out further, Calvin's multifaceted reception of, and attempt to emulate, Paul "derived from his reading of Erasmus."[14] The rich content of the unit comprising 1 Corinthians 1–4 provides us with an opportunity to examine some of the ways in which Erasmus' Paul was taken up and modified by the next generation's foremost interpreter. A comparison of their interpretations and use of Pauline folly will provide not only a portrait of the significance of a comparatively neglected Pauline text in the history of interpretation for the broader history of ideas in early modern Christian thought, but also a fertile context for studying the relationship between Erasmus and Calvin, two of the most influential readers of the Bible in the history of Christianity.

Sustained analysis of Erasmus' influence on one subsequent thread of the Protestant biblical-humanist exegetical tradition has several distinct advantages. First of all, the reception of a multivalent Pauline text has implications in a number of diverse areas of theology from a cross-confessional perspective. More broadly, it opens up the possibility for illuminating further the complexities involved in the relationship between the "Renaissance" and "Reformation" or "humanist" and "reformer" from an exegetical perspective – and it further exposes the problematic nature of using these terms and others related to them as exclusive categories. Finally, it allows us to take advantage of the relatively recent scholarly appreciation of Erasmus the theologian from the perspective of his reception in Calvin's thought, as well as his influence on other sixteenth-century thinkers. Such a study might take various forms, and a comparative analysis of the reception of Pauline folly and related texts is necessarily limited to certain themes and sixteenth-century works. This book is not meant to serve as a comprehensive study of Calvin's Erasmianism, nor as a comprehensive account of the exegetical influences on Calvin's reception of Pauline folly. Rather, it represents an attempt to demonstrate that Erasmus and Calvin were operating in a common interpretive and theological milieu in virtue of their understanding and use of certain New Testament texts, including 1 Corinthians 1–4, Colossians 2, and the Gethsemane scene in the synoptic gospels. This book, finally, is not only about reception history, but it takes biblical interpretation as a starting point from which to examine assumptions about the nature of theology in the sixteenth century, how it was understood by leading humanist reformers, and how ideas about philosophy and rhetoric were received, appropriated, and shared in a complex intellectual and religious context.

Chapter 1 introduces the historiographical and methodological questions of the book, and then considers Erasmus' and Calvin's dedicatory letters for their exegetical works on 1 Corinthians. Chapters 2, 3, and 4 consist of an analysis of the exegesis of Paul's discourse on folly in the first half of the sixteenth century. These chapters offer a close comparison of the translations and interpretations of Paul's letter by Erasmus and Calvin, but they also refer to other interpretations and sixteenth-century readings (primarily those of Heinrich Bullinger and Konrad Pellikan, who are clearly indebted to Erasmus' exegetical works, and whose works Calvin also would have read). Chapters 2 and 3 focus primarily on the question of the role of Pauline folly in the religious epistemologies of Erasmus and Calvin. The analysis follows the order and main themes of the first two chapters of 1 Corinthians in order to give readers an idea of the similarities and differences of the sixteenth-century reception of Paul in this respect.

Chapter 4 considers the implications of Paul's claims to ineloquence in Erasmus' and Calvin's reception of 1 Corinthians, and the importance of a shared conception of rhetorical and theological accommodation in their thought. The role of rhetoric in theological discourse and in Christian teaching and preaching comes to the fore here. I argue that Erasmus and Calvin advocated for a similar *theologia rhetorica* based on Paul's reformulations of eloquence rooted in his writing about the folly of the cross, which was to employ simple and unadulterated discourse that is, at least theoretically, altogether different from both philosophical dialectic (which, in the eyes of Erasmus and Calvin is often abstruse and superfluous) and classical rhetorical eloquence (which, to them, is overly ornate and distracting). In Calvin's commentary in particular it becomes clear that this issue needs to be handled with kid gloves, given, on the one hand, his biblical-humanist interest in learned piety (itself an Erasmian impetus, taken up by Melanchthon and a number of other sixteenth-century Protestants) and, on the other, Paul's explicitly stated rejection of classical eloquence. The significance of Pauline accommodation, an important aspect of these exegetes' reception of this text, is shown here to be a meaningful common factor in Erasmus' and Calvin's attempts to defend, and elevate as a model, Paul as the Christian pedagogue par excellence.

Chapters 5 and 6 examine the significance of a conception of the Christian philosophy from the perspective of works outside the commentaries on 1 Corinthians in the sixteenth century. They show how far-reaching the implications of taking Paul's discourse on folly seriously can be in the construction of Christian philosophies by the biblical humanists. Chapter 5 analyses the reception of Paul's use of the word *philosophia* in Colossians 2:8 by Erasmus, Melanchthon, Bullinger, Pellikan, and Calvin. It compares the translations and interpretations of key concepts from Colossians 2 in these authors' commentaries in order to provide a broader view of how Paul's ideas were understood in a wider Christian-humanist context, and also to connect the Pauline criticism of *philosophia* to the discourse on foolishness, which connection is explicit in the exegetical works themselves. It then turns to the definitions of the *philosophia Christiana* in Erasmus and Calvin in comparison with treatments of the concept in the twentieth century, and shows how the "Christian philosophy" was grounded in the Pauline texts under consideration in previous chapters.

Chapter 6 maps the connections between the reception of Pauline folly and the importance of affectivity in the exegetical theologies of Erasmus and Calvin. Affectivity plays a fundamental role in sixteenth-century religious thought, something increasingly appreciated by historians of the period, and thus I will consider its significance in the context of the Christian philosophy by examining the interpretation of Christ's emotions in the Gospels, in theological and exegetical works, and in a sermon. The diminution of reason as unequivocal hegemon in biblical-humanist anthropology and epistemology makes room for a fuller appreciation of the role of the emotions in piety and in theological discourse in their works. This becomes clear not only in Erasmus' and Calvin's criticisms of the "frigid" philosophizing of university theologians, but also in their understanding of certain New Testament scenes; for example, Christ's fear and sorrow in the Garden of Gethsemane.

An exhaustive reception history would consider not only the direct exegetical material on a passage, or textual unit, but its appearance (explicit or only through reverberation) in other contexts, whether theological, literary, or otherwise. However, the sheer volume of works produced by Erasmus and Calvin, and their persistent interest in issues relevant to their reception of Pauline folly, make a complete inventory of such references impracticable, much less a consideration of their unique contexts. That said, while the relevance of foolish wisdom in other exegetical settings will become apparent from our studies in chapters 5 and 6, there are notable texts in Erasmus' and Calvin's corpora where foolishness features heavily as an important rhetorical-theological device. Thus, at the end of chapters 2, 3, and 4, respectively, the reader will find brief excurses on the role of Pauline folly in Erasmus' immensely popular satire *The Praise of Folly*, in Calvin's theological masterwork the *Institutes of the Christian Religion*, and on its connection to Christ's kenosis (from Philippians 2). This will allow readers to see, if in a limited way, how ideas laid out in an exegetical context are carried over into broader literary and theological works (or vice versa), which further demonstrates their fundamental role in Erasmus' and Calvin's theologies in general, connects them to other areas of their thought, and situates them in the broader intellectual and religious context of sixteenth-century biblical humanism.

ERASMUS AND CALVIN ON THE FOOLISHNESS OF GOD

Reason and Emotion in the Christian Philosophy

Chapter One

Calvin's Erasmus, *Theologia Rhetorica,* and Pauline Folly

Thus is apparent the barbarous tyranny with which the *theologastri* violently castigated Erasmus for changing one word for the better.

– Calvin, *Commentary on John* 1:1

Calvin's Erasmus

Erasmus' New Testament scholarship was extraordinarily influential across Europe throughout the sixteenth century. In 1516 he provided the (highly) educated public with the first opportunity to consult the Greek original in printed form, complete with a controversial alternative Latin translation to the Vulgate, which latter had been the predominant version in the West since the early Middle Ages. From the first edition, he appended *annotationes* to the text, which consisted early on primarily of philological notes and justifications for his alternative translation, but through successive editions came to contain more and more theological and historical commentary.[1] These versions, with the notes, would become standard editions for Protestant exegetes as well as editors and translators of new Latin and/or vernacular editions. But also, beginning in 1517, with Paul's letter to the Romans, Erasmus began publishing *Paraphrases* of the books of the New Testament in Latin, all of which (excluding Revelation, which he never paraphrased) were in print by 1524, and they were followed closely by translations into vernacular languages.[2] The *Paraphrases* offer readers (ostensibly, at any rate) a more accessible version of the text – a 1522 Froben edition of paraphrases of all the NT epistles describes them on the title page as a *liberior ac dilucidior interpretatio* (a more free and clearer version) – but they also contain clear instances of Erasmus' own theological disposition through the translations themselves, in amplifications of the text, and in decidedly sixteenth-century theological determinations.[3] That they constitute a kind of commentary is not only confirmed by a number of recent scholarly studies,[4] but also in the fact that early modern readers recognized them as more than literal paraphrases. This is true not only of Erasmus' allies (in Konrad Pellikan's ample borrowings for his own commentaries, for example), but also of his enemies (Noel Beda, in the words of Erika Rummel, "found what he considered to be significant theological errors in the *Paraphrases*" and published a critical review of them at the behest of the faculty of theology at Paris in 1526).[5] Taking the vast influence of his New Testament works into account, and including his literary and polemical works as well as the substantial number of editions of classical and patristic authors he edited and published (to say nothing of widely published popular works like the *Adagia* and the *Moria*), all of which were ubiquitous in Northern Europe from the fifteen-teens onwards, it becomes clear that the towering figure of Erasmus would have been unavoidable.[6]

This is confirmed in the case of John Calvin, as Erasmus' name appears more frequently than that of any other exegete in his New Testament commentaries.[7] An accounting of all the instances where Calvin uses the texts of Erasmus, whether the Greek or Latin versions of his *Novum Testamentum* or the *Annotations* and *Paraphrases* Erasmus composed in order to aid readers of the sacred text, would be enormous (and perhaps not very interesting to read).[8] T.H.L. Parker has alerted us already to Calvin's continued use of Erasmus in his New Testament commentaries, with special attention to the explicit disagreements, and Anthony Lane has demonstrated how Calvin's use of the sources he often criticizes can be a sign of subtle appreciation.[9] Parker has provided many examples (and compiled statistics) of Calvin's use of Erasmus' New Testament Latin translation, although the fact that he focuses on the explicit cases where Calvin disagrees with Erasmus is somewhat misleading: after all, Calvin adopts Erasmus' translation vastly more often than he rejects it, but we would not expect him to point out each case.[10] Nevertheless, Parker documents twenty-two new citations of Erasmus in the 1556 revised edition of the Romans commentary alone, demonstrating that Calvin never abandoned the works of Erasmus as a valuable source for biblical studies. A quick glance at the footnotes of Helmut Feld's critical editions of Calvin's commentaries on some of Paul's letters gives the reader an idea of how much Erasmus figured into the Reformer's New Testament studies, especially in his attempts to offer his own translation. In his introduction to the critical edition of Calvin's commentaries on Galatians, Ephesians, Philippians, and Colossians, Feld suggests that, in terms of sources he's wrestling with, Erasmus' *Annotations* have the most import for Calvin's commentary.[11]

In terms of judgment, Calvin's use of Erasmus, in conformity with his use of extrabiblical sources in general, is varied: he will happily criticize him and borrow from him in the same breath. He dismisses the Dutchman's "cavils" regarding his refusal to use Philippians 2:6 against the Arians, but defends his translation of *Logos* as *Sermo* in the Johannine prologue against Erasmus' scholastic critics. He uses him most when composing his own translations of New Testament works, which are embedded in his running commentaries. Unlike with Beza, however, who voiced his opinion about Erasmus in print, we are unable to construct anything like a "portrait" of Erasmus from the mind of Calvin, which, in the case of analysing his debts to him, is probably in fact a benefit.[12] We are left, rather, with the assessment of Erasmus' work as a philologist and exegetical theologian as it might be discerned in Calvin's commentaries on the New Testament. The fact that Calvin read his works closely and continued reading them throughout his life itself warrants closer scholarly attention to the ways in which he might have been indebted to the great Dutch humanist.

While Erasmus' influence on Calvin has not gone unacknowledged, given the stature of the two figures in their own time as well as their importance for posterity, the relative paucity of direct studies of their relationship is surprising. Studies of Calvin's humanism have long recognized that any humanistic study in the first half of the sixteenth century would have meant a substantial acquaintance with Erasmus' works.[13] William Bouwsma has put forth the strongest case for Calvin's Erasmianism in terms of a shared *theologia rhetorica*, and his work is directly relevant to our study.[14] In an early study, Francois Wendel suggests a broad influence of Erasmus on Calvin, discernible from his Seneca commentary throughout his career.[15] Almost any study of Calvin's hermeneutics must reckon with the prospects of Erasmus' influence, at least in passing.[16] Olivier Millet's massive and thorough work is especially important in situating Calvin's understanding of Christian rhetoric in its humanist context; and Erasmus' works, according to Millet, would be put to use by Calvin throughout his career, even if they served the function more of "classical texts in a student's hand than a strong personal influence," and even if he opposed certain of Erasmus' ideas.[17] Debora Kuller Shuger has shown, among other things, how much there is to be learned from a comparison of Erasmian and Calvinist readings of the suffering of Christ.[18]

In one of the few direct case studies of the influence of Erasmus' exegesis on Calvin's on any biblical text (in this case Galatians), Riemer Faber suggests in his conclusion that the *nachleben* of Erasmus on the Reformation has been underappreciated, something suggested also by studies of Erasmus' influence on other Protestant thinkers.[19] Christine Christ-von Wedel, for example, has analysed the reception of Erasmus among Zurich Reformers.[20] Aside from his direct reading of Erasmus, Calvin was very much a part of a network of theologians who owed a great deal to Erasmus for their approach to theology and exegesis. Of course each of these exegetes also went their own way, and none was a slavish devotee: the "ambivalent" reception of Erasmus, as Hilmar Pabel refers to it, was a common phenomenon especially among sixteenth-century Protestants.[21] Nevertheless, as N. Scott Amos puts it, Erasmus "exercised an enormous influence in his time, and in particular upon many of the first generation of Reformers – not only in their exegetical practice (a commonly accepted point), but also in their assumptions as to what constituted the task and purpose of theology."[22] Both of these aspects of the reception of Erasmus will be under consideration in what follows.

Clarifying the relationship between Erasmus and Calvin, which is at many points positive, is also important for reasons extending beyond the continent. Gregory Dodds' book, *Exploiting Erasmus*, analyses the significance of the reception of the *Paraphrases* in England, where, in 1547 by order of Edward VI – and at the behest of Cranmer and Nicholas Udall, both Protestants – they were to be placed in churches throughout the kingdom. Alongside Foxe's *Book of Martyrs* and Calvin's *Institutes* lay Erasmus' *Paraphrases* as one of the most significant theological works accessible to the layman during the English Reformation.[23] Of course, the irony was not lost on the Protestant translators of Erasmus' works, as Dodds points out: Miles Coverdale, translator of the Romans paraphrase, included William Tyndale's overtly Lutheran prologue to Romans by way of introduction to Erasmus' rendering. In any case, and without delving into the labyrinth of "Calvin vs. Calvinism" scholarship,[24] what's important for our purposes is that Dodds' description of Erasmus' paraphrases as "non-Calvinist," or as put to use by anti-Calvinists, while no doubt meaningful in the context of sixteenth- and seventeenth-century religious debates in England, might not apply to John Calvin's own reception of Erasmus' theology as it appears in his

New Testament works.[25] In other words, a further contribution of our study lies in pointing out that the later judgment of Erasmus by Calvinists, prevalent and vocal as it may have been, cannot be confused with the reception of Erasmus by Calvin himself.

There is a methodological problem looming. Analyses of "Erasmianism" have a long history in scholarship on the early modern period, and the subfield has undergone some important methodological changes in recent years.[26] The term "Erasmianism" itself has fallen into disfavour for its nebulousness, and there has been encouragement to focus on the reception of Erasmus by subsequent thinkers in order to determine how his ideas are moulded and shaped in the varied contexts of later traditions.[27] Like many scholarly constructs, "Erasmianism" has become problematic when employed to pick out an essential cluster of characteristics embodied, ostensibly, in the historical person of Erasmus, which characteristics (perhaps not all of them) are then identified in later thinkers or even entire intellectual or political movements that themselves thus obtain the same label. The problem is clear for any student reared in a contemporary historicist intellectual milieu: a monolithic Erasmus, even if such a person could be circumscribed, certainly doesn't survive intact in the manifold ways and contexts in which his works and ideas are received. As Enenkel puts it, "numerous, totally different intellectuals with extremely different opinions and convictions may be labeled 'Erasmians'," and thus the term is judged useless.[28] The language of "reception" thereby becomes more appropriate, along with a focus on the recipients of Erasmus' ideas, for these ideas invariably take on different shades of significance when employed by another thinker in a wholly other context, whether political, religious, or literary.

This is a useful approach when considering Calvin, whose large and complex theology differs in many crucial ways from Erasmus'. Furthermore, while we will argue for Erasmus' influence, based on much exegetical and theological common ground related to the reception of Pauline folly, we will also point to areas of divergence in Calvin's thoughts on the matter. Moreover, reception history, it should be pointed out, is not a science – we are almost never dealing with straightforward instances of Calvin's copying sections of text from Erasmus' works (as we find in Pellikan's approach, for example). And because Calvin was not only reading Erasmus, but in addition reading other exegetes who were also demonstrably reading Erasmus very closely, in cases where specific linguistic evidence cannot be adduced but where the force of an idea appears to be the same, it often becomes more accurate to speak of a common intellectual, exegetical, or interpretative milieu, which is nonetheless "Erasmian." Indeed, the fact that Calvin himself lists three Protestants – Melanchthon, Bullinger, Bucer – as his exegetical forebears in an oft-cited passage from the dedicatory epistle that prefaces his Romans commentary of 1539 might suggest that Erasmus' influence could easily be overstated.

In the first place, however, Calvin is expressly speaking of exegetes alive in his day (*hodie vivunt*), while Erasmus had died three years earlier. Furthermore, as Bruce Gordon points out in his biography of Calvin, his dedicatory letter in this way was more a deft rhetorical and political move, tying Calvin and Geneva to the other major centres of reform, than a comprehensive genealogy of the origins of his exegesis.[29] This is further confirmed by Joel Kok's work, which argues, first with respect to Bucer and then Bullinger, that Calvin seems to have been less indebted in his exegesis of Romans to those mentioned in the letter to Grynaeus than he had insinuated.[30] While Calvin no doubt read and used the works of these exegetes, explicit references to Erasmus dwarf all three combined. It is only through close-reading and comparison of exegetical works that the true nature of these relationships can be established. As for examining 1 Corinthians 1–4, some further potential methodological confusion in this regard will be alleviated by the fact that some of the usual suspects for sixteenth-century influence on Calvin didn't compose commentaries on the text: Neither Bucer nor Luther, for example, composed one, and Melanchthon's *Annotationes* of 1522 are – aside from being published without his permission by Luther, and having been written in his very early days at Wittenberg – brief in the extreme (although we will have occasion to refer to them).[31]

The necessity and heuristic usefulness of using the language of an exegetical or interpretative milieu can be illustrated with a brief example: Erasmus, Heinrich Bullinger, and Calvin all repeatedly denounce the use of *adminiculis* and *praesidia humana* (i.e., human "aids" or "props") for the purpose of grounding theological truth, and they use this language in similar contexts to similar ends in their commentaries on 1 Corinthians (and elsewhere). We know that Calvin read Erasmus closely, and Calvin himself says that he used Bullinger's commentaries on some level for his own exegesis. It is also demonstrably true that Bullinger followed Erasmus' NT translation along with his *Annotations* and *Paraphrases* closely when writing his own commentaries – he reproduces Erasmus' Latin New Testament verbatim (at least for the passages we examined) for the text he comments upon, and cites whole swaths of text from Erasmus' exegetical works in the commentary itself. This can be said with even more emphasis of Konrad Pellikan, whose edition of commentaries on all of Paul's letters was published in Zurich in 1539, and who reproduces entire paragraphs of Erasmus' *Paraphrase* on 1 Corinthians in his commentary without notice.[32] While there might be certain specific cases where we can determine which exegete Calvin had most closely at hand when writing, it isn't possible to know definitively one way or another, and there are decent reasons for assuming either one: Calvin *says* he's reading Bullinger, after all, so perhaps we take him at his word. On the other hand, he almost never cites Bullinger in his commentaries, and he repeatedly cites Erasmus, in which case Ockham's Razor would seem to stipulate that we settle on Erasmus as the primary source in such cases. Ultimately, this is likely a false dichotomy, and the reality was no doubt more complicated – Calvin could have had multiple texts at hand or could have been relying on memory in a particular case – which further makes the language of a common interpretative milieu often more appropriate. Thus, in considering the commentaries of Bullinger and Pellikan, in addition to Calvin, we are able to show just how influential Erasmus was, not only in establishing philological and exegetical methods that were taken up by Protestant commentators – something long recognized – but in articulating a Pauline position on the nature of theology in relation to philosophy and rhetoric.

Erasmus Theologus

We must take seriously the idea of "Erasmus the theologian" in the context of reception history of his New Testament works and not only look to his influence in areas of philology and text-criticism. Work on Erasmus' theology, which came on in full force in the 1970s, especially in North America, has clarified the nature of Erasmus' thought by making available and analysing theological works (and, especially, exegetical works) that had been theretofore comparatively neglected.[33] In the work of Manfred Hoffmann, to take one prominent example, we find an Erasmus whose interest in faith and piety is not an afterthought, but a central and determining feature of all his intellectual endeavours.[34] More generally, work on Renaissance philosophy and theology has revealed that humanist theologians were not mere grammarians and metaphysical relativists, even if they did believe that the schools' *quaestiones* and *disputationes* were often deleterious to a theology of moral substance.

At the heart of the matter is the role of rhetoric in theological discourse in Renaissance thought, and this relationship has been clarified in a variety of ways in the scholarly literature. Susan Schreiner, in her excellent work on certainty in the early modern period, has taken cues from Ernesto Grassi in pointing out that even the most ostensibly "rhetorical" of early modern thinkers bore substantial philosophical predispositions.[35] As Schreiner puts it, the dispute over rhetoric and philosophy in the early modern period was really a dispute over "where truth lay," and not an argument over whether it was accessible.[36]

One particular obstacle that it is necessary to move past for our study is the tendency, once quite common among historians of the period, to understand Renaissance thinkers as subscribing to a form of rhetorical theology which eschews a commitment to dogmatic truth in favour of a kind of scepticism, and which is interested in *mere* persuasion rather than Truth (a theology which *moves* but does not necessarily *convince*). This issue has direct bearing on the reception of Paul's teachings on wisdom and folly, given the significance 1 Corinthians 1–4 has for questions surrounding religious epistemology. Erasmus in particular has long been misunderstood for his ostensible penchant for scepticism, and it would seem that his debate with Luther over the freedom of the will, where he obliquely voiced (with some irony) his own sceptical tendencies, has done much in the way of preventing his influence on Protestants in other areas of thought and method from being fully appreciated. It is no longer tenable, however, to understand thinkers along the humanist theological trajectory from Petrarch to Erasmus as hard sceptics interested in *mere* persuasion.[37]

The past few decades have seen scholarship on Renaissance philosophy in general and on Erasmus' theology in particular that has complicated such generalizing accounts. Even if we adhere to Erasmus' debate with Luther, where Erasmus himself claimed to side with the sceptics on certain questions (especially what he deemed *adiaphora*), we find recent revisions in the scholarship.[38] Irena Backus has argued convincingly that, though Erasmus purported that he would rather side with the sceptics than *assert*, the entirety of the rest of the treatise is good evidence that Erasmus isn't a sceptic about free will, and that Erasmus' tendency to use phrases like "I do not wish to debate," e.g., are rhetorical ploys to gain favour with his audience and not abstentions from truth-seeking.[39] Earlier, Marjorie O'Rourke Boyle had clarified Erasmus' relationship to different types of scepticism in antiquity, arguing that Erasmus' particular Ciceronian brand of scepticism did not entail a refusal to make truth-claims.[40] Recently, Greta Kroeker has outlined Erasmus' evolving ideas about grace (towards a "Protestant" understanding) in his exegesis on Romans in the wake of his debates with Luther, which further suggests the importance of eschewing assumptions about similarity and difference among groups or thinkers perceived as utterly antagonistic.[41] As she puts it more generally regarding Erasmus as a theologian, "Contrary to the outmoded characterization of Erasmus as a theological amateur or even a theological invertebrate, his theological works demonstrate that he was neither a defender of orthodox piety nor a pagan philologist in search of grammatical gaps in scripture."[42] Erasmus can no longer be ignored as a theologian in his own right who exerted theological influence over his close readers.

The tendency persists, nevertheless, in more muted forms: John Monfasani, for example, in an otherwise excellent overview of Erasmus' knowledge and use of ancient philosophy, writes that "if the one essential component of the Christian dispensation is a virtuous life, then the gap between pagan *philosophia* and the *philosophia Christi* comes close to disappearing apart from the insistence on faith in Jesus Christ."[43] The remark doesn't do justice to the significance of "faith in Jesus Christ" for Erasmus, how complicated a thing it really is, and just how thoroughgoing for Erasmus' thought and his conception of the "Christian philosophy." Indeed, the scope of the designation *philosophia Christiana* as Erasmus employs it and as I use it in this book is broader than the typical scholarly understanding of Erasmus' *philosophia Christi*, the latter of which is generally assumed to describe Erasmus' theology as a kind of pragmatic moralism grounded in the precepts of Christ's ethical teachings. Erasmus seems to employ *philosophia Christiana* much more often throughout his corpus, and especially after 1516, and he means something broader by it than what is usually understood in descriptions of his philosophy of Christ. It comes to bear, for example, on epistemological and anthropological questions in addition to ethical ones. Greta Kroeker suggests that Erasmus had perhaps left behind the ethical *philosophia Christi* as his primary mode of theological understanding in his later years, in light of a newfound appreciation of a theology of grace, after substantive theological engagment in the 1520s with Luther's interpretation of Paul.[44] This may be correct for other reasons as well, especially when considering Paul's Christian philosophy of First Corinthians in addition to Paul's theology of grace in Romans; and if so, we would seem to be justified in distinguishing between the Erasmian *philosophia Christi* and the Erasmian *philosophia Christiana*. The latter is pitted rhetorically against all forms of human philosophy, and I hope to make clear in the following chapters the ways in which the qualification *Christiana* on *philosophia* makes all the difference in the world for certain sixteenth-century thinkers. A fuller appreciation of this qualification, and of Erasmus as theologian, clears the way for more productive analyses of his reception by theologians in the early modern period.

This is all to say that any attempt at a fuller understanding Calvin's indebtedness to Erasmus necessitates first a better understanding of Erasmus' thought in its own right. As Erika Rummel has suggested, while there is a tendency among Christian intelligentsia in the Renaissance to downplay speculative forms of knowing in favour of practical ones and, in a certain sense, to privilege belief over knowledge, this doesn't necessarily mean that *certainty* was cast away in favour of nebulous feeling, for certainty can be grounded in ways other than by logical demonstration.[45] In other words, even if we take as an example Calvin's well-documented commitment to assurance, or his definition of faith as a certain kind of knowledge, this ought not to preclude us a priori from considering Erasmus and Calvin in the same intellectual milieu, even in areas such as religious epistemology.[46] Indeed, as will be shown in chapter 5, for example, it is just as possible to establish a line of continuity from Erasmus to Calvin on faith's certitude from the perspective of their exegetical analysis of the Greek word πληροφορία ("full or certain assurance") in Colossians 2:4. It is only through doing the painstaking work of examining the *Annotations* – and only those on Romans have, to date, been translated into English – alongside the *Paraphrases*, and further, through close reading, comparing Erasmus' exegetical work to the commentaries of those reading his texts, that we are able to determine the manner in and extent to which Erasmus' ideas were received. Furthermore, establishing such lines of continuity make this a study not only about Calvin, and incidentally about Erasmus, but one that rests on the assumption that in laying out and then comparing the sixteenth-century appropriations of certain aspects of Paul's theological approach, we are better placed to understand Erasmus' position in its own right as well.

Theologia Rhetorica

We are aided in this endeavour, I believe, by using a heuristic device put forth by Charles Trinkaus. While we must be wary of reductionism, the manner in which Trinkaus spells out the requirements of what he called a *theologia rhetorica* can attenuate some of the previous misunderstandings of Erasmus' thought, and can also be illuminating for understanding the sixteenth-century biblical-humanist reception of Paul's denunciations of human wisdom and eloquence. Trinkaus suggests this approach to theology begins in many ways with Lorenzo Valla (ca. 1407–57), who joins eloquence with wisdom, not permitting one to exist truly without the other. The same sort of caveat was issued by Valla's predecessors, such as Petrarch and, to return *ad fontes*, by Cicero and Augustine as well.[47] Trinkaus coined the term *theologia rhetorica* to describe the humanist theological method that begins with Valla and takes shape in various of his biblical-humanist heirs.[48] Describing Italian humanist Brandolini (ca. 1454–97), he writes, "*theologia rhetorica* meant the use of 'words that bite and sting' or gratify and cajole rather than tight logical arguments, although it would be a mistake to think that there was no intellectual content or logical core in his position or that of the other humanists."[49] The final clause is important, lest one think that this sort of theological method is *merely* rhetorical, or only concerned with adapting classical rhetorical forms and strategies for use in Christian theology:[50] while there is, perhaps, a touch of scepticism built into such an enterprise, when coupled with God's revelation in the Word, the language employed to "convert" the listener is, according to the biblical humanists, neither sophistical nor empty, but is substantiated in and by the *Logos*. It is worth quoting Trinkaus' description of Valla's theological vision:

> [It] may be arrived at by rhetorical rather than philosophical or dialectical means, thus rejecting both the attempted humanist version of Neo-Stoic theology and the Neo-Aristotelian theology of the scholastics. His preference is for a *theologia rhetorica*, as it were, and a *philosophia moralis Chrisiana modo rhetorico*. The nature and the requirements of such a *theologia rhetorica* are simple. A speaker on divine matters should exhibit modesty, not asseveration, fear, not audacity or confidence. He should have "knowledge of divine matters, integrity of life, gravity of character." These are an adaptation of the Ciceronian conception of the orator to Christian purposes, and they are spelled out. In place of Cicero's knowledge of philosophy the Christian rhetor has "*scientia divinorum*" by means of "that which the crowd calls 'faith'."… [Valla] proceeds to write as though all the theological complexities and epistemological difficulties of scholastic thought were completely non-existent and perfectly settled by the direct declaration of the divine Word.[51]

These criteria are important for what follows. The "knowledge of divine things" here is hardly a *scientia* at all in Valla's heirs, at least by traditional standards, and the investigation of theological minutiae is eschewed in favour of what Erasmus would call an "unadulterated" preaching of the gospel.

The requirements for Valla's rhetorical theology could just as well serve as an accurate recapitulation of the major themes of sixteenth-century biblical-humanist reception of the early chapters of 1 Corinthians. It is a moral-philosophical way of doing exegetical theology: the reader/theologian must approach the subject matter with epistemological humility and with an interest in cultivating piety, and the preacher must preach a humble gospel, accessible to all. John O'Malley connects Erasmus to Trinkaus' designation, usefully tying it to his understanding of *pietas*, and contrasting it with scholastic dialectical method:

> Dense though that expression [*theologia rhetorica*] is, and susceptible to further analysis, it points even in its raw designation to the 'persuasional' character to Erasmus' enterprise. Rhetoric in the strict or 'primary' sense is the tool of oratory, of public discourse in an assembly. Its aims are *docere, movere, delectare*. Erasmus' prose tries to embody and coordinate all three of these aims, whereas his scholastic contemporaries were concerned almost exclusively with the first, and that in a dialectical mode. That mode, central to their enterprise, was in fact inimical to *pietas*. More precisely, it was inimical to the pastoral dimension that marked Erasmian *pietas*. Erasmus wanted, while teaching, to persuade and please as well. To that extent his piety, although of course dealing with the soul's relationship to God, looked outward to the world of his fellows.[52]

Importantly for our purposes, William Bouwsma suggested that this approach might be useful in analysing Calvin's thought as well.[53]

It is crucial to understand the scope of this device properly insofar as it is really quite different from what is often characterized as the particularly humanist interest *merely to persuade*, or *only to delight*, regardless of the truth. Bouwsma's proposal, it should be noted, is quietly rejected by Richard Muller, who argues that Calvin's didactical use of rhetorical categories like *amplificatio* and *copia* distances him from an Erasmian *theologia rhetorica* and places him more firmly in the camp of Melanchthonian Christian humanism.[54] But even if this were true regarding those specific categories, it isn't clear why Muller imagines Erasmus' rhetorical theology to focus on the "ornamentation of discourse," as he puts it, and to lack a didactic element. One needn't look further than Erasmus' massive preaching manual, the *Ecclesiastes*, to realize the substantial weight he places on the importance of teaching as the primary goal of Christian rhetorical theology. Moreover, Erasmus, as we will see, repeatedly targets "ornamentation of discourse" in his interpretations of Paul's criticisms of human forms of wisdom. Indeed, Brian Cummings has shown just how deeply *literary* rather than *merely rhetorical* Erasmus' hermeneutic is, and his reading of Erasmus' use of affective mimesis is an eloquent exposition of issues related to those taken up in this book.[55] Muller's position is, in any case, more nuanced than two oft-cited scholars on Calvin's hermeneutics who tend to oversimplify, or misunderstand, the humanist interest in *persuasio*, which leads inevitably to a mischaracterization of Calvin's reception of it: Richard Gamble, for example, argues that Calvin's exegetical method is new because it is different from other Protestant exegetes'. However, he doesn't consider a single non-Protestant humanist as a possible influence on Calvin (and indeed all the items he lists as possibly new in Calvin are easily found in Erasmus), and he explicitly dismisses "humanist" influence by quoting T.F. Torrance: "Calvin has given up the rhetorical conception of *persuasion* beloved by the humanists, one that appeals to what is attractive and desirable, and substitutes for it a mode of *persuasion* which throws the reader back upon the truth itself and its inherent validity."[56] Several recent studies have made it clear that such a distinction cannot be maintained, and that the role of persuasion in, e.g., Erasmus' and Calvin's thought, has little to do with appeals to such criteria. Olivier Millet, to take a prominent example, has argued that Calvin shares with Catholic and Protestant biblical humanists a notion of *fides* which is strongly connected to *persuasio* (although he mistakenly distances Calvin from Erasmus here through a misreading of Calvin's commentary on Luke 2).[57]

Persuasion and assurance are intimately connected in *theologia rhetorica* and neither, in the case of the gospel, is accomplished without the work of the Spirit. This is made explicit in the Christian tradition since Augustine, as has been demonstrated in Paul Kolbet's work on the Bishop of Hippo's re-imagination of the appropriate uses of rhetoric in theology. He writes, for example, that "to understand ancient psychagogy requires one to set aside such polarities and imagine the possibility of a kind of speech whose persuasiveness does not diminish its truthfulness."[58] This is, perhaps, a healthier way of imagining rhetoric to have functioned as well in the imaginations of humanistically trained theologians, although we will have the opportunity to further clarify the matter as it arises in the sixteenth century when parsing out Paul's criticisms of eloquence in 1 Corinthians as they are received by Erasmus and Calvin: for both exegetes are at pains to find a balance between retaining Paul's criticisms of eloquence in Christian teaching and their own vested interests in developing an approach to Christian teaching that embodies learned piety as an ideal. Suffice it to say for now though that, as I am using the phrase, *theologia rhetorica* can be understood as a form of Christian theological discourse whose primary purpose is to teach by way of appealing to both the affective and cognitive aspects of the learner, and that embodies the Pauline ideals of simplicity and humility in its aim of instiling learned piety. The ways in which this is particularly so for Erasmus, Calvin, and other reform-minded biblical humanists, will become clear as this book progresses.

The Dedicatory Letter for Erasmus' *Paraphrase* on *First Corinthians*

By way of introduction to the reception of Pauline folly, it might be most appropriate to consult briefly the prefatory material from Erasmus' and Calvin's exegetical works on 1 Corinthians. Erasmus' *Paraphrases* of the Corinthian correspondence were first published in 1519 by Martens at Louvain. The final edition during Erasmus' lifetime appeared in 1532 from Froben, and this is the edition I follow throughout this book unless otherwise noted. In the dedicatory letter, Erasmus points out that Paul "fought the battles of the gospel with the resources that the gospel supplies – tentmaker and pontiff, offscouring of the world and chosen instrument of Christ, who wished by the Apostle's sublime humility and tongue-tied eloquence and stammering flow of words to spread the glory of his name through superstitious Jewry, clever Greece, and Rome, the queen of earthly kingdoms."[59] The imminently christological description of Paul himself conquering the world through paradoxical means becomes a *topos* in Erasmus' *Paraphrase*, as in Calvin's commentary. And Erasmus is not merely summarizing Paul's comparison of Christian and pagan worldviews, but he recognizes the value of the work as substantiating his criticisms of then-contemporary theologians, whom he himself had encountered in his time at the Collège de Montaigu as a student of theology, and whom he tirelessly satirizes in the *Praise of Folly* and elsewhere. Erasmus routinely glosses the dangers of philosophy for both the method and the content of Christian theology. The Italian Aristotelians come in for specific criticism regarding the latter in defending the resurrection in sermons on the basis that the Stagirite "did not entirely abolish the immortality of the soul."[60] As for the former, and with special reference to overwrought and ornate discourse, Erasmus writes: "The trumpet of the gospel which Isaiah bids sound to publish forth the glory of God, is turned into a lyre to tickle the ears of men." And poignantly: "not all who have a tongue have a heart and brains."[61] The upshot, of course, is that what had been a sort of purity in Christian teaching, advocated by Paul and rejected by certain members of the Corinthian churches, was rejected for similar reasons and corrupted by similar means in Erasmus' own day.

Erasmus further explains the way in which the Gentiles at Corinth had erred: "But the Corinthians swelled in pride not only from wealth, but also from the arrogance of Greek philosophy; they despised as barbarians the others who were utterly deficient in this."[62] It is significant that Paul is not overt in tying arrogance to worldly philosophy directly (although he does, of course, emphasize the humility of the preaching of the gospel), while for Erasmus the pride and haughtiness (*supercilium*) of the Greeks is precisely how they stray from Christian wisdom, which is, by definition, achieved only through humility.[63] This is an oft-repeated theme: "From the arrogance of worldly philosophy, he calls them back to the humility of the cross, which although it has no ostentation, nevertheless has power and effectiveness."[64] And he continues in the same vein: "Now it was partly the fault of pride and partly that of philosophy that certain of them were disdaining Paul as poor and lowly, and then as ineloquent and ignorant. But it was the particular result of philosophy alone that they were calling into doubt the resurrection of the dead, the foundation of our faith."[65]

Erasmus is making a point about the proper approach to Christian teaching and understanding: arrogance – *tumor, arrogantia, supercilium, superbia, turgidus* are all sprinkled liberally throughout Erasmus' exegetical works – in itself doesn't lead one astray from right belief, but "philosophy" does, for it operates with different epistemological axioms, and seeks to *know* in an intellective sense alone. Erasmus here uses a number of Pauline themes from the subsequent chapters pre-emptively. Indeed, these themes – the arrogance of philosophy, the modesty of true Christian wisdom, and the eschewal of human eloquence for the language of Christ and the apostles – are repeated over and over again in the paraphrase of the early chapters of the letter.

Erasmus' exegesis of this unit provides, in outline, all the necessary components of what Erasmus calls a *philosophia Christiana*, and in doing so Erasmus lays the foundations for a similar *ideal* Pauline rhetorical *and* theological methodology among sixteenth-century Protestantism, especially in Switzerland.

The Dedicatory Epistles and *Argumentum* of Calvin's Commentary on 1 Corinthians

Calvin wrote two separate dedicatory epistles for his commentary on 1 Corinthians: the first was to James of Burgundy, Lord of Falais, for the first (1546) edition. In it, he laments that "in the present time there are far too many people who turn the Gospel into a cold and academic philosophy, thinking that they have done all that is required of them, and done it properly, if they nod their heads in assent to what they are told," and not, like James himself, living out what is preached.[66] The target is twofold, it would seem, directed towards the doctrine of implicit faith of the Catholic church (repeatedly denounced in Calvin's works) and towards a cerebral, inefficacious form of theology. The 1556 edition was dedicated to Lord Caraccioli, after James of Burgundy apparently didn't live up to Calvin's expectations in the end – Calvin is forced, reluctantly and uncharacteristically (*morem meum invitus muto*), to remove the previous dedication (*inscriptum nunc delere cogor*), and refuses even to mention the first recipient by name![67] It isn't surprising, then, that the first dedication is not included in Estienne's 1556 edition of Calvin's commentaries on all of Paul's letters. The second dedication does retain, however, the earlier criticism of those who give "cold assent" to the gospel (*frigide multi Evangelii doctrinae annuunt*) without the accompanying willingness to give up any worldly comforts, much less their entire lives. Calvin writes further that the chief of virtues is self-denial.[68] It is clear that the importance of Paul's criticisms of worldly wisdom is readily available for Calvin's use in the context of sixteenth-century religious practice, and the distinction between frigid and efficacious forms of theological discourse will arise often in Calvin's work in this regard.

The *Argumentum* to Calvin's commentary is more elaborate in laying out the significance of Paul's discourse on folly. Calvin suggests that the Corinthians whom Paul criticizes (as being over-eager to accept the wisdom of the world, especially eloquence in this case) have not erred theologically (i.e., they don't *necessarily* maintain unorthodox views), but they have erred *methodologically* on account of their hubris and vainglory. This is also the substance of Erasmus' critique of the "Greeks" in his *Paraphrase*, and it is a significant distinction, as we will see Calvin interpreting Paul as denouncing overly sophisticated and overly eloquent theological method (*ratio docendi*) in more than one instance. Here Calvin seems in fact to be criticizing, if not *methodology* in a strictly technical sense, then the underpinnings of an approach to the *ratio* of those he refers to pejoratively as "schoolmen." This bears especially on a comment Richard Muller makes: "The polemical usage [of 'scholasticism'] denounces not the *method* but, instead, the theological and philosophical *content* of the writings of the scholastic era. In other words, Calvin seldom, if ever, inveighs against the use of distinctions in theological argumentation."[69] The distinction between method and content in theology, however, can be a rather subtle one, as Muller himself has demonstrated at length in his analysis of Calvin's thought in the context of contrived debates between humanists and scholastics in the sixteenth century.[70] Indeed, it would seem that the force of biblical-humanist rhetorical sallies against university theologians in some measure arises out of a notion that theological content cannot be totally divorced from the manner in which it is presented: method often determines the kinds of questions that are asked, which questions inevitably determine the sorts of answers given. Even if here Calvin does not mention the *scholastici* explicitly, in the commentary on 1 Corinthians Calvin often discusses the correct method of teaching (*ratio docendi*) in the context of denouncing frivolities and the emptiness of human wisdom, and sixteenth-century readers would have understood Calvin's rhetoric as arising out of the specific milieu of humanist anti-scholasticism.

This doesn't mean, of course, that Calvin didn't have scholastic tools in his theological toolbox, nor that he never wielded them. Muller has shown that the devil is in the details here, and that particular cases like Calvin's confound a generalized dichotomy between humanism and scholasticism.[71] The purpose of this book is not to describe early sixteenth-century Christianity via a contrived debate between constructed camps (humanists and scholastics), nor to answer the more particular question of whether Erasmus or Calvin employed "humanist" and/or "scholastic" categories; it is to examine the way in which Pauline folly is put to use rhetorically from the perspective of reception history in sixteenth-century constructions of *ideal* approaches to theology and Christian teaching. That said, it is often helpful to imagine

Calvin as participating in a form of biblical humanism, articulated most clearly and forcefully by Erasmus, which sought explicitly to distinguish itself from a form of speculative scholastic theology.[72]

Calvin continues to write that the preachers who followed Paul in Corinth, "did not come (in my opinion at any rate) to upset the Church with obviously unorthodox teaching, or to damage the orthodox teaching intentionally, as it were ... [but] being proud (*superbientes*) of their brilliant and showy oratory, one should rather say, being swollen-headed (*tumidi*) about their empty and bombastic language, they were out to treat the simplicity of Paul and even the very Gospel, with contempt."[73] This, of course, leads to strife in the Corinthian churches and the various factions Paul speaks of, and hinders the spreading of the gospel. Corinth, like most commercial cities, Calvin tells us, is "infested" with arrogance, vanity, and self-seeking, which are sins but not heresies. But Calvin also notes that this occasionally leads to fundamentals of the faith, like the resurrection of the dead, being questioned (which would seem to be a clear case of theological method and content converging).[74] Instead of pointing out false teaching, though, which in many other contexts Paul isn't hesitant to do, here he condemns the ambition of the "preposterous teachers and chattering speechmakers," who turn the gospel into a "man-made philosophy" (*humanam philosophiam*) through their "preoccupation with empty, bombastic language." These, Calvin tells us, have "devised a new method of teaching that was not consistent with the simplicity of Christ."[75]

Because of a desire to display their learning, they render the gospel useless: "Their preaching is dead, when it should be alive and producing results (*vivida et efficax*); and in order to be in the public eye themselves they disguise the Gospel, dressing it in different clothes, so that it may look like a worldly philosophy."[76] The contrast here is between a simple preaching of the gospel that – with the power of the Spirit – transforms, and an attempt to render the gospel compatible with worldly philosophy. When the gospel comes to be "on the level with any worldly philosophy," Calvin tells us, it is "adulterated," and its "natural purity is spoiled."[77] It is worth emphasizing Calvin's insistence that theological method has important implications not only for getting at the truth, but also in terms of the disposition of the theologian or evangelist (who succumbs to arrogance when attempting too much to rationalize or rhetorically adorn the gospel), and in terms of utility (the gospel is dead and fruitless when adorned with the language of rhetoricians and philosophers).

Not unexpectedly, one of Calvin's repeated themes in his exegesis of 1 Corinthians is, as for Erasmus, humility versus arrogance, and in those instances where Paul discusses wisdom and folly, humility as it relates to explaining, or understanding, the gospel:

> From this main evil [i.e., the evil of the Corinthians who were swollen with ambition 'ingratiating themselves by a show of words and a mask of human wisdom'] two others follow: (1) By those things, which we might call disguises, the simplicity of the Gospel was deformed and Christ was clothed, as it were, in a new and foreign garb, so that the pure and genuine knowledge of Him was hidden from view. Further (2) because men's minds were turned to the brilliancy and fineness of words, to clever speculations, to an empty show of rather uplifted teaching, the power of the Spirit vanished, and nothing was left except the dead letter. The majesty of God, which shines out in the Gospel, was blanked out, and, instead, only purple and fruitless pomp was visible.[78]

Calvin here is obviously worried about what too much eloquence and speculation might do to the simplicity of the preaching of Christ crucified. With an emphasis on the virtue of simplicity in theological understanding, Calvin castigates pompous eloquence and clever speculation (*acutas speculatione*), at least in part (and here again we find Calvin echoing Erasmus) because this sort of thing renders the gospel unfruitful (*infructuosa*) – what isn't practically effective ought to be avoided. The gospel is distorted – indeed, covered up by the masks of human wisdom (*larva humanae sapientiae*) – in the hands of philosophers and rhetoricians. Its inherent simplicity is hidden from view. Even before we've gotten to the meat of the commentaries themselves, then, we see already the richness of interpretative material Paul offers his readers in condemning worldly wisdom alongside human eloquence and elevating the humble foolishness of the cross as a model (with epistemological, ethical, and methodological implications) for Christian teaching. An in-depth analysis of the commentaries themselves will illuminate further the role of Pauline folly in the exegesis of Erasmus and Calvin, revealing in general the importance of the biblical text for the articulation of their ideas about the nature of theology, as well as the significance of their interpretations of the foolishness of God for what they called the *philosophia Christiana*.

Chapter Two

Foolishness as Religious Knowledge

A peasant may believe as much
As a great clerk, and reach the highest stature.
Thus dost thou make proud knowledge bend and crouch,
While grace fills up uneven nature.

– George Herbert

For Erasmus and Calvin, Paul has two targets in mind in the early chapters of his letter to the Corinthian churches: human reason and human eloquence. These he seeks to replace in the hearts and minds of the Corinthians with the wisdom of God and the preaching of the cross, respectively. Paul's division, of course, isn't quite so neat as this, but it is plain to see that Erasmus and Calvin do conceive of the role of reason and the role of eloquence in theological method to be different sorts of things, even if they both stem from the same root problem, viz. human arrogance and a misplaced trust in human ingenuity to comprehend and convey divine matters.[1] In the sixteenth century these themes have their own peculiar implications for theological method, especially in light of humanist critiques of scholastic speculative theology, on the one hand, and the newfound appreciation of classical forms of rhetoric and the subsequent attempts to employ these in Christian theology and exegesis on the other.[2] The purpose of this chapter is twofold: first, to offer a running exposition of the exegetical works of Erasmus and Calvin on the early chapters of 1 Corinthians, with reference to the commentaries of Heinrich Bullinger and Konrad Pellikan, in order to show how Erasmus' *Annotations* and *Paraphrase* on 1 Corinthians laid the foundations for later biblical-humanist commentaries on the text; and second, to provide an outline of Erasmus' and Calvin's reception of Pauline folly in the context of religious epistemology. The chapter is divided into two larger sections covering first the reception of 1 Corinthians 1:17–27, and then 1 Corinthians chapter 2. In each section I will consider Erasmus' *Annotations* and *Paraphrases* on Paul's text, then briefly the commentaries of Bullinger and Pellikan, and finally Calvin's commentary at length. In providing a running commentary on their exegetical works on this unit in Paul's letter, we will have a more complete portrait of the significance of Pauline folly in each exegete's approach, and a better idea of the consonance of their readings of Paul on the question of the relationship between worldly philosophy and Christian philosophy.

The Foolishness of God: 1 Cor. 1:17b–27[3]

Paraphrasing and Annotating the Folly of God:
Erasmus' Commentary

The discourse on wisdom, folly, and eloquence begins at verse 1:17, where Paul writes that he was sent by Christ not to baptize, but to preach the gospel, and to do this without σοφία λόγου, lest the cross of Christ be made void. Erasmus, in his Latin New Testament text, renders Paul's Greek σοφία λόγου as *erudito sermone* in order to emphasize the nature of speech he takes Paul to be avoiding here, and seemingly omitting Paul's criticism of *sapientia* which the Vulgate retains. He also here, as (infamously) elsewhere, modifies the Vulgate's preference for *verbum* as *sermo* to best capture what he perceives to be the discursive nature of the Greek *logos*.[4] We will have more opportunity in a later chapter to analyse the implications of Pauline folly for Christian rhetoric, but note here that in the paraphrase Erasmus retains Paul's denunciation of wisdom *and* of eloquence: "For [Paul] did not wish this [i.e., spreading the Gospel] to be accomplished by the sources of human wisdom or eloquence – resources that could provide nothing of this sort – but he wanted so arduous an exploit to be carried out by simple and unadorned speech so that all the praise for the feat may be assigned to God, whom it pleased to renew all the world through the despised and dishonored cross of Christ."[5] Indeed, he argues in his annotation on this verse that the semantic range of the Greek *sophia* covers not only *sapientia* but also *elegantia* and *eruditio,* and that the simplicity of the *sermonis de cruce* (preaching of the cross) is different from the arguments of the *sermone philosophorum et rhetorum* (discourse of the philosophers and orators).

In other words, Paul's condemnations here are far reaching: the whole world (*mundum universum*) is renewed through the cross, and it is made explicit that Paul's criticisms extend to philosophers and rhetoricians.

The implications for religious epistemology and for theological method become clear as the paraphrase progresses:

> The cross of Christ seems a low and worthless affair, but this lowliness subdues all the loftiness of this world. This crude and unpolished speech, by which we proclaim that Christ was fixed to the cross and died on the cross, seems to be a foolish and ignorant thing, but to whom, may I ask, does it seem so? Surely to those who, blinded by their old vices, do not hear the gospel word inwardly, and therefore perish because they have rejected that from which their salvation could arise. Those, however, who attain eternal salvation from this source understand indeed that it is no feeble thing, but one that is more efficacious than all human deployments and that proceeds directly from God.[6]

The cross, the symbol of redemption for Christians, is decidedly unphilosophical, and pride blinds the philosophers to this fact. After all, as Erasmus asks, "What is more humiliating than to be hanged on a cross as a criminal between criminals? What is more artless or belongs to ordinary people than the teaching of the gospel?"[7] All true wisdom is located in this moment of ostensible folly, and philosophy is rendered useless on account of the lowly humility of Christ and his having suffered the most humiliating of earthly punishments: "Through him has come true and saving wisdom, so that you have no need of philosophy."[8] The rejection of human *praesidiis* and *adminiculis* (here "deployments"), language Erasmus may have picked up from John Colet, is repeated often in his, Calvin's, and the Zurichers' commentaries on 1 Corinthians.[9]

All who have misguided approaches to the truth for Paul are misguided on account of their arrogance according to Erasmus: "Where, meanwhile, is the wise man swelling up with his knowledge of the Law? Where is the scribe haughty with his exposition of the Law? Where is the philosopher who explores the secrets of nature and, unmindful of the maker, marvels at created things?"[10] It is notable that Erasmus renders Paul's phrase here so explicitly to refer to the philosophers of this world who attempt to descry the *arcana naturae*, for Paul does not refer to natural philosophers in his letter, but merely to "disputers" (*suzetetes*). In his annotation on the verse, Erasmus offers a litany of renderings – Theophylact, Jerome, the Septuagint, Ambrose, the Constantinian Codex – in order to demonstrate the possibility of understanding a wide range of targets for Paul's rhetorical questions.[11] Also, importantly (and Calvin will follow Erasmus here), he modifes the Vulgate translation of verse 19 – "the prudence of the prudent [*prudentiam prudentium*] I will reject" – to *intellgentiam intelligentium*, which, as is pointed out by the editors of Erasmus' NT in the Amsterdam edition, results from his discerning "that the Greek terms have more to do with intelligence and understanding than with prudence or foresight."[12] In other words, Erasmus has turned the whole passage against "traditional" or classical Greek approaches to wisdom and knowledge, and invoked Paul against the possibilities of a natural knowledge of God on account of human sinfulness. Even though God had "shown his own wisdom through this most beautiful spectacle of the world [*pulcherrimum spectaculum mundi*]" that human beings "might be swept into love for the maker of the work" the outcome was different: "because of their own sin [*vitio*]" they "admired and worshipped created things, but scorned the author as if he were unknown."[13] Furthermore, the downfall of the misguided philosophers and scribes is described by Paul only by invoking a distinction between the wisdom of the world and the ostensible foolishness of God; but for Erasmus, again, God has used the philosophers' ostentatiousness against them as a way of condemnation: "God has allowed them through their blindness (and so did their presumption deserve) to go headlong into every kind of disgrace, so that he might show them to themselves, and in repenting they might at last understand that their claim to wisdom was hollow and powerless [*inanem et inefficacem*]. Has God therefore not shown the wisdom of the world to be foolish?"[14] That the wisdom of the world is empty and inefficacious is a common description for both Erasmus and Calvin; the Christian philosophy (especially as *theologia rhetorica*) is founded upon substance and efficacy.[15]

The demand, on the part of Jews for signs, and on the part of Greeks for philosophical wisdom is, again, an error of pride according to Erasmus' Paul in the *Paraphrase*: "Just as the Jews demand wondrous signs and pride themselves on their ancestors' miracles, so do the Greeks strive for erudition and for the knowledge of philosophy, assuring themselves that from this will come happiness and glory. Both have been deceived in their thinking. For the Jews through confidence in the Law have fallen away from Christ, and the philosophers, bloated with their belief in wisdom, do not accept the outwardly humble preaching of the cross."[16] It is noteworthy that in his translation of the New Testament, Erasmus opts for *Graecis* over the Vulgate's *gentibus*; the Greek manuscript witnesses are divided between reading "Hellenes" and "Gentiles," generally synonymous in the New Testament, but here, as the editors of the Amsterdam edition note, Paul "was referring to mental attitudes that were especially characteristic of Greek philosophy, rather than of pagan culture in general."[17] Erasmus understood the distinction, of course, but he also had a vested rhetorical and theological interest for making his choice. Furthermore, over-confidence and bloatedness (*turgidi*) prevent an adoption of humble Christian preaching. For Erasmus the orientation of confidence in the Law or in Knowledge for "salvation" rests on an anthropological claim: the fact that human beings are unable to adequately follow the Law, a classic Pauline theme that finds new life in the sixteenth century, necessitates that any attempt to do so be understood as misplaced pride in one's innate ability; and, by the same token, the Greeks' confidence in their own ability to be assured in the truth is not sufficiently humble nor appreciative of the absurdities of the Incarnation and the resurrection of the dead:[18] "To the Greeks who investigate all things with human reasoning [*rationibus humanis*], it seems foolish [*stultum*] that by heavenly power a maiden conceived a child, that God lay hidden under human form, that life has been restored by death, that he who was once dead has come to life again ..."[19] *Ratio* is simply not the appropriate means for comprehending the gospel.

Paul's use of the phrase "foolishness of God" (*stultitia Dei*, in Erasmus' rendering) at 1 Cor. 1:25 is related both to a serious transcendentalism and to Christ's self-emptying in Erasmus' *Annotations*. Commenting on the phrase *stultitia Dei* – which Erasmus has rendered more blatantly than the Vulgate's *quod stultum est Dei*[20] – he writes, "The foolishness and weakness of God [Paul] calls the preaching of the cross, either because it seems foolish and weak to the impious, or because, compared with the ineffable wisdom and power of God, it is in some way foolish and weak. Just as all the righteousness of men in the eyes of God is as a woman's soiled menstrual rag, so the entire wisdom of mortal men, if compared to that incomprehensible celestial wisdom, can be called a certain kind of folly."[21] And he continues on this note, citing Augustine and justifying the scandalous phrase "foolishness of God": "Nor is the phrase 'foolishness of God' an abomination: it didn't horrify Augustine, who wrote in his hundred and second letter: 'This foolishness of God and the foolishness of preaching draw many to salvation'. If God lowered himself to our weakness that he might make us strong, what is novel if he should lower himself to our foolishness, that out of fools he might make wise men?'"[22]

There is ample patristic evidence, aside from the Augustine reference, which no doubt influenced Erasmus in his reading. In the dedicatory preface he claims to have consulted "Ambrose" (i.e., Ambrosiaster) and Theophylact most often, and this is borne out in the number of references to each in comparison with other Fathers. The comparison with the ineffable wisdom and power of God is, moreover, "Origenesque," according to M.A. Screech. Origen writes, e.g., in his *Homily on the Song of Songs*, "What was Christ *not* made for our salvation? We were empty: he emptied himself, taking on the form of a slave. We were a people foolish and lacking wisdom: he was made the foolishness of preaching so that the silliness of God might be wiser than men. We were weak: the weakness of God was made stronger than men."[23] But Chrysostom's homilies on the early chapters of 1 Cor. abound with similar sentiments, and many are more forceful than Origen's here, including attacks on specific Greek philosophers, like Plato, who apparently dwelt too often on geometry for Chrysostom's tastes.[24] In any case, the force of Erasmus' considerations of the foolishness of human wisdom here are, at root, anthropological or perhaps, more broadly, ontological. There is, quite simply, a radical gulf between God and humanity. And it isn't only human wisdom that seems foolish when considered alongside the vast wisdom of God, for Erasmus. There is also something fundamentally christological at work here: Christ's self-emptying is, on the one hand, foolish according to the wisdom of the world, and on the other, it is precisely what makes the fools of the world wise who believe in it.

In the same section, Erasmus explains again that the error lies in an over-appreciation of human ability, and a resulting disjunction between the ways of God and man's ability to comprehend them:

What is more artless or belongs to ordinary people than the teaching of the gospel? It has renewed the world, a feat that before this nothing the philosophers professed was able to accomplish, to the end that none of the praise for this deed should be assigned to human supports. That would have happened if the affair had been conducted with the auxiliary props of wealth or erudition, through those in power or distinguished by their profession of wisdom. Because now, through uneducated folk and fishermen the pinnacle of human wisdom has been taken by storm, we realize that the glory of this whole work belongs to God alone, whose secret power has brought forth opposites from opposites.[25]

The philosophy of the fisherman has no use for the auxiliary props (*praesidiis* and *adminiculis*) of philosophical speculation. Here also lies the substance of Erasmus' criticism of errant theologizing, with its elite and learned distinctions that keep the unlettered from accessing that which is meant to be available to everyone in its divinely ordained simplicity. One cannot help but think, when reading this *Paraphrase*, of the debates over the requisite qualifications for theologians between the scholastics and humanists of Erasmus' day, which has been so well documented by Erika Rummel.[26] The continual castigation of humanist theologians as mere grammarians by scholastic theologians, such as Noel Beda of the Sorbonne and Edward Lee at Louvain, is objectionable to Erasmus, not only because he believed in the inherent value of the humanist enterprise to improve upon extant versions of the New Testament text through philological work, but because Christian theology itself is unphilosophical and its simplicity is betrayed by dialectic. Put another way, Erasmus doesn't believe the scholastics to be naive only in their rejection of the study of ancient languages, but naive also in their hubristic attempts to understand God through reason. God has specifically chosen such a humble and foolish way of revelation to confound just such "professors of wisdom," "so that they may be more ashamed at their trifling effort."[27] Christian revelation represents an absolute condemnation of human philosophy, both epistemologically and ethically.

Manfred Hoffmann sums this up nicely, and points to the connection to piety that will become clearer as we proceed: "[F]aith constitutes not only an objective assurance derived from the word itself. It connotes also the believer's commitment, both intellectual and moral, to the truth and its consequences."[28] The inseparability of faith and piety cannot be overstated in Erasmus' theology in general, and it is important to bear in mind when turning to Calvin that the assurance of faith has implications for both the intellectual and moral realms. And it isn't merely those with whom he has direct contact, but, like the schismatics mentioned by Paul in his letter (the followers of Apollo, Cephas, et al.), Erasmus recognizes in his own day a similar sort of division: In his annotation on 1 Cor. 1:10, where Paul encourages the Corinthians to agree with one another in speech (*idem loquamini omnes* in Erasmus' rendering) and to avoid dissension, Erasmus writes that Paul's rule had not been remembered in his own day and invokes the Thomists, Occamists, Albertists, and Scotists, along with the Nominalists and Realists as proof of unnecessary dissension in the Church.[29] In the *Paraphrase* on the same section, he takes liberty to gloss the Corinthian sects with reference to Pythagoreans, Platonists, Aristotelians, Stoics, and Epicureans.[30] It is a convenient passage for Erasmus to employ in his attacks on discord, and he lengthens the analogy further in his *Lingua* of 1525 to include the Paris theologians as well as those from Cologne, Lutherans, followers of Karlstadt, evangelists, and papists: all who are culpable in the construction of a "new Babel."[31]

"The Lord sent me to evangelize, not to philosophize":
Bullinger and Pellikan on 1 Cor. 1

It is helpful to point to certain common themes and vocabulary in other sixteenth-century commentaries on 1 Corinthians in order to demonstrate that they, too, help to make up a common interpretative milieu with respect to Pauline folly.[32] Zurich, the eventual home to both Pellikan and Bullinger, had long been friendly to Erasmus' works, many of which were printed there in the house of Christoph Froschauer throughout the middle decades of the sixteenth century (although controversy between Erasmus and the Zurichers did arise).[33] Zwingli was devoted to a form of Erasmian Christian humanism, and the two corresponded amicably. As early as 1521 the *Paraphrases* of Paul's epistles were translated in Zurich into German by Leo Jud and printed by Froschauer. Pellikan, who was a friend of Erasmus' during his time in Basel in the 1520s (he was lured to Zurich by Zwingli in 1526) and who also worked on Erasmus' editions of the Fathers in Froben's press, wrote to Erasmus in 1525 that he often kissed the *Paraphrases* as he read them.[34] In 1528, Leo Jud published a series of notes derived from Zwingli's lectures on 1 Corinthians, and it is clear that Zwingli was lecturing from Erasmus' New Testament text and using his *Annotations* as well.[35] In 1541, Jud and Pellikan would publish the complete *Paraphrases* of Erasmus in German, with Pellikan's own version of Revelation, which Erasmus had never rendered himself. Erasmus' exegetical works thus loomed large over the Zurichers.

As Peter Opitz has written of Bullinger, "The theological and ecclesiological parting of ways between Erasmus and the Reformation that ultimately took place in the mid-1520s did not prevent Bullinger from further and consciously using humanist methods in his biblical interpretation. Indeed, on the contrary, the Reformation principle of *sola scriptura* demanded a methodically thought-out 'philology,' as well as a 'rhetorical' analysis of biblical texts. Thus Bullinger relied on Erasmus very strongly in his exegetical work and also acknowledged this gratefully."[36] This is a specific aspect of a more general situation: Reformed humanist scholarship in Switzerland could never be fully divorced from the wider scholarly network of the *respublica litterarum*, nor did it intend to be. While the full picture of the reception of Erasmus' thought in Zurich is a complex matter, it is in large measure positive, as Bruce Gordon has noted: "Not only did Erasmus give rise to the humanist Christian culture central to the thought of Zwingli and the other Swiss reformers, but his sodality of scholars with himself at the centre provided the model for the Zurich Reformation."[37] There are indelible traces of Erasmus' influence in the Zurichers' commentaries on 1 Corinthians, and the *Paraphrase* especially came to be used in framing Bullinger's and Pellikan's understanding of the meaningfulness of Pauline folly for theological method.

Although Bullinger was the younger of the two, and was in fact Pellikan's student in Zurich, he had succeeded Zwingli as head of the Zurich church in 1531, and his commentary on 1 Corinthians was published five years earlier than Pellikan's. Bullinger's complete commentaries on the Pauline epistles would not appear until 1537, but there he explicitly acknowledged his indebtedness to Erasmus in the introduction to the volume.[38] The 1534 edition of Bullinger's commentary on 1 Corinthians has a textual division before the treatment of 1 Cor. 1:17, in all caps: SIMPLEX EVANGELII PRAEDICATIO, a signal that he (or his editor) is serious about the dangers of complicating the gospel message.[39] It should be noted first that, although Bullinger will consult the Greek New Testament in his commentaries, the Latin translation of the New Testament embedded in Bullinger's commentary is largely a verbatim reproduction of Erasmus' translation, which has inevitable consequences for the language and manner of his interpretation as well.[40] But the agreements are not accounted for by linguistic similarity alone. It is clear early on that Bullinger imagines Paul's censures to be relevant to contemporary concerns, and he rattles off the same list of modern schismatics that Erasmus had in his comment on 1 Cor. 1:10ff.: *Zenonis, Pythagorae, Aristotelis et Platonis ... Alberti, Thomae, Scoti, Occam et id genus alia.*[41] In the dedicatory epistle, he self-reflectively compares the factious Corinthian church to a contemporary schism between Zwinglians and Lutherans.[42] As for the role of reason in accessing divine truth, Bullinger's gloss on 1:17 takes aim at human philosophy (*humana philosophia*), interpreting Paul as warning the Corinthians against its "swollen and luxurious" manner and its pandering language (*verborum lenocinio*), and contrasts it with the simple preaching of the cross.[43] Erasmus, too, had advocated for preaching *sine lenociniis* (speech without "meretricious ornament," per Lewis and Short's dictionary) in his annotation on this verse, and he was followed by Zwingli, and eventually by Calvin as well.[44]

Joel Kok has argued that Bullinger may be more receptive to pagan philosophy than Calvin, judging from his commentary on Romans,[45] but here Bullinger repeatedly denounces the "painted" or "artificial" (*fucus*) human philosophy, modelled probably on Erasmus' "*sermone philosophorum et rhetorum fucato compositoque*" from the annotation cited above, and which word (*fucus*) becomes a favourite pejorative in Calvin's commentary. And, commenting upon Paul's *ouk en sophia logou*, Bullinger poetically rewrites Paul's declamation, which comes to read that he was sent to preach, not to philosophize: "Dominis (inquit) misit me evangelizare, non philosophare."[46] Admittedly with some repetition, he juxtaposes the simplicity of the cross with the *compositum praedicari sermonem* (as Erasmus had done), and warns against multiple forms of human wisdom and eloquence, all still commenting on verse 1:17: *eruditum sermonem, sapientia humana, elaboratae elegantiae*, and *orationis splendorem* each come in for condemnation.[47] He also contrasts the "inane" with the "solid" in the same context, and this we will find in both Erasmus and Calvin as well. In a nice turn of phrase, Bullinger sums up the relationship between simplicity and truth: *Quae enim vera sunt, simplicia sunt, quae falsa sunt medicamina poscunt* – True things are simple, false things demand an antidote.[48] Bullinger's gloss on 1 Cor. 1:17 is a mini-treatise on the perceived dangers of rhetoric and philosophy for the simple preaching of the cross. Significantly, on 1 Cor. 1:21, Bullinger also connects the foolishness of preaching to divine accommodation, an important aspect of Erasmian rhetorical theology: aside from accommodating himself to humanity in various other ways (*ad captum attempterat mortalium*), Paul also did so *per stultitiam praedicationis*, that is, through foolish preaching.[49] As will become clear in chapter 4, the Erasmian-Pauline accommodation in foolish preaching is emphasized in Calvin as well.

Konrad Pellikan, who enjoyed a sometime, if troubled, friendship with Erasmus during his years in Basel and would eventually sit by him on his deathbed, had moved from Basel to Zurich in 1526 to take over the position of professor of theology and resident expert in Hebrew from the recently deceased Jakob Ceporin.[50] While Pellikan's legacy is mostly one of helping to lay the groundwork for modern Christian Hebraica (he was the teacher and long-time colleague of Sebastian

Munster), he was also the first to publish Latin commentaries on the entire Bible, culminating in the seven-volume *Commentaria bibliorum*.[51] As Bruce Gordon has pointed out, Pellikan was concerned to produce biblical commentaries that moved beyond grammatical analysis and served the needs of the church.[52] This is no doubt part of the reason why Pellikan reproduces large amounts of Erasmus' *Paraphrase* verbatim in his commentary on 1 Corinthians, which was published alongside commentaries on the other apostolic epistles in 1539.[53] It is interesting to note, however, that, unlike in Bullinger's commentary, the New Testament version placed throughout Pellikan's commentary is the Vulgate and not Erasmus' version.[54]

The passages of the *Paraphrases* reproduced are pertinent to the same themes Bullinger and (later) Calvin pick up. Much of his borrowing is related to the desire for simplicity in preaching and an eschewing of eloquence. He copies the following passage from Erasmus' *Paraphrase* in his comment on 1:17: "For Paul did not wish this to be accomplished by the supports (*praesidiis*) of human wisdom or eloquence, which could not put forth anything like it, but he wanted so arduous an exploit to be carried out by simple and uncomplicated speech so that all the praise for the feat may be ascribed to God, whom it pleased to renew all the world through the despised and dishonored cross of Christ."[55] He then elaborates, noting that Paul had eschewed the *elegantia orationis* being peddled (*venditabant*) by the Corinthians, and warned further against *pompa verborum*, which Paul had replaced with *sermone simplici*.[56] Pellikan's comments on verse 1:18, with the exception of the final sentence (which was taken from Zwingli's lectures on 1 Corinthians), consist entirely of Erasmus' paraphrase.[57] On verse 1:19, he resumes immediately with the *Paraphrase*, interspersing his own comments, but including, for example, the questions of Erasmus' Paul critical of the natural philosophers: *Ubi philosophos, qui scrutatur arcana naturae, et opificis oblitus, res conditas admiratur?*[58] At any rate, to document all the instances of Pellikan's use of Erasmus, even if we kept to verbatim replication, would result in a book in itself, so we must confine ourselves to these few comments.

We should note also briefly for purposes of contrast that Melanchthon, in his early *Annotationes* on 1 Corinthians and in the posthumously published *brevis commentarius*, despite following Erasmus' translation (*in erudito sermone*) against the Vulgate's, glosses verse 1:17 as pertaining to philosophy specifically and its *probabiles et verisimiles rationes*, and doesn't mention the deleterious effects of ornamental rhetoric, in contrast with the rest of our interpreters. This conforms to a similar judgment, to be treated later, at Colossians 2:8, where Melanchthon's gloss attends directly to issues with philosophical reasoning and, as Wengert has pointed out, he rejects the Erasmian interpretation that has Paul also criticizing rhetoric.[59] There is, of course, overlap in other areas: Melanchthon, for example, offers a characteristically Lutheran focus on the entirety of Christian wisdom as contained in the cross, and gives a very strong reading of God's foolishness at 1 Cor. 1:21, and we shouldn't discount the possibilities of Melanchthon's influence on our commentators, and vice versa. But the sheer brevity of his notes on 1 Corinthians limits the possibilities of substantial comparative work.[60] Suffice it to say for now though that Bullinger and Pellikan have borrowed extensively from Erasmus' reception of Paul's discourse on folly and wisdom in the early chapters of 1 Corinthians, and that the language and emphases have much in common with Erasmus' reception and use of the text for establishing the contours of a Pauline Christian philosophy of foolishness.

Calvin on 1 Cor. 1:17–27

Despite the extensive treatment Bullinger gives to the questions that arise from Paul's warnings against human wisdom and eloquence, Calvin's comments on 1:17 dwarf them (and, less surprisingly given the genre, Erasmus' as well) by a decent margin. Calvin, while he does occasionally go his own way in translating the New Testament, follows Erasmus' New Testament here about ninety percent of the time. In interpreting Paul, Calvin's purpose, too, is to establish Paul's message against the haughty wisdom of the philosophers. All human wisdom is "dethroned," and pride is shamed before the contemptible nature of God-made-man and crucified. Moreover, Calvin suggests that there is something inherently unphilosophical or unclever about the cross:

"The cross of Christ would have been rendered useless," Paul says, "if my preaching had been tricked out with eloquence and brilliance." He has used the cross of Christ for the benefit of salvation, which must be sought from Christ crucified. But the teaching of the Gospel, which calls us to that benefit, ought to suggest the nature of the cross, so that, instead of being glorious, it might rather be despised and worthless, in the eyes of the world. The meaning therefore is that if Paul had used the acuteness of a philosopher and clever speeches in his dealings with the Corinthians, the power of the cross of Christ, in which the salvation of men consists, would have been buried, because it cannot reach us in that way.[61]

Language from both Erasmus' and Bullinger's commentaries is taken over by Calvin. *Eloquentia* and *ornata splendore* are rejected in favour of the "efficacy" of the cross. There is a built-in offensiveness (*abjecta coram mundo*) in the cross that cannot be appreciated by the wisdom of the world.[62]

Eloquence and brilliance are denounced. We are saved, not by anything glorious, but by the lowly and worthless elements of the Incarnation, and it is the lowly only who are able to appreciate it: *piscatores et idiotas* (fishermen and the simple minded), used by Calvin in his comments on this verse, is the precise formulation of Erasmus in his paraphrase.[63] Paul couldn't have used philosophical astuteness (*philosophico acumine*) to explicate the crucifixion because it lacks decorum with respect to its subject matter. It is not able to reach us in that way (*pervenire ad nos hac via non potest*). The concentration of all Christian wisdom in the cross, its reducibility to the cross, and repeated exhortations to humility in the context of the cross are all themes we have seen repeated in Erasmus' interpretations of 1 Corinthians, and elaborated on by Bullinger.

Continuing on 1:17, Calvin, too, explains the centrality of the lowliness of the cross:

> As Paul had so often before set the name of Christ in contrast to the proud wisdom of the flesh, so he now plants the cross of Christ right in the center, in order to dethrone all the haughtiness and superiority of that wisdom. For all the wisdom of believers is concentrated in the cross of Christ. And is there anything more contemptible than a cross? Therefore he who would be truly wise in the things of God must necessarily stoop to the humility of the cross. This will only be done by first of all renouncing his own understanding of things, and all the wisdom of the world. Indeed Paul is teaching here not only what sort of men the disciples of Christ ought to be, and the proper way by which they ought to learn, but also what the method of teaching should be in the school of Christ.[64]

Calvin's rhetorical question here reminds us of the question posed by Erasmus above in his paraphrase: "What is more humiliating than to be hanged on a cross as a criminal between criminals? What is more artless or belongs to ordinary people than the teaching of the gospel?"[65] So does his contrasting of the arrogance of worldly wisdom (*superbae sapientiae*) with the humility of the cross (*humilitatem crucis*). And, explicitly, Calvin argues that the very *method* of teaching (*docendi ratio*) must be modified in light of revelation. True wisdom does not seek to explain the cross philosophically – after the fact, so to speak – but it *begins* there. The student in the school of Christ (*schola Christi*) is not trained in philosophical dialectic, but is humble before the incomprehensible truth of Christ crucified. "Knowing God," writes T.H.L. Parker, expositing Calvin, "is a unique activity in man's experience, having its own categories. It runs the risk, if it borrows from the categories of general epistemology, of destroying itself by turning its direction from its true object, God, to an idol fabricated by itself."[66]

Calvin doesn't condemn all non-Christian philosophy as useless, however, and the *Institutes* has numerous non-pejorative references to ancient philosophers, even if these are typically invoked as *guides* rather than as authorities outright.[67] Calvin's problem with the philosophers is, as Charles Partee puts it, that they have "an overweening confidence" in reason, whereas Calvin, while not rejecting reason outright, wishes for it to be used "within its proper bounds."[68] At any rate, the remainder of Calvin's comments on 1 Cor. 1, which comprise several pages, constitute a treatise on the inability of human reason to comprehend divine matters. Reason's proper bounds are mundane. Calvin distinguishes between the things humans can't know as a result of original sin and the things humans can't know because God hasn't revealed them in comprehensible forms. Insofar as humans cannot comprehend God through his creation, for example, this is due to the Fall of Adam: Adam's original integrity permitted him to contemplate God through God's works, but through sin human reason has been seriously damaged in this regard. Insofar as man cannot understand various tenets of Christian revelation through reason, however – e.g., that God became man, that righteousness had been concealed under sin, that sinners might be redeemed thus, that bodies will be raised, etc. – this is due not explicitly to noetic damage which results from the Fall, but is so simply because God has decided to reveal these things in a manner that is absurd from the perspective of the *philosophia mundi*. Even the angels are astonished at the gospel (*angeli quoque obstupescant*), Calvin tells us, for its wisdom is a part of God's hidden counsel. In the *Argumentum*, Calvin sums up Paul's treatment of the relationship between the gospel and human reason thus:

> [Paul] goes on to develop the thought that the Gospel contains a heavenly and secret wisdom. It is something that neither man's natural ability,

however acute and penetrating, nor his physical senses, can grasp; something about which human argument can give no conviction; something which needs no flowery language and word-pictures. It is only by the revelation of the Spirit that it comes to be known by the minds of men, and sealed in their hearts. Finally, he concludes, not only that the preaching of the Gospel is poles apart from human wisdom, since it consists in the humiliation of the cross, but also that mere human judgment cannot determine what its real value is.[69]

The wisdom of the gospel comes to us in a different manner than philosophical knowledge does, and yet for all that it is still wise: "The preaching of the cross is regarded as foolishness by those who are perishing, just because it does not have the attractiveness of human wisdom to commend it. Be that as it may; in our view, however, the wisdom of God is shining from it."[70]

At times Calvin insinuates that it isn't the case that these two kinds of wisdom can exist side by side, as they might have for the Nominalists of the late medieval period, or for the so-called Averroists who allegedly preached a theory of double-truth. The wisdom of God confounds human wisdom and, what's more, God will destroy the wisdom of the wise. Calvin mentions Erasmus' translation of Paul's rendering of Isaiah at 1 Cor. 1:19, *the wisdom of the wise I will reject*, and suggests that something even stronger than *reiicere* (Erasmus' rendering) should be used to translate the Greek ἀθετεῖν – to destroy. Calvin would prefer, for example *delere* ("to efface"), *expungere* ("to expunge"), or *obliterare* ("to obliterate"), not only because he thinks it is more suitable to the meaning of Isaiah, but because "the idea of [merely] rejecting did not agree with the subject matter."[71] For the prophet is not only detailing an account of God rejecting wise rulers, but "wants to make it very clear that they will no longer have governors ... because the Lord will take away from them sound judgment and intelligence. For just as he threatens the whole people with blindness in another passage, so here it is the leaders, and it is just as if He were plucking out the eyes from the body."[72] In his action, God demonstrates the futility of the wisdom of the world compared with heavenly wisdom: "Paul makes use of this testimony of Isaiah's in order to prove that the wisdom of this world is useless and valueless, when it lifts itself up against God."[73] The purpose of Christ's humiliation is not only to suffer for the sins of humanity, but to reveal the mystery of God in such a way that the arrogant intelligentsia no longer have a monopoly on truth.

But who are the wise of this world (*sapientes saeculi*)? It is worth noting that, whereas Calvin elsewhere doesn't hesitate to denounce the "Sorbonnist sophists," or the scholastic theologians, in the commentary at this point he speaks at a rather general level (although he will go on to define the "Greeks" as those educated in the liberal sciences (*liberalibus doctrinis*) at *Comm. 1 Cor.* 1:22–3).[74] One reason for this, perhaps, is that Calvin wants to make it clear that reliance on human wisdom *in general*, and not only in the context of university theological disputes, is to miss the mark: "The words 'of this world' ought to be taken not only with the last term ('disputer') but should also be connected with the other two nouns ('wise man' and 'scribe'). For he calls the wise of this world those who are not enlightened in wisdom by the Word of God through the Spirit, but, being endowed with worldly insight only, place their trust in that."[75] The ones who trust in their own innate abilities do so hubristically, on the one hand, and uselessly on the other, focusing their attention on matters of no importance:

> Paul appropriately calls disputers those who display sharpness in handling thorny problems and intricate questions. So, generally speaking, he brings down all the natural ability of men, so that it counts for nothing in the kingdom of God. And he has good grounds for speaking so vehemently against human wisdom. For no words can describe how difficult it is to tear away from men's minds their misplaced confidence in the flesh, so that they may not arrogate to themselves more than is due. But it is going too far, if, relying even in the slightest degree on their own wisdom, they dare to form or pass judgments on their own.[76]

Totum hominis ingenium, all of natural human intelligence, counts for nothing in God's kingdom. To use even the smallest amount of their own wisdom (*minimum sua prudentia*) in attempts to discern divine truth is to err.[77] Certainly the language here of "thorny problems and intricate questions" (*scrupis perplexisque quaestionibus*) reminds us of his condemnations elsewhere of the overly speculative theologians of the schools, but Paul's condemnation of human wisdom is not confined to forms of meaningless speculation, as Calvin might have found among the logicians during his time as a student in Paris – human wisdom is just generally inappropriate when attempting to cultivate Christian piety.

Again, commenting on Paul's question at 1 Cor. 1:21, *Hath not God made foolish the wisdom of the world?* Calvin steps back a bit from his previous praise of the liberal arts (see below) as somehow worthwhile in the political or social sphere, and issues a sweeping condemnation of human ingenuity: "By *wisdom*, Paul means here whatever man can comprehend, not only by his own natural mental ability, but also by the help of experience, scholarship, and knowledge of the arts. For he contrasts the wisdom of the world with the wisdom of the Spirit. It follows that whatever knowledge a man may come by, apart from the enlightening of the Holy Spirit, is included in the wisdom of this world. He says that God has made all that ridiculous, or condemned it as foolish."[78] This is blanket criticism of human wisdom, for it includes whatever wisdom humans might innately have (*naturali ingenii facultate*) as well as that which they might acquire by their own means. Whatever knowledge man has that isn't derived from the Spirit, is of no more value (to use Calvin's metaphors) than the eye of a blind man for discerning colour, and is as inept in this regard "as an ass at conducting a symphony": "Knowledge of all the sciences [*cognitio scientiarum*] is so much smoke apart from the heavenly science of Christ [*coelestis Christi scientia*]."[79]

Calvin's metaphor (*asinus ineptus est ad symphoniam*) clearly invokes the proverbial 'ass at the lyre,' which features not only in Erasmus' *Adagia*, his massive and immensely popular collection of classical proverbs, but also in *The Praise of Folly*, complete with a marginal illustration in the famous edition marked up by Hans Holbein.[80] Indeed, Calvin's English translators of 1577 bring the classical adage back explicitly into play.[81] In any case, the *scientia Christi* is a divine science, imparted unto humans from without, not obtained by their own sophisticated striving. Paul's purpose here also, according to Calvin, is to condemn the haughtiness of the philosophical theologians: "Paul here gives lie to the consuming pride of those who exult in the wisdom of this world ... and checks the arrogance of those who, trusting in their own capability, seek to penetrate into heaven."[82] It is worth noting here again that Calvin's criticisms of human reason are not *only* rooted in his anthropology – that is, they do not only stem from an understanding of the human capacity of reason to have been damaged by the Fall; they are also onto-logico-metaphysical: humans qua finite beings are inherently incapable of comprehending the infinite.

But Calvin will offer a qualification. The wisdom of this world is in fact only utterly condemnable when it attempts to negotiate heavenly matters:

> At the same time an answer is given to the question, how it comes about that Paul throws to the ground, in this way, every kind of knowledge which exists apart from Christ, and, as it were, tramples under his feet what is well known to be the chief gift of God in this world. For what is

more noble than the reason of man, by which he stands out far above all other animals? How greatly deserving of honor are the liberal sciences, which refine man in such a way as to make him truly human! Besides, what a great number of rare products they yield! Who would not use the highest praise to extol statesmanship, by which states, empires and kingdoms are maintained? – to say nothing of other things. I maintain that the answer to this question is obvious from the fact that Paul does not utterly condemn, either the natural insight of men, or wisdom gained by practice and experience, or education of the mind through learning; but what he affirms is that all those things are useless for obtaining spiritual wisdom.[83]

He claims that the knowledge obtained through ordinary human means does indeed have *some* value, just not any value whatsoever for doing theology, or practicing piety. All the mysteries of the Kingdom of God are "hidden from human perception," and thus ought not to be striven for with human acumen. Human wisdom remains at the level of this world and "does not reach to heaven at all." Human effort has no efficacy in attempts to know God. "It is certainly madness (*insania*) for anyone to presume to ascend to heaven, relying on his own acumen, or the help of learning (*praesidio literarum*); in other words, to investigate the secret mysteries of the Kingdom of God, or force his way through to a knowledge of them, for they are hidden from human perception."[84] That they are hidden from human perception (*abscondita ab humano sensu*), it should be noted, is not a result, again, of human sinfulness, but of an active concealing on the part of the deity. Fallen or no, human wisdom is still just that – *human*. Aside from Christ, Calvin tells us, "every branch of human knowledge is futile." And finally, even when human wisdom is used to investigate the things of this world, if this is done without the wisdom of the Spirit (i.e., without knowledge of Christ), the endeavour is spoiled.[85] And so we have, on the one hand, the claim that knowledge of divine things is impossible through human wisdom without the Spirit (or Christ), and on the other hand (*a fortiori*), a spoiling of human wisdom itself when it is employed by the ungodly (*impios*), even when pursuing profane matters (so to speak).

The Inability to Know God Naturally:
Calvin on 1 Cor. 1:21–25

Calvin's commentary on verses 1:21–5 is, in the beginning, framed by a consideration of the relationship of human knowledge of God through creation, pre- and post-Fall – in other words, of the prospects of doing natural theology. There is a mass of scholarship on the issue in Calvin's thought, which dates to a debate between Barth and Brunner in the early twentieth century.[86] Here we only intend to address the issue insofar as it arises in Calvin's commentary, and to discern the role of Pauline folly for Calvin's approach. The question is, essentially, whether human beings can have meaningful knowledge of God without special revelation (through scripture or by the Spirit). A summary from Barbara Pitkin serves as a helpful model: she concludes, following Dowey and others, that there can be no knowledge of God whatever through nature without scripture – scripture is the always-necessary lens through which the Christian understands God so long as she is on earth. Pitkin's important contribution for our purposes, as it reflects Calvin's treatment of the matter in his commentary, is that all aspects of the knowledge of God, not only knowledge of God the redeemer, are mediated through Christ for Calvin: "The failure to understand the knowledge of God the creator as a christocentric knowledge in the broader sense reflects a one-sided emphasis on Christ's redemptive activity to the neglect of Christ's sustaining activity as head of the angels and all creation"[87] We might add Christ as an example of utmost humility as well, but in any case the general sense is one which Calvin can comfortably ground in his reading of the Pauline doctrine of the folly of the cross.

"The right order of things was surely this," Calvin writes, commenting on 1 Cor. 1:21, "that man, contemplating the wisdom of God in His works, by aid of the innate light of his own natural ability, might come to a knowledge of Him."[88] But, on account of our perverseness, God rendered us foolish, and then, beginning to "instruct us in the way of salvation," offers forth a *simulacrum stultitiae* – an image of folly. "The ingratitude of men deserved this inversion of things," Calvin writes. Human beings must be shamed on account of their presumptuousness before they can be instructed in true wisdom. All of creation was held out to us as "a clear mirror of God's wonderful wisdom," that the natural acquisition of the (still only partial) knowledge of God through his creation would be true wisdom. "Any man, who has even a spark of sound judgment, and pays attention to the earth and the other works of God, is bound to burst out in admiration of Him. If men were led to true knowledge of God by observation of His works, they would come to know God in a way that is wise, or by a way of acquiring wisdom that is natural and appropriate to them."[89] This was the state of Adam's knowledge of God through creation before the Fall. Furthermore, it describes in some sense the *potential* for human beings after the Fall to know God (e.g., the Greeks in Paul's letter to the Corinthians, for whom the cross is a stumbling block), even if, after the Fall, such knowledge can never become *actual*. "But because the whole world *learnt nothing at all from what God revealed of His wisdom in created things*, He then set about teaching men in another way."[90]

This is, in part, an anthropological issue with epistemological connotations: the human mind is blind and, though surrounded by light, perceives nothing. The entire world is a theatre displaying the glory of God, but it is all for naught: "we are blind, not because the revelation is obscure, but because our minds are alienated."[91] Calvin's use of the term *spectaculum* ("theatre") here, and the mention of blindness (a favourite term of Calvin's to describe humanity's theological insufficiencies), appear in Erasmus' *Paraphrase* on 1 Cor. 1:21 as well, also in the context of creation's beauty being rejected by human beings. And thus humans have only slight access to God even through faith, despite the fact that God shows himself openly. Citing Romans 1:20, Calvin tells us that we get just enough of an "inkling into his divine nature" to render us without excuse. A student of the *Institutes* is here reminded of its opening chapters. The theological framework in this section of the commentary, with its somber insistence on the incapacity of human reason in the face of the mysteries of God, is at least in this way different in terms of emphasis from the approach of Erasmus, which focuses more on the sheer impracticality of metaphysical speculation rather than dwelling on the depravity of humanity. Nevertheless, it is a difference of degree and not kind, as far as the exegesis goes: We've seen Erasmus invoke human sinfulness when Paul doesn't in his *Paraphrase*, and Calvin argues that even aside from their fallen nature, humans cannot comprehend the gospel without divine aid. Calvin betrays his indebtedness to his predecessor in other exegetical details as well, and even shows an appreciation for Erasmus' satirical puns when commenting on "the foolishness of preaching," which God uses to save believers: "Paul makes a concession when he calls the Gospel the *foolishness of preaching*, for that is precisely the light in which it is regarded by those 'foolish wise men' [*morosophoi*], who, intoxicated by a false confidence, have no fears about subjecting the inviolable truth of God to their own feeble censorship. And besides, there is no doubt that human reason finds nothing more absurd than the news that God became a mortal man, [etc.]."[92]

More broadly in conformity with the tendencies of Erasmian biblical humanism is the general scepticism which Calvin displays regarding knowledge of divine things apart from revelation, even if his is rooted more proximately in a robust understanding of the fallenness of humanity than his forebears (or most of his contemporaries) would be comfortable with. Practically speaking, though, with respect to theological method and practical piety, the results are identical: one ought to set aside any pretension to understand God on one's own, and ought instead to embrace Christ and his humility as both the object of theological discourse and the exemplum of Christian life. If anyone should offer forth the philosophers as exceptions to the rule that no one can know God through his creation, Calvin is explicit: "in their case especially there is a conspicuous example of our weakness, for you cannot find one of them who has not constantly fallen away from that principle of knowledge which I have already mentioned, to wanderings and misleading speculations. They are mostly sillier than old wives!"[93] We see here that a similar shortcoming prevents humans from understanding God through God's creation, as well as an explicit criticism of the *philosophi*. One cannot know God apart from Christ, but one also cannot know Christ in himself (as *Deus manifestus in carne*) via ordinary cognitive means. Knowledge as defined as something like comprehension solely through human noetic processes has virtually no role whatsoever in Calvin's theological epistemology.

We see this more fully in Calvin's attempt to define the "Greeks," who seek after wisdom (whom Paul distinguishes from the Jews, who seek after signs, at 1 Cor. 1:22–3), when paraphrasing Paul: "'The Greeks love what has the attraction of acuteness, and so pleases human cleverness. We in fact preach Christ crucified, and, at first glance, there seems to be nothing in that but weakness and foolishness ... The Greeks think it is like a fable to hear that this was the way of redemption.' In my opinion Paul means by the term *Greeks* not simply the heathen or the Gentiles, but those who were educated in the liberal sciences, or who were outstanding because of their superior intelligence."[94] Presumably the force of this last distinction is that Calvin is interested in criticizing not only pagan philosophers who might attempt to know God solely through reason, but also Christians who, though highly educated, have no sense of propriety in applying their learning to theology. That which is a stumbling block (*scandalon*) to the Jews and folly (*stultitia*) to the Greeks, Calvin describes as arising out of Christ's humility (*oriebatur ex humilitate*). This is really quite fundamental for our contention above that the entire problem is, at root, christologi-cal. The *humilitate crucis* is "derided by the Greeks" (*a Graecis autem derideatur*), for whom only an empty form of wisdom (*inani sapientiae specie*) can appease, and it simultaneously serves as the "wisdom of God for casting off the masks [of human wisdom]" (*quam sapientia ad excutiendam illam larvam*).[95]

At 1 Cor. 1:25, Paul writes that the foolishness of God is wiser than the wisdom of human beings, and that the weakness of God is stronger than human strength. Calvin's treatment of the verse, which comes on the heels of his treatment of the humility of Christ, which appears fool-ish to the Greeks, runs thus:

> When the Lord deals with us in such a way that He seems to act in an absurd way because he does not make His wisdom plain to see, neverthe-less what appears to be foolishness surpasses in wisdom all the shrewd-ness of men. Further, when God hides His power and seems to act in a weak way, what is imagined to be weakness is nevertheless stronger than any power of men. But we must always take note, in looking at these words, that there is a concession, as I noted a little earlier. For anyone can see quite clearly how improper it is to ascribe either foolishness or weak-ness to God, but it was necessary to use such ironic expressions in rebut-ting the insane arrogance of the flesh which does not hesitate to strip God of all His glory.[96]

The (*ironic*) inversion of values which attends God's confounding of human power and wisdom was expressed in such a way by Paul so as to confound human wisdom, and it also has social and soteriologi-cal implications for Calvin. Paul, he says, commenting on the follow-ing verse, does not exclude *all* high-born and powerful people from God's calling, but he doesn't include very many, because "the Lord, in preferring the contemptible to the great, might bring down the pride of men."[97] Calvin admits that God wishes all to be saved, but there is nevertheless a hierarchy, and it follows not the model of worldly virtue, but that of the humility of Christ: "shepherds are the first to be called to Christ; then afterwards come the philosophers; uneducated and despised fishermen hold the most honorable place, but, later, kings and their advisers."[98] Erasmus, too, had argued that gospel truth is more the province of idiots and fishermen than of philosophers in his comments on these verses, and Calvin will repeat the sentiment at least one other time in his commentary.[99]

Excursus: In Praise of Pauline Folly

The *Praise of Folly*, Erasmus' masterful satire first published in 1511, is a foundational text for considering foolishness in a sixteenth-century religious context, and its connections to his biblical humanism are mostly well established, even if disentangling Dame Folly's irony from Erasmus' theological vision has long proved difficult for students of the text.[100] It has long been noted that Pauline folly undergirds at least a good portion of Folly's philosophy in the *Moria*. Mark Vessey has argued more recently, in an analysis of Erasmus' paraphrases of the Pastoral and Catholic Epistles, that Dame Folly, the self-encomiastic narrative voice of the work, can be ascertained in the background, and that her "declamatory, cajoling, long-winded" style is the same one which Erasmus prefers in composing his paraphrases.[101] In the case of the early chapters of 1 Corinthians it is not only style, but also a great deal of theological substance, which Erasmus' Folly and Erasmus' Paul share. A brief overview of relevant aspects of Pauline folly in the *Praise of Folly*, with the help of Erasmus' defence of it as offered in a letter of 1515 to Martin Dorp, will focus on the major thematic theological context of Erasmus' deployment of the rhetoric of foolishness: the criticism of abstruse university theology.

The *recentiores* (modern theologians) are lampooned for their approach to theology by Folly:

> For that they have actually discovered nothing at all is clear enough from this fact alone: on every single point they disagree violently and irreconcilably among themselves. Though they know nothing at all, they profess to know everything; and though they do not know themselves, and sometimes can't see a ditch or a stone in their path (either because most of them are blear-eyed or because their minds are wool-gathering), nevertheless they claim that they can see ideas, universals, separate forms, prime matter, quiddities, ecceities, formalities, instants – things so fine-spun that no one, however 'eagle-eyed,' would be able, I think to perceive them.[102]

The "incredibly arrogant and touchy" theologians fair no better, who hedge themselves in by rows of "conclusions, corollaries, explicit and implicit propositions, ... distinctions, with which they cut all knots as cleanly as the fine-honed edge of 'the headman's axe' – so many new terms have they thought up and such monstrous jargon have they coined."[103]

What Folly (and no doubt Erasmus, here) considers to be "sacred mysteries" the theologians adjudicate with ease, explaining how the world was created, how Adam's sin is transmitted to posterity, how long it took for Christ to be fully formed in Mary's womb, "how accidents subsist in the Eucharist without any domicile," and even more absurdly, whether it's possible that God the Father could hate the Son, whether, instead of a man, God could have assumed the nature of "a woman, of the devil, of an ass, of a cucumber, of a piece of flint," and "what Peter would have consecrated (if he had consecrated) during the time Christ was hanging on the cross," and so on.[104] All of these "petty quibbles," the "deepest darkest things that are nowhere,"[105] parody questions from Lombard's *Sententiae* and the subsequent commentaries on them by theologians of the medieval university, even if it has been noted often that Erasmus' criticisms in general are leveled primarily at his contemporaries.[106] As for the foolishness endorsed by Paul, Erasmus clarifies his resuscitation of the idea in his apologia to Dorp:

> [Folly] went on to [describe] the apostles themselves and even Christ, for we find a certain folly attributed to them in Holy Scripture. Not that there is any danger that someone will think the apostles and Christ are really fools, but rather that they too have a certain infirmity, a sort of concession to our emotions, which, by comparison with the eternal and pure wisdom of God, might seem something less than wise. But it is this very folly that conquers all the wisdom of the world. So too the prophet compares all human justice to a woman's soiled menstrual rag. Not that the justice practiced by all good men is polluted, but because whatever is most pure among men is somehow impure compared to the ineffable purity of God.[107]

Folly's criticisms in cases like this are easily mapped onto the *stultitia Dei* of 1 Corinthians (indeed, portions of this passage are reproduced in the *Annotations*), and her voice becomes the *sermo* of Christ in the flesh. This is the substance of Marjorie O'Rourke Boyle's interpretation of Folly as the paradigmatic expression of Christian wisdom: "Moria, however, extends 'folly' to include even its antonym 'wisdom,' so that sinners and saints alike are legitimately predicated of her. The rationale for this license with language is Moria herself in her highest theophany, Christ as wisdom made foolish, and folly, wise, who as the Logos, the paradigm of speech, ultimately determines and interprets all meaning."[108] Erasmus' negative evaluation of the scholastic philosophical and theological enterprise – which to his mind leads to disharmony, which seeks (hubristically) to know the unknowable, which rejects the simplicity of the gospel – is rhetorically and theologically grounded in Paul's claim that the foolishness of God rendered meaningless all the wisdom of the world.

The early chapters of 1 Corinthians are in many ways a microcosm of Erasmus' entire theological program. Furthermore, what Christ and Paul did establish as the Christian philosophy to Erasmus' mind is sufficient in every period, and does not need to be redefined according to shifting philosophical paradigms. As Walter Kaiser pointed out some time ago, Dorp's plea, in a letter from 1514, that Erasmus write an encomium to wisdom to counterbalance what he'd done in the *Moria*, is to entirely miss the point – Folly *is* Wisdom.[109] The apostles themselves, indeed, Folly declares, couldn't comprehend the subtleties of school theology, nor would their definitions be "sufficiently magisterial," nor defined with "sufficient dialectical precision" for the modern theologians. Folly proceeds for pages explaining what the apostles *did* and what they *preached*, all without explaining it dialectically – indeed, all the while condemning *logomachia*, as Paul had done in his first letter to Timothy. They baptized, but didn't distinguish between the four Aristotelian causes in carrying out the act; they preached grace, but made no distinction between grace *gratis data* and grace *gratificans*; they exhorted to good works without distinguishing *opus operans* from *opus operatum*, and so on.[110] The condemnation of the stubbornness of the philosophers ought, according to Folly, to be done as the Fathers did it, "by the lives they led and the miracles they performed rather than by manufacturing syllogisms."[111]

Also to the chagrin of Folly is the dogmatic nature of the school theologians, who legislate on questions of heresy with respect to minute theological issues that were utterly foreign to the apostles and early fathers. As Atlas holds the world up on his shoulders, so do these theologians imagine themselves to support the entire Church, and to keep it from collapse, with their syllogistic props. Without their approval, no one, not even Thomas *Aristotelicissimus* (the "Aristotelianest" one) is considered to be truly Christian.[112] The theologians' investigations' trivial nature is proof of the theologians' arrogance, that oft-repeated insult of Erasmus' Paul against the Corinthian philosophers. Moreover, the cap which the doctor of theology wore also served a practical purpose, according to Folly: if a theologian didn't wear it, his head might explode, both from pride and on account of its being stuffed full of trifles. And not only in books, or scholastic disputations, does this sort of thing occur, but also in the sermons of the "most theological" monks, who esteem most highly what is most irrelevant. When preaching to the uneducated laity they pass by the gospel very quickly so as to "put on display their syllogisms, majors, minors, conclusions, corollaries, most jejune hypotheses and utterly pedantic quibbles."[113]

Erasmus represents well, on the one hand, humanists who spent much energy satirizing the impracticalities of school theology, which to their minds sought too often to convince rather than to convert; but he also represents, perhaps paradigmatically, the *theologia rhetorica* of biblical humanism which sought not only to replace school methods with a Pauline philosophical model for truth-seeking, but to ground Christian theological method in the special form of "simple" eloquence that can be found, according to Erasmus, in the Bible itself. Not only does too much learning and eloquence when applied to biblical exposition result in superfluities attached to something basically simple, but it forces the exegete to miss the mark altogether.[114]

An interpretative account of the themes of *Folly* pertinent to our study is conveniently given by Erasmus himself. In the letter to Dorp, Erasmus points out that he had actually held back in his satirical denigration of contemporary theologians, many of whose sins he had passed over when taking up the mantle of Folly.[115] Folly, for example, as Erasmus reminds Dorp, never touches upon the "bad morals" of the theologians, but she only satirizes the pettiness of their disputations and she only condemns those theologians "who think that such disputations constitute the whole of theology, 'from stem to stern,' so to speak, and who are so taken up with these wars of words, as St. Paul calls them, that they have no time to read the evangelists, prophets, and apostles."[116] Erasmus makes a further distinction between true theologians, who are "men of integrity, dignity, and learning who have assimilated the teaching of Christ" by actually reading the Bible, and the "modern" theologians, whom the proponents of "ancient" theology (Erasmus included) denounce on account of the "base monstrosities of [their theology's] barbarous and factitious language ... and its lack of literary culture, its ignorance of languages."[117] The humanist preference for a revival of "ancient theology," which includes an appreciation of the biblical texts and the commentaries upon them by the church fathers (embodied, indeed, in the person of Jerome himself) is contrasted with the newfangled appropriation of Aristotle's logic into scholastic theological method. Here Christ is pitted against Aristotle:

[Modern theology] is so contaminated with Aristotle, with trifling ideas thought up by men, even with secular laws, that I hardly see how it can preserve the true savor of Christ, who is pure and uncontaminated. For what happens is this: while it looks aside too often, gazing on man-made traditions, it is less able to follow its archetype, Christ ... What connection is there, I ask you, between Christ and Aristotle? or between sophistical quibbles and the mysteries of eternal wisdom? Where will these labyrinths of questions get us? How many of them are pointless! How many are downright noxious, by the very fact that they breed quarrels and dissension.[118]

Attempts to usher in Aristotelian language and categories constitute, for Erasmus, an adulteration and contamination of Christian theology. "Man-made" devices do not serve to explain, but to obscure and divide. In the adage *Dulce bellum inexpertis*, Erasmus traces the inexplicable propensity among Christians for war to the divisiveness introduced by the theologians, and points out that the introduction of Aristotle into the "heart of theology" was especially problematic. "We try to fuse together all his decrees and teachings of Christ, which is like mixing fire and water ... As if the teachings of Christ were not truly something that could be entirely shared by all, or had any kind of common ground with the wisdom of the philosophers."[119] As Manfred Hoffmann puts it, describing the error of scholastic exegesis as perceived by Erasmus, "human accretions, not least the presumptuous interpretations of the dialecticians, have burdened the sacred text so grievously as to sap its power to edify the church, confront the heretic, and convert the heathen. The simplicity of the biblical message has been distorted by the proliferation of complex readings."[120]

One of the motivations of the Christian philosophy for Erasmus is that it is more effectively collegial, which contrasts with the "proliferation of complex readings" inaugurated by scholastic disputation.[121] The result is a fractured church that parallels the church Paul attempts to mend in his letter to the Corinthians. Cephas and Apollos are paralleled by Aristotle and Zeno in Erasmus' paraphrase of 1 Cor. 1:11–13.[122] Human as opposed to Christian philosophy leads to discord: "Although there is a common source and ruler of all, still one of you says, 'I am a Pauline,' and another, 'I am an Apollonian.' For the students of human philosophy contend among themselves with labels of this same sort: 'I am an Aristotelian,' 'I a Platonist,' 'I a Stoic,' 'I an Epicurean'."[123] What ought to be the unifying nature of Christ as the head of the Church is dispersed when human systems of thought are applied to divine matters. The Neo-Aristotelians have the wrong *scopus*, and thus they "wander in a fog, they dream, they bump into things blindly, they produce nothing but monstrosities."[124] Erasmus' ideal of ecclesiastical consensus is also a criterion itself for determining whether something is true.[125] But, again, this scepticism is primarily aimed at over-speculation in theological matters, and does not entail that one cannot know the truth of revelation through the Word of God, for what has been revealed is in fact simple, and can be understood by all if approached in the proper manner. The fact that the philosophers can't agree on anything is proof that they know nothing (and, *a fortiori*, that they are unwise).[126]

While the *Moria* is perhaps an unsurprising place to find an emphasis on Pauline foolishness, there are less obvious places, too, in Erasmus' corpus, where we find significant use of Paul's contrast between human wisdom and divine folly. It pervades, for example, Erasmus' *Concio de puero Iesu*, a homily Erasmus composed so that it might be recited by one of the boys at John Colet's school, founded in 1510 at St Paul's in London. This text is not accorded a great deal of attention in modern scholarship, but it did occasion multiple editions and even more print runs during Erasmus' lifetime, along with early vernacular translations – a testament to its wider appeal in the sixteenth century.[127] That the child Jesus in Erasmus' homily is identified with Wisdom, as Kearns notes, immediately connects this text with the *Moria* and also, we might add, with the early chapters of 1 Corinthians.[128] Erasmus' literary conceit, the personification of Wisdom in the boy Jesus, a Lucan notion as well as a Pauline one (or perhaps a Pauline notion found in Luke's Gospel), already subverts the common idea of a sage and ushers in the association of Christian wisdom with paradox. The homily is redolent of themes commonly found in Erasmus' attempts to articulate a form of Christian humanism, defined by learned piety. There are a number of references in the text (at a rate of almost one per modern book page) to Pauline folly, both in the context of condemning worldly wisdom and of contrasting Christian with pagan eloquence.

The homily opens with a contrast between simple and Ciceronian discourse: "I, a child among children, shall now speak to you of the child Jesus, who cannot be expressed in words; so I should not wish to possess the eloquence of a Cicero, to delight the ears with a short-lived, meaningless pleasure. For Christian eloquence should be as far removed from the eloquence of the world as is the wisdom of Christ from the wisdom of the world, and such a distance is immeasurable."[129] The children are exhorted to pray to God the Father, for it is his Spirit that "makes eloquent the tongues of infants," and whose "living and efficacious discourse pierces deeper than any two-edged sword, reaching right to the inmost recesses of the heart."[130] The contrast between Christian and worldly eloquence here, further strengthened insofar as it's been put into the mouth of a child preaching about the child Jesus, prefigures Erasmus' somewhat more formal *Paraphrase* on 1 Corinthians, written many years later, especially in the assertion (which is also a paraphrase of Hebrews 4:12) of the divine *sermo* as *vivus et efficax* – a notion we have seen taken up by Pellikan, Bullinger, and Calvin as well.

The unsurpassable majesty of God is invoked here too in the context of Christian folly. In an elaborate display of apophasis, Erasmus poses a series of rhetorical questions regarding the ineffable nature of God, one of which alludes to 1 Corinthians: "What could be wiser than he, who created everything with such amazing order that even in the tiny bees he has left so great and so many wonderful traces of his wisdom ... and in whom the most foolish thing surpasses by far all the wisdom of human philosophers?"[131] This leads Erasmus to the child Jesus, who presents a similar problem of exposition, for his nature confounds description, it being easier to "drain the huge ocean using a tiny cup" than to "contain his greatness in speech." As with Folly's advice regarding the divine mysteries, the child Jesus' "boundlessness is rather to be adored than explained."[132] The natural link between the child Jesus and Paul's contrast between milk and solid food is appropriately invoked, too, in an appeal to the ideal of Christian simplicity as a form of infancy, followed shortly after by a shunning of the child with a "hairless chin but bearded mind," an image meant to evoke the university theologians, for example, biting off more than they can chew.[133]

Later in the text, alluding to Luke 2:52, the only appearance of the child Jesus in all the canonical Gospels, Erasmus writes: "Further, so that we do not strive to attain the foolish and specious wisdom of this world, there follows immediately 'and the favour of God was upon him.' He is truly wise who is foolish to the world and whose wisdom is in nothing but Christ. Such a man is not known by philosophers' tomes or from the subtleties of a Scotus; he is known by heartfelt faith, he is maintained in hope and bound in love."[134] The contrast between a childlike faith and scholastic theological knowledge is fleshed out with the familiar Pauline trope. Luke's tale of Jesus sitting among the learned at the Temple of Jerusalem, asking impressive questions, "was scarcely surprising, since this was he compared with whom all worldly wisdom is foolish," further demonstrating that "knowledge of philosophy is an outstanding achievement, attainments in theology are worthy of great respect; but if one hears Jesus, immediately they all seem foolish."[135] In this case even respectable forms of philosophy and theology pale in comparison to divine wisdom in the mouth of a child.

Chapter Three

Hidden Wisdom and the
Revelation of the Spirit

He saw God's foot upon the treadle of the loom, and spoke it; and therefore his
shipmates called him mad. So man's insanity is heaven's sense; and wander-
ing from all mortal reason, man comes at last to that celestial thought, which,
to reason, is absurd and frantic; and weal or woe, feels then uncompromised,
indifferent as his God.

– Herman Melville, Moby Dick

The second chapter of 1 Corinthians focuses on the role of the Spirit as
pedagogue, unveiling the mysteries of God to the ones who do not put
stock in worldly wisdom. It is an important chapter for considering the
relationship of Erasmus and Calvin on the manner in which the Christian comes to be illuminated with the truths of the Christian philosophy,
for *prima facie*, given Calvin's clear rejection of the validity of human
endeavour in coming to obtain meaningful theological knowledge, and
given the occasional caricatures of Erasmus as a detached rationalist
text-critic, we might expect their reception of this chapter to differ. In
the end, however, we find that rather than playing down the role of the
Spirit, Erasmus is keen to emphasize the importance of divine inspiration for unveiling the "secret and hidden wisdom of the gospel [*arcanam
et reconditam evangelii sapientiam*]."[1] 1 Cor. 2 also provides for some of Calvin's strongest formulations regarding humans' inability to know God
naturally. This chapter is fundamental for biblical-humanist attempts to
establish a Pauline religious epistemology which fully appreciates the
foolishness of God. In structure, this chapter will proceed in much the
same way as the previous one: by considering Erasmus' exegesis, then
that of Bullinger and Pellikan, and finally turning to Calvin's treatment.

"Lest we cast roses before swine": Erasmus on 1 Cor. 2:1–16[2]

Despite Erasmus' translation of the Greek *martyrion tou theou* ("witness/testimony of God") in chapter 2, verse 1 as *testimonium Dei* in his New Testament, in the paraphrase he emphasizes the valence found in Ambrosiaster's reading (and other Greek manuscript witnesses), the *mysterium Dei* ("mystery of God"), which he also glosses in the *Annotations*.[3] Expositing 1 Cor. 2:4, Paul, Erasmus paraphrases, did not come to teach either with the power of eloquence (*viribus eloquentiae*) or with a knowledge of philosophy (*cognitione philosophiae*), despite knowing that the Corinthians preferred this sort of thing.[4] Furthermore, even though he had not employed any "human defenses" (*praesidiis hominum*), nor the "ornaments of the rhetoricians or the arguments of philosophers ... nevertheless it had the efficacy to transform you, not through its display of learning, but through the Spirit and power of God."[5] More explicitly, Erasmus' Paul recognizes that the Corinthians had in fact been transformed, but warns them lest any "think that you owe this to human teaching or to eloquence, which we do not claim to have, but [you owe it to] divine power, through which our language was more effective than the philosophers' discourse, however subtly argued and embellished it might be."[6] Certainly many of Erasmus' readers would have understood the castigation of the subtle (*arguta*) arguments of the philosophers in the context of his other criticisms of the methods of university theologians writing in his own time, especially in light of the scathing criticisms he had offered in the *Praise of Folly*, treated above. Indeed, in his *Annotations* on verse 2:6, he appeals to patristic support in pointing out that while many interpreters had understood the *principes saeculi* to refer to *daemones*, both Chrysostom and Theophylact had interpreted them to be "the philosophers, orators, and other learned men who rule over the republic."[7] Erasmus has marshalled his extensive readings of the Church Fathers, which add such richness to his annotations, to justify his understanding of Paul's denunciations as directed at those learned in worldly philosophy and rhetoric.

Paraphrasing 1 Cor. 2:6, Erasmus attends to the obsolescence of human wisdom in the face of the folly of the cross:

Now among unbelievers we seem to teach foolishness when we preach the cross of Christ, but among those who fully believe we seem to preach an exceptional wisdom, but one far different from that which vainly explores through human reasoning the causes of this world. Nor is it the human wisdom on the basis of which those who are commonly called illustrious vaunt and advertise themselves. Their authority, along with their wisdom itself, is through Christ made null and obsolete since their foolishness has been disclosed.[8]

Understanding the gospel requires that the hearer approach the subject matter in a different way. Christian theology demands a different method from pagan philosophy, for it begins at an unreasonable starting point.

Erasmus will also occasionally interject a paraphrase into his *Annotations*, as he does on verse 2:7, *in mysterio quae abscondita* ("in a mystery which is hidden"): "But we speak not openly or indiscreetly, lest we be a stumbling-block, but in secret; not among anyone, lest we cast roses before swine, but among the perfect; and not just any wisdom, as the sort that is professed publicly by the other philosophers, but what is hidden and concealed and, so to speak, more obscure."[9] In the *Paraphrase*, he focuses extensively on the radical difference between the exalted rulers of this world, with their puffed-up knowledge of the Law (*turgidi scientia legis*) who have no access to the hidden mysteries of the humble cross of Christ, which latter has inestimable power for those of humble mind (*modestia animi*). The pompous philosophers (*tumidi philosophi*) cannot access through their *curiositas* what comes by the secret inbreathing of the Spirit (*per afflatum occultum spiritus*). God has reserved his revelation for those who philosophize in faith, not through reason (*qui fide philosophantur, non ratiocinationibus*).[10] His rejection of *doctrina humana* in this section of the paraphrase is also repeated in his annotation on 1 Cor. 2:13, *Sed in doctrina spiritus* ("but in the teaching of the Spirit"), where he argues that this verse proves that apostolic preaching is not consonant with human teaching, but is divinely inspired.[11] In the same note, just after criticizing the *theologici* for ushering the *philosophiam Aristotelicam* into their interpretations of sacred literature, Erasmus cites Chrysostom as confirming that the gospel is not a work of human philosophy (*non esse opus humana philosophia*) but is sufficient in the Word itself, for the philosophical method (*ratione philosophorum*) is not applicable to truths of Scripture, such as God creating trees without a seed or Adam from dust.[12] But as we've seen, when *philosophia* is employed properly, it can be used to describe the Pauline approach to Christian understanding as well. Erasmus defines the *philosophia Christiana* in his paraphrase here: "This is the philosophy which, as we have drawn it from the Spirit of

Christ, so we, in turn, impart it to simple and godly persons, not with artfully embellished words in the way those professing philosophy impart what they profess, but with words which, although indeed they are unpolished, yet impart spiritual teaching."[13]

Erasmus does not disparage scholastic theology in favour of ineffable subjective experience or contemplation of an unknown God. *Theologia rhetorica*, as it takes shape in Erasmus' approach, emphasizes the role of *oratio* over *ratio*, a preference which ostensibly leads to conversion rather than mere intellectual assent, as has been amply demonstrated in the work of O'Rourke Boyle and Hoffmann on the importance of rhetoric in Erasmus' theology.[14] But there is nevertheless a concrete theology here, and it is what Erasmus perceives to be the theology of the gospel. It is fundamental to recognize that the Incarnation of Christ and the teachings and example that accompany the story of his life on earth become simultaneously the *form* and the *content* of Christian theological discourse in this model. Paul is preaching the humble and foolish Word of God. The Christian experiences Christ not in seeking to understand God syllogistically, but through the preaching and hearing of the Word. And this leads to a vocational clarification regarding the task of theologians. In his annotation on 1 Cor. 2:13, where Paul distinguishes the learned words of human wisdom (here, too, we find a modification of the Vulgate's *verbi* to *sermones*) from those of the spirit, Erasmus writes that we thus know that "apostolic preaching does not agree with human learning, but rather with the divine spirit"; and then, citing Ambrose, Chrysostom, Theophylact, and Augustine for support, he asks: "What will certain theologians (as they call themselves) say here, who when teaching scripture prattle on about nothing except Aristotelian philosophy?"[15]

1 Cor. 2:13 in Erasmus' notes becomes a prooftext employed to undermine the validity of a very prominent form of late medieval university theological method. As Marjorie O'Rourke Boyle puts it, "The Christian theologian was therefore to be a rhetorician not a logician. This vocation distinguished the humanists from the scholastics (whom Erasmus aligned with the animals) in a methodological shift from inquiry to eloquence, from the dialectical question to the rhetorical period."[16] While, as we will see in a later chapter, the role of eloquence in Christian teaching is more complicated in Erasmus than Boyle's dichotomy in this quotation suggests, there is certainly a significant shift in tendency from *ratio* as an ideal to *oratio*. As Erasmus himself puts it in the *Paraphrase*, "Just as the kind of wisdom is different, so the method of

teaching is different."[17] And it isn't only the preacher, but the congregation, too, who must approach things differently: "The spiritual pupil must be suited to a spiritual philosophy in that understanding has been purified through faith and emotion corrected through love. The gross and natural person [*crassus et animalis homo*], who swells in pride from his knowledge of visible things and is governed by human affections does not accept things that belong to the divine Spirit ... he does not believe anything except what he has confirmed either by experience or proven by human reason."[18] This is highly reminiscent of Erasmus' definition of the *philosophia Christiana* in the *Paraclesis*, which served as a foreword to his New Testament, beginning with the first edition in 1516: it is "seated in emotions rather than in syllogisms, a life rather than a disputation, inspiration rather than erudition, transformation rather than reason."[19] It is worth pointing out, as well, that the human emotions (*humanis affectibus*) are here judged problematic alongside human knowledge (*scientia*), and that both can be chastened, or "spiritualized," when properly governed by faith and love. We will consider this more closely in the final chapter.

"Natural" (*animalis*) here doesn't refer to a type of philosophy as much as it does to the philosopher, who is contrasted, following the Pauline distinction, with the *spiritual* person. Although it is also true that Erasmus' "natural" philosopher, in one way at least, isn't all that different from a modern day natural philosopher, viz. in that he "does not believe anything except what he has either confirmed by experience or proven by human reasons." *Animalis* translates, quite literally, Paul's Greek ψυχικός, which refers, more or less neutrally in Paul's tripartite anthropology, to the merely human aspect of man governed by the rational soul (or, metonymously, to those kinds of people governed primarily by this part of the soul). The fleshly aspect (*carnalis*) is sinful while the spiritual aspect (*spiritualis*) is the highest in virtue. Thus note that Erasmus is not contrasting the spiritual philosophy with one governed by sin, or the flesh, but with the *human* philosophy, governed by the (morally neutral) rational soul, something also elaborated on in the *Annotations*.[20] We will see Calvin do something similar.

Both Erasmus and Calvin give a more robust account of the *psychical* aspect (or type) of human than did early Christian expositors, many of whom didn't account for this mediate aspect at all, but preferred the ease of the dichotomy between flesh and spirit.[21] Of interest here, in general, are the epistemological considerations that Erasmus draws our attention to. First, the definition given of *understanding* (*intellectus*) in the spiritual philosophy is "purified through faith," which is then contrasted with the natural (*crassus et animalis*) philosopher's demand for truths "confirmed by experience or proven by human reasons." This criterion precludes a proper understanding of a number of tenets of the Christian philosophy (*quod haec philosophiae*), from the virgin birth to the resurrection.[22] It is worth noting here, I think, that Erasmus does not seem to be describing a species of fideism whereby the Christian believes blindly things which are irrational, but which the Church teaches to be true. Rather (and this brings him close to Calvin on the point), the Christian does *comprehend*, but the understanding of the matters of the Christian philosophy is not arrived at by ordinary deductive processes (*non humana ratiocinatione*) – it is given through the inspiration of the Spirit.[23]

Erasmus wraps up his paraphrase of chapter 2 by repeating again that the things taught (*quae traduntur*) in the Christian philosophy are from the secrets of the divine mind (*divinae mentis arcanis*) and not from human reasoning (*non ex humanis ratiocinationibus*). "The divine mind wished to lay claim to its own people by a *new method* that would elude all human curiosity."[24] What has emerged from our exposition of Erasmus on chapter 2 is a profound and consistent rejection of the role of human reason in understanding the secret wisdom of the gospel. Both in the *Annotations* and in the *Paraphrases* we find substantial theological elaboration on the implications of the Pauline doctrine of the foolishness of the cross. Erasmus' Paul has initiated a new theological methodology, rooted in a robust appreciation of the insufficiencies of human reasoning and eloquence to comprehend and adequately interpret and convey divine wisdom. These themes will be taken up and strengthened by Erasmus' Protestant readers in Switzerland.

"Philosophy is destroyed": The Zurichers on 1 Cor. 2

Bullinger's interpretation of chapter 2 emphasizes early the transformative power of the Spirit's teaching, contrasted with the "strength of Persuasion" (*virtutem Persuasioni*), which "for a brief time caresses the ears of its listeners." The *sermo veritatis*, however, is "lively" itself, and also living and potent, transforming the heart of man; it stings, it maintains, it changes the hearer permanently.[25] This is part and parcel of the tradition of *theologia rhetorica*. Again, true faith is dependent on the power of God, not on human supports (*praesidio humano*).[26] Like Erasmus, Bullinger differentiates true wisdom also from the sort that relies on *ratiocinationes* and useless and superstitious *quaestiones*.[27] "Philosophy is destroyed" Bullinger proclaims, "and the ones who, in addition to God, cultivate the traditions of men, cultivate in error."[28] The artificial worldly philosophy (*fucum mundanae sapientiae philosophiam*) is again contrasted with the more simple and clear teachings of Christ.[29] We know Bullinger is reading Erasmus' *Annotations* for verse 2:13, for he lifts the line, without notice, against those who "prattle on about nothing except Aristotle."[30] The proclamation of the *destruction* of philosophy by God's foolishness along with the dismissal of Aristotelian theology situates Bullinger firmly on an Erasmian exegetical trajectory.

Pellikan begins his comments on chapter 2 with a section from Erasmus' *Paraphrase* on 2:1–3, emphasizing that the secret and hidden gospel wisdom (*arcanam et reconditam evangelii sapientiae*) was not taught by Paul with eloquence or a knowledge of philosophy, despite the Corinthians' proclivities towards these things.[31] He likewise reproduces, on 1 Cor. 2:3–4, Erasmus' paraphrase concerning the efficacious and transformative inspiration of the Spirit in contrast with the *rhetorum ornamentis* and *philosophorum argumentis*.[32] The subtleties and embellishments of philosophical discourse are denounced in Erasmian terms as well, along with the *lenocinio verborum* and *curiosis quaestionibus*, in a line taken directly from Zwingli's lectures.[33] Erasmus' Paul's notice that the secrets of the divine mind cannot be comprehended by *humanis ratiocinationibus* is picked up for verse 10.[34] Similar reproductions happen on almost every verse in Pellikan's commentary, sometimes more than once per verse. In short, as in chapter 1, Pellikan's commentary follows the contours of Erasmus' *Paraphrase* very closely. Pellikan's rejection of human reason in understanding divine things is as comprehensive and thoroughgoing as that of his counterparts. Crucially, as for the rest of our exegetes, Pellikan also borrows from Erasmus in his comment on 2:9 that a new method of teaching (*novo modo tradendo*) is required for heavenly and spiritual matters.[35] This recognition, along with the details of the new method, are precisely what joins biblical-humanist exegetes together in their attempts to establish a *philosophia Christiana* that approaches theological matters in a different manner from the philosophers.

"A Loftiness the Human Mind Cannot Reach": Calvin on 1 Cor. 2

Calvin's emphatic underscoring of the hiddenness of divine wisdom and of the inability of human reason to access it finds few rivals in the Christian tradition, and his comments on 1 Cor. 2 reveal the deep interest he has in these questions. Paul himself claims that he was without human wisdom, but nevertheless "proclaimed the testimony of God," and in mentioning both speech and wisdom (*logos* and *sophia*) in 1 Cor. 2:1, Calvin argues, Paul is not only condemning "empty chattering, but the whole culture of human learning" (*totum humanae doctrinae cultum*).[36] He then, commenting on a potential ambiguity in verse 2, viz. whether Paul decided to know nothing other than Christ (implying, presumably, that one could in fact *know* other things), or whether Paul counted nothing as knowledge outside of Christ (implying that actual knowledge is limited to Christ and him crucified), concludes that either is fine, as far as he is concerned, and paraphrases the verse as follows: "The reason why I lacked embellishments of speech, and did not argue with more refinement and subtlety, was because I did not strive after those things, in fact I rather disdained them, because only one thing mattered to me – to proclaim Christ with simplicity" (or to proclaim "Christ alone" – *Christum simpliciter*).[37] It is significant, of course, that Calvin doesn't rule out the second reading, for it is a much stronger claim. It's one thing to consider anything outside the knowledge of Christ as having little value, and quite another to claim that nothing is to be esteemed *as knowledge* "or as a substitute for knowledge except Christ alone."[38] This is, again, to understand Paul radically in his claims that God indeed has condemned all the wisdom of the world. However, Calvin does add that Paul's "Christ and him crucified" is not to be understood as an exhortation to preach nothing about Christ *other than the cross*. Rather, he paraphrases thus: "The disgrace of the cross will not prevent me from looking up to him who is the source of salvation, or make me ashamed of finding all my wisdom summed up in him – him, I say, whom proud men treat with disdain, and reject on account of the reproach of the cross ... No knowledge was of such importance to me, as to make me desire to know anything other than Christ, even if he was crucified."[39] This could be a qualification aimed, in part, at Luther's *theologia crucis*, which emphasizes so emphatically God hidden in the cross specifically (*CRUX sola est nostra theologia!*).[40] Calvin's God, too, is a *Deus absconditus*, but God's revelation in Christ extends beyond the cross.[41]

In any case, this verse (1 Cor. 2:2), which Calvin calls a beautiful one (*pulcher locus*), was aimed at those arrogant teachers whose "great desire was to be applauded for their reputation for some sort of higher wisdom." But the simple gospel is "what faithful ministers ought to teach, and what we must be learning throughout our life; and in comparison with that everything else is to be counted as *dung*."[42] Calvin elaborates on the idea of the hiddenness of the mystery of the gospel (1 Cor. 2:7), especially when it is considered from the perspective of human wisdom:

> The reason he gives for the small value put on the teaching of the Gospel by the rulers of this world is that it is wrapped up in mysteries, and for that reason concealed. For the Gospel towers over the insight of the human mind so that those who are considered intellectually of the first rank may look as high as they like, but they never reach its eminence. In the meantime, however, they look down upon its insignificance as if it were prostrate at their feet. In consequence the more haughtily they despise it the further they are from knowing it; more than that, they are standing at so great a distance from it that they are prevented from seeing it.[43]

The mystery of the gospel is concealed from the wise of this world (which, in this case, also consists of political and religious leaders like Pilate, also mentioned in Erasmus' *Paraphrase* and in Chrysostom's homilies on 2:8),[44] and it must come to humanity in a different manner than through intellectual attempts. "For if God established everything to some purpose, it follows that we will lose nothing in hearing the Gospel, which he intended for us, for when He speaks to us He accommodates Himself to our capacity."[45] The over-arching purpose of these sorts of comments seems to be an emphasis on the inability of human wisdom – and this includes what can be accomplished by "all the faculties of the mind," a gloss Calvin adds on Paul's quotation of Isaiah's "What no eye has seen, nor ear heard" – to appreciate the mysteries of God, with the consequence that illumination must come from the Holy Spirit, as we have seen elsewhere. (Incidentally, Calvin also points out that Paul, in using the phrase "those who love him" at verse 9, differs from the Hebrew because he was following the Septuagint, whose authors "translated it so because they were misled by the similarity of one letter to another." Fraser, in a footnote to his translation, points out that Calvin is actually wrong here, and offers an explanation why. What he doesn't point out is that Calvin was probably misled by Erasmus, who offers the exact same explanation in more detail in his annotation on the verse.)[46] Calvin insists that it is a matter of human reason, and not only knowledge via sensory perception, that is excluded from perceiving God: "For, since he ascribes this knowledge to God alone [i.e., knowledge of the will of God], he excludes from it not only the physical senses of man, but also all the ability of the mind. Therefore, although the prophet makes reference only to sight and hearing [i.e., Isaiah, whom Paul quotes in 1 Cor. 2:9], he implicitly includes all the faculties of the mind."[47] A full-scale condemnation of human ingenuity is also revealed by Calvin's use (with pejorative associations in this case) of a range of Latin words which have noetic connotations: *scientia, intelligentia, ratio, sapientia, cognitio, perspicacitas*, and others are all mixed in.

But the clearest condemnation comes in Calvin's comment on verse 2:10: "Having concluded that all men are blind, and having deprived the human mind of the power to rise up to knowledge of God, Paul now shows how the faithful are delivered from this blindness, viz. by the Lord honoring them with a special enlightenment of the Spirit. Therefore, the duller the human mind is for understanding the mysteries of God, and the greater its uncertainty, the surer is our faith, which is supported by the revelation of the Spirit of God."[48] This is a striking formulation: the greater the uncertainty, the more certain the faith (*quo maior est eius incertitudo, eo certior est fides nostra*). Rational certitude operates at an inversely proportional relationship to certainty through faith![49] But this latter sort of certainty is every bit as strong: "the teaching of the Gospel can only be understood by the witness of the Holy Spirit; and the assurance of those who have such witness from the Holy Spirit is as strong and firm as if they were actually touching with their hands what they believe, and that is because the Spirit is a faithful and reliable witness."[50]

Calvin goes on to provide a rather extended analogy, which is notable not only for its epistemological implications, but for his comments on the perceived problem, hinted at by Paul, of the ability of one person to understand another. 1 Cor. 2:11 reads: "Who among humans knows the things pertaining to each, if not the spirit inside them? Accordingly, the things which are of God no one knows except the Spirit of God."[51] Paul's comparison here affords Calvin the opportunity to indulge in a bit of psychologizing: "Everyone knows his own thoughts well. But others do not know what is hidden in his heart."[52] This hiddenness is akin to the hiddenness of the purpose and will of God, and yet after a while the analogy (*similitudine*) breaks down, according to Calvin: "For since speech represents the character of the mind, men convey their thoughts and feelings to each other, so that they come to know each other's minds well. Why may we not therefore understand from the Word of God what His will is? [... Because] the inner thought of a man, of which others know nothing, is clear to him alone. If, later, he reveals it to others, that does not alter the fact that his spirit [*spiritus*] alone knows what is in him."[53] This might be because he doesn't use persuasive language, or simply because he lacks the ability to "convey what he really means" (*fieri etiam poterit ut non bene exprimat sensum suum*). But even if he were able to accomplish both those things, "it is still the case that only his own spirit is truly familiar with it" (*quominus spiritus eius unicus sit verus cognitor*). In other words, despite the fact that language is in some way essentially productive of the speaker's inner cognitive *and* affective state (itself an Erasmian notion),[54] according to Calvin, one can never adequately convey, no matter how articulate, one's complete state of mind.[55] If this is the case, then it is true *a fortiori* that we can never comprehend the wisdom of God: even to the extent that humans can understand each other, there is still a difference between "the thoughts of God and men": "the Word of God is a kind of hidden wisdom [*arcana sapientia*], to whose loftiness the weak [*imbecillitas*] human mind does not reach."[56]

To summarize the foregoing argument here, God *does* accommodate himself to human capacity in his revelation of the Word of God through Christ, but this is still not sufficient for complete human comprehension of the mystery of the gospel. A further step is necessary, which consists of the specific revelation of the Holy Spirit to the individual. While Susan Schreiner argues importantly that Calvin was wary to place too much emphasis on an individual's claims to truth via the authority of the Spirit elsewhere, in the commentary on 1 Corinthians the Spirit serves an important functional response to natural human mental capacity:[57] "So light shines in darkness, until the Spirit opens the eyes of the blind."[58] This final step is significant, and is related to Calvin's doctrine of election and the concomitant notion that the elect themselves are *assured* and *certain* in their faith. As Randall Zachman puts it, glossing a different Calvin commentary, "The mind that is ultimately being revealed in Scripture is the mind of the Holy Spirit, but only those who are illumined by the Spirit can see that mind being disclosed in the words of the human authors of Scripture."[59] This position distinguishes Calvin, on his own account, from the "diabolical principle of sophists that believers are in a continual state of perplexity," for whom assurance can only rest on "moral or probable inference."[60] The elect, however, "have been given the Spirit by whose witness they know for a certainty that they have been adopted to the hope of eternal salvation."[61] In denying assurance, the "sophists" deny the efficacy of the work of the Spirit in the individual. Faith, for Calvin, includes this form of assurance, which places it "above the world" and far from "carnal arrogance."

The speculations of the sophists will always result in uncertainty, for human capacity is not such that it can obtain certainty on its own: "it will always be agitated and hesitant, because we see how audaciously human cleverness exalts itself; and the sons of God must tread upon this pride by an opposite kind of pride, heroic magnanimity."[62] And, finally, lest anyone confuse Paul's use of noetic language with natural forms of reason in the verse "That we might know what things have been given to us by Christ [etc.]," Calvin explains clearly that this knowledge is not obtained through human effort or innate ability: "the word *know* [*scientae vocabulum*] has been used in order to bring out better the assurance of faith. However let us note that it is not obtained in a natural way, or laid hold of by our mental power of comprehension [*mentis captu apprehendi*], but it depends altogether on the revelation of the Spirit."[63] It would be difficult to formulate a stronger wholesale rejection of natural theology than what is contained in these pages. But lest we overstate our case: Calvin argues clearly for an appreciation of God's creative works as necessary for true and complete faithful piety, but this appreciation must be subsumed to faith in God the redeemer as revealed in the Word. As Barbara Pitkin writes, "Though he cautions repeatedly against resting faith on God's works, he nonetheless argues that when faith properly relies on God's word and views God's works through the spectacles of scripture, believers are led to a fuller awareness of God's will *erga nos*. This deepened sense of God's fatherly benevolence and power is essential for the development of true piety. Saving faith and providential faith together constitute this attitude of reverence and love of God derived from the knowledge of God's benefits as both redeemer and creator."[64]

Paul writes in verse 2:13 that Christian wisdom is taught not by human wisdom, but by the Holy Spirit. Human wisdom is defined here, again, by Calvin as those words "which savor of human learning, and are polished according to the rules of the rhetoricians [*rhetorum normam*]; or are purposely and proudly overloaded with philosophy [*ampullis philosophicis*] in order to rush hearers into admiration. But the words 'taught by the Spirit' are suitable for a style which is sincere and simple, rather than empty and ostentatious."[65] Again we might point out, if for no other reason than that Calvin seems keen on repeating it, that this gap is not solely due to human sinfulness, but is rather ontological, for lack of a better way of putting it.[66] Calvin makes this clear in his comment on Paul's distinction between the natural man and the spiritual man at 1 Cor. 2:14: "By the *natural man* [*animalis homo*] Paul means, not, as is generally assumed, a man enslaved to gross desires, or, as they say, to his own sensuality, but any man endowed only with the powers of nature. This is clear from the opposite term, for he contrasts *the natural* with *the spiritual*. Since *the spiritual* refers to the man whose mind is directed by the illumination of the Spirit, there is no doubt that *the natural* means the man left in purely natural endowments [*in puris naturalibus*] as they are called. For the soul [*anima*] is bound up with nature, but the Spirit springs from a supernatural gift."[67] This is also Erasmus' reading, as we have seen, and Melanchthon uses the passage to condemn *ratio* and the "sophists" forcefully as well, in his *Annotations* published in 1522: "Here he calls that part of man the *animalem hominem* which we call 'reason' and the best part of nature, so that the *animalis homo* lives from the soul, not according to the crass pleasures of the body, but *secundum animam*, that is, by the use of reason [*rationis usum*], just as either Socrates or Zeno or Paul had done before the latter's conversion ... he calls it *animalem* to make a point, so as to emphatically signify that he is speaking particularly of man according to his higher faculties."[68] Calvin rounds off his own comments with a poetic meditation on the heights of divine wisdom: "What a wonderful wisdom this is," he writes, "which so far surpasses all human knowledge [*intelligentiam*], that men cannot have even the slightest taste of it!"[69]

Among sixteenth-century biblical humanists, interpreting the early chapters of 1 Corinthians furnishes an opportunity to clarify the deleterious impact human forms of reason have on Christian understanding. The folly of the cross serves to undermine ordinary philosophy and demands an altogether different form of wisdom for comprehending it. Erasmus' *Annotations* and *Paraphrase* on 1 Corinthians, along with his New Testament text, works used by each of the other exegetes considered here, serve an important role in laying the exegetical groundwork for subsequent interpreters. While it would be vastly oversimple to reduce Bullinger's, Pellikan's, or Calvin's theology to Erasmus' – for each exegete's reception of Pauline folly bears the distinctive traits of that theologian's larger theological interests, and each has its own emphases and unique contributions to Pauline interpretation – there is much common ground in vocabulary, in exegetical conclusions, and in attempts to constuct the Pauline foundations of a theological method for a peculiarly Christian philosophy, especially from the perspective of religious epistemology.

Excursus: Pauline Folly in Calvin's *Institutes*

The language of Paul's discourse on wisdom and folly reverberates throughout the *Institutes* as well. The very first sentence, from the very first edition, consists of a qualification we will find repeatedly in Calvin's formal handling of Pauline wisdom: "Nearly all of our wisdom – the things, at any rate, which ought to be assessed as true and solid wisdom [*vera ac solida sapientia*] – consists in two parts."[70] To trace Calvin's total debt to Pauline folly in the *Institutes* would be as tiresome as the results would be cumbersome. According to the index of the McNeill/Battles edition, there are 121 explicit references or citations to verses from 1 Cor. 1–4 in the final version, and this almost certainly doesn't account for many paraphrases or borrowings of Paul's language in less direct instances.[71] Nevertheless, a few instances illustrate the significance the themes of Paul's letter have for Calvin's thinking in general, and for his religious epistemology in particular. Very early (in section I.1.2, added in 1539) we find the first overt allusion to 1 Corinthians. Capping off an eloquent discussion of both the necessity and incapacity of humans to know God, Calvin writes that, on the assumption that we begin to contemplate God's righteousness, then "what wonderfully imposed itself under the title of wisdom will stink in its extreme foolishness."[72]

At *Institutes* II.6.1, a section added in the final edition of 1559, in the context of discussing the detrimental nature of the fall for human comprehension of God through nature, Calvin writes that "all our senses have become perverted, and we wickedly defraud God of his glory," and then quotes Paul directly:

> We must, for this reason, come to Paul's statement: "Since in the wisdom of God the world did not know God through wisdom, it pleased God through the folly of preaching to save those who believe" [1 Cor. 1:21]. This magnificent theater of heaven and earth, crammed with innumerable miracles, Paul calls the "wisdom of God." Contemplating it, we ought in wisdom to have known God. But because we have profited so little by it, he calls us to the faith of Christ, which, because it appears foolish, the unbelievers despise. Therefore, although the preaching of the cross does not agree with our human inclination, if we desire to return to God our Author and Maker, from whom we have been estranged, in order that he may again begin to be our Father, we ought nevertheless to embrace it humbly. Surely, after the fall of the first man no knowledge of God apart from the Mediator has had power unto salvation.[73]

With echoes of Romans 1:20ff., Calvin provides a similar interpretation of 1 Cor. 1:21 to the one we find in his commentary. The emphasis here is on the gap between God's creation as a mirror of his wisdom and humanity's inability to comprehend it, with the result that God chose to save the world through the foolishness of Christ. Knowledge of God can only come through Christ's mediation, which we might learn through the preaching of the cross should we set aside the human inclination to know God through reason or our senses.

Elsewhere, too, Calvin employs themes from 1 Corinthians to emphasize the incompatibility of human and divine wisdom. At III.2.34 (another addition to the final version), Calvin writes, "But if, as Paul preaches, no one 'except the spirit of man which is in him' [1 Cor. 2:11] witnesses the human will, what man would be sure of God's will? And if the truth of God be untrustworthy among us also in those things which we at present behold with our eyes, how could it be firm and steadfast when the Lord promises such things as neither eye can see nor understanding can grasp [cf. 1 Cor. 2:9]? But here man's discernment is so overwhelmed and so fails that the first degree of advancement in the school of the Lord is to renounce it."[74] Man's discernment is a veil that conceals the mysteries of God, and Calvin repeats here that the natural man does not perceive spiritual things, because God's teaching is "'foolish to him ... because it must be spiritually discerned.' Therefore, the support of the Holy Spirit is necessary, or rather, his power alone thrives here." Calvin argues in this section that the human mind is completely incapable of understanding without the illumination of the Spirit. Even the apostles, he says, who were taught directly by Christ, *still* needed the illumination of the Spirit for correct understanding, and this illumination seems to result almost in a form of *ecstasis*. When illuminated by the Spirit, Calvin writes, "we are lifted up in mind and heart above our understanding. For the soul, illumined by him, takes on a new keenness, as it were, to contemplate the heavenly mysteries, whose splendor had previously blinded it."[75]

Illumination by the Spirit of the heavenly mysteries is *beyond* understanding, according to Calvin. Not only is the human intellect in itself incapable of contemplating God on its own, but even when illuminated by the Spirit, there is something more going on than intellectual comprehension. The self is divided, or is taken beyond itself.[76] At III.2.35, Calvin rejects that the *initium fidei* rests with human agency, and then cites our text: "In the letter to the Corinthians he states that faith does not depend upon men's wisdom, but is founded upon the might of the

Spirit [1 Cor. 2:4-5]."[77] Calvin then cites Augustine's sermon 131, which is highly relevant to our theme: Augustine appeals to the "depth of the cross" to explain (or explain away) the problem of theodicy wherein faith is granted to one person and not another: "It is an abyss, the depth of the cross. I can exclaim in wonder; I cannot demonstrate it through disputation."[78] This then leads straight into a discussion of faith as a matter of the heart, rather than the brain, which theme we will examine more closely in chapter 6.

A final example must suffice: at section II.2.20, Calvin cites 1 Cor. 2:14 and 1 Cor. 1:20 explicitly; the passage is worth quoting in its entirety:

> It therefore remains for us to understand that the way to the Kingdom of God is open only to him whose mind has been made new by the illumination of the Holy Spirit. Paul, however, having expressly entered this discussion, speaks more clearly than all. After condemning the stupidity and vanity of all human wisdom and utterly reducing it to nothing [*exinanivit*], he concludes: "The natural man cannot receive the things of the Spirit of God, for they are folly to him, and he is not able to understand them because they are spiritually discerned." Whom does he call "natural"? The man who depends upon the light of nature. He, I say, comprehends nothing of God's spiritual mysteries. Why is this? Is it because he neglects them out of laziness? No, even though he try, he can do nothing, for "they are spiritually discerned." What does this mean? Because these mysteries are deeply hidden from human insight, they are disclosed solely by the revelation of the Spirit. Hence, where the Spirit of God does not illumine them, they are considered folly ... Indeed, [Paul] had likened human wisdom to a veil that hinders the mind from seeing God. What then? The apostle declares, "God has made foolish the wisdom of this world." Shall we then attribute to it the keen insight by which man can penetrate to God and to the secret places of the Kingdom of Heaven? Away with such madness![79]

Without the illumination of the Holy Spirit, the mysteries of God remain foolishness in the minds of humans. Human wisdom is here "utterly reduced to nothing," which translates the Latin verb *exinanire*, the same verb used in the Vulgate, and retained by Calvin in his rendering of Phil. 2:7 to describe Christ's *kenosis*, or self-emptying.[80] The connection between Christ's kenosis and Paul's theology of folly has been noted as a fundamental feature of Erasmus' thought by Screech, and it will be discussed briefly in an excursus at the end of chapter 4.

Chapter Four

Milk for Babes: A Pauline Eloquence[1]

Not all who have a tongue have a heart and brains.

        – Erasmus, *Paraphrase on First Corinthians*

In the same way that the cross renders foolish the wisdom of the world, it also confounds human forms of eloquence: a new method of teaching is required, and one that moves away, in large measure, not only from logico-dialectical forms of reasoning and discourse in theology, but also from the ornate and embellished language of classical rhetoric in preaching and teaching. The development of a notion of a peculiarly Christian form of discourse dates at least to Augustine's *De doctrina christiana* (a work with which our sixteenth-century exegetes were no doubt familiar), where he argues that the biblical authors "fashioned a new eloquence of their own (*alteram quandam eloquentiam suam*) from the language of the common people," and Erich Auerbach fifty years ago teased out the implications of an Augustinian *sermo humilis* within the history of rhetoric.[2] Marc Fumaroli has argued that Augustine is the founder of the idea of a Christian eloquence, recognizing his influence on Erasmus, and that book four of the *De doctrina christiana* is "à la fois la dernière rhétorique antique et la première rhétorique ecclésiastique."[3]

The questions that interested Augustine – who was a professional rhetorician before his conversion to Christianity and eventual tenure as a North African bishop – are rejuvenated in the Renaissance due to the renewed interest in classical rhetorical forms and the proliferation of ancient rhetorical texts from printing houses across Europe. Erasmus was highly attuned to the problems attendant to the relationship between pagan and Christian style. He published multiple works that attend to the issue in one way or another, culminating in his massive manual for preachers, the *Ecclesiastes* of 1535. While Fumaroli writes that the *Ecclesiastes*, "dans une grande mesure, était une amplification du L. IV du *De Doctrina Christiana*,"[4] standing at almost a thousand pages it is rather more than that, and, as Debora Shuger notes, constitutes a "serious exploration of the theological foundations of sacred rhetoric."[5] In 1528 Erasmus had published a lengthy satirical dialogue attacking those who attempted to model their discourse exclusively on Ciceronian style.[6] Erika Rummel, in describing the *Ciceronianus*, explains well Erasmus' attempts at conceiving of a Christian eloquence in this regard; it is worth quoting her at length:

> In a late work, *The Ciceronian* (1528), Erasmus made a remarkable effort to come to terms with the question of a "Christian style" and to present a solution palatable to both parties in the dispute. He suffered the fate of all moderates, however, and pleased neither side. In his view, the Christian style would be neither classical nor scholastic, but "something in between the extremes of Scotuses and Ciceronian apes": a style that was "appropriate and decorous." He insisted, moreover, that for Christians it was Christ, not Cicero, that set the standard of speaking. "And if your speech departs from that standard, you will prove neither to be a good orator nor a good man." Indeed, "the person who treats matters of the faith in the phrases of unbelievers and contaminates his Christian subject matter with pagan follies will be thought a positive monstrosity." This statement may surprise modern readers, who know Erasmus only as an advocate of classical learning. They may even argue that the character in the *Ciceronianus* does not represent Erasmus' opinion.[7]

In fact, Erasmus had been developing his thoughts on the matter for some time before these relatively late publications, and in the exegetical works on 1 Corinthians, Paul becomes the model for a lowly Christian eloquence.

The subject of this chapter is to assess how Erasmus and Calvin receive Paul's rejection of human eloquence in Christian teaching, and how this rejection forms their own understanding of the relationship between language and revelation.[8] This will involve determining both the reception, by Erasmus and Calvin, of Paul's negative assessment of human eloquence, and also an attempt to understand the function of calls for a more appropriately *Christian* rhetoric, made necessary by the humility of Christ and Paul's foolish preaching. We will try to understand how two luminaries, masters of rhetoric themselves, dealt (in theory if not in practice) with Paul's exhortations that Christian teaching ought to be simple as Christ was simple. This chapter is especially important from the standpoint of considering our exegetes as operating in the tradition of a *theologia rhetorica*. We will see that Erasmus, Bullinger, and Calvin had an explicit notion of divine linguistic accommodation, that God "babbled" to humanity when he revealed his mysteries. While Marjorie O'Rourke Boyle has considered the far-reaching theological implications of Erasmus' choice of *sermo* over Jerome's *verbum* when translating *logos* in John 1:1,[9] which is directly related to his interpretations of Pauline folly, the importance of Calvin's choice to follow Erasmus in this controversial translation, while pointed out by William Bouwsma, has not been given its full due.[10]

Indeed, some Calvin scholars have attempted to distance Calvin from his humanist heritage, from the specific perspective of his participation in the rhetorical world of the humanists. It is worth quoting an oft-cited example from T.F. Torrance, representative of this tendency, which suggests that Calvin's move away from putatively empty humanist forms of discourse to a more robust theological method grounded in truth:

> [Calvin] has ceased to operate with *aesthetic propriety* as a criterion for the relation of language to things but is concerned to discern the realities of things in their distinctness from speech, where – and this is certainly truth in knowledge of God – a measure of *impropriety* or inadequacy serves the manifestation of the truth. Second, he has given up the rhetorical conception of *persuasion* beloved by the humanists, one that appeals to what is attractive and desirable, and substitutes for it a mode of *persuasion* which throws the reader back upon the truth itself and its inherent validity. This being the case, a man must give ear to the truth if it is to have any force with him. But that is just the difficulty with humanists. They will listen to nothing but what pleases them; behind all their objections to Christian teaching there is this basic reason: *quoad non placet*.[11]

The sort of characterization of humanism on offer here, especially in defining persuasion as only interested in pleasing an audience, is complicated by a wealth of scholarship in recent decades, as was pointed out in the introduction. The relationship between Renaissance rhetoric and philosophy is much more complicated than Torrance's portrait allows, and Calvin cannot be extricated from the humanist realm on these grounds.[12] Renaissance humanists weren't Gorgiases only interested in pleasing rhetorical forms any more than university theologians were only interested in discovering how many angels could sit on the head of a pin. Relatedly, Richard Muller argues for the importance of appreciating the nuances of early modern scholasticism in Protestant theology so that we ought not to understand Calvin and his colleagues as wholly divorced from the scholastic enterprise:

> [T]he relationship of the Reformation to the eras immediately preceding and immediately following it cannot be reduced to a simple contrast between scholasticism and reform or scholasticism and humanism. The Reformation should not be reductionistically described as a humanist phenomenon. Scholasticism or, more precisely, aspects of scholastic thought should not be viewed as incapable of rapprochement with aspects of humanist methods or, indeed, as contributing to the theological and methodological assumptions of an individual trained in humanistic philology and dialectical method.[13]

Recent work on Melanchthon, too, has demonstrated the complex relationship that can exist between dialectic and rhetoric in sixteenth-century thought.[14] It is thus equally important, on the other side of the coin, to avoid the misleading reduction of all humanists to practitioners of "mere" rhetoric. Such a portrait oversimplifies the vastly complex world of Renaissance rhetoric and ideas about language that continued to evolve over the course of the sixteenth century.

Appreciation for a persuasive mode of discourse, accompanied by a dash of scepticism with respect to areas of theological speculation that humanist theologians deemed *adiaphora*, does not entail sophistry. Several substantial scholarly works have made this point in recent years, in one way or another. In the words of Debora Shuger, "Renaissance sacred rhetoric ... everywhere juxtaposes the language of ornamental, gratifying self-display with passionate and redemptive discourse."[15] Importantly, moreover, Shuger has argued that *movere* – the rhetorical principle that the orator ought to move or affect the emotions of his audience – in the Renaissance ought not to be associated with "subrational obfuscation," and that Christian sacred rhetoric "sets affective inwardness over dispassionate intellection," but in a way "that links rather than opposes emotion and reason."[16] This approach is rooted in a shift in understandings of anthropology, which Shuger suggests is part and parcel of a rejuvenation of Augustinianism in the early modern period, and it is crucial for understanding the function of rhetorical theology in thinkers such as Erasmus and Calvin. The gospel must *move* in order to *teach*, and we have seen this emphasized already in the commentaries of Erasmus, Pellikan, Bullinger, and Calvin in the second chapter. Olivier Millet has demonstrated in great detail Calvin's deep indebtedness to the humanist rhetorical tradition, not least in the area of forming a "biblical eloquence."[17] Ann Moss has shown more generally how an entirely new Latin idiom is coextensive with Christian humanist rhetoric, and she describes its fundamentally affective nature in the context of Erasmus' criticism of the Ciceronians thus: "To be a truly adequate speech for the present, the humanists' Latin must, to a judicious extent, accommodate the lexis and cultural markers developed in the Christian era. More fundamentally, it must articulate the characteristic affectivity of Christian sentiment, the devotion of the 'pectus vere christianum,' the truly Christian heart."[18] Finally, as Christophe Strohm writes of Calvin: "Calvin's emphasis, not least grounded in the heritage of rhetoric, on the interrelation of *doctrina* and *applicatio*, that is on the constitutive significance of the practical application of doctrine, has consequences for the form of theological language."[19] If, then, we understand humanist rhetorical theology as doing something rather different from putting forth only what is attractive, we clear the way for a more responsible assessment not only of Calvin's theological heritage and his relationship to Erasmus, but of the relationship between the Renaissance and Reformation as well.

"A Contrary Manner of Erudition": Erasmus on Eloquence in 1 Corinthians

In his *Annotations on 1 Corinthians*, where Erasmus is in general much briefer and less given to theological exposition than he is in the *Paraphrases*, we find the following note on verse 1:17 (*less the cross of Christ be made empty*):

> A thing is said to be vacuous [*inane*] because it is not solid but is made attractive in form. That incidentally, you will note, is the best reading, that the divine Paul anxiously took great care that the gospel of Christ be the most pure and kept from all human props, that this world not be able to lay claim to it, and thus so that it does not yoke itself to human eloquence or erudition. And in these times when we burden Christ with wealth, with profane business, with honor, with empire, with war, with pleasure, and with everything else: we curse eloquence alone. And here at least we go against the apostles, for they spoke simply, but wisely, without

flattery, and again without filth and without monstrosities: their speech was unaffected, but it was prudent: and if I may say so briefly, they were thus in a different way powerful and wealthy, in a different way noble and illustrious – in this contrary manner then they were erudite and eloquent.[20]

While it certainly has its own rhetorical flair, this note is significant for several reasons, not least of which is that Erasmus departs from his ordinary practice in the *Annotations* of providing mostly philological commentary, and moves beyond the first-century context to apply his interpretation to contemporary concerns. Erasmus' attempt to restore theology by restoring grammar was a lifelong endeavour and it pervades his corpus.[21] Furthermore, we find a number of requisite themes of *theologia rhetorica*: the eschewing of human props (*adminiculis*), the yoking of simplicity with wisdom and of unaffected speech with prudence, and the idea that the apostles were teaching with an altogether different sort of eloquence and erudition from what would pass in the schools of oratory.

Paul more than once emphasizes his own lack of eloquence in his first letter to the Corinthians, and suggests that it is a deliberate mode of preaching on his part, lest the gospel be corrupted. Erasmus, too, in his paraphrase, repeats Paul's denunciations of eloquence, and further distinguishes the eloquent and erudite from the philosophically wise (although no doubt all these traits might be found in one person). While philosophers might also be somehow eloquent, there is a distinction made between investigating the things of the gospel with human reason, which Erasmus criticizes when paraphrasing 1 Cor. 1:21–4, e.g., and in using eloquent speech to profess the cross of Christ. The apostles *were* erudite and eloquent, but in a different manner. Apostolic eloquence, like apostolic wisdom, is fundamentally something quite different from ordinary, human, run of the mill eloquence. Erasmus, here, has situated himself in the Augustinian tradition of reimagining the Ciceronian category of a lowly style (*sermo humilis*), which was ordinarily reserved for the most mundane of affairs (legal matters, accounting, etc.), so that it might be employed in teaching the most sublime of topics – a necessary move in light of the Incarnation, which renders foolish the wisdom of the world.[22] Mark Vessey, moreover, in explaining the significance of the Erasmian paraphrase as a genre, invokes Jerome's play on Horace's *ars rhetorica*, which Jerome renders *ars scripturarum*, inventing (at least rhetorically) a rhetorical method of explicating scripture that differs from classical rhetoric in some way. To quote

Vessey, citing John Bateman describing Erasmus' adoption of a similar distinction: "the classical or Renaissance *ars rhetorica* may not by itself fully account for the texture of an Erasmian paraphrase on the New Testament. For while paraphrase falls naturally within the province of rhetoric as a technical discipline, *biblical* paraphrase is subject to 'genre'-specific rules of its own."[23] We must think of Christian rhetoric as somehow different from pagan rhetoric, even if some tools acquired from the latter are employed in the former.[24] Erich Auerbach suggests that Augustine is the first Christian orator to make this distinction explicit: for Augustine, "the highest mysteries of the faith may be set forth in the simple words of the lowly style which everyone can understand," and this was "a radical departure from the rhetorical, and indeed from the entire literary, tradition."[25]

Erasmus is not attempting merely to replace scholastic dialectic with humanist rhetoric as a theological method, but imagines himself to be reclaiming a method established by Paul's understanding of the implications of the folly of the cross, which putatively attempts to employ the language and symbols of the biblical text itself (per the *ars scripturarum*) without foreign philosophical and rhetorical tools as "props." Erasmus' exhortations for a revolution in theology grounded in grammatical simplicity are well known, but probably their explicit connections to his Paulinism haven't been fully appreciated. While Rummel above doesn't connect the *Ciceronianus* to the *Paraphrases* or the *Praise of Folly*, her description here is clearly relevant to our purposes.[26] By taking on the persona of Paul, Erasmus is able explicitly to create the *ars scripturarum* – what better expositor of Paul could there be than Paul himself? And while it might be true that Erasmus grew steadily wearier, over the course of his life, of the "Ciceronian apes," we see already in his *Annotations* and *Paraphrase on 1 Cor.* the beginnings of the development of an argument for a "Christian style," for which he finds authority in Paul's letters. We can flesh this out further by examining more closely the manner in which Erasmus uses Paul in arguing for an unconventional Christian eloquence.

At the beginning of the paraphrase of 1 Corinthians 2, Erasmus' Paul contrasts eloquence and philosophical erudition with his own method of preaching the lowliness of the cross:

I did not come equipped with the power of some eloquence for you to marvel at, or deserving your respect for some exceptional acquaintance with philosophy, although I knew that you had the highest regard for people of this kind. So far was I from proclaiming any of these qualities that the world deemed excellent that among you I considered myself to know nothing other than Jesus Christ, and him indeed crucified. The one whom I preached was a human being, but one anointed by God and promised by the prophets for the redemption of the human race. It was from what was most lowly in him that I began the preaching of the gospel.[27]

The lowliness of the cross was Paul's starting point, and Christ's abasement is inherently opposed to human eloquence and wisdom.[28] The text here reinforces Erasmus' oft-repeated claim that the gospel must be preached simply and unadulterated. Erasmus then emphasizes the fact that, even though Paul did not come with eloquence and wisdom, his preaching was nonetheless efficacious:

> The character of my life was matched by my style of speaking. Just as my life had been fortified against the violence of the wicked by no human defenses, but by the protection of God alone, so my speech had not been furnished in any way with the ornaments of the rhetoricians or the arguments of philosophers that it might show how much I myself could do either with eloquence or with erudition. Nevertheless, it had the efficacy to transform you, not through its display of learning, but through the Spirit and power of God, who through inspiration and miracles was adding persuasive force to the speech, unpolished as it was.[29]

The speech (*sermo*) itself is ineloquent and unpolished, but this does not detract from the power of the message. Rhetorical ornamentation is superfluous, for divine power itself is sufficient for conversion of the hearers. Assaults from outsiders, both physical and philosophical, are thwarted not by a violent response (whether physical or philosophical), but by God alone. "For [Paul] did not wish this [i.e., spreading the gospel] to be accomplished by the sources of human wisdom or eloquence – resources that could provide nothing of this sort – but he wanted so arduous an exploit to be carried out by simple and unadorned speech so that all the praise for the feat may be assigned to God, whom it pleased to renew all the world through the despised and dishonored cross of Christ."[30] Again, in this regard, Erasmus' Paul insists that, properly, Christian preaching finds its persuasiveness not in subtle embellishments or classical rhetorical techniques, but somehow in divine power. The argument mirrors the criticisms of human reason addressed in previous chapters. Paul's preaching itself is considered an act of divine self-manifestation. Christ the *Sermo* becomes the *sermo* of Paul. Erasmus writes, in the *Paraphrase*, "But no one should think that you owe [your redemption] to human teaching or to eloquence, which we do not claim to have, but to divine power, through which our language was more effective than the philosophers' discourse, however subtly argued and embellished it might be."[31] One component of *theologia rhetorica* as Erasmus employs it rests on an assumption of the divine work involved in the propagation of the Word: the philosophical and rhetorical feebleness of the gospel (according to worldly, i.e., classical Greco-Roman, philosophical and rhetorical standards) is rendered efficacious through divine power.

This is significant insofar as it provides some resistance to the idea of Erasmus as the detached humanist text-critic: the principles of good philological and historical exegesis are not sufficient for properly understanding the Bible in every case. In the *Paraclesis*, for example, Erasmus claims that to read the Bible is, in fact, to encounter Christ, the transcendent Word, to an even greater extent than "if you gazed upon him with your very eyes."[32] To preach the gospel, or to read the Bible was, for Erasmus, not only to extract the principles of the *philosophia Christi*, or to understand the historical context of Christ's and the apostles' lives, but to actually come into contact with God. John Bateman describes Erasmus' position in paraphrasing 1 Corinthians as drawing attention to the "fundamental difference between two kinds of discourse, the seemingly inartistic and unlearned speech of Scripture and the wholly human speech of philosophers and orators which, for all of its logical subtlety or stylistic elegance, lacks this transforming power."[33] Also in this regard, with a fuller appreciation of the *Logos* as mediator, Hoffmann argues that Erasmus' hermeneutic is "governed by the idea of language as mediation. Language, especially God's speech in Scripture, draws the reader into the truth through the process of interpretation. And it is the peculiar drawing power of allegory (the middle between the historical/literal and the spiritual/mystical sense of Scripture) that performs this metaphorical function. Here the divine word intercedes between heaven and earth as it translates the reader from the flesh into the spirit."[34] This *theologia rhetorica* "runs afoul" of dialectical theology, and is, for Hoffmann, the foremost reason for Erasmus' rejection of scholastic theological disputation.

The Word of God in Paul's preaching eventually finds its analogue in the New Testament itself for Erasmus, according to Hoffmann: "In Scripture, the author of all speech, God, has so become flesh in the incarnate word, Christ, that the *philosophia Christi* bears the sign of divine authority. As a result, the word of Christ possesses also the supreme drawing power to persuade its readers and to transform them into itself, much more so than any human speech in good literature can achieve."[35] This is to say, presumably, that the first-century hearers of Paul's preaching were moved by its divine power and not its erudition, but also that the Word of God which comes to exist in written form as representative of that ancient preached Word has a similar relationship to modern (sixteenth-century) readers and listeners – it wasn't only first-century Corinthians who were moved by the divinely instituted gospel in all its simplicity, but Paul's method of teaching becomes the norm for Christian evangelism. As Bateman puts it, "Erasmus' own mind is obviously focused here not so much on Corinth in Paul's time as on his own contemporary world and the claims of scholastic theologians on the one hand and of humanist authors on the other."[36]

Erasmus expands on the Pauline approach in his paraphrase of chapter 3: "Among the simple I used simple language ... and I babbled as if I were among infants ... Since I saw that you were still infants in the philosophy of Christ, I fed you with the milk, so to speak, of less spiritual teaching, not with the solid food of more mature teaching."[37] Paul accommodates (*accommodandus est sermo*) himself to the capacity of his audience in much the same way that God has accommodated Godself to humanity in Christ. The context here is manifold, but Erasmus focuses on Paul's condemnation of Corinthian discord, comparing the Corinthians' "Apollonians" and "Paulines" with the Aristotelians, Platonists, Stoics, and Epicureans of the human philosophies.[38] It is important to note, moreover, that insofar as God accommodates himself to humanity in this way, for Erasmus God accommodates himself to *everyone*, not only to the learned; that is, the "human" form which theological truth takes is not to be confused with the profane philosophical and rhetorical inventions of the erudite. Weavers and prostitutes, with no advanced degrees, can comprehend the gospel in its simplicity because of the condescension of Christ in his folly, while the Sorbonne theologians cannot comprehend the simplicity of the gospel in their attempts at intellectual ascension. "But someone may object," Erasmus writes in the *Ratio*: "'What are you saying? Do you think Holy Writ is so easy and its meaning so evident that it can be understood without commentary?' Yes, it is – at least as far as we need to understand it for sound teaching rather than a theatrical display of learning."[39] As Mark Vessey argues, profane, anile, and vain speech is roundly and consistently condemned within the confines of the "Pauline-Erasmian worldview."[40]

The gospel is sufficiently simple that it doesn't need elaborate exposition, and in those cases where it needs to be explained, the expositor ought to avoid unnecessary difficulties and to explain simply. This is the force of Erasmus' vision for democratic ecclesiastical and theological reform.[41] And yet it seems that even if everyone had the capacity to render the gospel into fine language or valid syllogisms, it would be to miss the point: "For the strength of the gospel is not placed in splendid words, which may come to anyone, but in a heavenly force or power made evident by the endurance of evils, by concord, by the innocence of one's whole life, and by miracles."[42] There is something inherently *affective* about the gospel, and something that moves beyond language into the Christian's lived experience – "How are frigid ceremonies consonant with Christ's fiery love?"[43] In this way, too, the *theologia rhetorica* is only successful, or even comprehensible, if it finds "expression," somewhat paradoxically, in a non-linguistic, non-discursive form. As Hoffmann has put it, Erasmus' exegesis is predicated on the notion that "the spirit transcends the letter, even though it appears in the form of the letter."[44] No matter how eloquent or philosophically astute, the cross of Christ is empty until it is experienced. The *scopus* of theological discourse is in some way ineffable.

Continuing in his paraphrase and describing the manner in which the church at Corinth was built via an agricultural metaphor borrowed from 1 Cor. 3:8, Erasmus points out that after Paul had planted the seed and Apollo had watered it, nevertheless "the planter would labor in vain, and the waterer in vain, if heaven did not breathe its hidden force upon the plant – a force all the more effective because it is hidden."[45] And yet Christian teaching must involve upbuilding discourse in particular, and Erasmus understands Paul's metaphor of a building foundation in 1 Cor. 3 to relate to teaching directly: "It is a heavenly and spiritual foundation; a structure of carnal and earthly teaching does not suit it."[46] Paul is the *architectus sapiens* of 1 Cor. 3:10, and the Greek *sophon*, according to Erasmus in the *Annotations*, "clearly means teaching and understanding."[47] And the foundation is the life and teachings of Christ: "I placed before you Christ as your *scopus*."[48] The proof of a valid teaching method is in the results: if it leads to an embodiment of the *philosophia Christi*, it "adds a structure worthy of Christ"; if it leads to discord, frigid ceremonies, superstitions, then it is *adulteratinam doctrinam* – adulterated teaching.[49] Thus, in describing Paul as the "paragon of learned piety" for Erasmus, Riemer Faber writes that "Erasmus developed a 'Pauline Erasmianism,' that consists in the rejection of traditional ceremonialism and outward religiosity," and that Paul has become for Erasmus "the ideal proponent of *pietas litterata*, of learned devotion to Christ in a life of humility."[50]

Language is mediation, and the *logos ensarkos* is the perfect form of mediation of divine truth to humanity, but there is yet some transcendental/existential aspect of knowing Christ that confounds a perfect correspondence between *verba et res*. This is one of the necessary ingredients of a theology of praxis. Any reasonably strong notion of divine accommodation precludes a philosophy of language that perfectly represents truth. But this shouldn't be pressed too hard, for language is all we have, precisely *because* we only have partial epistemological access to the truth per se.[51] And, furthermore, so long as we put our trust in Christ and not in human inventions, we may rest assured: "Christ deceives no one who leans upon him. But let each take care lest in wrongly relying on human resources he deceive himself."[52] It is here, in a fuller appreciation of the need for an appropriate use of language in theology, where Erasmus differs from the "new" theologians he often criticizes. "There is no reason you should look to the resources of philosophy or the Law for your happiness. Nor should anyone value himself above the others because he excels in human learning. Rather, whoever deems himself wise in the estimation of the world, let him wisely become foolish so that he may truly become wise. Let him cease being the pompous professor of a foolish wisdom, and he will be fit to be a student of the wisest folly."[53] The paradoxes of Paul's discourse on folly lead to a recognition of human inability to ascend to grasp divine wisdom. One must rather eschew the "eyes of the body" for this kind of discernment, and embrace the "eyes of faith."[54]

The principle of *accommodatio*, which in Erasmus is both rhetorical and theological, is fundamental for understanding Erasmus' exegetical position on eloquence in 1 Corinthians. To quote Bateman further on divine accommodation, "This divine 'baby talk' which is likewise characteristic of the language of the omniscient Jesus in his speech with humans is part of the divine pedagogy through which God progressively reveals himself in the economy of salvation history and the means for drawing us to him and gradually perfecting us as we progress from spiritual childhood to the perfect knowledge of the beatific vision."[55] There is a bit of a tension in this fairly straightforward portrait of divine accommodation when it comes to applying it to the wisdom/ folly paradoxes of 1 Corinthians, for on the one hand God has confounded all worldly things in the absurdity of the cross of Christ, and yet according to the principle of accommodation God still has to reveal himself to human beings, earthly creatures, in terms that they can at least partially understand. So, while there is occasionally a tendency in Erasmus scholarship to overemphasize his appreciation of *nature* and of the *natural man* whose innate abilities serve as some sort of ground for philosophizing, in the *Paraphrase on First Corinthians* the heavenly Spirit irrupts into the profane world and teaches humans in an altogether different manner:

> Many people search out and contemplate created things, but no one knows matters deeply hidden in the mind and purpose of God except the eternal Spirit, which is innermost in God and on that account is inwardly aware in him of all things. A person imparts secret thoughts to another by a quiet whispering; God imparts his purpose to the godly through the Spirit; not through a human spirit, which, outside of human affairs, can contribute nothing except through God's. A spirit teaches things as match its nature. This world also has its own spirit, and those who are possessed by it not only savor of worldly things, but love them as well. But the inspiration of the divine Spirit feeds us with heavenly things so that we may understand how great are the blessings God has bestowed on us through the cross of Christ.[56]

This calls for a new method of teaching, as we've seen, for "just as the kind of wisdom is entirely different, so also is the method of teaching different."[57] Heavenly and spiritual matters, Erasmus' Paul tells us, must be taught in "a new way," and here only to "those who by imbibing the Spirit of Christ are now fit for spiritual teaching."[58] Thus, not only is proper Christian teaching not "this-worldly," but the recipient of it must undergo a transformation before she is fit for learning. This "spiritual philosophy" can only properly be conveyed to a "spiritual pupil," whose "understanding has been purified through faith and [whose] emotion corrected through love."[59] Thus, divine accommodation entails not only a condescension of God to humanity, but also a transformation (by God) of humans that they might become practitioners of the Christian philosophy.

But if there is a new manner of teaching and a different sort of erudition involved in preaching the gospel, what does this Christian eloquence look like to Erasmus? It doesn't mean only an application of classical rhetorical technique to theological problems or to biblical paraphrase. Erasmus was acutely aware of the attempts by the new Ciceronians to achieve something along those lines, and he came to reject it outright: "I am a Christian and I must talk of the Christian religion before Christians. If I am going to do so in a manner befitting my subject, surely I am not to imagine that I am living in the age of Cicero, and speaking in a crowded senate before the conscript fathers on the Tarpeian height?"[60] For Erasmus, theologian to prostitutes and farmers, to insist on a rhetorical theology that was always in conformity to Greco-Roman standards would be to violate his own theological ideals and the attendant understanding of Christian *decorum* and *accommodatio*. Marjorie O'Rourke Boyle puts it aptly: "When Erasmus writes that it is better to adopt the expressions of Thomas Aquinas and Duns Scotus than to pervert the creed to Ciceronian Latin, the reader knows how seriously the discrepancy between pagan vocabulary and the Christian lexicon can be."[61] In the end, a fully satisfactory definition of a Christian rhetoric will probably escape us, if for no other reason than that a properly Christian rhetoric is not universalizable: it must be ad hoc lest it violate its own ideal of decorum. In one sense, however, we find Erasmus' ideal Christian eloquence exhibited in his *Paraphrases*, especially those of the Pauline epistles, for Paul himself was the ideal Christian preacher. (And certainly Erasmus does outline some definitive features of Christian eloquence in the *Ciceronianus*.)[62] But it would not be lost on Erasmus, of all people, that these themselves were translations and paraphrases created for a specific audience (and not the audience of first-century Corinth). While he could write in defence of his Latin version of the New Testament that it was only fair that Paul address the Romans in better Latin than the translator of the Vulgate had provided, he also repeated a notion that "divine wisdom has its own special eloquence."[63] Nor would he have imagined these texts to be read in Latin by prostitutes and farmers, although he advocated that *someone* ought to make the gospel accessible to these people as well. The *scopus* of theology is Christ, and him both as object and as model. "Humble and suffering in ways undeserved," Erasmus paraphrases Paul, "we preached Christ to you without adulteration."[64] Ultimately, the success of any theological method, within the confines of a *theologia rhetorica*, depends on simplicity and the ability to convert the listener to the *philosophia Christiana*. The end and the means must be pragmatic.

Calvin on Eloquence: Pro et Contra

In comparing Calvin's understanding of the role of eloquence in Christian teaching with Erasmus', we see a number of striking similarities in their approaches to theological method. Commenting on verse 1:17 ("For Christ sent me not to baptize, but to preach the gospel: not with the wisdom of words, lest the cross of Christ be made of none effect"), Calvin writes that someone might accuse Paul himself of seeking glory in his proclamation of the gospel, but that for Paul, "since the method of teaching [*ratio docendi*], which he followed, was free of all brilliance, and revealed not a trace of ambition, it could not be suspect on that score."[65] We can infer from this, says Calvin, that the Corinthians, swollen as they were with ambition, "wanted to rush the people into admiration of them, and did it by ingratiating themselves with them by a show of words [*verborum pompa*] and a mask of human wisdom [*larva humanae sapientiae*]."[66] Paul's method of teaching, Calvin tells us, is "diametrically opposed to the ostentation of those self-seeking men." And his discussion of a transformation of theological method here, with his insistence that Christian preaching must be utterly different from human eloquence, is highly reminiscent of what we've seen in Erasmus' *Paraphrase*, complete with shared vocabulary. Nor is Calvin afraid to do some paraphrasing of his own:[67] "It is as though [Paul] said: 'I know how much those easy-going teachers of yours coax you with their high-sounding language. For my part, not only do I confess that my preaching is done in a style that is unpolished, clumsy [*rudi et crasso*][68] and far from cultivated, but I even glory in it. For it ought to have been like that, and indeed this method was prescribed to me by God'."[69] The foolishness of Paul's preaching, vulgar as it is, is divinely instituted.

Calvin is then led to consider two questions, still commenting on 1:17: First, does Paul *completely* condemn "wise words" (or the "wisdom of words" – σοφιᾳ λόγου) as something in opposition to the gospel? And, second, does Paul mean that the gospel must *always* be kept separate from eloquence lest it be distorted? He begins with a qualification, claiming that "the arts" (*artes*) are not per se irreligious, and that they can be useful in myriad human affairs, etc. – as we would expect from someone with Calvin's humanist training. Indeed, the *artes* come from the Holy Spirit, and are gifts from God to human beings for assistance in carrying out their affairs in the world. "Therefore what Paul says here is not to be taken as disparaging to the arts, as if they were adverse to piety" (*quasi pietati adversentur*).[70] On the question of whether "wise words" are to be employed when preaching or expositing the gospel, Calvin tells us that, on the one hand, we must consider Paul's audience here: the Corinthians were especially misguided in their attraction to pompous language (*cupiditate magniloquentiae*), and so Paul was trying to give balance to a particular situation – the Corinthians, more than others, needed to be reminded of the humility of the cross, "free from any adulteration."[71]

On the other hand, Calvin argues that the opposition between the cross and the wisdom of the world which Paul invokes here has a *permanent validity* (*perpetuam esse fateor*), as it is just a fact of the matter that the "preaching of Christ is bare and simple." There is an assiduous insistence in Calvin's commentary on the cross of Christ as not being *disguised*, or *masked* (Lat. *larva*), and that its bare and unadorned revelation is its virtue. The cross of Christ is not only made void by worldly wisdom (i.e., by human philosophy), but also by brilliant speech (*splendore verborum*).[72] This twofold consideration places Calvin firmly within the biblical-humanist milieu, and also allies him quite closely with Erasmus' version of the *theologia rhetorica* as we've seen it play out in his *Annotations* and *Paraphrases* on 1 Corinthians: the liberal arts are useful, and even necessary, but the preaching of the gospel itself must remain free from human eloquence as far as this is possible.[73] Classical rhetoric must serve the gospel and not the other way around. We can feel Calvin here attempting to reconcile Paul's seemingly unequivocal reproof of "wise words," interpreted by Calvin as pertaining to a certain kind of fruitless eloquence and Calvin's own commitment to the *bonae litterae*. He doesn't want his readers to confuse the deleterious use of eloquence in expositing the gospel with the liberal arts themselves, which latter might be useful in other spheres of life (or, indeed, when correcting Jerome's and Erasmus' translations of the New Testament, e.g., as Calvin himself enjoys doing). Nevertheless, he continues: "the characteristic work of the Gospel is to bring down the wisdom of the world in such a manner, that, deprived of our own understanding we become completely docile, and do not consider knowing, or even desire to know anything but what the Lord Himself teaches."[74]

Calvin, still unpacking 1 Cor 1:17, proceeds to explain why God chose to express himself ineloquently (even though he could have done otherwise, clearly, as it was he who "designed the tongues of men for eloquence" in the first place). Calvin can discern two reasons for God's withholding of fine speech in his arrangement of how the gospel would be preached: "The first is that the majesty of His truth might be all the clearer through the use of unpolished and unrefined language [*rudi et impolito sermoni*], and the efficacy [*efficacia*] of His Spirit might penetrate the minds of men, by itself, without external aids [*externis adminiculis*]."[75] Calvin then tells us that Paul himself didn't use rhetoric, even the not-so-vacuous kind: "By the *wisdom of words* he does not mean verbal legerdemain [*logodaidalian*], which is mere empty talk, but true eloquence [*eloquentiam veram*], which consists in skillful choice of subjects, in clever arrangement, and fineness of style [*elegantia sermonis*].[76] He declares that he did not have permissibly elegant eloquence, indeed that for his preaching it was neither suitable nor useful" (*neque aptem neque utilem*).[77] The second reason why God chooses to eschew eloquence, according to Calvin, is "that He might put our obedience and teachableness the better to the test, and, at the same time, instruct us in the way of true humility. For the Lord only admits little ones [*parvulos*] to His school."[78] Moreover, heavenly wisdom is only actually comprehended by those who are content with the abject form (*speciem abiecta*) of the gospel and who do not desire a "masked Christ" (*larvatum Christum*). This *larvatum Christum* is contrasted with the naked, or bare Christ (*nudum Christum*) in this section of the commentary. Preaching Christ unadulterated is, for our sixteenth-century exegetes, a crucial aspect of the model that Paul set forth for the Corinthians and Christians after them. Furthermore, eloquence precludes humility, which for Erasmus and for Calvin is the Christian virtue *par excellence*; on this ground alone, then, eloquence must not be used as a way of propagating the gospel. As Calvin puts it at the beginning of his comments on chapter 2:

> Having begun to speak of his own method of teaching, Paul proceeded almost at once to deal with the general character of evangelical preaching. Now he turns to himself again, to show that whatever is to be despised in him is bound up with the nature of the Gospel itself, and in a sense is inseparable from it. Therefore he acknowledges that he did not have the help of human eloquence or wisdom [*facundiae vel sapientiae praesidia*], the provision of which might enable him to accomplish something. But he goes on to add that from the very fact that he admits his lack of those resources, the power of God, which does not need such aids [*subsidiis*], is all the more evident in his ministry.[79]

But again Calvin is careful not to condemn rhetorical ability outright.

The ideal of learned piety that Calvin was committed to – following in the tradition(s) instituted by Erasmus and Melanchthon[80] – is a difficult balance, but he is at pains to protect it here. As Bouwsma puts it, Calvin was always concerned to combine *eruditio* with *persuasio*.[81] The pendulum must swing back in the other direction a bit, lest we imagine that a certain kind of eloquence cannot be responsibly used *in service* of the gospel. Calvin asks whether someone "in our day" who "makes the teaching of the Gospel sparkle with his eloquence" ought to be rejected for that reason alone. He answers, in the negative, that "eloquence is not in conflict with the simplicity of the Gospel at all, when, free from contempt of the Gospel, it not only gives it first place, and is subject to it, but also serves it as a handmaid serves her mistress."[82] Eloquence, if properly subsumed to the gospel, is fine, so long as it preaches "the cross and nothing else." For in this case it "calls us back to the original simplicity of the Gospel," on the one hand, and on the other it "obtains a hearing for those fisherman and uneducated common people, who have nothing attractive about them except the power of the Spirit."[83] (The doublet *piscatores et idiotae* is identical to that found in Erasmus' *Paraphrase* on 1 Cor. 1.) So long as it does not aim at "captivating Christians with an outward brilliancy of words, or at intoxicating them with empty delights, or at tickling their ears with its jingle, or at covering up the cross of Christ with its ostentation," and so long as its starting point is the cross, it can be useful.[84]

Calvin continues, however (and note the similarities to Erasmus' *Paraphrase*), to emphasize that the apostles, through the Spirit, used a particularly Christian form of eloquence: "the Spirit of God has also an eloquence of His own. It shines with a splendor that is natural to it, peculiar to itself, to use a better word, intrinsic (as they say), more than with assumed rhetorical ornaments."[85] The prophets, Moses, and even the apostles, Calvin tells us, have this sort of eloquence. The eloquence which "is suitable to the Spirit of God," is eloquence which is not "swollen with ostentation, and does not clatter with empty sounds, but is solid and efficacious, and is sincere rather than elegant."[86] The contrast between empty (*inane*) eloquence and solid, or substantial, or genuine (*solidus*) eloquence, made here, is the same contrast Erasmus makes in his annotation on this verse, cited earlier in the chapter.[87] In his commentary on Galatians 3, Calvin describes Paul's vivid and moving preaching, writing that (as Paul himself had suggested) Paul's preaching displayed Christ as accurately as if the Galatians had seen him crucified themselves, before their very eyes. Referring pejoratively to *eloquentia* and *rhetorum coloribus* (embellished rhetoric) with a direct reference to the Corinthian correspondence, Calvin continues, offering advice to prospective preachers: "Let those who want to discharge the ministry of the Gospel aright, learn not only to speak and declaim but also to penetrate into consciences, so that men may see Christ cruficied and that His blood may flow."[88] When the church has preachers who can, with the help of the Spirit, paint vivid pictures with words, they do not need "dead images" (*mortuis simulacris*). Here we find a striking paradoxical blend of a denunciation of colourful words with the simultaneous elevation of the preacher as painter (*pictor*), an uneasy use of an extended metaphor with conflicting purposes that can only be resolved by ultimate appeal to the efficacy of the Spirit, who is in the end the true rhetor.[89]

Calvin insists, moreover, in the 1 Corinthians commentary, that the preaching of the gospel must be concerned with truth, and that artificial adornments must not jeopardize this concern. "When he says, 'the persuasive words of human wisdom,' Paul means choice oratory, which strives and exerts itself with artifice rather than truth; and at the same time he means the appearance of acuteness, which attracts the minds of men."[90] While we have seen that efficacy is an essential aspect of Christian teaching, it must be efficacious in the right way. And Calvin of course realizes, with Paul, that oratorical persuasiveness, even of falsehood, is a commonplace: "He is justified in attributing persuasiveness [τὸ πιθανόν] to human wisdom. For, by its majesty, the Word of the Lord urges us, as by a violent force, to give obedience to it. On the other hand human wisdom has its charms with which it insinuates itself; and has its showy ornament [*lenocinium*], as it were, by which to win over the minds of its hearers to itself."[91] But properly oriented *persuasio* must be oriented to *veritas*.[92] Paul's preaching, which is substantiated not by sophistry, but by the Holy Spirit, is paradoxical insofar as it is powerful precisely when it shouldn't be:

> Over against [human rhetorical persuasiveness] Paul sets "demonstration of the Spirit and power," which most interpreters confine to miracles. But I understand it in a wider sense, viz. as the hand of God stretching itself out to act powerfully through the apostle in every way ... For our dullness, when we look closely at the works of God, is such that when He uses inferior instruments, his power is concealed as if by so many veils, so that it is not clearly evident to us. On the other hand, in promoting Paul's ministry, because no human or worldly help was at work, the hand of God stretched itself out, as it were, bare; certainly His power was more visible.[93]

As Calvin advocates a theological focus on the *nudum Christum*, so here he emphasizes the nakedness of the power of God (*nuda manus Dei*) as it can be discerned in the simplicity of Paul's preaching. This nakedness is a proof of Christian teaching's fidelity to truth: "If the apostle's preaching had been supported by the power of eloquence alone, he could have been overthrown by superior oratory. Further, the truth which relies on brilliance of oratory [*splendore orationis nitatur*[94]] no one will call genuine. Indeed it can be helped by it, but it ought not to depend on it. On the other hand, what stands on its own, independent of all support, must be more powerful."[95] The power of God and the power of Paul's preaching are both more efficacious precisely *because* they aren't reinforced by the aids of human wisdom and rhetorical adeptness. And finally, the manifestation of divine truth in the simplicity of Paul's preaching is an instance of God's accommodating himself to human capacity:

> He says therefore that he adjusts or adapts spiritual things to spiritual, when he accommodates the words to the reality [*verba rei accommodat*]. In other words he properly tempers that heavenly wisdom of the Spirit with plainness of speech, and in such a way that it shows openly the very power of the Spirit Himself. In the meantime he reprimands others, who with an assumed elegance of style and a great show of cleverness, strive after men's applause, as either completely lacking in the genuine truth, or corrupting the spiritual teaching of God with an unbecoming veneer [*indecoro fuco*].[96]

The words themselves, it seems, are insufficient as a medium for conveying heavenly truths, but the Incarnation of God as *Sermo* and the power of the Spirit manifest in the preaching of Paul gives meaning and power to plain speech.

The divine accommodation of "words to reality" (*verba rei accommodat*) and of heavenly wisdom to plainness of speech (*spiritus sapientiam temperat oratione simplici*) is, again, an essential aspect of the *theologia rhetorica* advocated by Erasmus and Calvin, and a necessary ingredient in Christian eloquence. The mechanism manages to allow our exegetes to criticize overly splendid forms of human eloquence while at the same time "rescuing" Paul from a kind of philistinism that would run counter to pious learning. We find in Calvin's own exegetical strategy here, as in Erasmus', an attempt to navigate the inevitable tension that arises out of an assertion of divine accommodation between truth and language. On the one hand, when God accommodates himself to human capacity *through preaching,* or *through the Logos* (both *linguistic* forms of accommodation) there is never an absolutely complete disclosure of the heavenly mysteries, if for no other reason than that Erasmus and Calvin both believe that the infinite cannot be adequately inscribed in the finite. Thus Calvin's insistence on the truth of Paul's discourse is still only a partial truth – and certain mysteries remain hidden. And yet (on the other hand), even though human language is technically inadequate in itself to convey divine things, because of the incarnation of the *Logos* and because of the power of the Spirit working in the preacher, theological discourse, if enacted with propriety, is the only way of getting at divine truth on earth. In this we find an approximate description of "Christian eloquence." It is the language of the Christian philosophy, its exposition, which rejects ostentation and abstruse dialectic in favour of simplicity and practical wisdom.

Bouwsma writes of Calvin that "his rhetorical Christianity is most profoundly apparent in his emphasis on Scripture as everywhere accommodated by God's decorum to human comprehension: God speaks to us of things 'according to our capacity to understand them, not according to what they are'."[97] And furthermore that "His esteem for decorum provides a clue, often ignored, to understanding much in his own discourse. He was more concerned to sway a particular audience than to achieve the 'absolute balance' of a detached systematic theology."[98] Moreover, the emphasis on the utility of knowledge in general, and of theological language in particular, that we find in Calvin, strengthens the deep connection he has with the rhetorical theologians of biblical humanism. Here we have found in Calvin's attitude towards the use of eloquence in theology and preaching a consonant position, and it seems that *theologia rhetorica* as a lens, at least in its Erasmian form of privileging a *Christian* rhetoric (an *ars scripturarum*), is useful for understanding Calvin's methodological tendencies. The "new method" of Christian teaching that both Erasmus and Calvin call for depends upon an appreciation of the limits of divine revelation and, consequently, the humility of the hearer and teacher. The limits of Christian theology, and therefore of Christian eloquence, are circumscribed by the gospel itself. T.F. Torrance summarizes this point nicely: "Calvin will not have it that eloquence is in conflict with the Gospel, but since the truth of the Gospel by its very nature must shine through the language used and convince us by its own majesty and splendor, we must not let it be obscured by the words proclaiming it. That is why the Word of God comes to us largely in mean and lowly words so that its certainty may rest upon its own truth and not on external props."[99] We might qualify this somewhat, however: while the plainness of speech is indeed meant to avoid superfluous distractions, language is not ancillary but it is appropriate to its subject matter in its humility; in other words, while Torrance seems to come close to arguing that the truth is somehow *extra*-linguistic – it shines *through* the language used – it would seem more appropriate to say that, for Erasmus and Calvin, the truth is better expressed *in* a certain kind of discourse (or, perhaps, that a certain kind of discourse is truer to the truth).

For Calvin, the gold, silver, and jewels of 1 Cor. 3:12 constitute teaching built on the foundation of Christ, while the wood, hay, and stubble refer to "what is fabricated in men's brains" (*quae in hominum cerebro fabrefacta*), which "does nothing in the way of upbuilding" (*quae nihil ad aedificationem facit*).[100] Note the similarities in emphasis to Erasmus' gloss of this metaphor above. The appeal to a sort of divine eloquence which is *efficacious* rather than *ostentatious*, and which is governed by the humility of Christ, is more or less *the* definition of *theologia rhetorica* as we've seen it discussed regarding Calvin's humanist predecessors. As far as classical forms of rhetoric go, these are only appropriate when they are useful for gospel preaching and biblical exposition, and when they do not distort. Indeed, *efficax*, *efficacia*, and their cognates pervade these parts of Calvin's commentary. So, in much the same way as Erasmus, Calvin is not suggesting that humanist rhetoric is per se to be preferred to scholastic logic and dialectic in theological methodology, but rather that human aids ought, in general, to be subsumed to biblical discursive revelation, and only then – and when they are *useful* – are they not detrimental to true Christian preaching.

Sweetening Wormwood with Honey: Accommodation in Pauline Teaching

Something more can be said about the function of divine linguistic accommodation in the theologies of Erasmus and Calvin. Divine accommodation as a general form of revelation has been recognized as significant in Calvin's theology for some time.[101] However, its relationship to, and implications for, theological discourse as it takes shape in the exegesis on 1 Corinthians, in both exegetes, can be given more clarity. For, as Jon Balserak has shown, Calvin's use of the principle of *accommodatio* is rather diverse and takes many forms.[102] Calvin's dependence on Erasmus for his doctrine of accommodation has been appreciated more lately. Olivier Millet considers Erasmus' role as a mediator of the concept significant, and David Wright finds Millet's suggestion "immediately attractive," although he pinpoints the influence to Erasmus' comments about Chrysostom as an adept accommodator, which description of Chrysostom ostensibly sparked in Calvin an interest in the principle of accommodation.[103] But references to divine accommodation run throughout Erasmus' corpus, featuring prominently both in his exegesis of Paul, but also heavily in his preaching manual, the *Ecclesiastes*. The failure to appreciate the complexity and prominence of theological accommodation in Erasmus' thought distorts a proper understanding of his influence. Manfred Hoffmann, for example, refers to accommodation as the single most important principle in Erasmus' hermeneutic.[104] Arnold Huijgen, in his thorough study of Calvin's doctrine of accommodation, has recognized the "striking" similarities between Calvin's language and Erasmus' and that "all of Calvin's main terms [pertaining to accommodation] have parallels in Erasmus' accommodation theory."[105] This leads him to conclude that "the terminological resemblance is to be explained as Erasmus' influence on Calvin's accommodation terminology."[106] However, Huijgen goes on to argue that the "substance" of Calvin's use differs widely from Erasmus', such that Calvin "was very unlikely to have been influenced by it," and cites as evidence the "platonic premises" of Erasmus' theology.[107] Explaining accommodation in Erasmus determined by the "platonic premises of his theology," however, does not do justice to its richness (as, in fact, Huijgen himself seems to recognize).[108] Also, and not to put too fine a point on things, while Huijgen may be correct that Calvin's total understanding of accommodation differs from Erasmus', he fails to take into account Erasmus' comments on divine linguistic accommodation as it comes to take shape in Paul's foolish preaching, where in fact this is one area where Erasmus' and Calvin's conceptions of accommodation converge substantially.

What I am interested in here is the specific form of accommodation wherein God reveals himself through speech, or, as Calvin puts it, when God "tempers" the "heavenly wisdom of the Spirit with plainness of speech." This is the sort of accommodation that demands an altogether different sort of discourse when discussing divine matters. Both Erasmus and Calvin after him claim that God "babbles" to humans in revelation, using the same Latin word (*balbutio*) when describing this form of accommodation.[109] Erasmus sums up his account nicely as early as the 1503 *Enchiridion*: "The divine Spirit has his own peculiar language and modes of speech, which you must learn through careful observation. Divine wisdom speaks to us in baby-talk and like a loving mother accommodates its words to our state of infancy. It offers milk to tiny infants in Christ, and herbs to the sick."[110] Divine linguistic accommodation can take place in a number of ways, for example in God speaking to Moses on Mount Sinai, or the *Logos* taking on flesh and preaching the Sermon on the Mount. But it also occurs in the preaching of Paul, the consummate Christian rhetorician. In the figure of Paul himself, accommodation is layered: not only does God accommodate himself to humanity through the preaching and letter-writing of Paul, but Paul also must accommodate himself to his listeners at Corinth, who are only babes in Christ, not fit yet for solid food; and further, the exegete must accommodate to his or her audience. As Kathy Eden has written, "Faced with the differences between first-century Corinth and sixteenth-century Europe, Erasmus argues, Paul, in keeping with his efforts to interpret his own words equitably, interprets these same words historically."[111] "Discourse," Erasmus himself writes, paraphrasing Paul at 1 Cor 3:1, "must be accommodated to each person's capacity."[112] This, coupled with the notion shared by Erasmus and Calvin that God himself was an orator, means that Paul's use of rhetorical *accommodatio* in his preaching of Christ becomes a synecdoche for a larger-scale divine revelation.

Erasmus describes in rich language Paul's ability to accommodate himself to his audience in the dedicatory letter of the *Paraphrase on 1 Corinthians*:

> This Paul of ours is always skillful and slippery, but in these two Epistles [1 & 2 Cor.] he is such a squid, such a chameleon – he plays the part of Proteus or Vertumnus to such a tune that in dealing with the Corinthians, who are more than Greeks, he seems somehow to exemplify the old proverb 'Cretan with Cretan stand,' turning himself into every shape that he may shape them anew for Christ; with such freedom does he himself twist and turn like a man who threads the windings of a maze, and appearing to us in a fresh guise every time.[113]

These descriptions are striking – and they drew the criticism of Noel Beda of the Sorbonne – but Erasmus is not criticizing Paul. "Always Christ's business is his main concern," he continues, "always he thinks of the well-being of his flock, like a true physician leaving no remedy untried that he may restore his patients to perfect health."[114] Erasmus' Paul, borrowing a metaphor from Lucretius, "sweetens the bitter drug of wormwood with a dab of honey" in order to more effectively persuade the Corinthians.[115] But to read Erasmus as only referring to Paul's rhetorical abilities while not appreciating the theological significance of his rhetorical theology would be to miss the point. Paul is Christ-like in his accommodation: "When I first came to you," Erasmus paraphrases Paul, "I could not teach you the highest truths, as if you were fully spiritual, but I lowered my speech to the level of your weakness. Among the simple I used simple language; to the unspiritual I spoke quite unspiritually; and I babbled as if I were among infants."[116] Erasmus's Paul here casts his speech down to the weakness of the Corinthians (*deieci sermonem meum vestram ad imbecillitatem*), and he "babbles" in the same way that Divine Wisdom does in the *Enchiridion*.[117]

Strikingly, this is precisely the same language Erasmus uses to describe Christ's condescension to our weakness in the *Paraphrase* and the *Annotations*: earlier in the *Paraphrase* (at 1:23ff.), Erasmus describes God casting himself down from his sublimity to our humility (*Deiecit se quodammodo deus a sua sublimitate ad nostram humilitatem*); and likewise in the annotation on 1 Cor. 1 ("quod stultum est Dei"), where God lowers himself to our weakness (*Si deus demisit se ad nostram imbecillitatem ...*). If we were to press the issue, or wax literary, we might point out the intertextual connections to Erasmus' famous retranslation of John 1:1: when Paul is casting his own speech down to the weakness of his auditors, it is his *sermo* that is cast down, the very word Erasmus prefers as a translation of *Logos* in the Johannine prologue. And it isn't the only instance of Erasmus describing Paul's preaching in incarnational language.[118] The *Sermo* is God accommodated to lowly humanity in the most profound sense, and Paul's *sermones* are procedures for accommodating the profundity of the Incarnation to the weakness of his prospective converts, too much bound by their "carnal affections" to be able to digest the "solid food of mature teaching."[119]

There are varying levels of accommodation operating in Erasmus' picture here: God accommodates himself to humanity in Christ, Christ accommodates himself in various ways to his followers, Paul accommodates himself to his hearers in his simple preaching style, and further accommodates the difficulties inherent in the theology of Christ by preaching a simple gospel. Moreover, as Eden points out further, describing Paul as "master-rhetorician and advocate of accommodation," and describing Erasmus' own practice of biblical hermeneutics as one of Pauline accommodation: "Like rhetoric imitation, then, biblical hermeneutics as both practiced and preached by Erasmus is an act of accommodation, one in which both writer and reader come to feel at home. Like Bulephorus, his spokesman in the *Ciceronianus*, Erasmus, in his own voice in his mature hermeneutical works, pleads a double case: both Paul's and his own."[120]

We have seen in the previous chapter that Bullinger and Pellikan read Paul on the role of ornate rhetoric in Christian teaching along Erasmian lines, but they also follow Erasmus' theology of divine linguistic accommodation as operative in Paul's preaching.[121] In his commentary on 1 Corinthians 3:1–2, Bullinger describes Paul's *sermo* as being cast down to our weakness, using language similar to Erasmus' *Annotations* and *Paraphrase*, and even writes that God was babbling to us as he would an infant in describing the heavenly mysteries.[122] Pellikan is less innovative and, again, simply copies the relevant section of the *Paraphrase* on Paul's babbling accommodation, with a slight modification to Erasmus' opening line on Paul's discourse accommodating itself to the Corinthians' capacity (and complete with an invocation of the *philosophia Christi*).[123]

Calvin, too, applies the language of the abject and humble Christ to Paul and Paul's preaching, and develops further the notion of Paul as a vessel for divine accommodation. Calvin's description of Paul's own humiliation, which parallels in many ways Christ's, is remarkable. Paul becomes here a model for Christian humility and for preaching the simplicity of the gospel: "Paul gives a full explanation of what he merely touched on before, that there was nothing splendid or distinguished about him in men's eyes, to make him a notable figure ... He appeared to be someone worthy of less honor, because he was so insignificant and humble, according to the flesh [*secundum carnem*] Nevertheless he shows that the power of God was all the more evident in his ability to do so much, although he did not have the support of any human aids."[124] And, he continues, "Therefore since they [the Corinthians] had neglected his [Paul's!] simplicity, and longed feverishly for wisdom of some kind or another, that would be more grandiose and more polished, and since they were captivated by outward appearances, and more than that, by an assumed disguise, rather than by the living Spirit, did they not make their own love of display plain enough?"[125] The insignificance and humility of Paul, *according to the flesh* (*abiectus erat ac humilis secundum carnem*), was a deterrent to the Corinthians' appreciation of him. And the reasons for the Corinthians' rejection of Paul's preaching are substantially the same as their rejection of Christ as God incarnate. Millet connects Calvin's attempt to capture the voice of the biblical author, relevant here, to Erasmus' paraphrases, and also points out that Calvin brings his interpretation of 1 Cor. 2:1ff. to bear on the issue of biblical eloquence.[126]

In Calvin's commentary on Philippians 2, on Christ's kenosis, we see near-identical language applied to Christ: "before He assumed our flesh, there was nothing mean or contemptible, but a magnificence worthy of God" (*priusquam carnem nostram indueret, nihil humile erat vel abiectum*). Of course, once Christ does assume our flesh, he becomes, as does Paul, *abiectus* and *humile*.[127] A desire for something more elevated prevents the Corinthians from accepting both Christ and Paul. The absurdity of the gospel is rejected by the philosophers on account of its unreasonable aspects, while Paul's preaching is rejected by the Corinthian aesthetes on account of its unadorned nature. Furthermore, the common language of Calvin's descriptions of Christ's kenosis and of Paul's disposition adds force to the idea that Paul is, for Calvin, the Christian preacher *par excellence*, and that his is the perfect Christian eloquence. As Bouwsma has it: "Calvin's belief in God's accommodation of his word to human weakness in every age was central to his understanding of the Incarnation, as it had been for Valla and Erasmus. He believed, with Irenaeus, 'that the Father, himself infinite, becomes finite in the Son, for he has accommodated himself to our little measure lest our minds be overwhelmed by the immensity of his glory.' Like Valla and Erasmus, too, he rendered *Logos* as *sermo*, God's 'speech,' *oratio* rather than *ratio*, rhetorical rather than philosophical discourse."[128] This is true, certainly, as a descriptive account of Calvin's theological method. But Calvin, along with the other Erasmian biblical humanists, might say that there is a caveat in order, viz. that merely replacing dialectic with rhetoric is insufficient, for there always remains the danger of that rhetoric becoming an end in itself in any individual theologian or preacher.

A truly Christian rhetoric imitates the virtues of Christ, and God's accommodation to humanity in condescending to take on human flesh is repeated in Paul's accommodation to his hearers through lowly and unadorned preaching, both in terms of form and in terms of content. This further complicates arguments put forth by scholars who seem wont to reduce Calvin's "humanism" to *mere* method, which insinuates that rhetoric has no bearing on doctrine.[129] While it may be true that scholastics and humanists differed primarily on methodological approach and believed many similar things in terms of "pure" doctrine, to bracket things off in such a way leaves no room for what Calvin (and other biblical humanists) clearly perceived to be the dangers of the *form* of Christian teaching on, for example, Christian piety, which itself is neither a doctrinal nor a methodological issue per se. Commenting on 1 Cor. 3:2 (*I fed you milk, not solid food*), Calvin understands Paul's distinction to be one of (both rhetorical and theological) accommodation:

> Here one may ask whether Paul presented a different Christ to different people. I answer that this refers to his manner or form of teaching, rather than to the substance of what he taught. For the same Christ is milk for babes, and solid food for adults. The same truth of the Gospel is handled for both, but so as to suit the capacity of each. Therefore a wise teacher has the responsibility of accommodating himself [*se attemperare*] to the power of comprehension of those whom he undertakes to teach, so as to begin with first principles when instructing the weak and ignorant [*infirmos et rudes*], and not to move any higher than they can follow.[130]

Here the principle of accommodation as it is embodied in Paul's preaching is *rhetorical* insofar as his example becomes the model for the duty of the preacher to temper his method of teaching so that the hearers understand fully, each as they are able. It is *theological* insofar as the truth (*doctrinae substantiam ... veritas evangelii*) persists in the preaching unaltered, and this is only possible because Christ is accommodated to all through the stultification of all worldly wisdom.[131] And both the manner of teaching and the substance of the thing taught are rejected by the Corinthians for the same reasons. Furthermore, while *prima facie* one might think that progress from spiritual childhood to spiritual adulthood would involve the ability to understand more and more complex doctrinal matters, it seems to be the exact opposite. The carnal nature of the Corinthians is what prevents them from being able to partake of solid food, and it is also from this nature that the desire arises to hear highly polished and sophisticated teaching.[132] The Lord, we remember, only admits little ones (*parvulos*) to His school.[133] And the context for this assertion is that heavenly wisdom is only actually comprehended by those who are content with the abject form (*speciem abiecta*), and with a naked Christ (*nudum Christum*).[134]

From the perspective of their reception of Paul's exhortations to the Corinthians to eschew embellished rhetorical teaching strategies and to model their own teaching and preaching methods after the lowly humility of Christ, Erasmus and John Calvin, along with Bullinger and Pellikan, embrace a similar theological methodology, and one that corresponds quite closely to that outlined by Charles Trinkaus in describing the tendencies of Italian humanist theologians, viz. a *theologia rhetorica*. Aside from quite specifically similar exegetical conclusions, and the use of the same language in their commentaries, we find these exegetes employing very similar hermeneutical and theological strategies here: 1) a new method of teaching is inaugurated in light of the Incarnation and subsequent humiliation of Christ, which events confound traditional forms of worldly wisdom; 2) the theological principle of accommodation is invoked repeatedly by both exegetes in order to navigate the tricky problem of the relationship between divine truths and the difficulty of conveying those truths in a fallen world with fallible human language; 3) Paul, who ostensibly modelled his own teaching method after the humility of Christ (to the point of being described with "kenotic" language by Erasmus and Calvin), is to serve as the Christian teacher *par excellence*; and 4), that legitimate Christian teaching is both efficacious on account of its being governed by the Holy Spirit, and eminently practical insofar as its principal aim is to move the listener to act. While there are many areas where we might find Erasmus and Calvin diverging theologically or in their exegetical conclusions, these are fruitful points of comparison when considering their New Testament exegesis, and especially their attempts to articulate a Pauline rhetorical approach to Christian teaching.

Excursus: A Kenotic Doctrine of Folly

M.A. Screech first argued that Erasmus' conception of Pauline folly is intimately linked to his understanding of Christ's kenosis – his self-emptying described in the hymn of Philippians 2 – based on a passage from the *Moria* where Folly says that Christ "became in some way a fool ... when he was found 'in the form of a man'," a reference to Phil. 2:8.[135] It is an association that drew the charge of blasphemy from Peter Sutor, but Erasmus insisted that he had the backing of Paul and the church fathers. We have seen in this chapter an application of the concept of kenosis to the accommodated discourse of Paul in the context of preaching the gospel. The "kenotic doctrine of folly," if we wish to maintain Screech's designation, entails that any application of human forms of wisdom – which include not only scholastic dialectic, but also eloquence and erudition more generally – is of no use as an aid for understanding the gospel, which is already simple and eloquent in its own way, and that humility reigns as the first virtue of Christian learning. Rather than modifying the gospel in order to accommodate it to human wisdom, Erasmus demands that Christians do precisely the opposite: wisdom itself must be redefined in light of the gospel. For Erasmus the possibility of theology begins and ends with the Incarnation, with the enfleshed *Sermo*: *theologia rhetorica* depends upon the fact that the Word was made flesh, which is an accommodation to human capacity – this is the foolish tenet which serves as a norm for theological discourse, and there cannot be any *scientia divinorum* apart from it. As Screech writes in his analysis of the *Praise of Folly*: "Erasmus' Christ is a person of the godhead who emptied himself for the redemption of the world. At best he might seem no different from ordinary men. At worst he seemed a raving lunatic – not least to his relatives – and that in the presence of his mother and brethren."[136]

We reproduce here a portion of Erasmus' annotation on 1 Cor. 1:25, which we referred to in the second chapter: "Nor is the phrase 'foolishness of God' an abomination: it didn't horrify Augustine, who wrote in his hundred and second letter: 'This foolishness of God and the foolishness of preaching draw many to salvation.' If God lowered himself to our weakness that he might make us strong, what is novel if he should lower himself to our foolishness, that out of fools he might make wise men?"[137] Erasmus' inclusion of christological themes from Philippians 2 into his comments on 1 Corinthians in this context allows him to provide a more robust account of how he imagines the role of the humility of Christ to serve as a model for theological practice: in kenosis, Christ's humility serves as both the *ontological* event which confounds humanity's rational capacity as it relates to divine matters, and as the *ethical* model as a prescription for how to do theology. In the *Paraphrase on First Corinthians*, Erasmus also makes the connection explicit: "God has in a way cast himself down from his sublime height to our lowliness; from his wisdom he came down to our foolishness. Nevertheless what seemed foolish in him surpasses all the wisdom of the world, and what seemed feeble in him has been sturdier than all human strength."[138] The weakness and infirmity of Christ here has an intellective component, so to speak: Christ condescended not only to confound the strong and wealthy by becoming weak and poor, but also to confound the wise by taking on foolishness. While Screech has detailed Erasmus' possible debts to Origen in his kenotic doctrine of folly, John Chrysostom, too, in his *Homily 4 on 1 Corinthians* (1:18–25), invokes Christ's kenosis in the context of wisdom and folly, quoting Phil. 2:7, and perhaps this is a more obvious source for Erasmus' exegesis of this passage. The kenotic moment, furthermore, is precisely what cannot be accounted for by philosophical speculation or expressed through ornate rhetorical discourse: "Through the lowly the glory of the gospel sprang forth; through the lowly it is being spread abroad so that, contrary to the normal course of events, lowliness overwhelms loftiness, and simplicity refutes human cunning."[139] There is no epistemological upheaval without Christ's radical self-emptying. Elsewhere in the *Paraphrase* he elaborates on the lowliness of Christ as antagonistic to human wisdom: "From the arrogance of worldly philosophy, he calls them back to the humility of the cross, which although it has no ostentation, nevertheless has power and effectiveness."[140] Here *humilitas*, contrasted with *supercilium* (arrogance), is a foil to worldly philosophical wisdom. This is the force of Paul's claim that he knows nothing other than Jesus Christ, and him crucified, and Erasmus interprets Paul at the beginning of chapter 2 so that he was preaching what was "most lowly" (*humillimus*) and "human" in Christ when he was preaching the gospel. This is an interpretation that resonates with Erasmus' understanding of the christological hymn in Philippians as glossed in the 1519 *Annotations*, where he also associates Christ's kenosis with his becoming *humillimum et nihili*.[141]

Walter Gordon has argued, furthermore, that Erasmus' Pauline kenotic ethical ideal is tantamount to a critique of Aristotle's ethics:

> Aristotle devotes the entire seventh book of the *Nicomachean Ethics* to the refinement of the concept of 'enkrateia,' a notion signifying human self-possession. The idea is not foreign to the New Testament, but it is not a master concept. In fact, a dominant idea arising from the Pauline meditation on the cross runs head-on into the concept of self-possession. M.A. Screech, in showing Erasmus' dependence on Origen for his theology of foolishness, indicates that the divine folly is made manifest in the kenosis of Christ, the self-emptying process which Paul beholds in the birth and the death of the saviour. The notion of kenosis, in so far as it rubs against the psychology of a Greek understanding of virtue, bears a resemblance to vice, without, of course, being so. The concept does not so much change the content of the moral order as revolutionize our whole way of viewing this order.[142]

There is a related anthropological claim here (which we explore in the final chapter), tied to Erasmus' rejection of the Stoic doctrine of *apatheia*, which seeks to subordinate all emotions to reason in order to achieve psychological tranquility. On the one hand, there is a kind of foreignness of the wisdom of God that is incomprehensible to human beings, but on the other hand, if we take the correct approach, which consists in adopting the strange and paradoxical virtues of Paul's christological formulations, we become united to Christ. Put another way, Christ's kenotic emptying into foolishness is, for Erasmus, anthropologically significant insofar as it entails that the Stoics were wrong in their assertion that what is essentially human is the ability to contemplate "apathetically," so to speak.[143] The Stoic doctrine of *apatheia* is bad Christology.[144]

While I have compared Erasmus' and Calvin's interpretations of the christological hymn in Philippians 2 elsewhere, and though we've briefly seen Calvin use kenotic language in his understanding of Paul's preaching method, it is worth noting that Calvin, too, in addition to the instance cited above in the section on the *Institutes*, connects kenosis to foolishness explicitly in his commentary.[145] The Christian philosophy, Calvin writes, demands that Christians empty themselves of wisdom and become, as Paul says, "fools in this world," which Calvin glosses, commenting on 1 Cor. 3:18, as "someone who renounces his own understanding and, as if he were blind, allows himself to be guided by the Lord; who, lacking confidence in himself, leans entirely upon the Lord; who bases all his wisdom on Him; who yields himself, obedient and willing to learn, to God. Our wisdom must vanish by this method, so that God's will may have sway over our lives; and we must be emptied of our own understanding, so that we may be filled with the wisdom of God."[146] Here Calvin argues that we must be emptied of our *reason* (*exinaniri ratione*), using the same verb he retains as a translation of the Greek ἐκένωσεν in his commentary on Phil. 2:7.[147] He continues, again using the Latin *exinanire*: "Let him who excels in the world because of a reputation for wisdom become a fool in his own eyes, emptying himself out."[148] Calvin, too, was a close reader of Chrysostom, and whether he was taking cues from the Greek father or from Erasmus in this case, it is impossible to say. Nevertheless, the connections between Christ's kenosis and Pauline folly, in both Erasmus' and Calvin's exegesis, are unmistakable, and the intertextual glosses bring together two of Paul's more striking christological formulations in order to expressly devalue the role of reason for Christian wisdom and piety. The next chapter will continue to examine the intertextual importance of Pauline folly for sixteenth-century interpretations of Paul's criticism of *philosophia* in Colossians 2.

Chapter Five

Blaming Philosophy, Praising Folly

O altitudo! Petrus negat, latro credit. O altitudo! Quaeris tu ratione? Ego expavescam altitudine. Tu ratiocinare, ego mirabor. Tu disputa, ego credam.
– Augustine, *De verb. Apost. serm.* 20

In his dedicatory letter to Cardinal Lorenzo Campeggi (1474–1539), which prefaces Erasmus' *Paraphrases* on Ephesians through 2 Thessalonians (first published in 1520), and which is a brief history of the slow degradation of theology in the hands of the university theologians as well as a brief overview of the contours of the humanist-scholastic debates, Erasmus digresses on the *philosophia Christiana*:

In the olden days the Christian philosophy was a matter of faith, not of disputation; men's simple piety was satisfied with the oracles of Holy Scripture, and charity, spontaneously responsive, had no need of complicated rules, believing all things, nowhere hesitating. Later, the management of theology was taken in hand by men nurtured in humane learning, but mainly in those fields of learning which today we commonly call rhetoric. Gradually philosophy came to be applied more and more, Platonic first and then Aristotelian, and questions began to be asked about many points which were thought to pertain either to morals or to the field of speculation and heavenly things. At first this seemed most fundamental; but it developed by stages until many, neglecting the study of ancient tongues and of polite literature and even of Holy Writ, grew old over questions meticulous, needless, and unreasonably minute, as if drawn to the rocks on which some Siren sang. By now theology began to be a form of skill, not wisdom; a show-piece, not a means towards true religion; and besides ambition and avarice it was spoilt by other pests, by flattery and strife and superstition.[1]

Here we have what, to Erasmus' mind, is a story of gradual (*magis quam magis*) decline in Christian theology (or of the *philosophia Christiana*), which coincides directly with the application of external aids, first by the rhetoricians (or simply those participating in the *humanis disciplinis*), and then by the philosophically minded theologians (*primum Platonica, mox Aristotelica*). The Sirens' song had long been a favourite metaphor of Erasmus' for describing the deleterious effects of scholastic quibbling.[2] In his brief history, the first stage was presumably more benign, to Erasmus' mind, than the second, but the ideal existed in the most simple time when the gospel stood on its own in the hearts of its devotees.

Generally speaking, however, it was a matter of human pride as much as anything else which had ruined the idyllic early days: "Thus at length it came about that the pure image of Christ was almost overlaid by human disputations; the crystal springs of the old gospel teaching were choked with sawdust by the Philistines; and the undeviating rule of Holy Scripture, bent this way and that, became the slave of our appetites rather than of the glory of Christ."[3] The occasion for the nature of this letter, which goes on for some time defending the use of language learning and the *bonae litterae* as handmaids to theology, reflects not only Erasmus' genuine interest in reviving theology, but also stems from published challenges by contemporary university theologians to Erasmus' work. While Erasmus had been contending against a certain kind of theology for quite a while, the publication of his new New Testament along with the notes brought new critics out of the woodwork, many of them conservative members of theology faculties who no doubt didn't feel the same sense of deterioration in the history of theological development.[4]

The notion of a "Christian philosophy," prominent in the discourse of sixteenth-century biblical humanists, has an interesting history in modern scholarship, and it may be illuminating at this stage to invoke its twentieth-century conception for comparative purposes.[5] Étienne Gilson (1884–1978), the eminent historian of philosophy, begins the first of his 1936 Gifford Lectures by outlining the methodological problems attendant to any discussion involving the designation "Christian philosophy." The question is not, he says, whether there were any philosophic Christians, but rather it is whether the systems of thought produced by philosophic Christians deserve to be called philosophies.[6] Certain historians, according to Gilson, answer negatively on account of their assessment that medieval Christian thought, to the extent that it is philosophical at all, is philosophical only insofar as it consists of "shreds of Greek thought" used to "clumsily patch up theology."[7] Such detractors reject outright even the possibility of a Christian philosophy, for reason and revelation are judged by them to be mutually exclusive.[8] Gilson, on the contrary, setting forth the example of Thomas Aquinas as the Christian philosopher *par excellence*, suggests that this is a false dichotomy.[9] The true Christian philosopher, for Gilson, follows the Anselmian formula, *fides quaerens intellectum*, and seeks to demonstrate through reason what she already believes through faith. For Gilson, in other words, what makes a Christian philosophy a philosophy at all are those moments when its practitioners seek to affirm what they already believe through rational processes: the rendering of *mere* faith into robust knowledge. The results of this process are undeniably beneficial from an epistemological standpoint, according to Gilson, who goes so far as to say that "there is no question of maintaining – *no one has ever maintained* – that faith is a kind of cognition superior to rational cognition. It is quite clear, on the contrary, that belief is a succedaneum of knowledge, and that to substitute science for belief, wherever possible, is always a positive gain for the understanding."[10] Of course, Gilson's prescriptions would make historians of a later period squirm, and apart from that, Paul Oscar Kristeller long ago pointed out that Aquinas never uses the term *philosophia Christiana* himself, and furthermore that Gilson neglects to cite anyone in the time between Augustine and Erasmus who did.[11] Nevertheless, Gilson's rather provocative formulations can serve as a foil for considering sixteenth-century thinkers who both did employ the term *philosophia Christiana* and meant something rather different by it than Gilson's imagined ideal.

Thus it is the aim of this chapter to elaborate on the relationship between Pauline folly and the Christian philosophy as it is understood primarily by Erasmus and Calvin. Aside from the fact that Calvin invokes 1 Corinthians and the folly of the cross in his commentary on Colossians chapter 2, an examination of the Pauline Christian philosophy in the sixteenth century would not be complete without an examination of the reception of Paul's use of the word *philosophia* at Colossians 2:8, where he warns that the Colossians not be deceived by philosophy and empty deception. It is the only instance of the word in the New Testament, and in sixteenth-century commentaries Colossians 2 serves as a focal point for discussions not only of the relationship between philosophy and Christian teaching, but also, more specifically, for issues surrounding the certainty of faith and rhetorical eloquence. In this last regard, Erasmus and Calvin deride ornate rhetoric alongside philosophy in their commentaries, which distinguishes their exegesis from Melanchthon's, providing an opportunity for further cross-confessional comparison on the reception of Paul's teaching. Thus, after a close comparison of the commentaries of Erasmus, Bullinger, Pellikan, Calvin, and Melanchthon, the chapter will end by considering how the reception of Paul's criticism of *philosophia* in Colossians relates to our earlier analysis of the reception of Pauline folly from the perspective of sixteenth-century conceptions of the *philosophia Christiana*.

Antiphilosophy in the *Argumenta* to Colossians of Erasmus and Calvin

Col. 2:8 does not stand alone, of course, and there is much relevant material in the commentaries running up to interpretations of this verse. Erasmus' *argumentum* to his *Paraphrase* opens with the consideration of how the pseudoapostles led the Colossians astray, to set the stage for his rendering. He delineates two errant paths: the ceremonies of Judaism and the superstitions of philosophy. A 1549 London printing of the English *Paraphrases* – the edition that every parish church in England was meant to have placed in an accessible location – renders Erasmus thus: "Beside this the same teachers with Christes doctrine mingled Jewishnes and supersticious Philosophie, observing and keeping certain poyntes of the lawe, supersticiously also honouring the Sonne, the Moone, and starres, with such other small trinkettes of this world, bearing the Colossians in hand that they were also bound to do the same."[12] Erasmus further disparages the *magniloquentia* of the pseudoapostles in the preface.[13] The "small trinkettes of this world" from the early English version renders *elementa mundi* of verse 2:8, which *philosophia* and *inane deceptio* (empty deceit) depend on. Indeed, paraphrasing Colossians 1:8–11, Erasmus links Colossians to the twofold concerns of 1 Corinthians 1–4, viz. that true discernment of God's will comes not through *humana philosophia* or *superstitiosa hominum persuasione*, but through *sapientia prudentiaque spirituali*.[14] Erasmus' gloss represents a cornucopia of potential false paths: the Law, philosophy, astrology, and excessively wrought eloquence. Paul's criticisms of philosophy in chapter 2 provide sixteenth-century exegetes a broad brush with which to paint perceived threats to gospel simplicity.

In Calvin's *argumentum* to his Colossians commentary – first published by Jean Girard in Geneva in 1548 – which is rather longer than Erasmus', he glosses Paul's use of the term *philosophy* to describe one of the problems facing the Phrygian Christians Paul is addressing in his letter: what Calvin's Paul calls a "vain philosophy" (*inanem philosophiam*)[15] issues only secondarily from the fact that certain Jews (in Calvin's opinion) in the Colossian church intended on "mixing up Christ with Moses" (*Christum cum Mose miscerunt*), combining Law and Gospel, but primarily from the fact that they "painted over their fallacies with specious colors" (*speciosis fucis pingebant suas fallacias*). That is, the manner in which they presented their position is the *inane* aspect of the philosophy in question, and not necessarily the substance of their ideas (although certainly Calvin isn't endorsing these either). We have seen Calvin's preference for *fucus* and its cognates in previous chapters, a word choice he shares not only with Erasmus, but also with Pellikan and Bullinger to describe a kind of colourful ornateness that doesn't contribute anything to the substance of the thing taught. Calvin distinguishes his own reading from those of other interpreters who think that Paul is issuing a two-pronged attack: against pagan philosophers arguing about the stars, e.g., on the one hand, and against Jews advocating superfluous ceremonies on the other. Helmut Feld, in the notes to his critical edition of Calvin's text, suggests he has in mind Pellikan and Bullinger here, which may very well be the case, but Erasmus also makes a similar distinction in the preface to his paraphrase that may serve as the basis for the subsequent Swiss readings.[16] At any rate, according to Calvin, Paul employs *inanem philosophiam* with further reference to the overly clever quibbles (*argutias*) that the false teachers were "playing around with" (*ludebant*). This conjures an image of sophistical wordplay. Despite their subtlety, Calvin writes, they nevertheless remained useless.[17]

But Calvin extends his argument beyond the first-century historical context, invoking Pseudo-Dionysius' *Celestial Hierarchy* as the sort of thing Paul is criticizing, on account of its proffering, among many other similar speculative ideas, a way of access to God via the angels (Col. 2:18).[18] Calvin further points out that these ideas derive from Plato's Academy (*ex schola Platonicorum haustae*), and so, importantly, we see that even though Calvin puts forth the interpretation that there aren't two groups of people misleading the Colossians (pagans *and* Jews), but a single group of philosophically minded Jews set on "mixing Christ with Moses," he yet widens his rhetorical lens by explicitly invoking the mystical Platonist tradition. This move ties the interpretation of Col. 2 to the interpretation of the early chapters of 1 Corinthians. While Calvin makes an historical point about the social context of the Colossian church, the metaphilosophical point is a broader one: fruitless philosophizing is deleterious to gospel teaching irrespective of who is carrying it out. Indeed, the bulk of the *argumentum* concerns itself with positioning Christ as *scopus* over and against various human intellectual distractions, and with establishing that all things ought to be taught with this aim in mind.[19] (Calvin also uses the Erasmian *scopus fidei* to describe Christ in his note on Col. 1:4.) Finally, we find in the preface a common refrain from Calvin's interpretation of the folly material, viz. the distinction between useful and empty teaching: Paul's is a model of Christ that is living and efficacious (*vivum ac efficacem*), not the Christ of the "papists," who has been deformed and emptied of his power (*deformatum, exinanitum sua virtute*). Paul's reproof of *philosophia* has more to do with a flawed method and an errant focus than with specific beliefs, a similar conclusion to the one drawn in the *argumentum* to the commentary on 1 Corinthians. In other words, in the minds of sixteenth-century biblical humanists, the Colossians letter is quite similar to and consonant with the Corinthian correspondence in its importance as establishing a Pauline method of teaching.

Col. 2:2–3: On Faith, Certainty, and Hidden Wisdom[20]

At Colossians 2:2, Paul states his wish that the Colossians receive consolation in their hearts, that they are joined together in love, and that they have all the riches of a certain persuasion, or conviction, of understanding (Erasmus: *omnem opulentiam certae persuasionis intelligentiae*), as well as a knowledge of the mysteries of God. The relevance of the verse for our purposes hinges on the translation and interpretation of the Greek word πληροφορίας, which is glossed explicitly by all our commentators. Relevant translations of the Greek (εἰς πᾶν πλοῦτος πληροφορίας) are as follows:

– Vulgate: *in omnes divitias plenitudinis intellectus*
– Stapulensis: *plenariae certitudinis intelligentiae*
– Erasmus: *in omnem opulentiam certae persuasionis intelligentiae*
– Calvin: *omnes divitias certitudinis intelligentiae*
– Stephanus (Estienne) (1541): *ad omnem abundantiam certitudinis intelligentiae*
– Pellikan = Vulgate
– Bullinger = Erasmus

We note first Erasmus' modification of the Vulgate's rendering, from "all the riches of a full/complete understanding" to "complete abundance of *a certain assurance* of understanding," not an extraordinary change, but one that emphasizes resolve and conviction over "fullness." As we see, Jacques Lefevre d'Etaples (Faber Stapulensis) had already moved some way in this direction in his 1512 commentary on and translation of Paul's letters, and the move has consequences which can be felt by comparison with Aquinas, for example, who interprets the verse (following the Vulgate) to mean that the intellect will be "filled up" (*implet*) with an understanding "in abundance" (*in copiam*).[21] Erasmus glosses the term πληροφορία with an eye towards certainty in multiple places in the *Annotations*, and provides an overview of the use of the word in various biblical texts in his note on Luke 1:1, where the word also appears.[22] At Luke 1:1, Erasmus' NT renders the Greek participle πεπληροφορημένον as *certissimae fidei sunt* ("having been most certainly assured of faith"); similarly, at Romans 4:21, πληροφορηθεὶς is *certa accepta persuasione* ("having acquired a firm conviction").[23] In other words, the Greek term denotes something specifically to do with firm assurance to Erasmus' mind, a valence not captured in the Vulgate translator's rendering in multiple instances.

On Col. 2:2, Erasmus defines πληροφορίας as a *certam persuasionem*, with the further comment that it "admits of no doubt whatsoever."[24] In his *Paraphrase*, Erasmus renders the phrase more elaborately as "understanding better and more certainly believing (*magis intelligant, ac certius credant*)."[25] While Timothy Wengert has argued that Melanchthon's ostensible implicit exegetical judgments on Colossians are aimed at Erasmus' lack of commitment to an assured and certain faith evident in his position in the free will debate with Luther, we see here, as well as in earlier chapters on Erasmus' exegesis of the Spirit as teacher, that the picture is more complicated.[26] Erasmus' judgment that disputes over the freedom of the will constituted disputes over *adiaphora* did not entail, to Erasmus' mind, that faith was a potentially shifting matter through and through, a point reflected both in his judgments as a translator and his glosses on Paul's targets in his letters. To paraphrase Susan Schreiner, the question in early modern theology was not over whether there was certainty, but where certainty lay. Erasmus goes on to define the contents of true wisdom, which Christians are to be certain of: All wisdom being in Christ alone, "we should seek nothing in human wisdom – whether some promise made by the philosophers of this world or some offer made by the teachers of the Mosaic law or by others who boast that they have been instructed by the conversations of angels – since in him alone are stored up and kept from view all the treasures of wisdom and of fruitful knowledge. From this source one may draw summarily whatever pertains to authentic salvation."[27]

Erasmus' Protestant biblical-humanist successors, too, focus on the indubitability of true faith, which, of course, becomes a crucial aspect of sixteenth-century Protestantism, a penchant connected as well to the insistence on the verifiable authority of scripture. Bullinger, whose commentary was first published in Zurich in 1535, and who in 1538 published a treatise on the subject of the certitude of the authority of scripture,[28] follows Erasmus both in his translation and in the language of his interpretation as *certa persuasio quoties alicui rei sit fides adeo ut de ipsa nihil dubitemus*.[29] In the preface to his 1538 treatise on the authority of scripture and the certitude of faith, he warns – citing Cicero – against the dangers of eloquence that doesn't contain wisdom as well.[30] Olivier Millet points out that this work, too, is important for understanding Calvin's exegetical method, not for its originality per se, but because it represents a movement in Swiss Protestantism that synthesizes "the purest Erasmian spirit with a substantially reformed perspective," given its twofold goal of establishing the principle of *sola scriptura* and a particular biblical style.[31] This is akin also to these exegetes' understanding of the guaranteed teaching of the Spirit in the exegesis of 1 Corinthians 2. The authority of the Spirit as teacher and the certainty that attends the Spirit's inbreathing, moreover, pertains most especially to gospel teaching in these cases and not explicitly to the truth of *sola scriptura*.[32]

Pellikan, despite his retention of the Vulgate version in the biblical text of his commentary (of, that is, *plenitudinis intellectus* for πληροφορίας), nevertheless reproduces Erasmus' *Paraphrase* of Paul's hopes for the Colossians to "understand better and more certainly to believe," along with the entire section quoted from the *Paraphrase* supra.[33] Melanchthon, in the 1528 *Scholia*, calls πληροφορία a "certain perception in the mind and not an ambiguous opinion."[34] And in the 1559 *Ennarationes* he writes that it signifies *Certitudinem*.[35] Wengert argues that Melanchthon nonetheless targets Erasmus with his comments in the *Scholia* linking a doubting faith to the freedom of the will, although this would seemingly be a strange place to do it, given Erasmus' translation and interpretation of the text.[36] It is important to note further that while for Melanchthon these texts hinge on this question, so important during the years following the debate between Luther and Erasmus, Calvin does not mention free will or justification in this section of his commentary, and instead focuses on the assurance of faith on the one hand,

and the possibility of demonstrating Christ's equality with the Father on the other.

On the phrase, the "riches of the certitude of understanding," which Calvin renders as *omnes divitias certitudinis intelligentiae*, he states, from the first edition of the Colossians commentary, that it means "full and clear perception" (*plenam et luculentam perceptionem*). And, as elsewhere, Calvin is keen to emphasize the distinction between a certain faith on the one hand and mere opinion on the other, arguing that the word *certitudinis* is used by Paul to distinguish faith from opinion (*fidem ab opinione*), a similar distinction to the one made by Melancththon. True knowledge of God is borne by the one who remains steadfast in a firm and constant persuasion (*stat in firma constantique persuasione*). Finally, Calvin explicitly glosses Paul's use of the Greek *plerophorias*, which here stands for that constancy and stability (*constantiam et stabilitatem*) that can no more be separated from faith than heat or light from the sun.[37] Here as elsewhere, Calvin's emphasis favours Erasmus' understanding of the term over the Vulgate's use of *plenitudinem*. Millet suggests that this term is important for Calvin in connection with his understanding of *fides* as *persuasio*, and also for the movement of the heart (à émouvoir les coeurs), but he strangely writes that Calvin, in his gloss on Luke 1:1, "reproaches Erasmus for having translated [πληροφορία] as *fullness*."[38] Calvin, however, is clearly not reproaching Erasmus but is criticizing the Vulgate translation in his comments on Luke 1:1. First of all, Erasmus renders the passage against the Vulgate as *certissimae fidei*, digressing on this valence of the word at length in his annotation on the verse; and second, Calvin refers not to Erasmus in his comments but explicitly to the *vetus interpres* (a common, indeed Erasmian, shorthand for the translator of the Vulgate).

Calvin goes on to denounce the "diabolic dogma of the scholastics" which privileges "moral conjecture" over true assurance.[39] Regarding the mysteries of God, mentioned at the end of the verse, Calvin distinguishes between the knowledge (*scientia*) Paul was speaking of, which is equivalent to assured faith, and what the pseudoapostles sell "under the trade name of wisdom (*imposturas sapientiae titulo*)."[40] "The Gospel can be understood by faith alone," Calvin continues, "not by reason, nor by the perspicacity of human understanding; because in itself it is a thing hidden from us."[41] The condemnation of human understanding, as in the commentary on 1 Corinthians, relates directly to Calvin's position that all wisdom is to be found in Christ. On verse 2:3 ("in whom are hidden all the treasures of wisdom and knowledge"),

Calvin prefers the reading which has it that the relative pronoun refers specifically to Christ: "By this he means that we are perfect in wisdom if we truly know Christ, so that it is madness to wish to know anything besides him."[42] Calvin then makes explicit the connection to Pauline folly: Paul calls the treasures of wisdom and knowledge "hidden," according to Calvin, "because they are not seen shining brightly, but rather, as it were, lie hidden under the contemptible humility and simplicity of the cross. For the preaching of the cross is always (as we find in Corinthians) foolish to the world."[43] Calvin seems rather to like Colossians 2:3, and the intertextual relationship runs the other way as well: he quotes it three times in his commentary on Pauline folly in 1 Corinthians 1–4.[44]

In his translation of Col. 2:3, Calvin has departed from the Vulgate's and Erasmus' rendering of "knowledge" (γνώσεως) as *scientia*, opting instead for *intelligentia*. He explains that one ought not to rigidly distinguish between *sapientia* and *intelligentia*, and that Paul here only uses different words for the purpose of effect (*duplicatio ad augendum*) – Paul may as well have said that no *scientia, eruditio, doctrina*, or *sapientia* can be found apart from Christ.[45] None of our other sixteenth-century exegetes make the distinction Calvin here criticizes (between wisdom and knowledge), although such a distinction is found in Aquinas' comments on this verse: "*sapientia* is the knowledge of divine things [*cognitio divinorum*]," he says, and "*scientia* is the knowledge of created things [*cognitio creaturarum*]."[46] It could be that Calvin has Thomas in mind here. Aquinas further interprets the passage to pertain to *God's* knowledge and wisdom with respect to divine and created things, while clearly for Calvin this passage has to do with delineating meaningful wisdom from a human perspective – to establish that all things apart from the *scientia Christi* are smoke. It may be mentioned that Calvin provides a slightly different take in his comments on 1 Corinthians 12:8 (on the Spirit-granted gifts of the "words of wisdom" and the "words of knowledge"), where he invokes Col. 2:3 in his argument that the terms denoting wisdom and knowledge for Paul mark a difference of degree, but not of kind – an important qualification when defining religious epistemology in the Christian philosophy. There he suggests that wisdom (*sapientia*) is a deeper form of spiritual understanding than knowledge (*scientia vel cognitio*).[47] Perhaps most important for our purposes is that, for Calvin, Paul's discourse on the folly of the cross becomes the exegetical ground for his interpretation of Paul's message to the Colossians about the mysteries of divine wisdom.

Col. 2:4: Denouncing Rhetoric: Erasmus, Bullinger, Calvin, (Not) Melanchthon

The textual history of Melanchthon's reception of Colossians 2 is long and complex, but it has, thankfully, been sorted out for us by Timothy Wengert, who writes, "Next to Paul's letter to the Romans, no book of the New Testament received more attention from Melanchthon than Colossians."[48] Wengert has studied, at length, Melanchthon's departures from Erasmus in his *Scholia* on Colossians, with special attention devoted to chapter 2 on the scope of Paul's warning against philosophy, and has even written that Melanchthon "seemed to have viewed [his *Scholia*] as Wittenberg's answer to Erasmus' *Hyperaspistes*," which constituted part of Erasmus' dispute with Luther over the freedom of the will that began in 1524 with the publication of Erasmus' *De libero arbitrio*.[49] A crucial moment of departure for Melanchthon, according to Wengert, comes in his refusal to take Paul's use of the Greek πιθανολογία (variously spelled by our exegetes as πειθανολογία) of Col. 2:4 to involve a denunciation of classical rhetoric. Melanchthon translates the term as *probabile ratione*, and he glosses it thus: "Some inept people have understood this as ornament of oratory, but Paul holds a completely different opinion. For when Christian teaching disagrees with reason, he enjoins us to beware, lest we are deceived by arguments derived from reason ... And the word πιθανολογία that the apostle uses here does not mean ornament of oratory or elocution, but cleverly thought out arguments that appear true."[50] Melanchthon has thus recast the Greek, as Wengert points out, "without any reference to speech (*sermo*) at all!"[51] This is presumably tantamount to a condemnation of sophistry in the classical sense (i.e., something along the lines of making the weaker argument the stronger irrespective of the truth of the matter), while stopping short of a condemnation of rhetorical elements. Melanchthon makes a similar move in his avoidance of criticizing rhetoric in his lectures on 1 Corinthians of 1521.[52] The Wittenberger doesn't seem as comfortable (or as interested) as our other exegetes in attempting to articulate a distinctive type of Christian eloquence that runs contrary to classical norms.

The implications of Wengert's analysis for our purposes are that Melanchthon was mounting a criticism against Erasmus by 1) refusing to condemn rhetoric, and 2) by outright condemning reason. As we see below, Melanchthon's understanding of πιθανολογία differs not only from Erasmus', but from a prominent thread in the biblical-humanist exegetical tradition:

- Augustine: *in verisimili sermone*[53]
- Vulgate: *in sublimitate sermonum*
- Erasmus' NT: *probabilitate sermonis*
  - *Ann. Col.* 2:4: *In sublimitate sermonum, id est, in persuasibili oratione, sive persuasibilitate, sive probabilitate*
- Faber Stapulensis: *in persuasione eloquentiae*
- Melanchthon: *probabile ratione*
- Bullinger = Erasmus
- Pellikan = Vulgate
- Calvin: *persuasorio sermone.*

In translating the term as he does, Melanchthon is the only one of our exegetes who endorses *ratio* as lexically highly relevant, and his is the only rendering that completely excludes any insinuation of rhetorical persuasion as associated with πιθανολογία. The commentaries are broader. Erasmus paraphrases the section as follows:

> Now these statements of ours have this objective: that you should take care again and again that no one, armed with human skills against the simplicity of gospel doctrine, should play a trick on you and deceive you with talk that is false, but to all appearances plausible and consistent with the facts. It is the custom of the world's sophists to ensnare the minds of simple people with some legal quirks and the clever arguments of human thinking. It is no secret to me that there are some people of this kind among you craftily aiming at the simplicity of your faith.[54]

In this case, in fact, Erasmus does not denounce the ornaments of oratory per se, but he targets the methods of the sophists, who martial human skill (*humanis artibus*), speech that is false but appears true (*probabili ac verisimili*), and, like Melanchthon, criticizes the *argutiis rationum humanarum*. From this perspective, Wengert's claim that Melanchthon imagined Erasmus as "loathe to admit" that reason was "the real culprit" in Paul's criticisms of the Colossian instigators would seem to also entail that, if these were his true intentions, Melanchthon didn't read Erasmus very closely on the matter. Erasmus is certainly quite comfortable disparaging human reason both in his *Paraphrase* here and in a number of other circumstances; this, coupled with the observation that a prominent understanding of πιθανολογία in the exegetical tradition involves persuasive rhetoric, or at least as a kind of speech that confines its aims to mere probability, might make it more accurate to say that Melanchthon was loathe to admit that Paul here was denouncing human forms of eloquence.

Moreover, Wengert's understanding of Melanchthon as defending rhetoric tooth and nail on the grounds that it was, in part, his vocational life-blood,[55] serves as a useful backdrop for analysing Erasmus' and Calvin's rhetorical denunciations of human rhetoric. Melanchthon seemed to think that dismissing rhetoric in theology entailed throwing the baby out with the bathwater, while Erasmus and Calvin were quick to dismiss superfluous rhetorical flair and to argue for a distinctively Christian form of eloquence, but clearly didn't thereby wish for the study of rhetoric to be altogether abolished. Ultimately, all our exegetes understand Paul to be condemning misleading forms of discourse that detract from certainty, whether via sophistical forms of argumentation or via ornate and inticing language (or some combination of both). The take away is that, while Melanchthon confines his criticism to a form of deceptive *ratio*, Erasmus' condemnation (formed through a combination of comments from the *Annotations* and *Paraphrase*) is more sweeping and includes other forms of empty deceit through speech. Of utmost importance for Erasmus is that Christian teaching is firm and solid: Erasmus modifies the Vulgate's more ambiguous rendering of *firmamentum* in Col. 2:5 to read *soliditatem* to reflect this interest in his version of the text, and Erasmus' Paul in the *Paraphrase* calls on the Colossians to persevere and, with an allusion to 1 Corinthians 3:10, to build onto the "solid foundation of gospel teaching" which had been presented to them previously, not vacillating, but remaining firm and immovable.[56]

Bullinger's interpretation is at least as wide in scope; he makes an explicit distinction between "the wiles of the Sophists, the syllogisms of the philosophers, the probability and delights of rhetoric [*probabilitate et delectione rhetorum*] and the intricacies of dialectic" on the one hand, and the "credible and true method of speaking" on the other hand. *Peithanologia* is not just any sort of rhetoric, according to Bullinger, but it is rhetoric that corrupts truth with deceitful artifice.[57] It signifies, explicitly, *probabilitatem et orationem persuasibilem*, and Bullinger connects the word etymologically with the Greek goddess *Peitho* – who personifies persuasion and seduction – providing a number of classical references.[58]

Clearly, then, for Bullinger, the valence of Paul's word choice here tends towards the pejoratively rhetorical, distinguishing his reading from Melanchthon's. Pellikan, by contrast, is more interested in condemning philosophical reason than eloquence: he sandwiches in a section from Erasmus' *Paraphrase* (where Paul denounces teachings by the *sophistae mundi* which have only a probable and likely form – *speciem probabili ac verisimili*) between criticisms of the philosophies of Epicurus, Plato, and Aristotle, many of whose teachings run counter to the simple teachings of the gospel.[59] But he also paraphrases a line from Melanchthon's 1527 *Disputatio* on Colossians 2:8: "Paul did not say 'philosophy is bad,' but he said, 'Beware lest you be deceived through philosophy,' as if saying, 'Beware lest you be deceived by wine'."[60] He then invokes specific philosophical errors (that Epicurus' god doesn't care for us, that Aristotle believed in the eternity of the world) and advocates that one not mix the *doctrinae Christianae* with philosophy, for the former properly pertains to the salvation of the soul, and the latter to (for example) the necessities of the res publica.[61]

Calvin's interpretation of the verse emphasizes, again, the importance of a certain persuasion, or assurance (*persuasione*), that all the wisdom of God is contained in Christ. The inventions of men (*figmenta hominum*) have only the form of wisdom (*speciem sapientiae*), and their rejection of the simplicity of the gospel has led them into impious opinions, idolatries, and foolish speculations.[62] "It is not lawful for the Christian to know anything apart from Christ," he writes. And, further, aside from the fact that anything added onto Christ is tantamount to nothing, once this is acknowledged, "there will be no *pithanologia* which can bend even a pinky finger's breadth the minds of those who have devoted themselves to Christ."[63] Certain assurance, for Calvin, protects the Christian against the clever speech of philosophers and orators. And while Calvin translates πιθανολογία as *persuasorio sermone* in his reproduction of the biblical text, indicating (at least in contrast with Melanchthon) that oratorical persuasive speech is at issue here, he neither explicitly condemns philosophical reason nor rhetorical ornament in his interpretation, even going so far as to leave πιθανολογία untranslated in his gloss. Instead, his argument remains broad enough to cover any form of distraction from Christ as the *scopus* of gospel teaching. This is, he says, a truly noteworthy locus.[64] In sum, construing the meaning of Paul's words so broadly, Calvin follows the Erasmian exegetical tradition, taken up especially by Bullinger, more closely than he does Melanchthon's assaults on reason alone, which Pellikan seemed to favour.

Beware the 'Small Trinkettes of This World': Colossians 2:8

This brings us to the primary verse in question, in which Paul explicitly condemns *philosophia* along with vain deception as noxious when admitted into Christian teaching. Erasmus paraphrases the section thus:

> Those who set traps for your simplicity keep watch. You must keep watch in return so that you are not, once captivated by some splendid guise of philosophy, seduced from the solidity of faith to the inane, petty comments of men, and become prey for the foe. That will happen, if, led astray from the precept of evangelical truth, you begin to be influenced by human precepts and regulations, which are based on visible realities and on the gross elements of this world. The doctrine of Christ, on the contrary, is heavenly.[65]

Erasmus here goes on to link Paul's warnings against "precepts and regulations" – the *constitutionem hominum* of verse 8 – explicitly to certain Jewish teachings, that the Colossians not concern themselves with "food or drink ... [or] the observance of days or the washing of hands." This, indeed, seems to be Erasmus' preference for understanding the *elementa mundi* (here and at Gal. 4:3) as Jewish ceremonies taught to children, following Jerome in understanding *elementa* as "rudimentary" and Ambrosiaster in associating this with Jewish practice.[66] But the earlier warning is against the "splendid appearance of philosophy" (*magnifica specie philosophiae*), which seduces the Christian from a solid faith to the empty *commentatiunculae* of humans. No doubt Erasmus here uses this word not only to refer to abstruse philosophical disquisition ("little comments or fabrications") but also overly complex biblical commentary that takes away from gospel simplicity. As in the *Argumentum*, both the "shadows of the Mosaic law and the illusions of human philosophy" are the targets of Erasmus' Paul's discourse.[67] Like his reading of the implications of Pauline folly in 1 Corinthians, human philosophizing has nothing to contribute to gospel teaching or Christian understanding.

Bullinger's comments on 2:8 are extensive. He is quick to clarify, as we saw in Melanchthon's and Pellikan's readings earlier, that philosophy does have some use in human affairs, but has no bearing on faith, which latter rests solely on Christ (*unice innitamur Christo domino*).[68] He criticizes the "Colossian sophists," on the one hand, for "mixing the preaching of the gospel of Christ with profane erudition," and the "Nazareans" for preaching that circumcision and the law ought to be retained, on the other.[69] And he suggests that Paul identifies *Philosophia* with *Pithanologia* "by catachresis or synecdoche," and repeats that Paul only condemns philosophy as *probabili specie* (what seems credible), and not insofar as it is necessary for the preparation of genuine erudition.[70] Is is especially those who out of "reckless insidiousness attack and lead astray" whom the Colossians ought to beware of, for they teach what has merely the form of truth, taking refuge in the *praesidia humanae sapientiae*, and so on.[71] Here, then, *philosophia* itself comes to represent all adverse accretions Bullinger had associated with πιθανολογία, but there is a sort of non-Christian philosophy that is amenable to the sort of erudition that doesn't threaten to undermine gospel simplicity. Bullinger also takes the opportunity to criticize his Catholic counterparts, who preach free will, meritorious works, indulgences, and monastic regulations as representative of the *constitutionem hominum*.[72] Finally, he reminds us again that "this locus is abused by those who hate true erudition and the study of language and *bonae litterae*," repeating Erasmus' point in his dedicatory epistle to Campeggi, thus circumscribing the range of his condemnations of *philosophia*.[73] In his own commentary on 2:8, Pellikan reproduces Erasmus' *Paraphrase* on philosophy with no elaboration, and focuses afterwards on a definition of the *elementa mundi* as *ordinationes civiles*.[74]

In Calvin's commentary, philosophy actually comes in for criticism in chapter 1. He there contrasts the "contents of the philosophers' books" with divine wisdom, where he employs Paul's distinction between wisdom and folly to shed light on verse 1:9's mention of "wisdom and spiritual understanding," complete with two references to 1 Corinthians:

By "in all wisdom" he means that the will of God, of which he had spoken, was the only rule of right knowledge. For he who desires in simplicity to know those things which it has pleased God to reveal, will know what it is to be truly wise. If we desire anything beyond that, we shall only become foolish, by not keeping within due bounds. By the [Greek] word *suneseos*, which we render *prudentiam*, I understand that discrimination which proceeds from understanding. Both are called spiritual by Paul, because they are not attained otherwise than by the guidance of the Spirit. For the natural man does not perceive the things that are of God. So long as men are regulated by their carnal perceptions, they have also their own wisdom, but it is mere vanity, however complacent they may be about it. We see what sort of theology there is under the Papacy, what is contained in the books of the philosophers, and what wisdom secular men esteem. Let us, however, bear in mind that the wisdom which is alone commended by Paul is comprehended in the will of God.[75]

Here we find a number of themes that coincide with what we've seen in earlier chapters: that the will of God is the only rule of true wisdom (*unicam recte sapiendi regulam esse voluntatem Dei*); that human attempts to know anything beyond the simplicity of the gospel which God has revealed to us result only in foolishness (literally devoid of wisdom: *desipientia*); that only the Spirit can provide true wisdom, for humans in their natural state cannot perceive divine things; that human wisdom is vanity; that (presumably contemporary) papal theology is closely connected to the sort of useless knowledge pursued by the philosophers; and that this sort of theology is misguided insofar as it attempts to reach beyond what has been divinely revealed. Paul's discourse on foolishness is here used as a hermeneutic lens to explain Paul's discussions of wisdom elsewhere.

Calvin, in his commentary on 2:8, as his exegetical forebears, also seeks to clarify what Paul means by "philosophy," so as to prevent readers from thinking that he condemns it altogether. For Calvin, Paul means "whatever humans contrive for themselves wishing to be wise in their own eyes, and here not without the false pretext of reason (*specioso praetextu rationis*) and the appearance of credibility (*speciem probabile*)."[76] "And it isn't a difficult thing," he continues, "to reject the human fabrications [*commentis hominum*] which have nothing to commend them, but rather those which capture minds with conjectures of false wisdom."[77] Calvin, like Bullinger, also identifies *philosophia* with πιθανολογία, albeit a little less obviously by employing his earlier translation of the πιθανολογία itself: *Philosophia* "is nothing other than" *persuasorius sermo*; this "persuasive speech" is further defined as what "insinuates itself in the minds of men through beautiful and plausible arguments."[78] The phrase *pulchris ac plausibilibus argumentis* here clarifies even further that Calvin is denouncing not only vapid dialectic – no biblical-humanist could refer to scholastic discourse as beautiful! – but also elegant rhetoric that leads astray. Indeed, he argues that all the clever arguments of the philosophers (*argutiae philosophorum*) which attempt to add to the pure word of God (*purum sermonem Dei*) ought to be understood along the lines of *philosophia* defined as "persuasive speech."[79]

"*Philosophia* is nothing other than a corruption of spiritual teaching when intermingled with Christ," Calvin continues.[80] Again, the gospel stands on its own for Calvin and his exegetical predecessors, and any attempt to improve upon it through "adulterated teachings which are born from human heads, whatever rational hue they may have," is a profanation.[81] Glossing the next clause, Calvin understands the *traditiones hominibus* and the *elementa mundi* as constitutive of a further elaboration on *philosophia*: these things consist of "whatever has been fabricated in the brain of man" and are opposed to Christ who has been "ordained as our only teacher" so that we retain the simplicity of the gospel.[82] He then connects the *elementa mundi*, in much the same way as Erasmus in his *Paraphrase*, to the ceremonies of Judaism, proof of which, he writes, can be found in Paul's mentioning circumcision not long after this section of his letter, although he suggests that the reason for Paul's use of the phrase is not (as some interpreters suppose) that they denote external and corruptible things, but rather that they do not lead to solid teaching (*solidam doctrinam*), "as in Galatians 4:3."[83]

In broad strokes, then, Calvin takes on various aspects from the antecedent biblical-humanist exegetical tradition in his interpretation of Paul's condemnation of philosophy while adding a few wrinkles of his own. The passage has even broader scope at *Inst.* IV.10.8, first added in the 1543 edition, where Calvin takes the opportunity to extend his interpretation of the passage by expanding the locus to bear on the question of religion and the state: he provides a brief exposition of Colossians 2 (paraphrasing both 2:3 and 2:8) in the context of a discussion on the manner in which "human constitutions" are impermissible for Christians, both legally and philosophically, if they run counter to the gospel. Even if he differs from his predecessors' opinion that Paul warns of two historical groups seeking to deceive the Colossians, in providing a lengthy definition covering not only speculative flights *and* ornate rhetoric, but also what he perceives to be the fruitless ceremonies of Jewish teaching – in short, anything that isn't derived from the "simple gospel" – Calvin's criticism of "philosophy" has a very wide scope. Indeed, in his comments on 2:8 Calvin creates a nice rhetorical triptych portrait of the toxic aspects of *philosophia* with the repeated use of the phrase *philosophia nihil aliud est quam...* ("Philosophy is nothing other than X"): philosophy is 1) nothing other than persuasive speech, which insinuates itself into men's minds by beautiful and plausible arguements; it is 2) nothing other than what corrupts spiritual teaching; and it is 3) nothing other than empty deception (*inanis deceptio*). *Philosophia* here, like πιθανολογία previously, becomes a convenient rhetorical catch-all that ultimately denotes whatever it is that these sixteenth-century exegetes deem unnecessary and even noxious to a stripped down form of Christian teaching consonant with the humility of Christ and Paul themselves.

The Intertextual Pauline Philosophy: Joining Colossians and 1 Corinthians

What none of our thinkers does, it can be mentioned at this point, is to imagine a sort of *philosophia Christiana* in the vein of Gilson's "Christian philosophy," whereby one sets out, in a two-step process as it were, to demonstrate by reason what one already believes by faith. Quite the contrary, true faith itself, for many sixteenth-century thinkers, brings along with it the requisite sort of certainty that Gilson ascribes to knowledge. Indeed, *assurance* of the sort that we have seen emphasized above is a more certain form of knowing than human reason can offer, and precisely because it subsists in divine inspiration and eschews "what is born from the brains of humans." The exegetes whose readings of Colossians 2 we've considered make a special point to argue that true faith itself brings with it the certitude Gilson would seem to be after in calling for rational proofs after the *initium fidei*. However, any attempt to tack onto what is already offered by the *Christus doctor* is an adulteration, a distraction. In the remainder of this chapter, we will flesh out how the deleterious philosophy of Colossians relates to Paul's discourse on folly in First Corinthians in the context of defining the *philosophia Christiana* in the sixteenth century.

While in his exegesis of Paul, Thomas Aquinas does not always offer as radical a rationalist position as Gilson ascribes to him, Gilson's account reflects at least a portion of Thomas' reading of 1 Corinthians. On 1 Cor. 1:17, Aquinas plays down Paul's eschewing of σοφια λόγου, or *sapientia verbi* – wise words, or eloquent wisdom, which Paul says empty the cross of its power: he cites Jerome and Augustine in favour of the method of augmenting faithful teaching with worldly wisdom. Human *sapientia verbi* are permissible when they support the *fundamentis fidei*, and one might reasonably use the teachings of the philosophers, if true, in the service of faith.[84] This is a rather different reading from the one we've seen in the commentaries of the Erasmian biblical humanists in the sixteenth century. Compared with Erasmus' and Calvin's much stronger readings, which at times emphasize an unequivocal rejection of human wisdom, Thomas has brought in a softer interpretation of Paul's proscriptions in order to retain some use for the approaches of the philosophers in doing theology. Our sixteenth-century interpreters' repeated concerns about the frivolous and empty nature of a certain approach to theological questions are not present in Thomas' interpretation (this, of course, in part for historical reasons: this sort of criticism is borne from the rhetoric of humanist antischolasticism, long after Aquinas' time, much of it geared towards later-medieval "frigid" *quaestiones*).[85] While Aquinas clearly recognizes that the cross of Christ is the primary focus of Paul's conception of wisdom, and that Paul's criticisms are twofold (of reason and of eloquence), he focuses primarily on the fact that Paul himself did not use these supports, and rarely extends his comments to a more general criticism of human forms of reason and eloquence in theology. In other words, the impetus to model a theological method after the teachings of Paul himself, in abundant evidence in Erasmus and Calvin, did not manifest itself similarly in Thomas' thought.

Incidentally, Gilson begins his second Gifford lecture, entitled "The Concept of Christian Philosophy," by invoking Paul, and recites 1 Cor. 1:19–25 in full. He then provides a comment in the form of a scholastic *quaestione*. The question, or "article" (should we stay true to the scholastic form), as stated at the beginning of this chapter, is whether there might be such a thing as a Christian philosophy. What we might call the first objection, after the model of Aquinas' *Summa Theologiae*, follows: "What St. Paul has laid down, what no Christian can henceforth dispute, is this: that to have faith in Jesus Christ is *a fortiori* to achieve wisdom, in this sense at least, that as far as concerns the interests of salvation, faith really and totally absolves us from all need of philosophy."[86] This summarizes well the biblical-humanist understanding of wisdom from Erasmus to Calvin. But then comes Gilson's rebuttal, the *sed contra*:

On the contrary, if we have religion we have also the essential truth of science, art and philosophy, all of them admirable things no doubt, but rather poor consolations when religion is wanting. But then, if this be true, if to possess religion is to possess all the rest, the thing must nevertheless be demonstrated. An Apostle like St. Paul may be content to preach it, a philosopher will wish to assure himself of the fact. It is not enough to assert that a believer can dispense with philosophy because the whole content of philosophy, and much more beside, is given implicitly in his belief; some kind of proof is required.[87]

This is, in fact, a much stronger reading of Paul than Thomas Aquinas (Gilson's ideal Christian philosopher) himself puts forth in his commentary on the passage. But in any case, what is important for our purposes is to point out that Erasmus and Calvin had very different ideas from Gilson about the need for demonstrations and proofs as guarantors of assurance, and also about the meaningful role "philosophy" might play in such demonstrations, if not about the need for assurance itself. Erasmus paraphrases Paul in precisely the manner Gilson wishes to move past, viz. in stating unequivocally that the Christian has "no need of philosophy." And while it doesn't explicitly follow from this that philosophical demonstrations *after the fact* – under the rubric, say, of the Anselmian *fides quaerens intellectum* – are utterly forbidden on a biblical-humanist model, they are not necessary for assurance nor for piety and, more often than not, they're a distraction or even a profanation. The vehemence with which Erasmus and Calvin denounce human forms of reasoning in the theological realm, and the strength with which they exhort their readers to have a passionate, as opposed to a cerebral, approach to the Word of God, places them on a different epistemological and methodological trajectory than Gilson's Thomist ideal. For sixteenth-century biblical humanists St Paul the humble preacher of the simple gospel *is* St Paul the philosopher.

Gilson's isn't the only modern account of the "Christian philosophy" at odds with our interpreters', however. More descriptive accounts, too, seem to have missed the mark when the question is viewed from the perspective of interpretations of Pauline folly. Charles Partee begins his book on Calvin's reception of ancient philosophy by setting the sixteenth-century use of the term "Christian philosophy" apart from Gilson's Thomistic account: "In the sixteenth century," Partee writes, "the term 'Christian philosophy' is used in a different and important sense by some of the Christian humanists in referring to their program of reforming Christian thought by returning to the correct understanding of Holy Scripture and purer Christianity in opposition to what they consider to be the fruitless speculations and philosophical accretions of scholastic theology."[88] This, no doubt, conforms generally to the interests of Erasmus and Calvin. However, Partee goes on to give an account of what he considers to be the sixteenth-century version of Christian philosophy as an enterprise that endorses engagement with classical philosophy and whose practitioners "discuss philosophical insights in their writings with a strong sense of appreciation."[89] He writes:

> Christian philosophy was indeed focused on God's revelation and accepted by faith, but it was not simply biblical theology because the humanists thought that the faithful could, and should, make a proper use of reason and therefore correctly appreciate the insights of the classical philosophers without becoming unduly dependent upon them. Thus, in historical terms, Christian philosophy in the high Renaissance, especially in Erasmus and Calvin, was a return to 'Christian' Platonism by way of Augustine in opposition to the 'Christian' Aristotelianism of Aquinas.[90]

Whether or not Erasmus' and Calvin's thought can be appropriately understood as a return to Christian Platonism over and against Christian Aristotelianism is rather beside the point for our purposes. The point to be made here, rather, is one about the sixteenth-century use of the term "Christian philosophy" by those who employed it to describe their own theological program. If we want to appreciate the *philosophia Christiana* as a sixteenth-century category, we must take seriously the ways in which those who used it understood the term. From this perspective, Partee's account confuses matters – very much like Gilson's – insofar as it defines the Christian philosophy in a manner rather different from how biblical humanists discuss the *philosophia Christiana* as it arises out of the exegesis of Paul's understanding of wisdom and folly. When Erasmus and Calvin employ the phrase, it isn't in order to assure their readers of their appreciation of the insights of ancient philosophers (Plato, Aristotle, or otherwise) or of their usefulness in Christian theology. It is to set their worldview(s) apart from both "worldly" philosophical systems of thought and Christian systems of thought that rely too heavily on precisely the sort of wisdom offered by the Greeks and their later acolytes.

Erasmus more than once in the *Paraphrase on 1 Corinthians* defines the Christian philosophy against the pursuit of wisdom through the knowledge of created things. Paraphrasing 1 Cor. 2:7–9, he writes that the folly of the cross is "far different from that which vainly explores through human reasoning the causes of this world," which latter "is through Christ made null and obsolete."[91] This is not only because the aims of the two types of philosophy are completely different, but primarily because one relies on the abilities of human reason, while the other humbly resigns itself to what God has chosen to reveal: "However learned they were in their comprehension of visible things, however swollen in their knowledge of the Law, nevertheless, they failed to perceive this mystery [i.e., of the cross of Christ], which was to be shared only with those whom humility of mind had reconciled to God."[92] On this reading of Paul, what human reason can accomplish is of no value to the Christian philosophy, and is even detrimental to its practitioners because the pursuits of worldly wisdom are incompatible with humility. "We do not preach the movements of heavenly spheres or the influence of constellations or the causes of lightning. Knowledge of such phenomena leads to arrogance in the Greeks."[93] And, as we have seen previously, paraphrasing 1 Cor. 1:20, where Paul asks, "Where is the wise person?" Erasmus defines the *sophos* as a natural philosopher: "Where is the philosopher who explores the secrets of nature and, unmindful of the maker, marvels at created things?"[94]

Instead of wisdom resulting from attempts to explore the secrets of nature, "this wisdom about which we are speaking was breathed secretly into minds ... Exalted rulers were not worthy of this mystery [i.e., of the cross], nor were pompous philosophers."[95] This is the wisdom, Erasmus tells us in the *Annotations*, which justifies Paul's attribution of foolishness to God.[96] It is also a secret wisdom, and can only be given fully to the perfect, "lest we cast roses before swine."[97] Human reason has no access to the mysteries of the Christian philosophy, and thus these must be given from without: "Since this Spirit is divine and has proceeded from God, it probes even the most deeply hidden and remote of God's secrets, where human curiosity does not reach."[98] It is simply the nature of the object of the Christian philosophy that it can't be gotten at by human reason in the same way that knowledge of created things can: "Many people search out and contemplate created things, but no one knows matters deeply hidden in the mind and purpose of God except the eternal Spirit, which is innermost in God and on that account is inwardly aware in him of all things."[99] And yet, as Erasmus paraphrases 1 Cor. 2:10, the Spirit does reveal these things to the adherents of the true philosophy: "To us, as if to friends, God revealed it, not through human teaching, but through the secret inbreathing of his Spirit."[100] Finally, an essential aspect of the Christian philosophy is that it isn't, unlike worldly wisdom, splintered into various teachings, precisely because its wisdom comes from a single author. "It does not know the rivulets of human sects and opinions."[101]

Turning now to Calvin, Mary Potter Engel has argued for three ways in which Calvin's Christian philosophy is closer to Bude's than to Erasmus': (1) "For Calvin the heavenly philosophy contained knowledge about doctrine as well as morals" (while Erasmus', she intimates, consisted only of morals); (2) "Calvin sees a great discontinuity between heavenly and earthly philosophy," which contrast "is not emphasized by Erasmus"; and (3) that Calvin, "following Bude, presents heavenly philosophy as a rival body of certain knowledge ... [which] certain knowledge consists of two parts, the knowledge of God and knowledge of ourselves."[102] While the final clause of the third way *may* hold water, the first two cannot be maintained on the basis of the extensive evidence we've provided up to this point as distinguishing Calvin from Erasmus. In Engel's first point, we find the oft-repeated theme in Protestant historiography of understanding Erasmus as merely a moral theologian, who apparently didn't believe anything at all, a point no longer tenable in accounts of Erasmus' thought. As for the second, not only are Erasmus' works replete with contrasts between the heavenly and earthly philosophies, but Calvin's own conception of the Christian philosophy is itself in the main an Erasmian one.

Aside from other instances we have noted, Calvin also employs the term "Philosophie Chrestienne" in the *Argument du Present Livre* that introduces the 1541 French translation of his *Institutes*.[103] He suggests that he has been called to lead more simple people to understand the main principles of the Christian philosophy through Scripture, which he has summarized in the work, and futher that once one has a handle on these, they can "benefit more from a single day in the school of God than from three months in any other."[104] In the 1536 Latin edition, at III.xx.1, Calvin had described the "secret and hidden philosophy which cannot be wrested from syllogisms" as the philosophy which, rooted in the understanding that the Christian, upon realizing "how destitute and devoid of all good things man is," seeks everything in Christ.[105] Some years later, in the final (1559) edition – demonstrating that this was of interest to Calvin throughout his career – he provides a more extensive definition at *Inst.* III.vii.1, which is worth quoting at length:

> Let this therefore be the first step, that a man depart from himself in order that he may apply the whole force of his ability in the service of the Lord. I call "service" not only what lies in obedience to God's Word but what turns the mind of man, empty in its own carnal sense, wholly to the bidding of God's Spirit. While it is the first entrance to life, all philosophers were ignorant of this transformation, which Paul calls "renewal of the mind" [Eph. 4:23]. For they set up reason alone as the ruling principle in

man, and think that it alone should be listened to; to it alone, in short, they entrust the conduct of life. But the Christian philosophy bids reason give way to, submit and subject itself to, the Holy Spirit so that the man himself may no longer live but hear Christ living and reigning within him.[106]

Reason is demoted as hegemon in Calvin's theological anthropology, and it isn't until one's mind is renewed by the Spirit that one is practicing the Christian philosophy.[107]

In the *Argumentum* to the commentary on 1 Corinthians, Calvin writes further that the real problem of the Corinthians whom Paul is denouncing is that the "preposterous teachers and chattering speechmakers" have invented a new method of teaching which is rooted in a "passionate desire for prominence." This new method of teaching, which turned the gospel into a "man-made philosophy," was "not consistent with the simplicity of Christ," and they hoped that "it would make them the objects of people's admiration." "This is what inevitably happens to all those who have not yet got rid of self-concern." The Corinthian teachers "dress the gospel in different clothes so that it may look like a worldly philosophy," whereas one must "enter into the Lord's work with absolutely no encumbrances."[108] The "natural purity" of the gospel is tainted when it is made to be "on the level with any worldly philosophy."[109] But, as Paul argues in the second chapter, the gospel, which contains a "heavenly and secret wisdom," is something that neither "man's natural ability, however acute and penetrating, nor his physical senses, can grasp; something about which no human argument can give conviction."[110] Paul argues, Calvin says, that "mere human judgment cannot determine what the real value" of the gospel is. This for two reasons: first, "the preaching of the gospel is poles apart from human wisdom, since it consists in the humiliation of the cross," and second, that human understanding "gives wrong assessments of everything."[111]

The Christian philosophy differs from worldly philosophy in that it rests on the humiliation of the cross (which itself is an aspect of that secret and heavenly wisdom which cannot be comprehended by human reason), and in that it moves far beyond ordinary cognitive assent. In his comment on 1 Cor. 1:6 ("Even as the testimony of Christ was confirmed in you ..."), Calvin writes that Paul means here to convey first that the testimony is granted through the Holy Spirit, but also that "the Corinthians were rich in knowledge, inasmuch as from the beginning God had made his gospel yield results among them."[112] To know Christianly, for Calvin, means that assent must be accompanied by practical results. David Willis, describing the Christian philosophy among Christian humanists, summarizes this tendency nicely: "There is considerable difference among the Christian humanists about how Christian philosophy comes about, and there is considerable latitude in the way they related intellect and will. They share, however, the conviction that self-knowledge and human happiness are not to be divorced from the knowledge of God, and that this knowledge involves a conversion of the will by divine instruction and persuasion."[113]

Commenting on 1 Cor. 1:21, Calvin provides a list of credenda which cannot be apprehended by human reason: "There is no doubt that human reason finds nothing more absurd than the news that God became a mortal man, that life is submissive to death, that righteousness has been concealed under the likeness of sin, that the source of blessing has been subjected to the curse, that by this means men might be redeemed from death and be sharers in blessed immortality, that they might gain possession of life, that, sin being abolished, righteousness might reign, that death and the curse might be swallowed up."[114] Erasmus, too, provides a list of credenda offensive to the Greeks in his paraphrase of the same verse: "To the Greeks, however, who investigate all things with human reasoning, it seems foolish that by heavenly power a maiden conceived a child, that God lay hidden under human form, that life has been restored by death, that he who was once dead has come to life again."[115] Another way in which the Corinthians had gone astray in listening too closely to the philosophers' teaching is that they began to doubt the resurrection. Erasmus and Calvin, like Paul, emphasize this as one of the more pernicious results of over-philosophizing, and both posit the resurrection as an essential yet *unreasonable* tenet of the Christian philosophy.[116] Belief in these things, at which "even the angels are astonished," is then contrasted with attempts to come to know God through nature. God, in fact, reveals himself clearly in nature – creation is a "theatre of His glory" – yet it is "only by the eye of faith that we can look at Him."[117]

Humans must be "emptied of their own understanding" before arriving at a "saving knowledge of God."[118] Calvin puts it even more strongly when commenting on 1 Cor. 2:10: "The duller the human mind is for understanding the mysteries of God, and the greater its uncertainty, the more certain is our faith, which is supported by the revelation of the Spirit of God."[119] Certainty in faith has an inversely proportional relationship to the ability of human understanding here for comprehending divine matters. And again, the knowledge of Christ, revealed to the individual by the Spirit, is the whole of the Christian philosophy: "The one who has learned Christ has already learned all of heavenly teaching."[120] To add to the *scientia Christi* is to distort, and to "turn aside to some extent from the strict purity of the Word of God."[121] A Christocentrism, albeit one which ultimately manifests itself in different ways, is what sets Erasmus' and Calvin's Christian philosophy apart from Gilson's Thomism. If Christ is the *scopus* of all theology, and if Christ's nature and crucifixion cannot be comprehended by human forms of reasoning, then the very centre of the Christian philosophy is non-rational.

The spiritual person becomes, necessarily, a fool to the world, for Christian wisdom and human wisdom are diametrically opposed to one another. Probably the strongest statement to this effect comes in Calvin's paraphrase of Paul's ironic contention that the apostles are different from the Corinthians: *We are fools for Christ's sake, but ye are wise in Christ.*

> [Paul] is being ironical in conceding that the Corinthians are wise in Christ, and strong and illustrious. It is as if he said: "You desire to keep a reputation for wisdom along with the Gospel, whereas I have been able to preach Christ to you only by becoming a fool in this world. Now, when I have willingly put up with being a fool or having that reputation, turn it over in your minds whether it is fair that you wish to be looked upon as wise. You can hardly say these two things go well together: that I, who have been your teacher, am a fool for Christ's sake, while you remain wise." It follows that being wise in Christ has not got a good connotation here, for he laughs at the Corinthians in their desire to mingle Christ and human wisdom together, because, in effect, they were wanting to join things which are totally dissimilar.[122]

That all necessary knowledge is contained in Christ is a theme repeated often in Calvin's commentaries on 1 Corinthians and Colossians 2, not to mention in the *Institutes*, as seen in foregoing chapters, and he is indebted to Erasmus and the Erasmian exegetical tradition for much of the vocabulary and conceptual language surrounding discussions of the Christian philosophy.[123] For Erasmus and Calvin, along with Bullinger and Pellikan, *philosophia Christiana* denotes an understanding of the Christian philosophy rooted in a similar reading of certain relevant loci from the New Testament, especially Paul's discourse on foolishness in the early chapters of First Corinthians, but completed in the reception of what they read as Paul's affirmation of a certain assurance and his criticisms of *philosophia* in Colossians 2. It remains in the following chapter to examine a final aspect of the sixteenth-century Christian philosophy, viz. the implications of the folly of the cross on the role of the passions in the Christian life and the language of what we might call "theologies of the heart" in sixteenth-century biblical interpretation.

Chapter Six

The Affective Christian Philosophy

By Stoic definition wisdom means nothing else but being ruled by reason; and
folly, by contrast, is being swayed by the dictates of the passions.

— Erasmus, *Praise of Folly*

Christ's example alone should be sufficient for rejecting the unbending hard-
ness of the Stoics; for where should we seek for the rule of supreme perfection
but in Him?

— Calvin, *Commentary on John*

In most exegetical accounts of Christ's psychological anguish in the Garden of Gethsemane (recounted in Matthew 26, Mark 14, and Luke 22),
there arises the inevitable comparison between Christ's human passions
and everyone else's, and in these comparisons one typically finds both
prescriptive and descriptive accounts of the emotions along with implicit
and explicit considerations of their relationship to reason. In the long history of interpretation of the scene, there exists an exegetical back and
forth between those who want to explain Christ's seemingly gratuitous
emotions away and those who endorse them as an ordinary, and even
necessary, aspect of his human nature. The *object* of Christ's sorrow (or
sadness, fear, agony, anxiety) receives special attention from this perspective from the patristic period into the sixteenth century, and the interpretation that Christ was deeply troubled at the prospect *of his own death* was
not a foregone conclusion among either patristic or early modern exegetes. Questions about the ethics of Christ's emotions at Gethsemane and
elsewhere are, of course, ancient in the history of interpretation: Jerome
and Augustine, for example, argued that it would have been unbecoming

of Christ to have feared death, given that alacrity for expunging human guilt would be more appropriate given the cosmic circumstances, and that the object of his sorrowful trepidation must have been something else (the impending destruction of the Jews, for example).[1]

By the sixteenth century, apologiae for his fear of death were much more common: Christ's grief was an important aspect of the affective piety of late medieval devotion to the *imitatio Christi,* and this way of thinking – along with medieval scholastic interpretations of Christ's agony that had the benefit of pronouncements at ecumenical councils regarding Christ's nature not available to the Fathers in the third and fourth centuries – had influence on biblical humanists in the sixteenth century as well.[2] In his New Testament, Erasmus had even modified Mark 14:33, changing the Vulgate's *pavere,* which could mean "to be alarmed," to the much more emphatic *expavescere,* "to dread exceedingly." Calvin would follow suit. In England, Thomas More's last work, the *De Tristitia Christi,* perhaps the most poignant and extended homage to Gethsemane, attempts to defend the ethical possibility of a balance between reason and fear with an eye towards the importance of their interplay in martyrdom. More was long preceded by Erasmus in labouring over the Gospel passage, however, and the Dutchman had kicked off the sixteenth-century discussion of Christ's emotions in his 1503 publication, the *Disputatiuncula de taedio Iesu,* which recounts a debate Erasmus himself had with John Colet at Oxford in 1499 over the theological problem of Christ's affections in the Garden.[3] The essence of the debate consists in Erasmus' attempt to refute Colet's contention that Christ's sorrow and fear couldn't have resulted from the thought of his own impending suffering and death, for this would contravene the supposed eagerness and even joy with which he faced his self-sacrifice. The divinely heroic Christ of the ancient martyrs is pitted against the lowly, humble, humiliated, and *human* Jesus of medieval devotional piety.[4] But the dispute is intricately theological and it serves as Erasmus' attempt to undergird an already present form of devotion with nuanced theological and exegetical reasoning. It also had an indelible influence on Calvin's understanding of Christ's emotions and of the ethics of emotion in the Christian life. Alongside the contemporaneous Renaissance revival of Stoicism, the Gethsemane scene stands in the sixteenth century as a repeatedly invoked locus used to combat the perceived threat of the Stoic doctrine of *apatheia* against a Christian humanist appreciation of affectivity.

The scene is also best understood, to Calvin's mind, as an example of Paul's foolish wisdom. In his first sermon on Christ's passion, delivered either in 1557 or 1558[5] and first published in 1558 in a collection of sermons on the humanity, divinity, and nativity of Christ, Calvin makes an explicit connection between Christ's sorrow and fear in the Garden of Gethsemane and Paul's preaching the folly of the cross:

> [Christ] did not refuse to sustain the anguishes, which were prepared for all whose consciences are rebuked and feel themselves guilty of eternal death and condemnation before God ... and therefore we must not be ashamed seeing that the Son of God assumed to himself such an infirmity. *Neither was it without cause that Saint Paul exhorted us through his example not to be ashamed of the preaching of the cross, even though it is foolishness to some and an offense to many.* For the more that our Lord Jesus Christ abased himself, we see thereby that the offences for which we were indebted to God, could not be abolished without great extremity ... For if he had not himself felt the fears, doubts, and torments that we endure, he would not be so inclined to be as merciful to us as he is.[6]

It is a significant reference for understanding the broader contours of Calvin's theology of the heart as it relates to Pauline folly. There are important connections between Christ's emotions, Pauline folly, and the role of the heart in Calvin's understanding of Christian teaching, and it provides us with an entry point for exploring the ethics of emotion in conceptions of the "Christian philosophy." Throughout this study I have considered the reception of Pauline folly as it pertains to Christ and the cross in a relatively abstract manner, primarily with respect to the confounding of worldly wisdom that takes an abstract cross as its rhetorical starting point. Here, I would like to use Calvin's intertextual reference as an entree into an examination of the way in which the interpretations of Christ's emotions are a constitutive, if not immediately obvious, aspect of the Christian philosophies of Erasmus and Calvin. Christ's voluntary submission to human experience, in all its physical and psychological verities, constitutes the supreme moment of folly from the perspective of worldly wisdom. That he felt extreme forms of human emotion in the face of death – an expression of his full humanity – is, to Calvin's thinking, a feature of Paul's "preaching of the cross," which itself has a fundamental affective component, thus far only hinted at, in sixteenth-century rhetorical theology.

Theological discourse heavily laden with language of the heart and of affectivity is, of course, by no means new in the sixteenth century. It has a long and vivid history in medieval forms of affective piety, some of which no doubt undergird similar sixteenth-century approaches. But even these forms have their roots in the language of the biblical text, which might be the more proximate source for thinkers like Erasmus and Calvin. Paul's letters are riddled with language of the heart, much of it derived from the Old Testament, a fact not lost on sixteenth-century readers who find many such heart-related references to be examples of Paul's penchant for "Hebraisms." Indeed, in one way, this is the crucial point: for sixteenth-century biblical humanists, a renovation of theological discourse to mirror more approximately the Word of God is an important underlying feature of a modified approach to Christian teaching. Debora Shuger has outlined the importance of affectivity in Christian rhetoric in the fifteenth and sixteenth centuries, a newly refined tradition of "sacred rhetoric" that Calvin is indebted to; and we have argued likewise, following Trinkaus and Bouwsma, that Calvin's approach has much in common with the *theologia rhetorica* inaugurated by Valla and taken up by Erasmus.[7] But how does this approach come to bear on understanding the ethics of emotion in practice? Does an appreciation of the heart in terms of its metaphorical orientation to religious knowledge entail an endorsement of emotional expression in other contexts? How does the critique of what might be called rationalist approaches to religious epistemology relate to rationalist approaches to the ethics of emotion? In this chapter, I'd like to explore these and similar questions, along with further consideration of Calvin's reception of Erasmus through another exegetical test-case. New Testament evidence of Christ's suffering deep emotional pain in the Garden of Gethsemane, and the consequent implication that the rest of us might thereby emote without fault, are invoked to level criticism at the *novi Stoici*, or "new Stoics" – as Calvin calls them – who argue that the passions are to be suppressed altogether.

My purpose here is not to give a complete account of the revised anthropological or psychological tendencies of Erasmus and Calvin, but rather to use the history of biblical interpretation as an avenue for considering their relationship to antecedent, and in some ways regnant, anthropological thinking about the ethics of emotion. Calvin's christological anti-Stoicism has many Erasmian features, and teasing these out will provide another aspect of how he received the antecedent exegetical tradition. It will be shown how comparative exegesis can serve as a fruitful mode of analysis as well for historians of emotion and religion, and likewise how the questions and approaches developed in the increasingly important field of the history of emotions can sharpen our approaches to reception history. The rise of the history of emotions as an interdisciplinary force, and the development of the study of "religion and emotion" as a distinct sub-discipline, has illuminated fresh avenues of inquiry for analysing texts, understanding individual thinkers, and assessing social relationships for historians. The underlying assumption that affectivity or emotionality is a sine qua non of all human experience – a fact perhaps taken for granted to the point of neglect until fairly recently by Anglophone intellectual historians – and that it should therefore be an integral aspect of any history (social, cultural, intellectual, literary, or otherwise), further necessitates a reassessment of the history of theological anthropology, religious epistemology, and religious ethics with a view to the role of emotions and conceptions of emotion in the past.

It is also incumbent upon historians of religion to map out the emotional landscape with respect to their particular subjects, groups, or texts, lest misunderstandings be perpetuated in other fields. The importance of the biblical text in sixteenth-century Christianity needs no argument, of course, and analysing reception history with an eye on emotion does indeed illuminate an important facet of Christian thought in this period.[8] Moreover, we have abundant evidence that neither Erasmus nor Calvin thought the hardline Stoic position on the emotions to be compatible with Christian teaching. Christian humanists took a broadly Aristotelian conception of emotions as conducive to virtue and fleshed it out with language and examples from biblical texts (or vice versa). Additionally, humanist appreciation of rhetorical *persuasio* as crucial for Christian teaching and understanding brought the heart and its affections to the forefront of conceptions of faith and piety. What Christopher Tilmouth has called "passion's triumph over reason" in his study of a newfound appreciation of the emotions in the seventeenth century is set in motion by humanist exegetes in the sixteenth.[9]

Revising Philosophical Anthropology

Before we look more closely at the exegesis of the Gethsemane scene, we should first outline the classical background with respect to the question of reason's relationship to the passions.[10] Throughout Erasmus' and Calvin's writings one finds anthropological constructions derived quite clearly from ancient philosophy, and occasionally one even finds explicit invocations of ancient philosophical notions as important guides for Christian virtue.[11] The substrate of anthropological and psychological thinking in sixteenth-century humanism typically represented a learned hybrid of Platonist, Aristotelian, and Stoic views on the body, the soul, the intellect, the will, and the passions.[12] And yet these notions were not taken over by Christian humanists at face value or without substantial revision. While there are a number of ways in which sixteenth-century humanists positively received and used ancient philosophical concepts, the conscious rejection of the eminently rational man as ideal is linked directly to the reception of certain biblical texts, as we've already seen. Examining the understandings of Christ's emotions, which are almost always couched in discourse about human emotions generally, can be revealing of shifting anthropological tendencies and language in the Renaissance and Reformation. First, a brief overview of Stoic and Peripatetic tendencies, which are being simultaneously adopted and responded to, will help to frame the relevant issues involved.

For Aristotle, and also for the Stoic and subsequent Peripatetic tradition, the essence of a human being (what sets humans apart from animals) is that humans have a rational soul – a soul governed by *nous* (Latin *intellectus*).[13] While this descriptive aspect of classical anthropology isn't especially problematic for Erasmus and Calvin[14] (who, though, refrain from engaging in lengthy discussions of faculty psychology), problematic is the position (common in both the Peripatetic and Stoic traditions) that the *telos* of the human being is to maximize rationality and to unequivocally subsume the will and the emotions to the intellect. This classical model is an ethical rationality – it is the duty therein of the virtuous person to seek to maximize his or her rationality in all spheres of life. Aristotle, for example, writes in the *Nicomachean Ethics*, "[Contemplation] is best, since not only is reason the best thing in us, but the objects of reason are the best of knowable objects."[15] And, teleologically, "That which is proper to each thing is by nature best and most pleasant for each thing; for man, therefore, the life according to reason is best and pleasantest, since reason more than anything else *is* man."[16] We might, I think, just take these two quotations from Aristotle as representative of a long-standing (indeed, in many ways still-standing) intellectual tradition in Western culture, which bears two important claims: (1) the contemplative (i.e., rational) life is best because we are rational animals – that is, the potential for rationality is the essence of human life, meaning the *telos* of human life is to be as reasonable as possible, and this is how one achieves happiness (*eudaimonia* in Aristotelian parlance);[17] (2) the objects of reason are the best knowable objects, which

seems *prima facie* tautological, but perhaps Aristotle means to differentiate objects of contemplation from something like objects of (mere) sense
perception, belying his indebtedness in this regard to Plato – in other
words, what corresponds to the highest part of the intellect (abstracted
non-material essences, or *forms* in Aristotle's account) are of higher
ontological and therefore epistemological value than other objects, and
are thus worth spending more time trying to get to know.

Importantly, the strong form of Stoicism differs from Aristotelianism
most explicitly in its (Stoicism's) rejection of the ethical permissibility
of the passions.[18] As a generalization, Stoics in the Hellenistic period
thought that the human, as an infant, has similar capacities to those of
an animal, but as the infant becomes a well-formed adult, reason takes
over and thoroughly governs the individual's non-rational impulses.
A.A. Long describes the Stoic account of the reasonable man thus: "Reason, the late developer, is a faculty which shapes but does not destroy
those faculties that precede its emergence. In the Stoic view of human
development, innate impulses are so transformed by the flowering
of reason that they cease to exist as an independent faculty. They are
taken over by reason. Human nature is so constituted that it develops
from something non-rational and animal-like into a structure which is
governed throughout by reason."[19] Indeed, it is important to note that
certain Stoics actually have a stronger position regarding reason as gov-
ernor of the soul than do both traditional Platonists and Aristotelians:
"There is no such thing," writes Chrysippus, "as the appetitive and the
spirited elements, for the whole of the human governing-principle is
rational."[20] This means, not that there are no emotional or "passionate"
human beings, but that the relationship of reason to the other aspects
of human experience shifts such that *right reason* becomes the ideal of
the Stoic sage who lives his life always on an even keel in terms of emotion, which also means that, more or less, he lives his life free of those
things – *wrong reason*, or *bad reason* becoming synonymous with *passion*,
affection, etc. The passions are constitutive of errant judgments and thus
ought to be avoided.[21] While there is room in the Stoic tradition for
properly oriented impulses, which we might call emotions, the *telos* of
the Stoic sage is *apatheia*, or, literally, to be without passion or emotional
experience so that one's reason is undisturbed.[22]

Sixteenth-century humanists, like Erasmus and Calvin, knew these
traditions well, and they were also fully aware of the nuances within the
traditions.[23] Rhetorically, however, in the same way that we've seen Aristotelianism come to metonymically represent school theology, Stoicism

comes to serve the same function for anti-emotionalism. The Stoic man of iron is also frequently a man of straw. Our purpose here, though, is not to understand the ways in which these traditions were or weren't correctly received – good work has been done on this question elsewhere[24] – but how Erasmus and Calvin used biblical texts to construct philosophies that run counter to the rhetorical foils they created out of classical philosophical traditions. At this point it should be obvious that, as far as theological knowledge is concerned, in their conception of the Christian philosophy, Erasmus and Calvin both reject outright that the *telos* of human life is to be as rational as possible, and that the objects of reason are the best sorts of objects one can contemplate.[25] The folly of the cross, as Erasmus and Calvin see it, is at odds with both these claims. And if reason's status as unequivocal hegemon is diminished, an anthropological restructuring is in order, which impacts the valuation of emotion in the Christian life. Given that the suffering and humiliation of Christ and his existence as a model for Christian life is the substantive element of Christian foolishness, the emphasis on Christ's radical humility, and on the reality of his psychological suffering, which we have seen crop up from time to time in our study, clears the way for a fuller appreciation of the human passions.

As Richard Strier has recently written, "The Renaissance revived anti-Stoicism as well as Stoicism," and it could be further added that this duality, given the complexities of Stoicism and its reception, could comfortably exist in a single thinker.[26] Invoking examples from Petrarch through to Erasmus, Luther, and Calvin, Strier also notes – and here he was preceded notably by Debora Shuger – that "both the humanist and the Reformation traditions provided powerful defenses of the validity and even the desirability of ordinary human emotions and passions."[27] Erasmus' and Calvin's relationship to Stoicism broadly construed is complicated and debated in the literature.[28] Barbara Pitkin, using William Bouwsma's famous article on the two faces of Renaissance humanism as a launching point, has recently compared Erasmus and Calvin on their respective Stoic tendencies, noting importantly that "the relationship of both Erasmus and Calvin to the early modern receptions of Stoicism was extremely complex, highly eclectic, and dependent on the topic in question."[29] Erasmus notably defends the very general Stoic and Peripatetic position on reason as ruler over the passions in the *Enchiridion*, for example. Calvin in the *Institutes* offers a qualified Aristotelian description of faculty psychology, and once refers to the ruling part of the soul (i.e., the *mens*) in Greek as ἡγεμονικόν (a Stoic designation), and even defines man as a *rationale animal*; but elsewhere, throughout their careers, they routinely condemn Stoic hyper-rationalism and the doctrine of *apatheia*.[30]

The classical philosophical idea of the intellect as unequivocal hegemon, which was increasingly and widely questioned during the Renaissance, is heavily qualified and at times seemingly undone in biblical-humanist writings, making way for a Renaissance affective piety and a conception of faith that involves the entirety of the individual. Implicit criticisms of Greco-Roman anthropological constructions, moreover, are often made explicit in the form of anti-Stoic rhetoric. In the *Praise of Folly*, for example, Erasmus has Folly outline the Stoic position on emotion, with an obvious critical bent and with clear Pauline overtones relevant to our study:

> First of all, it's admitted that all the emotions belong to Folly, and this is what marks the wise man off from the fool; he is ruled by reason, the fool by his emotions. This is why the Stoics segregate all passions from the wise man, as if they were diseases. But in fact these emotions not only act as guides to those hastening towards the haven of wisdom, but also wherever virtue is put into practice they are always present to act like spurs and goads as incentives towards good deeds. Yet this is hotly denied by that double-dyed Stoic Seneca who strips his wise man of every emotion. In doing so he leaves nothing at all of the man, and has to fabricate in his place a new sort of god who never was and never will be in existence anywhere. Indeed, if I may be frank, what he created was a kind of marble statue of a man, devoid of sense and any sort of human feeling.[31]

The Listrius commentary on this passage, some of which was composed by Erasmus himself, notes that the notion of emotions as guides to wisdom (as opposed to hindrances) is Aristotelian: *haec est opinio peripateticorum* ("this is the opinion of the Peripitatics").[32]

The anti-Stoic sentiment found here, and even some of the language, may have been inspired by Valla, and importantly it represents the position adopted by Calvin and other Protestants. In other words, to assume that occasional descriptive accounts of the rational man, with their appeals to philosophical terminology, entail the sort of ethical rationality that attends similar descriptions among the ancients, would be to badly miss the mark. Throughout Calvin's corpus one finds a persistent reference to frigidity and coldness in the context of criticism of what he deems to be an improperly intellectualist approach to knowing

God. The rhetoric against frigidity in the context of Christian religious epistemology is an important recurring feature of rhetorical theology among the biblical humanists, and Erasmus' use of it in the *Paraclesis* carries over into the earliest formative works of Protestant thought (it appears, for example, in Luther's preface to his Romans commentary, and in the first version of Melanchthon's *Loci Communes*). The tendency in Calvin to blur the lines between anthropological categories has been pointed out before. As Richard Muller writes, "Calvin does not oblige any neat 'head/heart', intellective/affective, rational/experiential dichotomy," his ultimate point being that Calvin's understanding of faith must involve the whole person. Muller attributes this tendency of "balancing of the mind and heart" to an indebtedness to Melanchthon's *Loci Communes*, which may very well be.[33] He suggests further that Calvin leans more towards endorsing a voluntarist account of faith, and plots him on an Augustinian-Melanchthonian trajectory in this regard. In doing so, he has also clarified the relationship between the intellect and the will in Calvin's conception of faith, demonstrating as well that Calvin's interest in the heart as a fundamental aspect of his theological anthropology and religious epistemology comes to the fore in the second (1539) version of the Institutes.

What Muller doesn't acknowledge is that Melanchthon's own emphases in this regard are constitutive of a broader Renaissance, and even Erasmian, trend. Calvin's increasing deployment of biblical language as normative for theological discourse is part and parcel of the rhetorical theologies of Italian and Northern European biblical humanism, and it cannot be confined to Melanchthonian influence. There are a number of explicit instances of Erasmus outlining the importance of affectivity in the Christian philosophy. In the *Paraclesis*, his exhortation to the *philosophia Christiana* appended to the first edition of his New Testament, he writes that the Christian philosophy "is seated in emotions rather than in syllogisms, a life rather than a disputation, inspiration rather than erudition, transformation rather than reason."[34] In his treatise on theological method, the *Ratio* (also a prefatory work to the New Testament), he writes that the "particular aim of the theologian is to interpret the divine writings wisely, from faith and not via the method of the *frivolis quaestionibus*, with grave piety and effective discourse, bringing forth tears and kindling the heavenly spirit." His enormous and influential manual for preachers, the *Ecclesiastes* of 1535, is replete with language of the heart and advice for preachers on the best and most appropriate way of stirring the emotions of the congregation.[35] There he writes that preachers need "a heart trained in a philosophy like no other," and that a pure heart is necessary "not only for teaching and inflaming the minds of the audience ... but also for acquiring knowledge of the heavenly philosophy."[36] In the *Lingua*, a treatise on the tongue (i.e., as synecdoche for discourse) composed in 1525, he writes, "We need not investigate here whether the seat of the human mind is in the brain or the heart, because their relationship is so close that if one is damaged the other instantly fails," and in his *Paraphrase on Ephesians* he has Paul speak of fortifying the heart of the understanding (*mentis praecordia*).[37] This *affective* language, which resists frigidity, emphasizes the importance of the heart as the locus for true religious activity and is a fundamental aspect of the Christian philosophy in the Erasmian biblical-humanist tradition.

Thus the outlines of this approach, taken up by several reformers, can be found scattered throughout Erasmus' corpus. Moreover, as Russ Leo has argued, the centrality of *affectus* and its more positive evaluation in Calvin makes for a stronger appreciation of the connection between affectivity and faith than is found in Melanchthon's *Loci Communes*, where *affectus* is located under the headings of "The Powers of Man" and "Sin."[38] Indeed, Calvin seems to go beyond his biblical-humanist predecessors in his appreciation of the affective component of religious knowledge. A balanced faculty psychology, along with an expressly affective understanding of faith, are borne out in several statements Calvin makes, many of which seem to privilege the affective over the intellectual aspect of the person. "The Word of God," Calvin writes in the *Institutes*, "is not received by faith if it flits about in the top of the brain [*in summo cerebro volutatur*], but when it takes root in the depths of the heart [*in imo corde radices egit*] that it may be an invincible defense to withstand and drive off all the stratagems of temptation" (III.ii.36).[39] In other words, the *telos* of religious knowledge is not contemplation, as it might be for, say, a good Christian-Aristotelian, but it must rather be conducive to, or even derivative of, a pious affective orientation toward God. Furthermore, Calvin writes that, "God's power is much more clearly manifested in the confirmation of the heart than in the illumination of the mind, to the extent that the heart's distrust is greater than the mind's blindness. It is harder for the heart [*animum*] to be furnished with assurance than for the mind to be endowed with thought."[40] This is a striking and rather complicated formulation, and it shouldn't be overlooked. The *completion* of religious knowing, for Calvin, actually takes place in the heart. Affectivity thus lies at the very centre of Calvin's conception of faith, and this has implications for a number of other areas of his thought.

Also in the *Institutes* (at III.vi.4), Calvin writes that the gospel "is a teaching not of the tongue but of life. It is not apprehended by the understanding and memory alone [*intellectu memoriaque*], as other disciplines are, but it is received only when it possesses the *whole soul* [*totam animam*], and finds a seat and resting place in the inmost affection of the heart [*intimo cordis affectu*]."[41] There is no intellective assent for Calvin where there is not already pious affective inclination.[42] "The very assent itself ... is more of the heart than of the brain [*cordis quam cerebri*], and more of the *affectus* than of the understanding [*intelligentiae*]."[43] *Affectus* is typically translated as "disposition" in this passage, but it seems clearly to have a more explicitly emotional valence than the common rendering allows. The gospel ought, Calvin continues in this section, "to penetrate the inmost affections of the heart, take its seat in the soul, and affect the whole man a hundred times more deeply than the cold exhortations of the philosophers!"[44] Coldness and frigidness are terms repeated often by Calvin in his excoriations of what he deems to be ineffective academic theologizing, and they imply, of course, non-affectivity. As Bouwsma puts it, "Here then lies the significance of Calvin's frequent attacks on *frigidity*; knowing, for Calvin, was frigid if it lacked that involvement of the affections which distinguishes really knowing from merely knowing."[45]

Christian discourse, likewise, must *move* as well as *teach*, and in the concrete example of Christ's emotions we find the possibility of concomitant ethical and anthropological components of an affective Christian philosophy. We've documented in an earlier chapter biblical-humanist calls for a new method of teaching (*ratio docendi*), which for Calvin needed to be "free of all brilliance, and revealed not a trace of ambition."[46] It is crucial for Calvin that a true convincing, a real movement of the heart, not be reducible to worldly rhetorical ability, as can be seen by his repeated dismissal in the commentary of superfluous elegance as an empty distraction through the employment of a variety of constructions: *pompa verborum, cupiditate magniloquentia, splendore verborum, elegantia sermonis, colore verborum, logodaidalian*. Even "true eloquence" (*vera eloquentia*) was eschewed by Paul in favour of unrefined speech (*rudi et impolito sermoni*), and of preaching that conformed instead to simplicity, utility, and efficacy (*simplicitas, utilitas, efficacia*). And for preaching to have utility, or to be efficacious, for Calvin, it must involve the emotions. While Calvin doesn't discuss this affective rhetorical approach explicitly in his sermon on Gethsemane, which focuses instead on the soteriological and ethical import of Christ's emotions for his congregation, in a sermon on 1 Timothy he describes the exhortatory task of the preacher as one of profitable instruction, and the church as a place not for farce and laughter, but where God's word "moves and touches" (*esmeus et touchez*) the congregation.[47] More apt to the themes of this book, in his *Argumentum* to the commentary on 1 Corinthians, Calvin writes, "no one will be suited for teaching unless they have first imbibed of the power of the gospel, so that they are speaking not from the mouth, but from the affections of the heart."[48] The purpose of what follows is to show how these varied concerns regarding emotion in the Christian life are also evident, or even grounded, in anthropological conceptions that are often most clearly laid out in exegetical and pastoral considerations of Christ's emotions.

Erasmus on Gethsemane

Aside from in the *Paraphrases*, the Gethsemane scene features heavily also in Erasmus' *De preparatio ad mortem* (1533), and features centrally in his *Disputatiuncula de taedio Iesu* (1503). The *De taedio*, comprising a series of letters between Erasmus and Colet born out of an argument they had in person at Oxford in 1499, and then edited and compiled by Erasmus himself, analyses the problem of Christ's fear at Gethsemane from nearly every conceivable angle. As mentioned previously, Erasmus takes up the position of defending the reality of Christ's fear of his own death, which he thinks is a natural and inextricable inclination in all humans, sinful or not. At issue here is a question specifically of mental anguish, a point of significance for understanding a range of sixteenth-century readings of Gethsemane. Gethsemane is in many ways the psychological counterpart to Christ's corporeal suffering on the cross, a point to be made explicit by Calvin. The fear of death is variously categorized by Erasmus as an *affectus* and a *passio naturalis* (Erasmus makes no firm distinction between the two terms in this early work),[49] and Erasmus argues against any notion of the fear of death, along with Christ's sorrow, as reducible to a physical response: *apatheia* refers to a lack of "pain in the mind" (*animi dolorem*) while *anaisthesia* refers to a lack of bodily pain (*corporis dolorem*).[50] In response to the implication that human affections are always tainted by sin, Erasmus argues that while original sin did reorient human passions towards a sinful inclination, that "in the best of us" the passions are neutral because they are natural and, *a fortiori*, that Christ's affections were ordered and sinless.

Recognizing that among human beings after the Fall we find a fractured psychological constitution (torn between reason and the passions, for example), Erasmus argues that "no one is so irreverent as to attribute to Christ this dissension and endless strife between reason and passion, spirit and flesh."[51] Nevertheless, Christ did assume all the weaknesses of man excepting sin, and for Erasmus this includes the affections: "Since Christ took nothing from fallen nature except the handicaps imposed on us as chastisement, and there was in him no capacity for sin, I shall boldly ascribe to him the natural passions [*passiones naturales*] appropriate to mind [*animi*] and body [*corporis*], respectively: grief, joy, hatred, fear, and anger in the mind; in the body, hunger, thirst, drowsiness, weariness, suffering, death [*animi, ut dolere, gaudere, odisse, sperare, metuere, irasci; corporis, ut esurire, sitire, dormiturire, lassari, affligi, more*]."[52] Christ took on all the emotions (*omnibus affectibus*) that Adam, had he "continued in his original state," would have borne, along with the corresponding faculties: "a sensible body [*corpus sensibile*] and a sensible soul [*animam sensibilem*] subject to the natural passions [*naturalibus passionibus obnoxiam*]."[53] In other words, pre-lapsarian Adam was a fully formed emotional human being who experienced the full range of mental and bodily affections.

Following a Pauline tripartite anthropological schema,[54] Erasmus argues further that there are three kinds of "impulses" (*nisus*) in humans: a virtuous, or spiritual, impulse; a sinful, or fleshly, impulse; and a morally neutral, or natural, impulse that is "attracted neither towards good for its own sake, nor towards evil for its own sake, but instead towards anything that is favourable to nature; and it recoils from anything that threatens our survival, or even our peace of mind."[55] Affections such as hunger and fear of death are not, according to Erasmus, sinful in themselves. Christ, moreover, does not possess the second sort of impulse, but he does possess the first and the third. And if the third, neutral, sort is not necessarily connected to the flesh or the spirit, and is *merely natural* (*mere naturalis*), then we ought not to hesitate in ascribing it to Christ, who is fully human while sinless. It was this neutral kind of "will" which was in Christ that made him fearful of death (*quae illa voluntas in Christo, qua mori noluit*).[56] Put another way, before the Fall Adam was not an exclusively rational being, embodying the Stoic ideal of *apatheia*, but he also *felt*; and in the same way Christ dreaded his death not out of fear resulting from a sinfully disordered soul, but simply because fearing death is something all humans do.[57] Erasmus assigns to Christ and to humans a set of emotional dispositions that are not in themselves sinful, thereby complicating the Stoic anthropological schema wherein anything non-rational is to be avoided.[58] Indeed, to the contrary, at times Erasmus contends that Jesus' emotions did overwhelm him in the Garden:

> That is why Jerome's interpretation holds no great attraction for me. He calls the Redeemer's suffering 'propassion' rather than passion, something that, to use St Bernard's distinction, overtook but did not overwhelm him. If they define 'passion' as something that dethrones reason, and 'overwhelm' as being driven out of one's mind, I do not object. But I should not hesitate also to call 'passion' these feelings which not only overtook Jesus' mind (or at least the lower part of it), but most violently overwhelmed it.[59]

While the passions don't completely dethrone *ratio* on Erasmus' reading (and here he follows, more or less, Aquinas),[60] they do overwhelm the *mens* of Christ. Erasmus deliberately "softens" the definition of *passio* here against Jerome and Bernard so that it doesn't bear the uniquivocal deleterious connotations assigned to it by a major thread of the antecedent tradition. More generally, Erasmus' attitude towards Stoicism in this early treatise is complicated, rather than simply antagonistic, and he reveals his awareness of the nuances of the Stoic tradition. He invokes the Stoics against Colet and argues that even they have a fear of death, whether they show it or not. But most importantly, he explicitly invokes particular Stoics to support his arguments, such as Panaetius, who does "not insist that his wise man should practice *analgesia*, or insensibility, and *apatheia*, or lack of feeling, and indeed considers them incompatible with being human."[61] In other words, the Stoics Erasmus appreciates, even at this early date, are the ones who are least Stoic, so to speak, in their anthropologies.

Erasmus never abandons his early position against Colet, and in his paraphrases of the synoptic Gospel scenes on Gethsemane, he goes on to make explicit his reading that Jesus was fearful of his own imminent suffering and death.[62] In his *Paraphrase on Matthew*, Erasmus writes – following Theophylact – that Jesus brought the same three disciples, to whom he had previously (at the Transfiguration) revealed his divine nature, into Gethsemane to demonstrate his human nature, to "have them as witnesses to his extreme human weakness."[63] Aside from the christological purpose of the passage, it also served "to teach that as often as any tempest of troubles is at hand greater than what human strength can bear, that we, utterly distrusting ourselves, commit ourselves totally to divine aid. And the fear of death, when it seizes a man, is harsher than death itself."[64] (This last sentence finds its way into Bullinger's commentary on Matthew unacknowledged.[65]) While he makes no overt references to Stoicism in the *Paraphrases*, in the *Paraphrase on Mark*, he uses a favourite phrase to castigate human philosophy – *praesidiis superbiae humanae* – in the context of Jesus' desolation in Gethsemane.[66] While Erasmus occasionally describes Christ's aversion to death as something physical or corporeal, he doesn't reduce the affections to physical impulses. "My Father, if it be possible take away this cup of death from me, for I feel the bodily affection vehemently recoiling from death," Christ says in the *Paraphrase on Matthew*.[67] In *Mark*, he writes that "His bodily nature recoiled from suffering and imminent death."[68]

However, Erasmus here also underscores the fact that these emotions affect both mind and body in Christ: "Therefore this [anguish] began then to come upon Jesus, and he felt great sorrow and was troubled in spirit. For he did not wish to hide the mental anguish from his friends, so that they would plainly see that he was truly human, equally disturbed by the affections of both mind and body."[69] Indeed, he often focuses on the psychological aspect of Christ's suffering at Gethsemane, and he argues more than once in the *De taedio* against the danger of mistaking extrinsic (physical, bodily) signs of emotion as meaningful indicators on which to ground judgments of praise or blame (pallor does not entail cowardice, for example).[70] Erasmus' understanding of the situation of the passions in both body and mind serves to complicate recent scholarly oversimplifications of premodern conceptions of emotion as thoroughly Galenic and inextricably bound to the humors.[71] Moreover, aside from the *De taedio* and *Paraphrases*, Erasmus also dealt with the Gethsemane scene in his 1533 *De preparatione ad mortem* – a work that enjoyed large and multiple early print runs (twenty in the first six years) and translations into the vernacular.[72] Here he emphasizes the psychological aspects of Christ's passion: "We must not immediately despair if consolation does not come at once. Again and again we must return to call out, not with our voice, but with our heart. To be sure, if we imitate spiritually what the Lord did openly, a good angel will be with us to *wipe away the bloody sweat from our mind*. He either will snatch us away from death or will add strength to our spirit so that we may endure death bravely."[73] The corporeal bloody sweat of the garden, itself representative of mental anguish, is here transformed completely into a psychological metaphor.

Sarah Covington has outlined the importance of Christ's psychological suffering in English interpretations of the passion, and these had sixteenth-century precedents not only in Calvin but also in Erasmus and Luther.[74] In Erasmus, the clearest example of what is often glossed as a specifically Protestant association of Christ's agony with grief over human sinfulness, and also the torments of Hell, comes in the *De preparatione ad mortem*:

> Fear of hell surpasses all fear, but our most compassionate Redeemer deigned to subject himself to it so that he might lessen it for us. When he felt fear in the garden and was so seized by anguish that he sweated blood, this was the infirmity of our nature. When he was fixed to the cross and called out, 'My God, my God, why have you forsaken me and far from my salvation are the words of my sins,' he seems to have felt the horror of hell in his mind. For what is left for those abandoned by God except extreme despair? It ought not to seem strange that he showed this most distressing state of mind when he had taken upon himself the sins of all so that each evil that could not be overcome by the strength in us could be overcome by his compassion ... We had deserved hell, he in his innocence feels dread on our behalf so that, if a similar emotion invades our mind either from awareness of our crimes or from the weakness of our nature, we shall not abandon all hope, but with our eyes set on Christ shall have hope even in despair.[75]

This association of Christ's agony with our sins in this late text, found earlier in Luther's *Commentary on the Psalms*, is stronger than anything found in the *De taedio*, and it could be that this work, especially in its emphasis on despair, belies Lutheran influence (even if in other ways the formulation of some questions in Luther's commentary looks to be indebted to Erasmus' *De taedio*).[76] But even in the *De taedio* Erasmus could wax emphatic about the extent of Christ's psychological suffering: "It is logical to suppose that if his death was more painful physically than any other, then his dread of it must have been more excruciating mentally than any other."[77] What is clear, at any rate, is that Christ's mental anguish had cross-confessional interest.[78]

Erasmus' theological appropriation of Christ's emotions, which consists of an implicit and multifaceted apologia for Christian emotion broadly speaking, represents a departure from classical models of philosophical anthropology, a departure that conforms to the broader attempts by biblical humanists to re-orient the "Christian philosophy" to abide more explicitly particular biblical norms. Furthermore, the specific questions and formulations of the *De taedio*, which become more pronounced and refined in later works, would seem to have a strong impact on subsequent sixteenth-century exegeses of the Gethsemane scene in particular, and in understanding Christ's emotions in general, for both Catholics and Protestants.

Calvin's *Premier sermon de la Passion sur Matthieu 26*

Much of Calvin's engagement with the Gethsemane scene took place late in his career, when he published a sermon on the subject (1558)[79] and wrote his commentary on the harmony of the Gospels (1555), but the substance of his understanding of this pericope, for our purposes, is already established in the 1539 *Institutes* (III.8, sections 8–10). The details of the sermon, however, are rich and worth considering in detail, and they will serve as the focal point for this chapter. Calvin's *First Sermon on the Passion*, which is the longest engagement he published on Gethsemane, focuses less on fine-grained christological nuance and more on the role of emotion in Christian piety. Calvin takes up many of Erasmus' arguments and concerns regarding the emotions and Christ's human nature.[80] As mentioned, Calvin follows Erasmus in all of the above works that consider Gethsemane in understanding the passage in its most straightforward sense: Christ was afraid, sad, and anxious about his impending suffering and death – with an added emphasis that death for Christ entailed facing divine wrath – all signs of his truly human nature.[81] And partly because of the flexibility of different genres, Calvin is more explicit in his condemnations of Stoicism in the context of interpreting Gethsemane in his commentaries and in the *Institutes*. In the sermon he is more emphatic in offering Christ's example of sorrow as a model of Christian emotionality, and in arguing for the salvific efficacy of Christ's psychological agony.

The extensive and varied engagement with Christ's emotions in this sermon offers students of Calvin substantial insight into his judgment of affectivity from several angles. Susan Karant-Nunn, in her account of Calvin's use of the emotions in his sermons, fails to do justice to the multifaceted way in which Calvin employs Christ's emotions as consolatory and exemplary, but focuses instead on Calvin's shaming techniques and inattention to Christ's bodily suffering in a bid to emphasize confessional difference in early modern attitudes towards feeling.[82] While the christological issues mentioned above often feature heavily in formal biblical exegesis in the sixteenth century (including in Calvin's commentary), Calvin in his sermon on the scene focuses rather on the way in which Christ's emotions may be used for ethical ends by relating them to the emotions of his congregation.[83] Nevertheless, the *Institutes* and his *Commentary on the Gospel Harmony* allow us to consider the theological and exegetical underpinnings of Calvin's position on the emotions vis-à-vis Christ's experience, in relation to the way in which Calvin relates Christ's passions rhetorically to the emotions of the Geneva congregation in his sermon.[84] The three primary aims of Calvin's *First Sermon on the Passion* follow the trends of his exegetical predecessors: 1) to establish Christ's psychological suffering as a crucial and necessary aspect of his suffering as a substitutionary sacrifice for humanity's sins; 2) to put forth Christ as an ethical example for human beings in his grief in general and in his prayer for God's mercy, with the somewhat related aim of putting forth Christ's grief as impetus for Christians to grieve over their own shortcomings; and 3) despite setting up Christ as an ethical exemplum, to argue for a great difference between Christ's passions and the sinful passions of all other humans.

The Salvific Power of Christ's Emotions

Throughout the sermon Calvin emphasizes the soteriological aspects of the Gethsemane scene, pointing out first that the sinfulness of humanity was such that it required Christ to undergo deep psychological torments, and that this fact ought to encourage his followers, in acknowledging their sinfulness, not to fall asleep on their obligations to God (an allusion, no doubt, to the disciples falling asleep during these moments in the Gospel):

> But we, however, see that the price of our redemption was very high when our Lord Jesus Christ was tormented so much when he sustained the fear of death that he sweat drops of blood; it was as though he were out of his mind, desiring that he might escape such a distress. When we see these things, it is good for us to come to an acknowledgment of our sins, and it is no time for us to rock ourselves to sleep through flattery when we see the Son of God plunged into such extremity, suffering, as it were, as though he were in a deep abyss.[85]

The extreme and profound abyss Calvin refers to here is constitutive of the emotional agony Christ is experiencing in the garden. The image of Christ agonizing to the point of sweating blood ought to serve, Calvin thinks, to awaken in Christians a renewed sense simultaneously of their own sins and of the fact that these do not excuse them of their religious duty.[86] In this way, then, Christ's undergoing an extreme form of psychological agony (to the point, Calvin will remind us, that he sweats blood, a most forceful somatic expression of emotion, even if Calvin typically avoids such corporeal imagery)[87] serves to ground an explicitly affective form of religious piety. Calvin goes to great lengths to convince his audience of the reality of Christ's passions before his Passion, which serve both an ethical and a soteriological purpose.

Strikingly, Calvin even insinuates in the sermon that it is Christ's fear of death that frees sinners from the wrath of God, and not only his suffering and death on the cross: "And surely we cannot wait for our Lord Jesus Christ without being persuaded that he has fought against the fears of death in such a way that we are thereby made free, and that he attained victory for us."[88] Christ's wrestling in emotional turmoil – his fear and sorrow at the prospect of death – has soteriological significance. This exegetical line is overt in the 1559 *Institutes*, where he writes, glossing the Gethsemane scene, that "unless [Christ's] soul shared in the punishment, he would have been a redeemer of bodies alone."[89] Thus, the psychological aspects of Christ's suffering are of utmost importance. Calvin argues further in the *Institutes* that the *descensus ad infernum* described in the Apostle's Creed is purely psychological – not in the sense that only the soul descended, for many in the tradition believed this, but in the sense that it is to be taken as a metaphor[90] – and he suggests that the *descensus* actually begins at Gethsemane and reaches its climax in Christ's plea on the cross.[91] Christ, Calvin repeats, "paid a greater and more excellent price in suffering in his soul the terrible torments of a condemned and forsaken man."[92] We gain insight into Calvin's understanding of the passions or emotions here as essentially incorporeal, for his insistence that Christ's sorrow and fear were necessary in order to redeem the whole human being entails that he understands them to pertain primarily to the immaterial soul. Moreover, the *active* force of Christ's emotions in their soteriological effectiveness – keeping in mind, too, that his suffering was voluntary – as this plays out in Calvin's reading would seem to prefigure an aspect of Renaissance thought in the seventeenth century outlined by Christopher Tilmouth.[93] Tilmouth's description of Crashaw's Christ having "transformed a passive emotional experience into an active one, making of imposed grief a source of outward-moving love," is quite readily applicable to Calvin's account of Gethsemane as well, written a century earlier (and, for that matter, in Erasmus' before him).[94] Either way, what's crucial is to understand the emotions here in a manner other than as pathologized and conceived as passive (bodily) reactions – again contrary to a tendency in recent scholarship on emotion in the early modern period that Richard Strier has referred to as the "new humoralism," whose proponents conceive of early modern emotions primarily insofar as they are signified in the bodily humours.[95]

Aside from salvific efficacy, Christ's emotions, on Calvin's reading, also have an effect on Christian experience. Mitigating the severity of Karant-Nunn's argument, which focuses extensively on Calvin's penchant for shaming and instiling fear into his congregation, and even suggests that Calvin did not seek to offer consolation to his parishioners,[96] Calvin repeats several times that "by this means we may overcome all anxieties, all fears, all terrors, and we are able to call upon God with the assurance that he continually stretches out his arms to embrace us."[97] Calvin insists that it is "no speculative doctrine, when it is said that our Lord Jesus Christ has experienced the horrible fears of death," in order to convince his parishioners that they can be assured of God's aid, should they ask. This aspect of Calvin's pastoral application of Christ's grief brings us to the more explicit assessment of Christ's fear and sorrow in the face of death as an example for Christians to follow.

Christ's Emotions as a Mirror

Calvin more than once in the sermon sets Christ's sorrow forth as an example of a permissible form of emoting and Christ's trust as an example of faith in divine consolation:

> Moreover, he showed for us, in addressing the Father, the remedy for the easing of all our griefs, for mitigating our sorrows, and even for pulling ourselves up out of the abyss. For when we are grieved and vexed, we remember that God is not in vain named the father of consolation. Again, if we are separated from him, where will we find power and strength but in him? ... Let us then hear and behold the Son of God, who, when we are in sorrow and anguish, guides us to true refuge by his example.[98]

Christ's approaching God the Father in prayer in order to alleviate his sorrow is set forth by Calvin as a model for all Christians undergoing forms of psychic anguish. While Karant-Nunn is correct in suggesting that Calvin's keenness to impress upon his audience a sense of their sinfulness leads to his use of the "emotive vocabulary of shaming and condemnation," it is important not to neglect that Calvin's use of emotional language in his analysis of Christ's psychological agonies in Gethsemane also serves the purpose of reminding his audience that Christ underwent such suffering in order to redeem Adam's descendants on the one hand, and, on the other, that his fear and sadness in some way permit our own. (Kyle Fedler refers to these two aspects, respectively, as the objective and subjective benefits of Christ's emotional suffering.)[99] Indeed, in her contrast of Luther and Calvin, the former who allegedly portrays God as a loving father and the latter who only emphasizes God's distance from us, Karant-Nunn continually overlooks Calvin's repeated injunctions for his congregation to identify with Christ the Mediator in his sorrows. The negative fear of God's wrath is transformed into a positive fear of God as awe and obedience.

While Calvin may indeed be unrivalled in his appreciation of the *Deus absconditus* and in the vast gulf between God's goodness and humanity's depravity, he finds in the example of Christ an ethical example of emotionality. Implicit here in Calvin's emotional-ethical prescriptions is a predisposition against the Stoic doctrine of *apatheia*, which is made explicit in connection with Gethsemane both in the *Institutes* and in his commentary on the passage. The abstract and general rejection of a radical Stoic philosophy of emotion is given concrete form in the example of the Christ of Gethsemane. The Genevan reformer condemns the Stoic position – that "iron philosophy" (*ferrea philosophia*) – and the Christian "new Stoics" who have adopted it, in the *Institutes*.[100] It is worth reproducing the passage at length:

You see that to bear the cross patiently is not to be stupified and altogether deprived of a sense of sorrow. In this manner the Stoics of old foolishly described the great-spirited man who was devoid of humanity, moved alike in prosperity and adversity, affected similarly by joy and by sadness, indeed one who was as a stone, affected by nothing at all. And what did this sublime wisdom accomplish? They painted rather a *simulacrum sapientiae*, which has never been discovered among humans, nor is it even possible. Now there are new Stoics among Christians, for whom not only to groan and weep, but also to be sad and care-ridden is to be sinful. These paradoxes, however, proceed from idle men, who in spending their time speculating rather than acting, are able to provide us with nothing other than paradoxes. But we have nothing to do with that iron philosophy, which our master and Lord condemned not only in word, but also by his example.[101]

Calvin ushers in prooftexts here which also refer to Christ's agony at Gethsemane in order to establish, against the Stoic ideal man, the *Christus exemplum* who experiences a full range of human emotions. The Stoic philosopher, in setting up *apatheia* as an ideal, merely paints a picture of an unattainable wisdom that, aside from being unrealizable in this world, is condemned by Christ in both word and deed. "For if all tears are blamed," Calvin asks, "what shall we judge of the Lord himself, out of whose body dropped bloody tears? If every fear is judged unfaithful, what shall we judge of that horror of which we read that he was not lightly stricken? If all sadness is unpleasing, how shall we like the fact that he confessed his soul to be sorrowful even unto death?"[102] Calvin's audience must bear Christ in mind as an emotional exemplar.

The contrast between speculation and action invoked here, along with the contrast in the following sections between "Christian and philosophic patience," brings Calvin's discussion in the *Institutes* in line with other aspects of his Christian philosophy, notably the theology of the heart and advocacy of practical piety over theological intellectualism. A common way in which Calvin specifically attempts to rewrite anthropological language is in his exhortations to Christians to subsume their passions to the obedience of God, rather than to the rational faculty. This isn't universal in Calvin, as we'll see below, but *Institutes* III.8.10 provides a good example of this tendency. It also appears to follow a specific section of Erasmus' *De taedio* quite closely in its description of the tension in the pious person between a "natural sense" or "natural feeling" (*sensus naturalis* and *affectus naturalis*) to flee the cross in times of despair and the "disposition to godliness" (*pietatis affectus*) that constitutes obedience to God, complete with the same reference to Peter's divided will at John 21:18 in order to illustrate the possibility of a sinless sort of *automachia*.[103] Here, according to Calvin, even in the saints we will find a contradiction in their hearts between the *sensus naturae* and the *pietatis affectus ad obedientiam divinae voluntatis* ("pious disposition to obedience of the divine will"). Erasmus had also repeated the phrases *sensus naturalis* and *affectus naturalis* describing Peter's and Christ's humanity, and in describing Christ's human propensity to have a divided will, writes that he demonstrates his "subordination of a natural disposition to the divine will" (*naturalem affectum submittentis voluntati divinae*) when Christ says "Not my will, but thine be done" while praying in the garden.[104] In other words, again, we find both exegetes describing a natural sort of affection that, albeit not sinful, needs to be aligned with God's will rather than in perfect accord with the rational faculty or suppressed altogether.

In preaching that the sorrow of Christ is justified given that the wrath of God was imminently upon him (seemingly taking up Luther's understanding), Calvin says both that we ought to fear death, and that we ought to be assured in the face of it on account of what Christ underwent – all of which results from our knowledge of his experience at Gethsemane: "Let us rejoice when we see that death has no more power over us. It is true that we will always naturally fear and flee from death, but with the purpose that we should consider the inestimable benefit which the Son of God purchased through his death. And keep in mind that this comes through death itself, which death takes away the wrath of God, and which wrath is the gulf of hell."[105] Here the objective benefits and the subjective benefits are collapsed together, for the fact that Christ has undergone such a grave terror in the face of death means that Christians can approach it with more assurance, thereby tempering our fear. Calvin continues along these lines:

> Moreover, we know when we are fighting against this fear that our Lord Jesus Christ has so provided for all these fears that we might now come boldly before God in the face of death. It is true that we ought to humble ourselves above all else, and, as we have said previously, if we intend to hate our sins and if we are displeased with them, we must be touched by the judgment of God, and to be afraid. Meanwhile, we must come with a cheerful countenance when God calls us to him.[106]

Christ's example of overcoming the fear of death and divine wrath and submitting in obedience to the divine will should serve as a model for Calvin's parishioners. But there is a less appealing way in which Christ's emotions may serve as an example or *miroir*. The fear and grief Christ undergoes in relation to God's wrath is also employed as a warning to the parishioners that, unless they forego their sinfulness, they will face the same sorts of emotional torments many times over: "in death we see the depths of the curse and the gulf of the wrath of God devour us, and that not only one, but a million fears have taken hold of us, and all of creation cries out for vengeance against us."[107] This dual role of Christ's emotions, the objective and the subjective, governs Calvin's sermon throughout in a more explicit and emphatic way than we find in the works of Erasmus, and he bounces back and forth between these two lessons through rhetorical antithesis, occasionally splitting the difference: After a long digression on the deeply entrenched nature of human sinfulness, Calvin says, "we must continually remember here that the Son of God set himself before us not only as an example or a mirror, but also to show us how much our salvation cost him."[108]

Christ's Emotions and Ours

Calvin is keen on establishing for his congregation the *humanness* of Christ's emotions, for only by doing so may he both refute what he perceived to be unorthodox notions of Christ's nature and at the same time set Christ forth as a more or less imitable example that, in the broader context of Renaissance philosophy, cuts against Stoic tendencies in ethics and anthropology. A consequence of Calvin's reading is that he must also carve out space for a conception of emotions as sinless *in themselves*, as we've hinted at previously, which means granting a prelapsarian Adam the ability to emote without fault, without at the same time conceding the same ability to his audience:

> But we who are encompassed with this lump of sin are so block-headed that we are very distant from God's will. Our desires are in excess and are often manifestly rebellious. But if we consider man in his original state, before his sinful corruption, it is certain that his affections were very far from God, but they were not corrupt. And if Adam had not been corrupted as he was, but had continued in the state in which he was created, he would have felt hot and cold, and could have suffered anxieties, fears, and similar things.[109]

Emotion is a built-in feature of human nature, in the same way that susceptibility to temperature is for Calvin. And thus Christ, the second Adam, cannot be faulted for his emotions alone in themselves: "Thus was our Lord Jesus Christ. For we know that his affections were without stain and were immaculate, and they were all regulated unto the obedience of God, but yet (because he had taken on our nature) he was subject to fear and to this terror which is mentioned, and to anxieties and similar emotions."[110] In other words, emotions *qua* emotions aren't sinful: they become sinful for a fallen humanity.

There arises an awkward tension between advocating Christ in his grave emotional state as an example for Christians to follow and Calvin's commitment to distinguishing between Christ's sinless emotions and the emotions of all other humans. It is a tension that pervades Erasmus' *De taedio* as well. It comes to bear on Calvin's handling of Christ's prayer, for even if the fear of death and other forms of strong affection are naturally human, the Gospel writers tell us that they were so strong that Christ prayed that "the cup be removed from him," which cup Calvin defines as not only death and bodily suffering but incurring the full wrath of God in order to serve as a substitution for all sinners. Here it would seem that Christ's human will was not in accord with the will of the Father. Calvin is thus forced to go back and forth between emphasizing the extremely strong effect Christ's emotions had on his psyche in Gethsemane in order to explain the prayer, and distinguishing the orderedness of his passions in comparison with other humans'. Lest anyone hearing (or reading) his sermon think that Christ, in showing such fear and in asking that the cup be removed, had "forgotten our salvation" or "had intended to leave us in destruction," he argues that extraordinary forms of psychological anguish can block out all other concerns. We've already seen Calvin describe Christ earlier in the sermon as "like one out of his mind," and here, too, he explains the extreme form of anguish Christ underwent:

> Because we know that a passion often ravishes the mind of a man to the extent that he thinks neither of one thing or another: But being pressed with the present malady, he is thrown around and is unable to hold himself up. When our minds are likewise ravished, we cannot say that everything is effaced from our hearts and that we have no affection.[111]

Calvin is appealing to the emotional experience of his audience so that they might understand how Christ felt in order that they not judge his actions remiss. In doing so, he again equates Christ's emotions with theirs, in this case, however, with reverse expectations.

Continuing from the idea that Christ's emotions remained in obedience to God, Calvin expounds on our inability truly to relate:

> We cannot perceive this in ourselves any more than we can see clearly in muddy water. And we see how our human affections cause us to drift from one side to the other, and that they give us such movement [*nous donner telles esmotions*] that God has to hold us up: But the affections which

the descendants of Adam have are like clay, exceedingly tempered with infection, and they make us unable to contemplate what the passion of our Lord Jesus Christ was when we consider it from a human perspective.[112]

The rhetorical force (and complication) of the sermon is in essence determined by Calvin's oscillation between insisting on the difference between Christ's emotions and the emotions of fallen human beings on the one hand, and, on the other, his descriptions of the various ways in which his congregation ought to identify with Christ's emotional experience, whether through his example of seeking God's aid when fearing death, or through grieving for the sinfulness of humankind. As in Erasmus' interpretations of Gethsemane, the *human* nature of Christ is demonstrated in Calvin's sermon forcefully by his emotionality, but in a way that goes beyond anything Erasmus writes relating Christ's emotions to other humans', and Calvin's congregation and readers are called forth to understand their own emotions in a manner appropriate to piety. Calvin's sermon on Gethsemane is rich and complex in attempting to parse out the ways in which Christ's psychological agony can be properly invoked in an articulation of the importance of emotion for Christian piety, and it provides more concrete form to the affective aspects of the Christian philosophy.

Jesus Wept: Christ's Tears and the Ambivalent Reception of Stoicism

While the Gethsemane scene is the locus classicus for exegetical consideration of the role of emotions in the Christian life, Jesus' weeping at the scene of Lazarus' death in John 11 constitutes another significant pericope for analysing the interpretation of Christ's emotions, and a few remarks from sixteenth-century commentaries are worth considering briefly here. In his *Paraphrase* on John 11:23ff. (first published in 1523),[113] Erasmus expands the original Gospel text significantly to cover the potential problems that might arise from a misunderstanding of Christ's weeping with the family of the recently deceased Lazarus.

But when Jesus saw Mary completely caught up in grief and the Jews who accompanied her also weeping, he did not reason with her, as he had done with her sister Martha, with whom he had spoken without an attendant crowd; nor did he make any promises, since now the time and place were at hand for performing what he had promised Martha. First he groaned in spirit, and became distressed, displaying of course the reality of his human nature, while soon to give evidence of his divine might.[114]

Erasmus' rendering is a straightforward defence of Chalcedonian christology, concommitant with his christological position in the *De taedio*. What distinguishes Christ's expression of emotion here from the scene in the garden, however, to Erasmus' mind, is that in the case in John, Jesus took the emotions upon himself voluntarily in that moment – they did not result from his weak human nature unlike his fear of death at Gethsemane.[115] Moreover, Christ did not weep for the same reasons as the others present at the scene. As the paraphrase progresses, Erasmus is also keen to emphasize that Christ's sadness was not – or at least was not only – for Lazarus:

> That he shuddered in his heart and that he was distressed were not pretended emotions; yet the important point was that he took these feelings to himself not from the weakness of nature but by his deliberate choice. And the reasons for the others' tears and for Jesus' distress were not the same. They mourned with a purely human emotion for the death of the body; Jesus rather was moved to indignation at the sins of mankind, through which so many souls were perishing.[116]

This is, perhaps, a surprising reading given Erasmus' more straightforward interpretation of Christ's agony at Gethsemane in the *De taedio*, and it anticipates a common Reformed sentiment that Christ's grief ought to be placed in front of his followers as a mirror to induce lamentation at human sinfulness. However, what may seem like equivocation on Erasmus' part from the perspective of his cumulative position on Christ's emotions can more readily be ascribed to his awareness – following a long tradition of interpreting John – of the endeavours of the author of John to emphasize the divinity of Christ, a fact made clear in Erasmus' dedicatory letter to Prince Ferdinand, where he argues that the chief reason for John's writing a new Gospel was to assert Christ's divinity in the face of new christological heresies.[117] With this in mind, Erasmus' faithfulness in this case to the mind of the author in his *Paraphrases* is quite remarkable. In any case, as Jane Phillips points out in the notes to her translation, the interpretation has similar but no exact precedents. Nicholas of Lyra suggested that Christ's weeping represented his indignation at the devil for bringing death into the world, and Augustine long before him had seen in Christ's weeping a model for us to follow in considering our own sinfulness, a gloss Erasmus will apply even more clearly a bit later in the paraphrase, and one which Calvin uses extensively when considering Christ's grief, as we have seen. First, however, Erasmus reiterates that Christ had shown emotion not for Lazarus, but for us:

> So after he had given plain proof of his human nature in the shuddering of his spirit and the distress of his heart, in his face, his eyes, and the whole look of his body, now teaching us that there should be no succumbing to emotions of this kind or distraction from the things that concern power, he curbed his heart's distress and said, 'Where have you laid him?' – not that he did not know, but so that he could exclude from the miracle any suspicion of deceit. The relatives replied, 'Lord, come and see.' That remark indicated that the tomb was not far off, and now, as if this grief was renewed at being shown the grave, Jesus wept. Groaning and distress had come first, a mark of grief breaking in upon the heart. Tears are as it were the blood of the already wounded and vanquished heart; but these tears did not come from a vanquished heart. For they were not spent for the dead Lazarus, but for us, so that we might believe Jesus was truly a man, and at the same time we might learn how pitiable, how lamentable, is the death of the soul, though humankind neither loathes nor laments it.[118]

As with the Gethsemane scene, the exegetical use of Christ's emotions is manifold. Erasmus suggests that too much emotion would be unbecoming, and Christ sets forth an example for us in his eventual restraint, though the biblical text doesn't recount such a moment explicitly.[119] The notion that Christ more or less opted to show emotion, potentially as an "exceptional" moment of his humanity, is also reflected in an argument Erasmus sets forth in the *De taedio*, following Ambrose.[120] It represents an interesting example of the relationship between the will and the affections, and it confounds generalizations in the historiography about early modern emotions as inherently passive experiences, even if the subject in this case is Christ. Erasmus then paraphrases John in even closer accord with Augustine's gloss:

> But Jesus was now close to the tomb. Wanting to show clearly that the state of a person long practised in sin is to be abhorred and how much repentance, how many tears are needed to reform and return to the life of innocence through the mercy of God, he again groaned and was distressed,

demonstrating in himself, of course, a model of that which must be shown in us if we wish to reform from the evils to which we have been long accustomed.[121]

In Erasmus' expansions on the Gospel text we find many of the same elements as in his glosses on the Gethsemane scene, but with more of an emphasis on Christ's lamentations over the sins of humanity. In the *Paraphrase on John* we also find a distinction between the objective and subjective benefits of Christ's emotions, although in this case the objective benefits are christological rather than soteriological. Erasmus' understanding of Christ's weeping as an example for sorrowful repentance here is a weaker version of his association of Christ's emotional agony with hell in his gloss on Gethsemane in the *De preparatione ad mortem*, written a decade later.

Craig Farmer has shown that Christ's weeping in John 11 was commonly interpreted as demonstrating Christ's true humanity in Reformed commentaries in the first half of the sixteenth century, and further that his emotions serve as an exemplary safeguard against rampant Stoicism.[122] Zwingli, Oecolampadius, Bullinger, Bucer, and Musculus all read the text in this way. Bullinger, for example, repeats the common refrain that "the Christian religion does not make human beings into stones or tree trunks," and he lifts the line from Erasmus' paraphrase that Christ's tears flow from his heart as blood from a wound. (The association of the Stoic *sapiens* with a tree trunk dates at least to Valla's *De Voluptate*.)[123] In addition, as Farmer points out, he uses Christ's sorrow as an example for later Christians to grieve over their own sins.[124] Bucer suggests that Christ's compassion and sadness at the grief of his friends and death of Lazarus refutes not only the Marcionite heresy, but also Stoic unfeeling: "For Bucer," writes Farmer, "the scene of the mourners and Jesus openly weeping over Lazarus's death paints a portrait of the kind of love required by God, a love that is not 'senseless' (*stupentem*) but 'living and ardent, which stirs up the heart and shows itself in the whole body'."[125] Bucer writes, "Therefore some of our Catabaptists are Stoics more than Christians, who permit no mourning, no tears for the dead or for brothers afflicted in other ways."[126] The interpretation that Christ is weeping over Lazarus, along with explicit mentions of Stoicism, mark a departure from Erasmus' *Paraphrase*, and reflect a common preoccupation with condemning Anabaptist neostoicism. Musculus takes cues from his predecessors in this way; as Farmer translates, "The Stoic *apatheia*, which the Anabaptists are once again attempting to introduce into the Church, is entirely foreign to the Saints." The Anabaptists, he says, *magis Stoicismus quam Christianismus dici debet*.[127]

Barbara Pitkin has shown that Calvin's interest in Johannine christology, including the pericope containing Jesus' weeping, is often anthropologically oriented.[128] As she notes, Calvin is also keen (as he is in expositing Gethsemane, and as his exegetical forebears are in expositing John 11) to establish Christ's humanity, to condemn Stoic unfeeling, and to argue that Christ's emotions are sinless. Calvin writes that when Christ "groaned in spirit" (John 11:33) he showed three things: his *sumpatheia* with the other mourners over Lazarus, his awareness of the "common misery of the human race," and the fact that "in feeling grief and through tears he shows that he is as affected by our sins as if he had suffered them in himself."[129] He also rejects Augustine's contention that Christ had only taken on human passions voluntarily for a time in this case and was "otherwise free from passion," arguing rather that his sympathetic reaction is just one example of a lifelong assumption of humanity: "he was similar to us in the affections of the soul" (*in animae affectibus nobis similis esset*).[130] In other words, Christ wept for the same reasons as the others at the scene, and for reasons in addition to those. We find in Calvin's commentary a mélange of elements from the glosses of his predecessors. He does not, it may be noted, mention the Anabaptists as adherents to a species of neostoicism, suggesting, perhaps, that his concerns regarding the impropriety of Christian unfeeling were not confined to sectarian concerns.

Calvin is also concerned with the other end of the emotional spectrum. Before he considers Christ's emotions he gives an extended gloss on what he considers to be Mary's excessive form of grieving. He writes that it is a "common illness" that people grieving over dead loved ones "eagerly increase their grief in whatever way possible."[131] Thus, Calvin blames those who were with Mary for allowing her to go to the tomb for encouraging her to excessive grieving (*fovent intemperantiam doloris*), for they ought to have applied a "harsher remedy" (*acre remedium*), and he issues a general scolding of those who indulge their friends in excessive consolation.[132] While Calvin's reading may come off as harsh at first glance, one cannot accuse Calvin of attempting to do away altogether with deathbed grief or of advocating Stoic unfeeling when faced with the prospect of a dying loved one. In general, his advice in *Comm. John* is in keeping with the advice Calvin gives in consolatory letters to his friends, which urge moderation of strong feeling but not suppression of it. In a letter from 1541 to a friend whose son had died from a plague in

Basel, Calvin writes: "When I first received the intelligence of the death of Claude and of your son Louis, I was so utterly overpowered that for many days I was fit for nothing but to grieve; and albeit I was somehow upheld before the Lord by those aids wherewith he sustains our souls in affliction, among men, however, I was almost a nonentity; so far at least as regards my discharge of duty, I appeared to myself quite as unfit for it as if I had been half dead."[133] While Calvin is no stranger to the rhetorical flourishes of Renaissance epistolography, to which some of this pathos may be chalked up, one would nevertheless be hard-pressed to paint Calvin as stern and lacking empathy after reading his letters. He ends the letter with a bit of practical advice, which, in context, may also temper his interpretation above: "It is difficult, you will say, so to shake off or supress the love of a father, as not to experience grief on occasion of losing a son. Neither do I insist upon your laying aside all grief. Nor, in the school of Christ, do we learn any such philosophy as requires us to put off that common humanity with which God has endowed us, that being men, we should be turned into stones. These considerations reach only so far as this, that you do set bounds, and, as it were, temper even your most reasonable sadness; that, having shed those tears which were due to nature and to fatherly affection, you by no means give way to senseless wailing."[134]

Calvin's affective ideal would seem to fall along a Peripatetic trajectory wherein the passions are not eschewed altogether, but are understood to be appropriate within certain bounds – submissive, if not to reason, then at least to the will of God.[135] Irena Backus has argued, however, that while Calvin appropriates many aspects of Greco-Roman philosophical anthropology, his own position has it that reason and the passions work together harmoniously in pre-lapsarian Adam, rather than the passions being ideally governed by reason, as in the Peripatetic and Stoic positions.[136] Similarly, describing Calvin in an article on Reformed affections, Elizabeth Agnew Cochran writes that "virtue, rather than reason, offers a standard that moderates and directs the appropriate exercise of the emotions."[137] This seems generally to be the case, and it is an absolutely fundamental qualification: Calvin will speak often of the emotions exceeding moderation, or going against the will of God, but typically doesn't appeal to reason as the hegemon in discussion of the disordered passions. He writes, for instance, in his comments on Gethsemane in the 1555 *Commentary on the Gospel Harmony*: "The weakness of the flesh that Christ assumed ought to be distinguished from ours, for it stands far apart. There is no affection in us devoid of sin, because they all exceed proper limits and moderation; but when Christ had been troubled by sorrow and fear, he did not rise against God, but remained composed toward the true rule of moderation."[138]

However, in his gloss on Jesus' weeping over the death of Lazarus – similarly comparing Christ's regulated emotions to everyone else's unregulated ones – Calvin writes that human emotions are never directed towards a proper end, and that no one rejoices or grieves appropriately or as far as God permits, except Christ, who never had a passion which exceeded its limits, nor one that was not "grounded in right reason and judgment" (*ex ratione rectoque iudicio suscepta*). He suggests further that Adam's prelapsarian affections "yielded and submitted to reason" (*affectus ... morigeros et rationi obsequentes*).[139] Moreover, "Christ assumed human affections, but without *ataxia*"; he was disordered in himself and vehemently shaken but did not transgress the Father's will; and his passions are to ours "as a clear and tranquil stream is to a wild and muddy spume."[140] Calvin here presents a fairly conventional classical account of the relationship between reason and the passions, one that was presented in popular Renaissance Christian works such as Erasmus' *Enchiridion*. But the "baptism" of the emotions becomes clearer in the following lines, where Calvin reverts to an understanding of emotion as appropriate within the bounds of Christian piety. The goal is not to eradicate the emotions, Calvin continues, but to order them in conformity with the will of God. In the next paragraph Calvin invokes 1 Thess. 4:13 and Paul's advice that we ought to grieve in moderation, an explicit instance of the tendency, described by Pitkin, of Calvin's reading of John's Gospel through "Pauline lenses."[141] He concludes his annotation with a condemnation of the "unbending iron of Stoicism" with its "stone-like insensibility," and, despite the great gulf between Christ's emotions and ours, advocates following Christ's example.[142] Because Christ has taken on human affection (*in se recepit Christus nostros affectus*), he has made it possible that his followers might subdue the sinfulness of their emotions (*ut eius virtute subigere possimus, quicquid in illis vitiosum est*).[143] This is a multilayered gloss with several aims, much like the diversity Calvin employs in his sermon on Gethsemane, and it cannot be mapped neatly onto any of the previously regnant conceptions of theological anthropology inherited from antiquity and perpetuated through the Christian tradition.

What, then, do we make of this complicated confluence of the ethics of emotion? William Bouwsma argued that a tension between Stoicism and Augustinianism had displaced in the Renaissance the older competition between Aristotelianism and Platonism, and this gets us some way to accounting for some of the tendencies we've traced in this chapter. Contrasting Augustinian with Stoic anthropology, Bouwsma writes that "the primary organ in Augustinian anthropology is not so much that which is highest as that which is central; it is literally the heart (*cor*), whose quality determines the quality of the whole."[144] We have seen how Calvin at times elevates the heart to serve as the primary organ of piety, and at others how he intimates that the passions ought to be subservient to reason, a tension that was common in sixteenth-century attempts to navigate competing philosophies of emotion. It should be noted that any history of emotion's "triumph over reason" that characterizes "humanism" as a movement that embraces "rationalist self-determination," and "Calvinism" as one that is opposed to such a movement on account of its recognition of human depravity, does not adequately account for the complexities of the relationship between reason and emotion in Erasmus and Calvin.[145] Instead, an affective rhetorical theology finds robust representation in the sixteenth-century biblical-humanist conceptions of a Christian philosophy grounded on Paul's foolishness of God and folly of the cross. More specifically, it must also be admitted that the language and conception of emotion found in the texts considered here is also not systematic, but rhetorical. There are felt anxieties about conceding too much to classical philosophical conceptions, and there are clear attempts to reformulate descriptive anthropological language in biblical terms, but there is also some hedging, which makes it difficult at times to pin down exactly what operative conceptions underlie these biblical-humanist attempts to adjudicate an ethics of emotion in the context of New Testament exegesis. Nevertheless, while the richly complex accounts considered above derive their rich complexity from the competing schools of thought that make the sixteenth century such a fascinating and fertile time in intellectual history, I hope to have shown that there are clear connections between the more abstract positive evaluations of affectivity associated with sixteenth-century Pauline denunciations of frigid intellectualism in theological discourse and the ways in which emotionality in a concrete form also features as a part of the grounding of the Christian philosophy for Erasmus, Calvin, and other sixteenth-century biblical humanists.

Conclusion

I have attempted in this book to trace the ways in which a small but prominent group of northern European Christian humanists and reformers sought to articulate a robust *philosophia Christiana* as a kind of theology that is constitutive of biblical and, more specifically, Pauline discourse and method. The foolishness of God, as outlined originally by Paul in his first letter to the Corinthians, came to serve as a foundational feature of biblical-humanist theology in the sixteenth century as well as a lens through which to interpret competing philosophies, theological approaches, and other biblical texts. Erasmus articulated the most comprehensive biblical-humanist theology of foolishness, and I have thus also attempted to mark out several of the ways in which the reception of Erasmus, whether direct or mediated, heavily informed the exegesis and theology of Reformed Protestant exegetes in the first half of the sixteenth century, most notably John Calvin. Erasmus' unparalleled appreciation of the multiform usefulness of Pauline folly and his repeated attempts to outline a properly Christian approach to philosophy and rhetoric provided an extraordinarily rich backdrop for exegetes in his wake to articulate their own versions of the Christian philosophy. Erasmus' interpretations of the early chapters of First Corinthians, of Colossians 2, and of Christ's emotional agony in the Gospels, in his *Annotations*, *Paraphrases*, and elsewhere, constituted a theological and methodological framework for anyone who looked to his exegesis for guidance.

Calvin, far from confining himself to an exegetical circle made up of Protestants (like those mentioned in his dedicatory letter to the Romans commentary), is constantly engaged with the works of Erasmus in his exegetical endeavours on the New Testament, and a closer examination of this relationship through his commentaries reveals Erasmus to have been an underappreciated influence on his thought. Perhaps Erasmus' fallout with Luther over such a crucial question as the freedom of the will contributed to obscuring the lines of explicit reception and influence that can be drawn from Erasmus' exegetical works in second-generation Protestant circles, but if we read his New Testament scholarship closely alongside the commentaries of biblical humanists working in his wake, we find substantial confluence, often in surprising areas of thought. I hope to have made clear that cross-confessional influence was abundant in sixteenth-century exegesis, and that Erasmian Christian humanism loomed large over biblical scholars for several decades after his death, and despite formal and informal pronouncements against him on both sides of the Protestant/Catholic divide.

As a coda to the book, let us consider a final example. Calvin's commentary on the prologue to the Gospel of John illustrates nicely the complex religious context in which Erasmus' exegetical works were received in the decades after they were first published, and it also links Calvin explicitly to an Erasmian *theologia rhetorica*. As was mentioned previously, Calvin defends Erasmus' translation of *logos* as *sermo* in John 1:1, a translation that directly bears on the foundations of a humanist rhetorical theology insofar as it designates God's revelation in Christ as continuous discourse rather than as a single word, contrary to the Vulgate's *verbum*.[1] "If theology is the verbal imitation of the divine *Logos*," writes Marjorie O'Rourke Boyle, "then it matters profoundly to know whether this paradigm is one single word of a complete oration."[2] Erasmus himself sided firmly with the latter, and he had defended his translation in an ever-expanding annotation on the verse through successive editions of his New Testament notes, and had also published, in 1520, a treatise solely dedicated to the translation of this word. In his own commentary, Calvin economically summarizes the importance of Erasmus' defence of his translation, complete with Erasmian language of Pauline accommodation, in an exegetical context of utmost doctrinal importance. Christine Christ-von Wedel has noted the controversy that arises from Erasmus' translation, but in arguing that certain Protestant exegetes follow Erasmus' *meaning* while retaining the translation of *verbum*, she claims that, aside from Zwingli and Beza, "only the radical Antitrinitarians adopted Erasmus' translation."[3]

Calvin, though, also follows Erasmus' rendering not only in his gloss but in his biblical text as well (as had Oecolampadius, it may be noted), and Calvin's choice no doubt influenced Beza's decision to include *sermo* in his edition of the New Testament printed by Estienne in 1556, along with the accompanying footnote of approbation: *recte mutavit Erasmus*.[4] In his gloss, Calvin reiterates several points Erasmus had made in his *Apologia* and in his *Paraphrase on John* 1:1; for instance, that speech is truly the image of the mind, and that it is thus appropriate for God to have expressed his hidden wisdom and his will to us specifically via his *Sermo*.[5] Erasmus' *Paraphrase* is replete with strong pronouncements against human ingenuity in attempting to understand the divine mysteries, much like his exegesis of Paul's discourse on folly, a theme that would have resonated strongly with Calvin. Relatedly, for Calvin, other renderings of *logos*, such as *definitio*, *ratio*, or *supputatio*, are lexically *possible*, as Erasmus too had noted,[6] but are especially inappropriate on account of their sophistical overtones: "I do not wish," Calvin writes, "for my faith to be overtaken by subtle philosophizing. We see moreover that the Spirit of God is so far from approving of such quibbling, that in babbling to us he proclaims how sober-minded we should be in pursuing wisdom regarding divine mysteries."[7] These lines abound with Erasmianisms, and they resonate heavily with themes considered above in the exegesis of Pauline folly, effectively providing a bridge between Pauline and Johannine approaches to divine discursive revelation.

Calvin's invocation of the notion that speech is the image of the mind, crucial for understanding the full force of this novel departure from the Vulgate, is found repeatedly in Erasmus' attempts to articulate the substantial importance of discursive modes for proper Christian teaching. It is also linked to the broader affective aspects of biblical-humanist rhetorical theology, as we have seen Calvin indicate earlier in the commentary on 1 Cor. 2:11: *Lingua*, he writes there, is the *character mentis*, which makes it possible for humans to communicate their *affectus* to one another.[8] In the adage *Muti magistri* (silent teachers), Erasmus attributes the idea to Aristotle (although it isn't clear where he found it): "Just as the spoken words, according to Aristotle, are a kind of image of the meaning in the mind, so the shapes of letters can properly be called reflections, as it were, of the sounds of speech. Nor is it to be wondered at if that direct image of the heart proves a better way of reproducing and communicating the soul's intentions than that other method, writing, which imitates the imitation rather than the thing itself."[9] As early as the *Enchiridion* (1503), Erasmus describes the *imago mentis* of Christ as explicated in the words of the Gospels, and writes that *oratio* reveals the image of the mind more aptly than Apelles could represent the body in painting.[10] "There could be no dissimilarity between the archetype of the divine mind [*pectoris*] and the form of speech [*imaginem sermonis*] that issued from it."[11] A similar sentiment is repeated throughout the *Ciceronianus*, Erasmus' dialogue condemning an over-eager reliance on classical forms of rhetoric. There Erasmus expands on the fact that speech is truly reflective of the very personal, subjective and affective essence of the person speaking: "All that you have devoured in a long course of varied reading must be thoroughly digested and by the action of thought incorporated into your deepest mental processes ... Then your mind, fattened on fodder of all kinds, will generate out of its own resources not a speech redolent of this or that flower or leaf or herb, but one redolent of your personality, your sensitivities, your feelings [*indolem affectusque pectoris tui*]."[12]

Erasmus' point here is that the affective interior comprising the speaking subject can be genuinely revealed through speech that is free of superfluous (in this case Ciceronian) devices: "Your speech will not be a patchwork or a mosaic, but a lifelike portrait of the person you really are, a river welling out from your inmost being."[13] In the *Ecclesiastes*, his manual for preachers and last published major work, Erasmus writes (echoing Augustine's *De Trinitate* rather more than anything in Aristotle), "A man's speech is the truthful image of his mind, reflected in his words as in a mirror; 'for thoughts proceed from the heart'."[14] In these later works on Christian rhetoric, the *affective* connection between truth and language is striking. Thomas Aquinas is chided in the *Ciceronianus* for being ἀπαθὴς *in dicendo* – passionless in his speech (i.e., his writing) – so that he only teaches, but does not also move the reader, an insufficient approach for the Christian teacher. Aquinas had avoided the Scylla of Ciceronianism but had been swallowed up by the Charybdis of cold and dry scholastic discourse. Furthermore, and conversely, echoing Bulephorus in the *Ciceronianus*, Erasmus writes in the *Ecclesiastes*, "if it differs from the heart from which it proceeds, it does not even deserve the name of speech, no more indeed than a mask deserves to be called a face."[15] Speech is the *imago mentis* and likewise the heart is the *fons orationis* for Erasmus. When this conception of the role of language is then coupled with God's revelation in Christ as *Sermo*, the substance of the Erasmian *theologia rhetorica* is more plainly in view.[16]

Moreover, and like Erasmus' *Paraphrase*, Calvin's commentary on John 1:1 is preoccupied with establishing orthodox Trinitarianism against heretical accounts.[17] Thus, after a lengthy digression attacking the contemporary antitrinitarian Michael Servetus' position, Calvin writes, "I wonder what moved the Latins to translate λόγος as 'verbum.' Such a rendering would have been more appropriate for ῥῆμα. But even granting that 'verbum' is a permissible rendering, it is not possible to deny that 'Sermo' is a much better translation. Thus is made evident the sort of barbarous tyranny exercised by the pseudo-theologians, who relentlessly harassed Erasmus for changing one word for the better."[18] In this note we find Calvin castigating the theologasters of the universities while defending Erasmus for a translation conducive to establishing a *theologia rhetorica* for its reconceptualization of divine discursive revelation incarnate in the humble person of Christ, the Speech of God. Calvin is, moreover, no doubt well aware of the far-reaching implications and previous controversy attendant to changing merely one word. It is worth noting that the complexity of Erasmus' influence is perhaps nowhere more evident, or ironic, than in the fact that Calvin's criticisms of Servetus are grounded in Erasmus' famously controversial translation, couched in Erasmian language, and finished off with a positive reference to the Dutchman himself. For Servetus was, after all, also an "Erasmian" of sorts, and he too had quoted from Erasmus' *Annotations* on John in his *De Trinitatis erroribus* of 1531, a work that would ultimately contribute to his being burned at the stake in Calvin's Geneva, just a few months after Calvin's own commentary on John was published.[19] It is a striking, if troubling, example of the richly diverse way in which Erasmus was received in the sixteenth century.

Whether or not we wish to employ the term "Erasmianism," intellectual historians, theologians, and historians of biblical interpretation in the sixteenth century must keep Erasmus (and especially the still under-studied *Annotations* and *Paraphrases*) in mind as possibly influential at almost every turn when reading exegetes and theologians who would have had access to Erasmus' works, regardless of what became of them confessionally in their later careers. While this is true especially of exegetical and theological conclusions, it also holds for literary trivia. A final example that encompasses both conclusions in Calvin's thought comes in the 1559 *Institutes*: arguing against the intellectual possibility of atheism, Calvin writes that when Diagoras of Melos and Dionysius of Syracuse "jest at whatever has been believed in every age" and "mock the heavenly judgment," it is a form of "sardonic laughter" (*sardonius risus*), "for the worm of conscience, sharper than any cauterizing iron, gnaws away within."[20] In an editorial note in his English edition of the *Institutes*, John McNeill suggests that Calvin uses the expression *sardonius risus* "probably with a recollection" of a proverb from Virgil about the bitterness of Sardinian herbs. Much more likely, however, is that Calvin had found the reference in Erasmus' *Adages*, where we find a lengthy entry precisely on *Risus Sardonius*, and even more specifically a reference to Plutarch's *De Superstitione* in the context of atheism: "Note therefore," Erasmus quotes Plutarch as writing, "on these occasions that the man who believes there are no gods laughs with a mad, sardonic laugh."[21] As with the example of Calvin's use of the term *morosophos* and his revision of the adage "ass at the lyre" mentioned earlier, Calvin's literary wit, too, is often derived from his reading of Erasmus' works, even if his debts go unacknowledged.

As interesting as these moments are, and they can no doubt be multiplied, I have attempted in the preceding chapters to disclose through close-reading some continuities of thought regarding the reception and rejection of classical philosophical norms in biblical-humanist exegetical texts, as well as a shared discourse in the articulation of a theological method in these works. While Erasmus' glosses show up repeatedly in the works of Protestants in Switzerland, and explicitly and unrepentantly in those of the Zurich reformers, a theological approach informed by an Erasmian-Pauline rhetorical theology is taken up extensively by Calvin as well. From the perspective of a *philosophia Christiana*, all these exegetes thrived in a common intellectual and, more specifically, exegetical milieu. If debts are not often explicitly acknowledged, it may perhaps be that the rhetorical costs of citing Erasmus as an influence outweighed the advantages for someone like Calvin, who spent much of his energy attempting to unify the Protestant cause.[22] Indeed, Erasmus died in the same year that Calvin published his first edition of the *Institutes*, and by that time vocal enthusiasm for a distinctively Erasmian Christian humanism was no longer fashionable in Protestant circles.

Nevertheless, if we peer through the cracks, we find that the force of Erasmus' interpretations of Pauline folly, his endeavours at establishing a kind of rhetorical theology with the intention of displacing a particular kind of university theological method, and his integration of his reading of Paul into other exegetical and theological works are fundamental to the continued development of biblical humanism in the decades after his death. As N. Scott Amos describes Bucer and other participants in the "Rhenish school" of exegetical theology (a group of theologians to which Calvin himself was intimately linked from his time in Strasbourg in the late 1530s), they "heeded Erasmus' plea for a reorientation of theology away from a focus on abstract, speculative questions and towards one centered on exegesis of the Bible."[23] This is a very different conclusion than the one put forth by other historiographical approaches that too readily imagine Erasmus and Calvin as inhabiting totally different theological worldviews, as Robert Coogan does when he writes that "Calvin could not, like Erasmus, be at ease in Hellas."[24] The ostensible implication of such a claim is that while Erasmus attempted to straddle the boundary between the proverbial domains of Athens and Jerusalem, his "conservative" critics, like Lee, Beda, Luther, and apparently Calvin, settled firmly in Jerusalem. I hope the analysis of Pauline folly and the Christian philosophy provided here has nuanced any such narrative about theological relationships in the sixteenth century. When one examines closely certain exegetical and theological works of many biblical humanists in the period, it becomes very difficult to draw firm lines between "Renaissance" and "Reformation," or "humanist" and "Protestant," or to carve up large and complicated intellectual trends along confessional lines.

The reorientation of theology in the sixteenth century among biblical humanists is part and parcel of an understanding of the theological enterprise as foolish to the world. It is, I'd suggest, at this point in the history of biblical interpretation that biblical humanism and the Christian philosophy cohere. Thus, at another level of reception history, this book has sought to outline the ways in which Paul's discourse on foolishness and wisdom grounded early sixteenth-century biblical-humanist Christian philosophy in fundamental ways. It is not only an epistemological reorientation that can be substantiated in the discourse of foolishness; the effects of foolishness are felt strongly elsewhere. The epistemological is intimately connected with the anthropological, and with the diminution of the significance of reason we find an increasing appreciation of the affective elements of Christian life and discourse. While in future studies I hope to tease out this connection further, the final chapter aimed to show how the concrete example of Christ's emotions offered sixteenth-century thinkers some interesting dilemmas, and to make explicit certain aspects of an already implicit affective theology.

Attending to biblical commentaries and other theological works with an eye towards how the emotions and affectivity are understood can thus also be illuminating and can reveal new contours of thought and influence that have been hitherto neglected in intellectual history. In the early modern period it is especially revealing of the ways in which theologians with humanist training navigated available philosophical discourses (in this case especially the tension between Stoic and Aristotelian accounts) in the context of their own attempts to appreciate what the biblical text had to offer in terms of constructing a normative account of the ethics of emotion. Christ's emotions become both the model that justifies Christian emotion and at the same time the one impossible to imitate. Christ's humility is in this way yet another example of the foolishness of God that proves problematic for the – in this case Stoic – wisdom of this world. And here again the lines of influence and corroboration in biblical commentary can only be comprehended through close reading.

Finally, we have seen that it was not only Paul's letter to the Romans that had a profound impact on sixteenth-century Christian thought, even if interpretations of it rested at the centre of Catholic and Protestant disputes over the issue of justification which ultimately proved an insurmountable ecclesiastical obstacle. Pauline folly shapes the language of religious epistemology, ethics, and anthropology, especially for those who considered a certain kind of theological methodology prominent among university theologians to be inhibitive of true piety and the spreading of a simple gospel. The way in which theology and theological method is conceived by Erasmus, determined as it is by his Pauline understanding of wisdom, which puts limits on approaches to theology as an abstract scholarly discipline, would come to have palpable influence on the evangelical philosophies of early Protestants. In terms of theological discourse, Erasmus' Pauline Christian philosophy, as it is grounded in the early chapters of 1 Corinthians, is articulated so as to preclude "Aristotelianism" (as metonymy for abstruse dialectical theology) as well as "Ciceronianism" (as metonymy for slavish devotion to classical rhetoric) as conducive scaffolding for doing theology. That is, the philosophies and rhetorical strategies of pagan antiquity are denounced in favour of a Pauline philosophy and rhetoric of simplicity. *Philosophia* and *persuasio* are redefined in a way that results in scholastic argumentation and extravagant rhetoric being ideally displaced, methodologically, by Christian affective mimesis: Paul, as the consummate rhetorical theologian, becomes the model of the Christian teacher whose duty is to *transform* as much as to *teach*; or, rather, whose duty is to teach by way of transformation.

Christian antiphilosophy is an essential aspect of the Christian philosophy in this period. It is remarkable, then, that much more recently we find Étienne Gilson arguing on the one hand that any Christian philosophy worth its name must be immenently rational, and Alain Badiou arguing on the other that Paul's discourse on foolishness is "incompatible with any prospect ... of a 'Christian philosophy'."[25] The approach of Erasmus and Calvin diverges from both of these paths: the substance of the Christian philosophy is found precisely in the foolishness of God.

Notes

Preface

1 *Paraphrase on First Corinthians*, from *Collected Works of Erasmus*, vol. 43:11; The Latin is provided from *Tomus secundus continens Paraphrasim in omneis epistolas apostolicas* (Basel: Froben, 1532, 75): Tanta zizaniorum vis coorta est, quae teneram etiamnum, et herbescentem Christi sementem penem obruit, mox philosophia mundana, mox Iudaica superstitio, reus de composito iunctis copiis in Christum conspirabat, philosophia dissuadebat resurrectionem, et humanis argutiis nonnihil vitiare coepit Evangelii synceritatem ... Philosophia tum per morosophos suos libris ac linguis, per tyrannos gladiis etiam grassabatur in pusillum ac simplicem Christi gregem, vestigiis et in haec usque tempora relictis.

2 *Paraclesis* (trans. John Olin [1975]), 93. At ego sane si quid huiusmodi votis proficitur, tantisper dum mortales omneis, ad sanctissimum ac saluberrimum Christiane philosophiae studium adhortor, ac veluti classicum canens evoco, vehementer optarim eloquentiam mihi dari, longe aliam quam fuerit Ciceroni. Si minus picturatam quam fuit illius, certe multo magis efficacem (*Novum Instrumentum omne*, Froben: 1516, aaa3.

3 Si qua Pitho vere flexanima, eam mihi cupiam in praesentia supperere, quo rem omnium saluberrimam omnibus persuadeam. Quorum illud potius optandum ut Christus ipse cuius negocium agitur, ita citharae nostrae chordas temperet, ut haec cantilena penitus afficiat ac moveat animos omnium. Ad quod quidem efficiendum, nihil opus rhetorum epicherematis, aut epiphonematis (*Novum Instrumentum omne*, Froben: 1516, aaa3).

4 Exhortations to the *philosophia Christiana* also come in the dedicatory letter of the *Novum Instrumentum*, addressed to Pope Leo X; see Ep. 384 in CWE

3:221–4. And similar themes – with references to the *philosophia Christiana*, the foolishness of God, and to *pia curiositas* – resonate through Erasmus' letter to the reader for the *Paraphrase on Matthew* (see CWE 45).

5 *Paraclesis* (trans. Olin), 96. Praesertim cum hoc sapientiae genus, tam eximium ut semel stultam reddiderit universam huius mundi sapientiam, ex paucis hisce libris, velut e limpidissimis fontibus haurire liceat, longe minore negocio, quam ex tot voluminibus spinosis, extam immensis, iisque inter se pugnantibus interpretum commentariis Aristotelicam doctrinam (*Novum Instrumentum omne*, Froben: 1516, aaa4).

6 *Paraclesis* (trans. Olin), 96. Haec omnibus ex aequo sese accommodat, submittit se parvulis, ad illorum modulum sese attemperat, lacte illos alens, etc. (*Novum Instrumentum omne*, Froben, 1516).

7 Hoc philosophiae genus in affectibus situm verius, quam in syllogismis, vita magis est quam disputatio, afflatus potius quam eruditio, transformatio magis quam ratio (*Novum Instrumentum omne*, Froben, 1516).

8 *Comm. 1 Cor.* 1:21 (my translation); *In omnes Pauli epistolas ...* (Estienne, 1556, ad loc.): Concessio est, quod evangelium stultitiam praedicationis vocat, quae in speciem talis consetur istis *morosophois*, qui falsa confidentia ebrii nihil verentur sacrosanctam Dei veritatem insipidae suae censurae subiicere. Et sane alioqui humanae rationi absurdius nihil est quam audire Deum mortalem, vitam morti obnoxiam, iustitiam peccati similitudine obtectam, benedictionem subiectam maledictioni ...

9 See, e.g., *The Praise of Folly* (trans. Clarence Miller), 13n8. "Foolosophers," Miller notes, was actually in the first English translation of the *Moria* by Thomas Chaloner (1549). Miller also notes that the word appears in the *De copia* and the *Adagia*, and it also appears in the dedicatory letter of the *Paraphrase on First Corinthians* as well as in the *De immensa dei misericordia* (CWE 70:123).

10 Welborn, *Paul, the Fool of Christ*, 6. See also Bruce Winter, *Philo and Paul Among the Sophists* (Cambridge, 1997); Daniel Boyarin, "Paul Among the Antiphilosophers; Or, Saul Among the Sophists," in *St. Paul Among the Philosophers*, ed. John D. Caputo and Linda Martín Alcoff (Indiana UP, 2009), 109–41; also Margaret Mitchell's work on 1 Corinthians itself and its reception by some of the early fathers (especially Chrysostom) for a substantial contribution to understanding the reception history of this text: *Paul, the Corinthians and the Birth of Christian Hermeneutics; The Heavenly Trumpet: John Chrysostom and the Art of Biblical Interpretation;* and *Paul and the Rhetoric of Reconciliation.*

11 *Comm. 1 Cor.* 3:19 (trans. Fraser, 81); Estienne, 1556, fol. 173: Argumentum est a contrariis. Positio unius contrarii alterum destruit. Quum ergo

sapientia mundi, stultitia sit apud Deum: sequitur non posse aliter nos sapere coram Deo, nisi secundum mundum stulti simus. Iam exposuimus quid significet per mundi sapientiam: naturalis enim perspicacia, Dei donum est. Artes ingenuae, et doctrinae omnes, quibus prudentia colligitur, Dei sunt dona. At suis limitibus continentur: neque enim usque ad caeleste Dei regnum penetrant: quare pedisequas esse oportet, non dominas: imo inanes et nihili reputari convenit, donec verbo Spirituique Dei subiectae prorsus fuerint. Si autem se Christo opponant, noxias esse pestes: si per se valere aliquid contendant, pessima esse impedimenta sentiendum est.

12 On the diversity of "Pauls" in the sixteenth century, see especially R. Ward Holder's introduction to, and the collection of essays in *A Companion to Paul in the Reformation* (ed. Holder).

13 Gordon, *Calvin*, 109.

14 Gordon, *Calvin*, 110.

1. Calvin's Erasmus, *Theologia Rhetorica*, and Pauline Folly

1 See, especially, Rummel, *Erasmus'* Annotations *on the New Testament*. Commemorating the 2016 quincentennial of Erasmus' *Novum Instrumentum*, multiple essay collections and journal special issues dealing with Erasmus' NT and its reception were yet forthcoming when this book was going to press. But see the helpful essays in Wallraff et al., *Basel 1516: Erasmus' Edition of the New Testament* (Mohr Siebeck, 2016).

2 For the history, see the introduction to CWE, vol. 42.

3 *In universas epistolas apostolorum ab ecclesia receptas, hoc est, Pauli quatuordecim, Petri duas, Iudae unam, Iacobi unam, Ioannis treis, paraphrasis, hoc est, liberior ac dilucidior interpretatio ...* (Froben, 1522).

4 See esp. CWE, vol. 42, xv–xvi; CWE, vol. 43, xii–xiii; Cottier, "Erasmus' Paraphrase: A New Kind of Commentary?" in Pabel and Vessey, *Holy Scripture Speaks*. See also Chomarat, *Grammaire et rhétorique*, esp. 593–604.

5 Rummel, "Why Noel Beda Did Not Like Erasmus' *Paraphrases*," 265ff. Beda's work, *Annotationum libri duo* (1526), was also directed at Lefevre d'Etaples' notes on the New Testament.

6 For Calvin's association with such circles before landing in Geneva, see Gordon's recent biography, *Calvin*.

7 Chrysostom outpaces him occasionally in individual commentaries.

8 As for Calvin's biblical text, we can say that Calvin is obviously reading the Greek (and Hebrew, in the case of the OT) original in offering his own translation and commentary, which he would have had access to

in Erasmus' various editions; these contained Erasmus' Greek edition and Erasmus' Latin translation in parallel columns, and the 1527 version also included the Vulgate in a third column. There was also a student edition published by Colinaeus in Paris in 1534 – which Parker shows Calvin did use through the 1540s but that gradually gave way to Erasmus' 1527 edition – and Estienne included a Greek text in his 1546 *Biblia*, both of which were dependent in large part, but not solely, on Erasmus' editions. As far as the Latin goes, Calvin obviously knew well the Vulgate and Erasmus' editions, for he engages with both often (and the latter became the *textus receptus* for Estienne and Beza; see Gilmont, *John Calvin and the Printed Book*, 147). He also would have known and used Estienne's marginalia and the *Biblia*. Other textual variants, in Greek and Latin, would have been found in the Church Fathers and in Erasmus' *Annotations*. In short, apart from the question of which he preferred (for this differed over the course of his composing the commentaries), Calvin had and used several sources for the Greek and the Latin of the New Testament. For an analysis of the various versions available to Calvin (Greek and Latin), see Parker, *Calvin's New Testament Commentaries*, 119–91. Also Gilmont, *John Calvin and the Printed Book*, esp. 143–56, and Engammare, "Cinquante ans de révision de la traduction biblique d'Olivetan," 347–77, and "Calvin connaissait-il la Bible?" 163–84.

9 See Parker, *Calvin's New Testament Commentaries*, 158–84, and Lane, *John Calvin: Student of the Church Fathers*, e.g., 4; Lane's work also mentions Erasmus as a source for Calvin in the context of his reception of the Fathers, variously throughout his book.

10 See Parker, *Calvin's New Testament Commentaries*, 158–84.

11 Die weitaus größte Bedeutung hat für Calvin die Auslegung des Erasmus in dessen "Annotationes," mit der er sich beständig, zustimmend und ablehnend, auseinandersetzt (p. XXIII).

12 See, e.g., Mansfield, *Phoenix of His Age*, 93–7.

13 See the early, but still good, example of Wendel, *Calvin: The Origins and Development of His Religious Thought*; also Ganoczy, *The Young Calvin*. The best biography is Gordon, *Calvin*, esp. 1–63. And see the extensive work of Millet, *Calvin et la dynamique de la parole*.

14 See, especially, "Calvinism as Theologia Rhetorica?"; also "Calvin and the Renaissance Crisis of Knowing," 190–211, and his biography *John Calvin: A Sixteenth-Century Portrait* (esp. ch. 7).

15 Wendel, *Calvin: Origins and Development of His Religious Thought*, esp. 31; also Battles and Hugo, *Calvin's Commentary on Seneca's De Clementia*, 79–81.

16 For explicit comparisons, see Compier, "The Independent Pupil: Calvin's Transformation of Erasmus' Theological Hermeneutics," 217–33; and Brashler, "From Calvin to Erasmus: Exploring the Roots of Reformed Hermeneutics"; Ganoczy and Scheld, *Die Hermeneutik Calvins*, esp. 83ff. See also Holder, *John Calvin and the Grounding of Interpretation*, passim.

17 *Calvin et la dynamique de la parole: Étude de rhétorique réformée*, 154–5, 575–6, 874. See also idem, "*Docere/movere*: les catégories rhétoriques et leurs sources humanistes dans la doctrine calvinienne de la foi," 35–51. See also Huijgen, *Divine Accommodation in John Calvin's Theology*, 126–31, and our treatment of the issue of accommodation in ch. 3 below, which diverges from Huijgen's analysis.

18 *The Renaissance Bible: Scholarship, Sacrifice, and Subjectivity*.

19 In "The Influence of Erasmus' *Annotationes* on Calvin's Galatians Commentary," 268–83. See also the valuable articles by Mellinghoff-Bourgerie: "De la 'philosophie du Christ' d'Erasme à la doctrine de Calvin," 99–126 and "Calvin emule d'Erasme: L'irriducibilitie d'une conscience humaniste" in *Calvin et ses contemporains* (ed. Olivier Millet) 225–45; also Backus, "L'influence de l'exégèse d'Erasme sur le milieu calvinien à Genève," 141–7; Kirk Essary, "The Radical Humility of Christ in the 16th Century: Erasmus and Calvin on Philippians 2:6–7"; idem, "Milk for Babes: Erasmus and Calvin on the Problem of Christian Eloquence"; and idem, "Calvin's Interpretation of Christ's Agony at Gethsemane: An Erasmian Reading?".

20 See Christ-von Wedel, *Erasmus of Rotterdam: Advocate of a New Christianity*, 183–202; idem, "Erasmus und die Zurcher Reformatoren: Huldrich Zwingli, Leo Jud, Konrad Pellikan, Heinrich Bullinger und Theodor Bibliander," *Erasmus in Zurich*. Also Wengert, *Human Freedom, Christian Righteousness: Melanchthon's Exegetical Dispute with Erasmus of Rotterdam*; John Payne, "Erasmus' Influence on Zwingli and Bullinger," in *Biblical Interpretation in the Era of the Reformation* (ed. Muller and Thompson); Farmer, *The Gospel of John in the Sixteenth Century*, ch. 4; and, most recently, Amos, *Bucer, Ephesians and Biblical Humanism*.

21 See also Pabel, "Praise and Blame: Peter Canisius' Ambivalent Reception of Erasmus," *The Reception of Erasmus in the Early Modern Period*.

22 Amos, *Bucer, Ephesians and Biblical Humanism*, 38.

23 See Dodds, *Exploiting Erasmus*, 14ff.

24 For a recent analysis with bibliography, see Muller, *Calvin and the Reformed Tradition*.

25 See, e.g., Dodds, *Exploiting Erasmus*, 3.

26 The extensive bibliography cannot be reproduced wholly here, but far and away the most comprehensive overview of Erasmus' influence and reception are Bruce Mansfield's invaluable three volumes: *Phoenix of His Age*, *Man on His Own*, and *Erasmus in the Twentieth Century*. The field begins, in many ways, with Marcel Bataillon's enormously influential *Erasme et l'Espagne*; see also more recently Seidel Menchi, *Erasmo in Italia: 1520–1580*; Bietenholz, *Encounters with a Radical Erasmus*; Dodds, *Exploiting Erasmus*; Enenkel, ed., *The Reception of Erasmus in the Early Modern Period*. For a nice recent overview of Erasmus' uneasy place in the contemporary humanities, see Cummings, "Erasmus and the Invention of Literature," 23–54.

27 For recent discussion and bibliography, see the introduction to Enenkel, ed., *The Reception of Erasmus in the Early Modern Period*, 1–10.

28 Enenkel, ed., *The Reception*, 10.

29 Gordon, *Calvin*, 104–5.

30 Kok, *The Influence of Martin Bucer on John Calvin's Interpretation of Romans*; and Kolbet, "Heinrich Bullinger's Exegetical Method: The Model For John Calvin's?" On Melanchthon's influence, see especially Muller, "*Scimus enim quod lex spiritualis est*: Melanchthon and Calvin on the Interpretation of Romans 7:14–23"; and on method, idem, *The Unaccommodated Calvin*, 118–59.

31 Melanchthon also wrote a *brevis commentarius*, but it wasn't published until 1561, and he gave lectures on 1 and 2 Corinthians in 1521 and 1522 – an unauthorized version of the latter was printed by his students; for analysis, see Weaver, "A More Excellent Way: Philip Melanchthon's Corinthians Lectures of 1521–1522."

32 He also uses the phrase *philosophia Christiana* to differentiate Paul's teachings from the philosophers of this world in his comment on 1 Cor. 1:10 (*In omnes apostolicas epistolas* [Zurich: Froschauer, 1539]). At any rate, documenting all of the instances of Pellikan's borrowings from Erasmus would be a monumental undertaking, and would take us far beyond our goals here, but we will occasionally note cases where substantial borrowing has taken place.

33 For an overview of trends in Erasmus scholarship in the twentieth century, see the indispensable study by Mansfield, *Erasmus in the Twentieth Century*.

34 See "Faith and Piety in Erasmus' Thought," and *Rhetoric and Theology: The Hermeneutic of Erasmus*; also "Rhetoric and Dialectic in Erasmus' and Melanchthon's Interpretation of John's Gospel."

35 For Grassi the more important question was ontological: the nominalist dethroning of a transcendental *res* as the object of philosophical knowledge, and the Renaissance interest in the particular/situational/ historical realm gave rise to a skepticism towards a particular kind of philosophizing, but not an eschewing of truth-seeking. See *Rhetoric as Philosophy: The Humanist Tradition*; cf. Schreiner, *Are You Alone Wise?* 28ff. The bibliography is large, but, aside from the following notes, see Shuger, "The Philosophical Foundations of Sacred Rhetoric," Khan, *Rhetoric, Prudence and Skepticism in the Renaissance*, and Seigel, *Rhetoric and Philosophy in Renaissance Humanism*.

36 Schreiner, *Are You Alone Wise?* 30.

37 The most prominent scholarly portrait of Erasmus as a theological skeptic is Chomarat, *Grammaire et rhétorique chez Érasme*.

38 See especially O'Rourke Boyle, *Rhetoric and Reform: Erasmus' Civil Dispute with Luther*. Boyle clarifies Erasmus' relationship to scepticism masterfully here. See also Kahn, *Rhetoric, Prudence, and Skepticism in the Renaissance*, esp. 89ff., for a partial treatment of the relationship of rhetoric and skepticism in Erasmus' *Praise of Folly* with reference to his dispute with Luther.

39 See "The Issue of Reformation and Skepticism Revisited: What Erasmus and Sebastian Castellio Did and Did Not Know," 61–90, along with the other essays in that volume, which are useful on the question of the influence of especially Pyrrhonistic skepticism in the early modern period, which wasn't available until printed editions of Sextus Empiricus appeared in 1562. Delineations between Academic and Pyrronistic skepticism in the early modern period are still only recently being appreciated and investigated in the scholarly literature. See also Hoffmann, *Rhetoric and Theology*, 18ff., for a discussion of Erasmus' rhetorical theology and its relationship to skepticism in the context of humanist-scholastic debates. Also, Marjorie O'Rourke Boyle, *Rhetoric and Reform*, chapters 1 and 2.

40 O'Rourke Boyle, *Rhetoric and Reform*, 23ff.

41 Kroeker, *Erasmus in the Footsteps of Paul*.

42 Kroeker, *Erasmus*, 7.

43 Monfasani, "Erasmus and the Philosophers," 62–3.

44 See Kroeker, *Erasmus*, 139–40.

45 Rummel, *The Humanist-Scholastic Debate in the Renaissance and Reformation*, 193. See also Moss, *Renaissance Truth and the Latin Language Turn*, 168, who points out that Erasmus in the *Ecclesiastes* has formulated a system loosely based around *loci communes* from which the preacher may "defend the truth and banish doubt."

46 For Calvin on assurance, see Zachman, *The Assurance of Faith: Conscience in the Theology of Martin Luther and John Calvin* and *Image and Word in the Theology of John Calvin*, and Schreiner, *Are You Alone Wise?*.

47 Augustine also makes the important distinction, at *De doctr. chr.* IV.75–6, between persuading of truth and moving the hearer to act upon what she already knows – to make an audience do what they already know must be done. Instruction is only one aspect of persuasion.

48 The "anti-scholastic" tendencies of the *theologia rhetorica*, which has its roots in the humanist-scholastic debates of the Renaissance more generally, are alive and well in Petrarch, although his own preference was for mysticism; see Rummel, *The Humanist-Scholastic Debate*, esp. 30–5. For the relevant implications of a broader shift from medieval Latin to a classicizing-humanist Latin idiom at this time, see Moss, *Renaissance Truth and the Latin Language Turn*.

49 Trinkaus, *Image and Likeness*, 306–7.

50 Although this latter is also important. We focus in this book rather on the implications for theological method and epistemology than on how Erasmus or Calvin used rhetorical categories in themselves (*inventio, elocutio, amplificatio, copia, dispositio*, etc.). For very good treatments of the latter, see Hoffmann, *Rhetoric and Theology* (esp. 135ff.), and also Hoffmann, "Erasmus: Rhetorical Theologian," 136–61. See also Rummel, "St. Paul in Plain Latin: Erasmus' Philological Annotations on 1 Corinthians," for an analysis of how Erasmus sought to render the Latin New Testament in a modern and intelligible style. On Calvin, see especially the final part of Millet, *Calvin*, and also Jones, *Calvin and the Rhetoric of Piety*.

51 Trinkaus, *Image and Likeness*, 126–7. On the difference between Ciceronian and Augustinian humble eloquence, see Auerbach, "*Sermo Humilis*," in his *Literary Language and Its Public in Late Latin Antiquity and in the Middle Ages*, 35ff., but note also Auerbach's suggestion that Cicero's category of lowly eloquence, too, isn't merely persuasive: "his conception of [the lowly style] is barely distinguishable from the Attic ideal (*deloun*: to make manifest – not *psychagogein*: to seduce)" (37).

52 See the introduction to CWE, vol. 66, xxviii–xxix.

53 On Calvin's understanding of *pietas*, which no doubt differs from Erasmus' in certain emphases (especially in its orientation to fearing God), see Lee, "Calvin's Understanding of Pietas," 225–40.

54 Muller, *The Unaccommodated Calvin*, 177.

55 Cummings, "Erasmus and the Invention of Literature," 23–54. I don't think I mean anything different by "rhetorical" in "rhetorical theology"

than Cummings means by "literary," although Cummings deliberately distances his own approach from rhetorical approaches to Erasmus, such as Jacques Chomarat's. As will become clear, my understanding of Erasmus' rhetorical theology is rather closer to Cummings' understanding of Erasmus' literary theology than to Chomarat's approach.

56 Gamble, "Calvin as Theologian and Exegete: Is There Anything New?" 191, quoting Torrance, *The Hermeneutics of John Calvin*, 148.

57 See Millet, "*Docere/movere*," 35–51. Millet only names Valla and Bude, and in fact errs in suggesting that Calvin "reproaches" Erasmus' translation of *plerophoria* at Luke 1:1 as "plenitude" – Calvin here reproaches the Vulgate (*vetus interpretatio*), rather: Erasmus renders it as *certissimae fidei* (see also Millet, *Calvin et la dynamique*, 212–13). See further discussion in ch. 5 below.

58 *Augustine and the Cure of Souls*, 9.

59 CWE 43:10.

60 CWE 43:10.

61 CWE 43:16.

62 CWE 43:20; from the *Argumentum* (1532, 80). Neque vero solum tumebant opibus Corinthii, verum etiam Graecanicae philosophiae supercilio, qua destitutos caeteros ut barbaros despiciebant.

63 Of course Erasmus was indebted to ancient philosophy for his own thought at various levels, which is not specifically at issue here. For a good recent assessment, see Monfasani, "Erasmus and the Philosophers," 47–68.

64 CWE 43:22; from the *Argumentum* (1532, 81): Proinde a supercilio mundanae philosophiae ad crucis humilitatem revocat, quae licet ostentationem non habeat, vim tamen et energiam habet.

65 CWE 43:21; from the *Argumentum* (1532, 81). Iam partim tumoris, partim philosophiae vitium erat, quod Paulum quidam illorum, ut tenuem atque humilem, deinde ineloquentem et imperitum fastidirent. Proptium vero philosophiae fuit, quod resurrectionem mortuorum, fidei nostrae basim, in dubium vocarent.

66 *Comm. 1 Cor.* (trans. Fraser), 1–2; I've often availed myself of Fraser's usually quite good translation of Calvin's commentary, although at times I have provided my own translations (always noted), and in every case I've checked the early modern Latin editions. Reproduced in the notes is the final version, published by Robert Estienne in 1556.

67 For an interesting study of the occasional pitfalls of book dedications in the early modern period (including for Calvin), see White, "The Perils and Possibilities of the Book Dedication."

68 Estienne, 1556, fol. 141: Sed, quae nostra omnium tarditas est vel potius
   socordia, dum frigide multi Evangelii doctrinae annuunt, vix centesimus
   quisque eius causa, si praediolum nescio quod possideat, ab ipso avelli se
   sustinet: vix quisquam, nisi aegerrime, ut minimis commodis renuntiet,
   adducitur: tantum abest ut se vita abdicare parati sint, ut decebat.
   Imprimis vero cunctos in sui abnegatione (quod est virtutum omnium
   caput) optarim tui esse similes.
69 Muller, *The Unaccommodated Calvin*, 176.
70 See also, with the important conclusion that Calvin's negative rhetorical
   sallies against the scholastics only constitute one aspect of his relationship
   to the medieval schools, Muller, "Scholasticism in Calvin: A Question of
   Relation and Disjunction," 247–65.
71 For an overview, see esp. Muller, *The Unaccommodated Calvin*, 174ff.
72 For a recent and deft handling of Erasmian biblical humanism in the
   theological method of Martin Bucer, a close colleague of Calvin's, see
   Amos, *Bucer, Ephesians and Biblical Humanism*.
73 *Comm. 1 Cor.* (trans. Fraser), 7; Estienne, 1556: Absente Paulo, subingressi
   erant pseudoapostoli, non qui dogmatibus palam impiis (meo quidem
   iudicio) turbarent ecclesiam, aut sanam doctrinam quasi ex professo
   labefactarent: sed qui verborum splendore et pompa superbientes, vel
   potius inani magniloquentia tumidi, Pauli simplicitatem, adeoque ipsum
   evangelium contemptui habarent.
74 Quin etiam doctrinae puritas concidere iam coeperat, ut praecipuum
   religionis caput, resurrectio mortuorum in dubium vocaretur.
75 *Comm. 1 Cor.* (trans. Fraser), 8; Estienne, 1556: Praeterea multum alioqui
   verborum adversus praeposteros illos doctores vel garrulos rhetores
   disputando, consumit. Perstringit eorum ambitionem: reprehendit quod
   evangelium in humanam philosophiam transfigurent.
76 *Comm. 1 Cor.* (trans. Fraser), 9; Estienne, 1556: Mortuam habent
   praedicationem, quae vivida et efficax esse debebat: et ut scenae serviant,
   evangelium fucando deformant, ut sit instar mundanae philosophiae.
77 *Comm. 1 Cor.* (trans. Fraser), 9; Estienne, 1556: Siquidem adulteratur quum
   ita inficitur nativa eius simplicitas, et quasi fucatur, ut nihil a mundana
   philosophia differat.
78 *Comm. 1 Cor.* (trans. Fraser), 10; Estienne, 1556: Ex hoc summo malo duo
   alia consequebantur: quod his quasi integumentis evangelii simplicitas
   deformabatur, et Christus tanquam nova et extranea forma induebatur, ne
   pura et nativa eius notitia exstaret. Deinde quod conversis ad verborum
   nitorem et elegantiam, ad acutas speculationes, ad inanem sublimioris
   doctrinae speciem hominum animis, spiritus energia evanescebat: nec

quidquam relinquebatur praeter mortuam literam: non apparebat Dei
maiestas, qualis in evangelio elucet, sed fucus tantum et infructuosa
pompa.

2. Foolishness as Religious Knowledge

1 Bullinger, too, discerns these as being the two primary targets in the
  argumentum to his 1534 commentary on 1 Corinthians (Prior philosophiam
  humanam, grandiloquentiam atque speculationes istas subtiliores,
  etc.). Melanchthon does not make the same distinction and, as Timothy
  Wengert has pointed out in his study on the Colossians *Scholia*, he shies
  away from condemning rhetoric too overtly (*Human Freedom, Christian
  Righteousness*, 42ff.); this is further confirmed by William Weaver's
  analysis of Melanchthon's lectures on 1 Corinthians, where on 1 Cor.
  4:20 he understands Paul's distinction between "speech" and "power" as
  pertaining to the "probable reasons of philosophy," a move he will also
  make in his exegesis of Colossians 2. See ch. 5 below, and Weaver, "A More
  Excellent Way," 31–63.
2 There is a large and ever-growing bibliography here, but for an overview
  of the debates, see Rummel, *The Humanist-Scholastic Debate*; for Erasmus'
  anti-scholasticism, see O'Rourke Boyle, *Erasmus on Language and Method in
  Theology*; for nuanced treatments in Calvin, see Muller, *The Unaccommodated
  Calvin*, esp. 39–62, and Steinmetz, *Calvin in Context*, 247–62.
3 For purposes of comparison, we reproduce the Vulgate, Erasmus' 1535
  Latin translation (available in ASD VI.3), and Calvin's translation from
  his commentary (the Estienne, 1556 edition) for each section of Paul's text
  throughout this chapter.
     Vulgate: 1:17 Non in sapientia verbi ut non evacuet crux Christi. **18**
  Verbum enim crucis pereuntibus quidem stultitia est: his autem qui salui
  fiunt: id est nobis, dei virtus est. **19** Scriptum est enim: Perdam sapientiam
  sapientium: et prudentiam prudentium reprobabo. **20** Ubi sapiens, ubi
  scriba, ubi inquisitor huius saeculi? Nonne stultam fecit deus sapientiam
  huius mundi? **21** Nam quia in dei sapientia non cognovit mundus
  per sapientiam deum: placuit deo per stultitiam praedicationis salvos
  facere credentes, **22** quoniam et Iudaei signa petunt et graeci sapientiam
  quaerunt: **23** nos autem praedicamus Christum crucifixum iudeis quidem
  scandalum gentibus autem stultitiam **24** ipsis autem vocatis Iudaeis atque
  Gracis Christum dei virtutem et dei sapientiam. **25** Quia quod stultum
  est dei: sapientius est hominibus, et quod infirmum est dei: fortius est
  hominibus. **26** Videte enim vocationem vestram fratres quia non multi

sapientes secundum carnem non multi potentes non multi nobiles: **27** sed quod stulta sunt mundi elegit deus: ut confundat sapientes, et infirma mundi elegit deus ut confundat fortia.

Erasmus (1535): 1:17 Non erudito sermone, ne inanis reddatur crux Christi. **18** Nam sermo crucis, iis quidem qui pereunt, stultitia est, at nobis qui salutem consequimur, potentia dei est. **19** Scriptum est enim: Perdam sapientiam sapientium, et intelligentiam intelligentium reiiciam. **20** Ubi sapiens? Ubi scriba? Ubi disputator seculi huius? Nonne infatuavit deus sapientiam mundi huius? **21** Nam postquem in sapientiae dei, non cognovit mundus per sapientiam deum, visum est deo, per stultitiam praedicationis salvos facere credentes. **22** Quando quidem et Iudaei signum postulant, et Graeci sapientiam quaerunt. **23** Nos autem praedicamus Christum crucifixum Iudaeis quidem offendiculum, Graecis vero stultitiam, **24** sed iisdem vocatis, Iudaies pariter et Graecis, Christum dei potentiam, ac dei sapientiam. **25** Quoniam stultitia dei sapientior est quam homines, et imbecillitas dei robustior est quae homines. **26** Videtis enim vocationem vestra fratres, quod non multi sapientes secundum carnem, non multi potentes non multi claro genere nati: **27** verum quae stulta erant secundum mundum, delegit deus, ut pudefaceret sapientes. et quae erant imbecillia in mundo, delegit deus, ut pudefaceret ea quaesunt robusta.

Calvin (1556): 1:17 Non in sapientia sermonis, ne inanis reddatur crux Christi. **18** Nam sermo crucis, iis qui pereunt, stultitia est: at nobis qui salutem consequimur, potentia dei est. **19** Scriptum est enim, Perdam sapientiam sapientum, et intelligentiam intelligentium auferam e medio. **20** Ubi sapiens? ubi scriba? ubi disputator huius seculi? Nonne infatuavit deus sapientiam mundi huius? **21** Quoniam enim in sapientia Dei, non cognovit mundus per sapientiam Deum: placuit Deo per stultitiam praedicationis salvos facere credentes, **22** Siquidem et Iudaei signum petunt et Graeci sapientiam quaerunt. **23** Nos autem praedicamus Christum crucifixum, Iudaeis quidem scandalum, Graecis autem stultitiam: **24** Ipsis autem vocatis tam Iudais quam Graecis, Christum Dei potentiam et Dei sapientiam. **25** Nam stultitia Dei, sapientior est hominibus: et informitas Dei robustior est hominibus. **26** Videte vocationem vestram fratres, quod non multi sapientes secundum carnem, non multi potentes, non multi nobiles: **27** sed stulta mundi elegit Deus, ut sapientes pudefaciat: et infirma mundi elegit Deus, ut pudefaciat fortia.

4 *Ann.* 1 Cor. 1:17, ad loc. (all translations of the *Annotations* of 1 Corinthians are mine; the Latin text is from the 1535 edition, available in facsimile

with all earlier variants noted in Reeve and Screech (1990), and in ASD
VI.8): "Furthermore when *logos* is better translated by 'sermonem'
than 'verbum' ['speech' than 'word'], why in this place is it agreeable
to use 'verbo' improperly? And presently [i.e., in v. 1:18], in the same
manner, it is in fact equivalent to the word (i.e., preaching) of the cross,
but it does not here refer to the Son of God. And it ought to be noted in
passing that later a pair of articles is added, *ho logos gar ho tou staurou.*
From this it is evident that there should be a distinction between the
straightforward and simple preaching of the cross, in itself an agreeable
proof, and the discourse of the philosophers and rhetoricians with their
complex counterfeits." (Siquidem *sophon* appellant non solum quod
sapit, verumetiam quicquid elegans est et eruditum ... Ubi et illud
obiter annotandum hic geminum addi articulum *ho logos gar ho tou
staurou*, quo sit evidentior discretio huius sermonis de cruce simplicis et
incompositi suoque congruentis argumento a sermone philosophorum
et rhetorum fucato compositoque.) See also Erasmus, *Apologia de 'In
principio erat sermo'* (LB IX 11B–122F); Jarrott, "Erasmus' 'In Principio Erat
Sermo': A Controversial Translation," 35–40; O'Rourke Boyle, "Sermo:
Reopening the Conversation on Translating JN 1,1," 161–8; and Christ-
von Wedel, *Erasmus of Rotterdam*, 133–44 (Christ-von Wedel notes the
controversy arising from Erasmus' translation, and that certain Protestant
exegetes follow Erasmus' *meaning* while retaining the translation of
verbum, claiming that, aside from Zwingli and Beza, "only the radical
Antitrinitarians adopted Erasmus' translation." Calvin, though, not only
follows Erasmus' translation in *Comm. John*, but also defends Erasmus
explicitly against the *theologastri*).

5 *Paraphrase* 1 Cor. 1:17–20. The English translations of the *Paraphrase on 1
Corinthians* are, unless otherwise noted, from the *Collected Works of Erasmus*
series (CWE), vol. 43; the Latin text is the 1532 Froben edition, the final
edition printed during Erasmus' lifetime, available at www.e-rara.ch;
CWE 43:37; Froben, 1532: Neque enim id fieri voluit humanae sapientiae,
facundiaeve praesidiis, quibus nihil huiusmodi praestari poterat, sed
incomposito simplicisque sermone rem tam arduam geri voluit, ut tota
laus facti deo transcribatur, cui placuit per contemptam et ignominiosam
Christi crucem innovare mundum universum.

6 *Paraphrase* 1 Cor. 1:17–20; CWE 43:37; Froben, 1532: Humilis et abiecta
res videtur Christi crux, sed haec humilitas vincit omnem huius mundi
celsitudinem. Stulta quaepiam et indocta res videtur sermo rudis et
inconditus, quo Christus praedicamus cruci affixum, et in cruce mortuum,
sed quibus tandem ita videtur? Nimirum iis, qui pristinis excaecati vitiis,

non audiunt intus sermonem Evangelicum, et ideo pereunt, eo reiecto, unde poterat salus obtingere. Caeterum ii, qui salutem aeternam hinc consequuntur, profecto sentiunt non esse rem imbecillam, sed omnibus humanis praesidiis efficaciorem, ac processus a deo profectam. Konrad Pellikan, in the 1539 edition of his commentaries on Paul's epistles, reproduces this entire paragraph verbatim in his comment on v. 1:18 (*In Omnes Apostolicas Epistolas ...* Zurich: Froschauer, 1539, 183v).

7 *Paraphrase* 1 Cor. 1:23–5; CWE 43:40; Froben, 1532: Quid abiectus, quam inter maleficos ut maleficum tolli in crucem? Atqui hoc pacto mortem, nulli non invictam, solus devicit. Quid simplicius aut popularius Evangelica doctrina?

8 *Paraphrase* 1 Cor. 1:29–31; CWE 43:42; Froben, 1532: Per hunc contigit salutaris ac vera sapientia, ut philosophia non sit opus.

9 John Colet, in his commentary on 1 Corinthians 2, uses the phrase *adminiculis humane doctrine ac eloquentie*. Erasmus didn't read it there, however, for Colet's work wasn't published until the nineteenth century – Erasmus didn't believe Colet had written any books at all – but he did hear Colet lecture on Paul's epistles at Oxford (see the Introduction to *John Colet's Commentary on First Corinthians*, 9 and 19; and see 98–9 for Colet's use of *adminiculis*). The phrase *praesidia humana* also appears in *Quaestiones Veteris et Novi Testamenti*, a work once attributed to Augustine, but discovered by Erasmus to belong (perhaps) to "Ambrosiaster," also the author of commentaries on Paul's letters once attributed to Ambrose, and cited often by Erasmus (see *quaestio* 112, par. 11 in CPL 185). The phrase *humanis adminiculis* appears in Rufinus' translation of Origen's homily on Jude (*Hom. in Iud.* 9.1); and *adminiculo humani* appears in Augustine, *Confessiones*, 13.iv.16. Tracy suggests that Erasmus began using this language in the late fifteen-'teens, when he also began to use the phrase *philosophia Christi* to describe his ideal theological program; see Tracy, *Erasmus: The Growth of a Mind*, 158ff. Calvin, Bullinger, and Pellikan will employ both *adminiculis* and *praesidia*, like Erasmus, to make similar points.

10 *Paraphrase* 1 Cor. 1:17–20; CWE 43:37; Froben, 1532: Ubi interim sapiens legis scientia tumens? ubi scriba legis interpretatione superbus? ubi philosophus, qui scrutatur arcana naturae, et opificis oblitus, res conditas admiratur? See also footnote 40 of the CWE for cross-references to other paraphrases/annotations.

11 *Ann. 1 Cor.* "Ubi scriba?" ad loc.

12 ASD VI.3, 193.

13 CWE 43:38; Froben, 1532: Declararat et antea suam sapientiam per hoc pulcherrimum spectaculum mundi, summa ratione conditi, ut ex operis

admiratione raperentur in amorem opificis. At ea res ipsorum vitio cessit in diversum. Res conditas admirati veneratique sunt, autorem velut incognitum contempserunt, itaque vixerunt, quasi deus aut faveret vitiis, aut quod condidisset non idem moderaretur.

14 *Paraphrase* 1 Cor. 1:20–1; CWE 43:38; Froben, 1532: Passus est illos deus (sic merebatur illorum arrogantia) per caecitatem ire praecipites in omne dedecoris genus, ut illos sibi ipsis ostenderet, ac resipiscentes tandem intelligerent inanem esse sapientiae professionem et inefficacem. An non igitur deus, huius mundi sapientiam stultam esse declaravit?

15 Pellikan, too, contrasts the *vanitates et pompam mundi* with the *efficacius praedicando* of the apostles in the preface to his commentaries on the apostolic letters (Zurich: Froschauer, 1539, fol. 12). In the *Paraphrase on Matthew*, Erasmus refers to gospel teaching as the "truly salvific and efficacious philosophy" (see CWE 45:30).

16 *Paraphrase* 1 Cor. 1:21–3; CWE 43:39; Froben, 1532: Etenim ut Iudaei prodigia postulant, ac maiorum suorum miraculis sese iactitant, ita Graeci sectantur eruditionem, ac philosophiae cognitionem, ab hac sibi pollicentes felicitatem et gloriam. Utrosque sua fefelit opinio. Nam et Iudaei fiducia legis, exciderunt a Christo, et philosophi sapientiae persuasione turgidi, non recipiunt humilem in speciem crucis praedicationem.

17 ASD VI.3, 194.

18 The stumbling blocks of ineloquence and simplicity are also of course highly relevant here, but will be dealt with more fully below.

19 *Paraphrase* 1 Cor. 1:21–4; CWE 43:39–40; Froben, 1532: Graecis vero, qui rationibus humanis vestigant omnia, stultum videtur virginem coelitus concepisse foetum, sub homine latuisse deum, morte vitam esse restitutam, revixisse qui semel esset mortuus.

20 Erasmus' rendering follows Lefevre here, although in the *Annotations* he cites Augustine, *Ep.* 102 (now 169). Cf. ASD VI.3, 195n.25. See also Screech, *Ecstasy*, 38–9.

21 *Ann. 1 Cor.* 1:25 ("quod stultum est Dei"): Porro stultitiam et imbecillitatem dei, vocat praedicationem crucis, siue quod ea res stulta et imbecillis uideretur impiis, siue quod ad ineffabilem illam dei sapientiam ac potentiam, haec quodammodo stulta esset et imbecillis. Ut enim omnes iustitiae hominum coram deo sunt veluti pannus milieris menstruo fluxu pollutae, ita universa mortalium sapientia, si componatur ad incoitabilem illam ac coelestem sapientiam, stultitia quaedam dici possit.

22 *Ann. 1 Cor.* 1:25 ("quod stultum est Dei"), ad loc.: Nec est quod abominemur hunc sermonem, stultitia dei: quam non horruit Augustinus epistola centesima secunda, scribens ad hunc modum: Haec stultitia dei,

et stultitia praedicationis multos contrahit ad salutem. Si deus demisit se ad nostram imbecillitatem, ut fortes redderet, quid onvum si se demisit ad nostram stultitiam, ut ex stultis redderet sapientes?

23 Screech, *Ecstasy*, 24; for Origen, see *PG* 13.49A. Rufinus' Latin runs thus: Quid enim pro nostra salute non factus est? Nos inanes, et ille exinanivit semetipsum formam servi accipiens. Nos populus stultus et non sapiens, et ille factus est stultitia praedicationis, ut fatuum Dei sapientius fieret hominibus. Nos infirmi, infirmum Dei fortius hominibus factum est. On Erasmus' Origenism, see especially Godin, *Érasme, Lecteur d'Origène*.

24 See *Homily 4 on 1 Corinthians*. See also the notes in the CWE English edition of Erasmus' *Paraphrase on 1 Corinthians*, ad loc., which contain many useful patristic references that might have influenced Erasmus' interpretation.

25 *Paraphrase* 1 Cor. 1:23–5; CWE 43:40; Froben, 1532: Quid simplicius aut popularius Evangelica doctrina? Haec orbem totus innovavit, quod antehac nulla philosophorum professio valuit efficere, ne quid huius laudis humanis praesidiis ascriberetur. Id erat futurum, si opus, aut eruditionis adminiculis, per potentes ac sapientiae professione celebres res administrata fuisset. Nunc cum per idiotas et piscatores expugnatus sit humanae sapientiae fastigium, totius huius negocii gloriam intelligimus uni deberi deo, cuius occulta vis contrariis rebus, contraria praestitit.

26 See Rummel, *The Humanist-Scholastic Debate*, esp. 86ff; and *Erasmus and His Catholic Critics*; also her *Biblical Humanism and Scholasticism in the Age of Erasmus*. For a short overview of Beda's criticisms of Erasmus' *Paraphrases* specifically, see Rummel, "Why Noel Beda Did Not Like Erasmus' *Paraphrases*," 265–78.

27 *Paraphrase* 1 Cor. 1:28–30; CWE 43:41–2; Froben, 1532: Ac proinde quae rudia indoctaque videntur apud mundum, ea potissimus delegit deus, quo magis pudeat humanae sapientiae professores frovoli contatus.

28 Hoffmann, "Faith and Piety," 249.

29 *Ann.* 1 Cor. 1:10, ad loc.: At huius praecepti non meminerunt quidam, quorum alius mordicus tenet Scotisticam sectam, alius Thomisticam, alius Occanisticam, alius Albertisticam. Aliud loquuntur Nominales, aliud Reales, aliud iurisperiti, aliud theologi, rursus aliud Transalpini, aliud Cisalpini.

30 *Paraphrase* 1 Cor. 1:11–13, 1532: Quid? an non haec factionem et sectarum sunt nomina? Sic ex his, qui stultam huius mundi sapientiam sectantur, alius Pythagoram, alius Platonem, alius Aristotelem, alius Zenonem, alius Epicurum, alius alium [etc.]. On a major focal point of Erasmus' theology

as avoiding dissension, see McConica, "Erasmus and the Grammar of Consent," 77–99.

31 See CWE 29: 406–7.

32 See Christ-von Wedel and Leu, eds., *Erasmus in Zurich*, for an examination of Erasmus' influence on the Zurich Reformers. Also Lucia Felici, "Universalism and Tolerance in a Follower of Erasmus from Zurich: Theodor Bibliander," *The Reception of Erasmus in the Early Modern Period*, ed. Enenkel (2014). For a recent paper on the relationship between Bullinger and Calvin with bibliography, see Campi, "Probing Similarities and differences between John Calvin and Heinrich Bullinger"; see also Kok – who focuses on the Romans commentary, and argues that Bullinger was more faithful to Erasmus than was Calvin – in "Heinrich Bullinger's Exegetical Method: The Model For John Calvin's?" in *Biblical Interpretation in the Era of the Reformation*, ed. Muller and Thompson (Eerdmans, 1996), 241–55.

33 See especially the works in CWE, vol. 78, which consist of various controversies between Erasmus and the southern German and Swiss Protestants after Erasmus left Basel in 1529.

34 Ep. 1638 (CWE 11: 352); See, further, Christ-von Wedel, "The Vernacular Paraphrases of Erasmus in Zurich," *Erasmus Studies* 24:1 (2004), 71–88. For more details on Pellikan as scholar and theologian, and as situated within the broader confines of a network of the *respublica litterarum*, see the recent essays by Matthew McLean and Bruce Gordon in *Following Zwingli*, ed. Baschera, Gordon, and Moser.

35 *Annotatiunculae per Leonem Iudae, ex ore Zvinglij in utranq; Pauli ad Corinthios Epistolam publice exponentis conceptae* (Zurich: Froschauer, 1528). I have not compared these annotations extensively with the other commentaries, but I have noticed that Pellikan quotes from them multiple times verbatim in his own commentary (see below).

36 See Peter Opitz, "Bullinger and Paul," in *A Companion to Paul in the Reformation*, ed. Holder, 244. Opitz also argues that Bullinger's approach to exegesis and Pauline theology is "rhetorical" (ibid., passim). See also Christ-von Wedel, *Erasmus of Rotterdam*, 193–4.

37 Gordon, *The Swiss Reformation*, 40. See also, on Bullinger's humanist background, Peter Stotz, "Heinrich Bullinger (1504–1575) and the ancient languages," in *Scholarly Knowledge: Textbooks in Early Modern Europe*, ed. Emidio Campi et al. (Droz, 2008), 113–38.

38 Deinde quanta potui diligentia curavi, ut bona fide recitarem tibi apostolorum verba: qua quidem parte potissimum sequutus sum beatae memoriae D. Erasmi Roterodami aeditionem (*In omnes apostolicas epistolas*; Zurich: Froschauer, 1537, aaa4). Cf. Opitz, "Bullinger and Paul," 244ff.

39 *In priorem D. Pauli ad Corinthios epistolam, Heinrychi Bullingeri commentarius* (Zurich: Froschauer, 1534), fol. 30.

40 On Bullinger's relationship to Latin versions of the Bible, see Stotz, "Heinrich Bullinger," 136–7.

41 Zurich: Froschauer, 1534, fol. 26.

42 Zurich: Froschauer, 1534, fol. 2: adeo ut iam nobis Lutheranorum et Zvinglianorum nomina non minus celebria vulgataque sint quam Corinthiis erant Cephistarum atque Paulianorum factiosa vocabula.

43 Zurich: Froschauer, 1534, fol. 30: Monui autem in argumento, quo totam huius epistolae structuram ob oculos, ceu in tabula spectandam, proposui, Pseudoapostolos maxima iactasse mysteria, quae Paulus fugerint hactenus, quaeque verborum lenocinio et humanae philosophiae fuco instructa mirifice Corinthiis humana philosophia turgidis et lascivientibus, proponebant, aspernantes interim simplicem de incarnatione morte et redemptione Christi praedicationem: qua in re complures invenerint asseeclas. Proinde Paulus commoda connectendi formula transiens, ostendit quod deus citra fucum humanae philosophiae, sapientiam suam orbi simpliciter et per simplices simplici et exposita dicendi docendique ratione proponere voluerit. Semel enim uno verbo omnia dicens subiungit.

44 For Zwingli, see *Annotatiunculae per Leonem Iudae, ex ore Zvinglij in utranq; Pauli ad Corinthios Epistolam publice exponentis conceptae* (Froschauer, 1528), fol. 10.

45 Kok, "Heinrich Bullinger's Exegetical Method," 251–3.

46 Zurich: Froschauer, 1534: fol. 31.

47 Zurich: Froschauer, 1534: fol. 31–2.

48 Zurich: Froschauer, 1534: fol. 32.

49 Zurich: Froschauer, 1534: fol. 35–6; Proinde cum hac non successisset, deus qui genus mortalium perire non vult, quin potius se ad captum attempterat mortalium, et in omnes formas se, nativa bonitate ductus, vertit, ut servet, etiam hic diversa negotium istud aggressus est, nempe per stultitiam praedicationis, id est, per stultam praedicationem.

50 See Gordon, *The Swiss Reformation*, 233–6.

51 On Pellikan's relationship with Munster, see McLean, "'Praeceptor amicissimus': Konrad Pellikan, and Models of Teacher, Student and the Ideal of Scholarship," *Following Zwingli*, 233–56.

52 See Gordon, "Fathers and Sons," *Following Zwingli*, 273ff.

53 He had done similarly for his commentaries on the Gospels; see Christ-von Wedel, *Erasmus*, 191ff., for a discussion of Erasmus' relationship with the Zurich Reformers.

54 Pellikan, along with his Zurich colleagues, would go on to publish a revised version of Erasmus' Latin NT in 1539, and would also eventually put out a new Latin version (the *Biblia Sacrosancta*) in 1543. For details, see Gordon, *The Swiss Reformation*, 239–44.

55 *In omnes apostolicas epistolas* (Zurich: Froschauer, 1539), fol. 183. Trans. modified from CWE 43:37; cf. Erasmus, *Paraphrase* (Froben, 1532), fol. 36v.

56 Zurich: Froschauer, 1539, 183.

57 Zurich: Froschauer, 1539, ad loc., and cf. Erasmus, *Paraphrase* (Froben, 1532), fol. 36v–37r.; and Zwingli, *Annotatiunculae per Leonem Iudae* (Froschauer, 1528), 10. Zwingli, too, uses the phrase *praesidiis humanis* in his notes on this verse.

58 Zurich: Froschauer, 1539, 184.

59 *Annotations on First Corinthians*, ed. Patrick Donnely, S.J. (Marquette UP, 1995), 39–40. See Wengert, *Human Freedom*, 33. Christian eloquence will be treated in ch. 4, and Colossians 2:8 in ch. 5.

60 See *Annotations on First Corinthians*, 43: Spiritualis cognoscit stultum deum per stultitiam. In the CR edition of the *brevis explicatio* (the posthumously published explication of 1 Corinthians), the introduction *plus* the explication of the first two chapters of Paul's text (those at issue here) constitutes only a single, two-column page.

61 *Comm. 1 Cor.* 1:17 (trans. Fraser), 33; Estienne, 1556: The Latin text provided in the notes is the 1556 Estienne edition, the final edition to appear in Calvin's lifetime (there is not yet a modern critical edition in the Droz series of the commentary on 1 Corinthians): Exinanitia, inquit, fuisset crux Christi, si eloquentia et splendore ornata fuisset mea praedicatio. Crucem Christi hic posuit pro redemptionis beneficio, quod a Christo crucifixo petendum est. Doctrina autem evangelii, quae illuc nos vocat, debet sapere crucis naturam: ut scilicet despecta sit magis et abiecta coram mundo quam gloriosa. Sensus ergo est, quod si Paulus philosophico acumine et dicendi artificio usus esset apud Corinthos, sepulta fuisset efficacia crucis Christi, in qua consistit salus hominum: quia pervenire ad nos hac via non potest.

62 See Torrance, *The Hermeneutics of John Calvin*, 145ff., for a discussion of this aspect of Calvin's thought in his *De scandalis*. Torrance affirms the point that "it is not only the plebeian and unostentatious simplicity of the gospel that scandalizes, but that it contains much that is absurd and even ridiculous to the human mind (*quae humano iudicio valde sunt non absurda modo, sed etiam ridicula*)" (146).

63 See above, *Paraphrase* 1 Cor. 1:23–5.

64 *Comm. 1 Cor.* 1:17 (trans. Fraser), 33; Estienne, 1556: Quemadmodum supra toties nomen Christi superbae carnis sapientiae opposuit, ita

nunc in medium adducit Christi crucem, qua fastum illius omnem ac
sublimitatem deiiciat. Tota enim fidelium sapientia in Christi cruce inclusa
est: quid autem cruce contemptibilius? Ergo qui vere Deo vult sapere,
necesse est ut ad hanc crucis humilitatem descendat: hoc porro non fiet,
quin se prius et proprio sensu et tota mundi sapientia abdicaverit. Verum
non hic tantum quales esse Christi discipulos, et quam discendi viam
tenere conveniat, sed etiam quae sit docendi ratio in schola Christi, tradit
Paulus.

65 *Paraphrase* 1 Cor. 1:23–5; CWE 43:40; LB VII 863.

66 Fraser, *Calvin's Doctrine of the Knowledge of God*, 106.

67 An entirely different question is Calvin's indebtedness to philosophy,
ancient or otherwise, in cases where he doesn't cite anyone at all, or simply
in broader trends in his theology. See Partee, *Calvin and Classical Philosophy*
(1977), for a good, clear overview of a few ways in which Calvin is related
to certain ancient Greco-Roman philosophers.

68 Partee, *Calvin and Classical Philosophy*, 29.

69 *Comm. 1 Cor., Argumentum* (trans. Fraser), 10; Estienne, 1556: Ac interim
sententiam illam fusius explicat, contineri in evangelio coelestem
arcanamque sapientiam: quae nec ingenii acumine aut perspicacia, nec
toto carnis sensu apprehendatur, nec persuadeatur rationibus humanis,
nec verborum lenocinio aut pictura indigeat: sed una duntaxat spiritus
revelatione mentibus hominum innotescat, et cordibus obsignetur.
Tandem concludit, non tantum a carnis prudentia remotam esse evangelii
praedicationem et in crucis humilitate positam, sed etiam carnis iudicio
non posse aestimari qualis sit. This passage is, in fact, remarkably similar
to the opening of Erasmus' *Paraphrase on John*. CWE translates it thus:
"Since the nature of God surpasses immeasurably the feebleness of human
intelligence, however talented and acute that intelligence may otherwise
be, its reality cannot be perceived by our senses, or conceived by our mind,
or represented by our imagination, or set out in words" (Froben, 1535, fol.
13: Natura divina quoniam in immensum superat imbecillitatem humani
ingenii, quamlibet alioqui felicis ac perspicacis: nec sensibus nostris, ut
est, potest percipi: nec animo concipi, nec imaginatione fingi, nec verbis
explicari).

70 *Comm. 1 Cor.* 1:18 (trans. Fraser), 35; Estienne, 1556: Utcunque sermo
crucis, quia non est humanae sapientiae commendatione gratiosus, stultitia
reputetur ab iis qui pereunt: nobis tamen illic sapientia Dei elucet.

71 Calvin actually chooses *auferare* in his own translation. *Obliterare*, it might
be noted, is the verb that Erasmus uses to describe a similar action on the
part of the deity at 1 Cor. 1:28 (but to translate the Greek *katargese*). On the

related question of Calvin's relationship to the biblical text, and of which
Bibles he worked with in forming his own judgments, see Fraser, *Calvin's
New Testament Commentaries*, 119–91; Gilmont, *John Calvin and the Printed
Book* (2005), esp. 143–56; also Engammare, "Cinquante ans de révision de
la traduction biblique d'Olivetan," 347–77, and "Calvin connaissait-il la
Bible?".

72 *Comm. 1 Cor.* 1:18 (trans. Fraser), 36; Estienne, 1556: Secundum verbum
athetein, quod Erasmus vertit reiicere, quum ambiguam habeat
significationem, et aliquando sumatur pro delere, vel expungere, aut
obliterare: in hoc sensu accipere hic malo, ut respondeat verbo prophetae
evanescere aut abscondi ... Nihil certe aliud vult propheta quam nullos
amplius fore gubernatores, qui iustam regendi rationem teneant: quia
Dominus eos privabit sano iudicio et intelligentia. Quemadmodum enim
alibi universo populo excaecationem minatur, ita hic ducibus: quod est
veluti oculos ex corpore eruere.

73 *Comm. 1 Cor.* 1:19 (trans. Fraser), 37; Estienne, 1556: Paulus, ut a vanidam
nihilique esse huius mundi sapientiam probet, quum se effert adversus
Deum, testimonium illud Iesaiae adducit.

74 The most obvious and extended example of Calvin connecting the
Sorbonne "sophists" to Paul's denunciations of frivolous questions comes
in his commentary on 1 Tim. 6:4–5.

75 *Comm. 1 Cor.* 1:20 (trans. Fraser), 37; Estienne, 1556: Nomen saeculi
non tantum ad postremum, sed etiam ad alia duo nomina adiungi
debet. Vocat autem sapientes saeculi, qui non e Dei verbo per spiritum
illuminati sapiunt: sed mundana tantum perspicacia praediti eius fiduciae
innituntur.

76 *Comm. 1 Cor.* 1:20 (trans. Fraser), 37–8; Estienne, 1556: Inquisitores apposite
nominat, qui movendis scrupis perplexisque quaestionibus acumen
ostentant. Ita generaliter in nihilum redigit totum hominis ingenium, ne
quid valeat in regno Dei. Nec sine causa tam vehementer in hominum
prudentiam insurgit. Dici enim non potest quam difficile sit revellere
ex hominum animis perversam carnis confidentiam, ne sibi plus aequo
arrogent. Id autem iam nimium est, si vel minimum freti sua prudentia
iudicare a se ipsis audeant.

77 Cf. Bullinger, *Comm. 1 Cor.* (Zurich: Froschauer, 1534) fol. 47: Philosophia
aboletur. Et qui deum secundum traditiones hominum colunt, frustra colunt.

78 *Comm. 1 Cor.* 1:20 (trans. Fraser), 38; Estienne, 1556: Hic per sapientiam
intelligit quidquid comprehendere potest homo, tam naturali ingenii
facultate, quam usu et literis atque artium scientia adiutus. Name mundi
sapientiam spiritus sapientia opponit. Proinde quidquid intelligentiae in

hominem cadit absque spiritus sancti illustratione, id sub mundi sapientia continetur. Eam totam dicit infatuatam esse a Deo, hoc est, damnatam stultitiae.

79 *Comm. 1 Cor.* 1:20 (trans. Fraser), 38; Estienne, 1556: Nam et mera est vanitas quidquid scit homo ac intelligit, nisi vera sapientia fulciatur: et nihilo plus valet ad comprehensionem spiritualis doctrinae quam caici oculos ad colores discernendos. Utrumque istorum diligenter notandum, quod fumus est omnium scientiarum cognitio, ubi abest coelestis Christi scientia: et homo cum toto suo acumine perinde est stupidus ad intelligenda per se Dei mysteria atque asinus ineptus est ad symphoniam. Cf. *Institutes* I.viii.1 (McNeill/Battles): "When we read Demonsthenes or Cicero, Plato or Aristotle, or some others of their kind, I confess indeed that they wonderfully attract, delight and move us, even ravish our minds. But if from them we turn to reading the Holy Scriptures, whether we will or no they will so pierce us to the heart and fix themselves within us that all the power of the rhetoricians and philosophers, compared with them, seems no more than smoke."

80 See adage I iv 35, *Asinus ad lyram*. He could also have picked up the proverb about a blind man discerning colour from Erasmus' adage I vi 16 (*Ne sutor ultra crepidam*), where he refers to a saying of Aristotle from the *Physics* regarding "a blind man disputing about colors – words which have become proverbial among academics of our own day for disputing on subjects of which a man knows nothing." See William Barker, *The Adages of Erasmus* (Toronto, 2001), 95; cf. Aristotle, *Physics* 2.1 (192a7).

81 "[man on his own is] as blockish and senseles to comprehend and understand to hym selfe the Misteryes of God, as is the foolish asse to play uppon the Harpe."

82 *Comm. 1 Cor.* 1:20 (trans. Fraser), 38; Estienne, 1556: Nam eo modo redarguitur exitialis eorum superbia, qui in mundi sapientia sic gloriantur, ut Christum et totam salutis doctrinam despiciant, beatos se putantes, si in creaturis haereant: et retunditur eorum supercilium, qui proprio ingenio confisi in coelum penetrare tenant.

83 *Comm. 1 Cor.* 1:20 (trans. Fraser), 38; Estienne, 1556: Simul etiam solvitur illa quaestio: qui fiat ut quidquid est scientiae extra Christum, hic Paulus ita prosternat humi et quasi pedibus conculcet, quod constat esse praecipuum in hoc mundo Dei donum. Quid enim hominis ratione nobilius, qua homo reliquis animantibus praecellit? doctrinae liberales quantum honoris merentur, quae hominem ita expoliunt, ut reddant vere humanum? Praeterea quantos et quam eximios fructus pariunt? Quis civilem prudentiam, qua respublicae, principatus et regna sustinentur

non summis laudibus extollat? ut de reliquis taceam. Huius, inquam, quaestionis solutio inde patet, quod non simpliciter damnat Paulus aut naturalem perspicaciam hominis, aut prudentiam usu et experientia collectam, aut cultum ingenii literis comparatum: sed hoc totum ad percipiendam spiritualem sapientiam nullius esse momenti affirmat.

84 *Comm. 1 Cor.* 1:20 (trans. Fraser), 38; Estienne, 1556: Et certe insania est, si vel proprio acumine, vel literarum praesidio quispiam fretus in coelum evolare conetur: hoc est, de arcanis regni Dei mysteriis iudicare, aut ad eorum cognitionem perrumpere: sunt enim abscondita ab humano sensu.

85 *Comm. 1 Cor.* 1:20 (trans. Fraser), 39; Estienne, 1556: Alioqui illud etiam verum est, sine Christo vanas esse rerum omnium scientias, vanumque esse hominem, qui doctrinis omnibus instructus Deum ignoret. Quin etiam hoc quoque vere dicetur, quodammodo profanari haec praeclara Dei dona, ut sunt ingenii dexteritas, acutum iudicium, doctrinae liberales, linguarum cognitio: quoties in homines impios inciderint.

86 Perhaps still the best and clearest exposition of this issue in Calvin, which incorporates both the *Institutes* and the commentaries, but which focuses primarily on the function of the *imago Dei* after the Fall, is to be found in the final two chapters of Torrance, *Calvin's Doctrine of Man*. But see also the more recent discussions in Schreiner, *In The Theatre of His Glory*; Pitkin, *What Pure Eyes Could See*, 159ff., and Zachman, *Image and Word in the Theology of John Calvin* and, idem, the first chapter of *Reconsidering John Calvin*.

87 Pitkin, *What Pure Eyes Could See*, 160. Zachman's position on Calvin, which is akin to Pitkin's, states that, while fallen humans cannot know God through creation by itself, once they have the revelation of the word of God in Christ, they can fully appreciate the work of God the Creator through the "spectacles" provided in Christ and in the Bible.

88 *Comm. 1 Cor.* 1:20–1 (trans. Fraser), 39; Estienne, 1556: Erat hic certe legitimus ordo, ut homo ingenita sibi ingenii luce sapientiam Dei in eius operibus contemplatus ad eius notitiam perveniret.

89 *Comm. 1 Cor.* 1:21 (trans. Fraser), 39; Estienne, 1556: Deus ergo in creaturis praeclarum admirabilis suae sapientiae speculum nobis profert, ut quicunque mundum et reliqua Dei opera intuetur, necese habeat, si vel scintillam unam sani iudicii habet, in eius admirationem prorumpere. Si ab operum Dei intuitu homines ad veram eius notitiam dirigerentur, sapienter Deum cognoscerent, vel naturali et proprio sapiendi modo.

90 *Comm. 1 Cor.* 1:21 (trans. Fraser), 39; Estienne, 1556: Sed quia toti mundo nihil ad eruditionem profuit, quod Deus sapientiam suam exseruerat in creaturis: alia via deinde aggressus est ad homines docendos.

91 Nos tamen, quum tale spectaculum nobis ante oculos pateat, caecutimus, non quia obscura sit revelatio, sed quia nos mente alienati sumus.
92 *Comm. 1 Cor.* 1:21 (trans. Fraser), 40; Estienne, 1556: Concessio est, quod evangelium stultitiam praedicationis vocat, quae in speciem talis consetur istis *morosophois*, qui falsa confidentia ebrii nihil verentur sacrosanctam Dei veritatem insipidae suae censurae subiicere. Et sane alioqui humanae rationi absurdius nihil est quam audire Deum mortalem, vitam morti obnoxiam, iustitiam peccati similitudine obtectam, benedictionem subiectam maledictioni ...
93 *Comm. 1 Cor.* 1:21 (trans. Fraser), 40; Estienne, 1556: Si quis philosophos obiiciat: respondeo, in ipsis potissimum exstare insigne huius nostrae imbecillitatis documentum. Nemo enim illorum reperietur qui non ex illo cognitionis principio quod dixi, protinus ad vagas et erroneas speculationes delapsus sit. Bona autem ex arte plus quam aniliter delirant.
94 *Comm. 1 Cor.* 1:22 (trans. Fraser), 41; Estienne, 1556: Graeci amant quae commendatione acuminis arrideant humano ingenio. Nos vero Christum crucifixum praedicamus, in quo nihil quam imbecillitas, prima specie, et stultitia apparet ... Graecis instar fabulae est, audire talem fuisse redeptionis modum. Graecorum nomine non gentes hic simplicter (meo iudicio) significat: sed eos notat, qui liberalibus doctrinis erant expoliti, vel altiore intelligentia pollebant.
95 *Comm. 1 Cor.* 1:24; my translation.
96 *Comm. 1 Cor.* 1:25 (trans. Fraser), 43; Estienne, 1556: Ubi sic nobiscum agit Dominus ut videatur ineptire, quia sapientiam suam non profert, quod tamen videtur stultitia, omnem hominum solertiam sapientia superat. Et ubi Deus virtutem suam occultando infirmiter agere videtur, robustior est tamen illa quae putatur imbecillitas quavis hominum virtute. Semper autem in his verbis notanda est quam nuper attigi concessio. Nemini enim obscurum est quam improprie vel stultitia vel infirmitas Deo adscribatur: sed necesse fuit talibus ironiis insanam carnis arrogantiam refutare, quae Deum omni sua gloria spoliare non dubitat.
97 *Comm. 1 Cor.* 1:26–8 (trans. Fraser), 44; Estienne, 1556: Finem indicat, ut Dominus contemptibiles magnis praeferendo gloriam carnis deiiceret.
98 *Comm. 1 Cor.* 1:26–8 (trans. Fraser), 44; Estienne, 1556: Vocantur ad Christum primo loco pastores, sequuntur tamen postea philosophi: piscatores indocti et contempti summum honoris gradum occupant, sed in eorum scholam deinde recipiuntur reges eorumque consiliarii, senatores, rhetores.
99 For Erasmus, see *Paraphrase* 1 Cor. 1:23–5.

100 A complete bibliography is not possible here, but for works particularly relevant to our project (i.e., the theology of folly), see Screech, *Ecstasy and the Praise of Folly*; Kaiser, *Praisers of Folly*, 84ff., for a treatment of Folly as the "Fool in Christ"; and Gordon, *Humanist Play and Belief*, ch. 1.

101 "The Tongue and the Book: Erasmus' *Paraphrases on the New Testament* and the Arts of Scripture," *Holy Scripture Speaks*, ed. Pabel and Vessey, 29–58; and "'Lingua Christi Praedicatrix': The Tongue and the Book in Erasmus' Paraphrases on the Pastoral and Catholic Epistles," *ERSY* 17 (1997), 70–97. See also the preface in Screech, *Ecstasy*, where it is argued that the Erasmus of the *Praise of Folly* is no different from the Erasmus of any of his other works or letters.

102 Erasmus, *Praise of Folly* (trans. Miller), 86; ASD IV-3, 144: Ii cum nihil omnino sciant, tamen omnia se scire profitentur, cumque seipsos ignorent neque fossam aliquoties aut saxum obvium videant, vel quia lippiunt plerique vel quia peregrinantur animi, tamen ideas, universalia, formas separatas, primas materias quidditates, ecceitates, formalitates, instantia videre se praedicant, res adeo tenues, ut neque Lynceus, opinor, possit perspicere.

103 *Praise of Folly* (trans. Miller), 87–8; ASD IV-3, 144–5: Porro theologos silentio transire fortasse praestiterit, *kai tauten kamarinan me kinein* nec hanc anagyrim tangere, utpote genus hominum mire superciliosum atque irritabile, ne forte turmatim sexcentis conclusionibus adoriantur et ad palinodiam adigant, quod si recusem, protinus haereticam clamitent.

104 *Praise of Folly* (trans. Miller), 88–9; ASD IV-3, 148: Num deus potuerit suppositare mulierem, num diabolum, num asinum, num cucurbitam, num cilicem? Tum quemadmodum cucurbita fuerit concionatura, editura miracula, figenda cruci. Et quid consecrasset Petrus, si consecrasset eo tempore, quo corpus Christi pendebat in cruce?

105 *Praise of Folly* (trans. Miller), 88–9; ASD IV-3, 148: his quoque multo subtiliores ... ea quoque per altissimas tenebras videat quae nusquam sunt.

106 See ASD IV-3, 148nn. for references to the original *quaestiones*. On his contemporaries, see Rummel, *The Humanist-Scholastic Debate* and *Erasmus and His Catholic Critics*. For an examination of Erasmus' reception of the Middle Ages, see Bejczy, *Erasmus and the Middle Ages*; for the critique of scholastic theology in particular, but also his occasional use of it, see 73–96.

107 *Praise of Folly* (trans. Miller), 157.

108 O'Rourke Boyle, "Fools and Schools," 187.

109 See Kaiser, *Praisers of Folly*, 23. And see Dorp's letter in *Ep.* 304 with Erasmus' response in *Ep.* 337 in CWE, vol. 3.

110 *Praise of Folly* (trans. Miller), 91–3.
111 *Praise of Folly* (trans. Miller), 94.
112 *Praise of Folly* (trans. Miller), 95–6.
113 *Praise of Folly* (trans. Miller), 104–5.
114 James Simpson has argued that the rhetoric of simplicity, especially as
     propagated by, for example, William Tyndale, is disingenuous insofar
     as the conceit of the simplicity of the biblical text is confounded by the
     lengths that English Protestants must go to in order to clarify it (see
     Burning to Read). Whether or not that's true of English Protestants,
     one might distinguish between an argument for the simplicity of the
     Word of God, meaning the biblical text itself, and the simplicity of the
     gospel, meaning the fundamental teachings of Jesus and the Apostles
     that are ostensibly accessible to everyone. Erasmus will readily admit
     to difficulties in the biblical text, some even insurmountable, but the
     simplicity of the gospel is another matter.
115 See Dorp's letter in *Ep.* 304 with Erasmus' response in *Ep.* 337 in CWE,
     vol. 3.
116 Erasmus to Dorp, in *Praise of Folly* (trans. Miller), 154.
117 Erasmus to Dorp, in *Praise of Folly* (trans. Miller), 154–5.
118 Erasmus to Dorp, in *Praise of Folly* (trans. Miller), 155.
119 *Adages* IV i 1 (CWE 35, 419–20).
120 Hoffmann, *Rhetoric and Theology*, 85.
121 On Erasmus' theology as aiming at avoiding dissension, see McConica,
     "Erasmus and the Grammar of Consent," 77–99.
122 Quid? an non haec factionum et sectarum sunt nomina? Sic ex his, qui
     stultam huius mundi sapientiam sectantur, alius Pythagoram, alius
     Platonem, alius Aristotelem, alius Zenonem, alius Epicurum, alius alium
     atque alium autorum iactat [etc.].
123 *Paraphrase* 1 Cor 3:2–4; CWE 43:52; (1532) Cum autor ac princeps
     communis sit omnium, tamen alius apud vos dicit: Ego sum Paulines:
     rursum alius, ego sum Apollonius, nam istiusmodi titulis inter sese
     decertant humanae philosophiae discipuli: Ego sum Aristotelicus, ego
     Platonicus, ego Stoicus, ego Epicurus.
124 *Praise of Folly* (trans. Miller), 166.
125 McConica puts it thus: "without *consensus* and concord, its social concomitant,
     no dogmatic certainty could be had about anything, and no problem of
     faith could be solved. The *consensus*, in Erasmus' thought, is the principle
     of intelligibility itself" ("Erasmus and the Grammar of Consent," 89).
126 This is also a reason he gives against joining the Protestant movement.
     The dissension among Protestants is proof in itself that they are not
     adequately following the gospel, according to Erasmus. In a letter to

Bucer, he writes, "You say that you are convinced that what you profess
is the teaching of Christ. If I could convince myself of that, no one among
you would profess it more readily than I. But if you are convinced, how
is it that you cannot agree among yourselves?" (qtd. in Rummel, *The
Humanist-Scholastic Debate*, 39).

127 Walter Gordon points out the connections of this work to the *Moria* in
Humanist Play and Belief, 95–8. A recent critical edition appears in ASD
V-7; for the English, see CWE 29. See the helpful introductory notes in
each edition for the compositional background and early printing history.
Also, James Rieger, "Erasmus, Colet, and the Schoolboy Jesus," *Studies in
the Renaissance*, vol. 9 (1962), 187–94.

128 ASD V-7, 159.

129 CWE 29:56; ASD V-7, 171: Puer apud ueros verba facturus de ineffabili
puero Iesu non optarim mihi Tullianam illam eloquentiam quae brevi
atque inani voluptate aures deliniat. Quantum enim abest Christi
sapientia a sapientia mundi (abest autem immenso intervallo), tantum
oportet christianam eloquentiam a mundana differre eloquentia.

130 CWE 29:56; ASD V-7, 171: cuius sermo vivus et efficax penetrantior est
quovis gladio ancipiti, ad intimos etiam cordis recessus penetrans.

131 CWE 29:58; ASD V-7, 173: Quid illo sapientius qui tam admirabili ratione
cuncta condidit ut vel in apiculis tot tantaque suae sapientiae reliquerit
miracula ... postremo in quo id quod stutissimum est universam mortalium
sophorum sapientiam longo superat intervallo?

132 CWE 29:58–9; ASD V-7, 174: Adoranda est eius immensitas magis quam
explicanda.

133 See CWE 29:62; ASD V-7, 178: mento levi mente sunt hirsuta.

134 CWE 29:65; ASD V-7, 182: Porro ne stultam huius mundi ac fucatam
sapientiam affectaremus protinus adjecit *Et gratia Dei erat in illo*. Is vero
demum sapit qui mundo desipit et nil nisi Christum sapit. Is non e
philosophorum libris, non e sciticis argutiis, sed syncera fide cognoscitur,
spe tenetur, charitate devincitur.

135 CWE 29:66; ASD V-7, 171: Neque id mirum, cum is esset ad quem omnis
mundi esapientia stulta est. Praeclara res legum prudentia, egregia res
philosophiae cognitio, suspicienda res theologiae professio, verum si quis
Iesum audiat ilico stultescunt omnia.

3. Hidden Wisdom and the Revelation of the Spirit

1 *Paraphrase* 1 Cor. 1:2; CWE 43:43.
2 **Vulgate: 2:1** Et ego, cum venissem ad vos, fratres, veni non per
sublimitatem sermonis aut sapientiae annuntians vobis mysterium Dei.

2 Non enim iudicavi scire me aliquid inter vos nisi Iesum Christum et hunc crucifixum. **3** Et ego in infirmitate et timore et tremore multo fui apud vos, **4** et sermo meus et praedicatio mea non in persuasibilibus sapientiae verbis, sed in ostentatione Spiritus et virtutis, **5** ut fides vestra non sit in sapientia hominum sed in virtute Dei. **6** Sapientiam autem loquimur inter perfectos, sapientiam vero non huius saeculi neque principum huius saeculi, qui destruuntur, **7** sed loquimur Dei sapientiam in mysterio, quae abscondita est, quam praedestinavit Deus ante saecula in gloriam nostram, **8** quam nemo principum huius saeculi cognovit; si enim cognovissent, numquam Dominum gloriae crucifixissent. **9** Sed sicut scriptum est: Quod oculus non vidit, nec auris audivit, nec in cor hominis ascendit, quae praeparavit Deus his, qui diligunt illum. **10** Nobis autem revelavit Deus per Spiritum; Spiritus enim omnia scrutatur, etiam profunda Dei. **11** Quis enim scit hominum, quae sint hominis nisi spiritus hominis, qui in ipso est? Ita et, quae Dei sunt, nemo cognovit nisi Spiritus Dei. **12** Nos autem non spiritum mundi accepimus, sed Spiritum, qui ex Deo est, ut sciamus, quae a Deo donata sunt nobis; **13** quae et loquimur non in doctis humanae sapientiae, sed in doctis Spiritus verbis, spiritalibus spiritalia comparantes. **14** Animalis autem homo non percipit, quae sunt Spiritus Dei, stultitia enim sunt illi, et non potest intellegere, quia spiritaliter examinantur; **15** spiritalis autem iudicat omnia, et ipse a nemine iudicatur. **16** Quis enim cognovit sensum Domini, qui instruat eum? Nos autem sensum Christi habemus.

Erasmus (1535): 2:1 Et ego quum venirem ad vos, fratres, non veniebam cum eminentia sermonis aut sapientiae, annuncians vobis testimonium dei. **2** Non enim me iudicavi quicquam scire inter vos, nisi Iesum Christum, et hunc crucifixum. **3** Et ego per infirmitatem, et cum timore, ac in tremore multo apud vos versatus sum: **4** et sermo meus, et praedicatio mea, non erat in persuasoriis humanae sapientiae verbis, sed in ostensione spiritus ac potentiae, **5** ut fides vestra non sit in sapientia hominum, sed in potentia dei. **6** Porro sapientiam loquimur inter perfectos: sapientiam autem non seculi huius, neque principum seculi huius qui abolentur: **7** sed loquimur sapientiam dei in mysterio, quae est recondita, quam praefinierat deus ante secula, in gloriam nostram, **8** quam nemo principum seculi huius cognovit: nam si cognovissent, haudquaquam dominum gloriae crucifixissent: **9** sed quemadmodum scriptum est: Quae oculus non vidit, et auris non audivit, et in cor hominis non ascenderunt, quae praeparavit deus diligentibus se. **10** Nobis autem deus revelavit per spiritum suum. Spiritus enim omnia scrutatur, etiam profunditates dei. **11** Quis enim hominum novit ea quae

sunt hominis, nisi spiritus hominis qui est in eo? Sic et ea quae sunt dei
nemo novit, nisi spiritus dei. **12** Nos vero non spiritum mundi accepimus,
sed spiritum qui est ex deo, ut sciamus quae a Christo donata sint nobis,
13 quae et loquimur non sermonibus quos docet humana sapientia,
sed quos docet spiritus sanctus, spiriualibus spiritualia comparantes.
14 Animalis autem homo non accipit ea quae sunt spiritus dei: stultitia
siquidem illi sunt: nec potest cognoscere quod spiritualiter diiudicatur.
15 At spiritualis diiudicat quidem omnia: ipse vero a nemine diiudicatur.
16 Quis enim cognovit mentem domini, qui consilium daturus sit illi?
Nos autem mentem Christi tenemus.

    Calvin (1556): 2:1 Et ego quum venissem ad vos, fratres, veni, non in
excellentia sermonis vel sapientiae, annuntians vobis testimonium Dei. **2**
Non enim eximium duxi, scire quicquam inter vos, nisi Iesum Christum,
et hunc crucifixum. **3** Et ego in infirmitate et in timore et in tremore multo
sui apud vos: **4** Et sermo meus, et praedicatio mea, non in persuasioriis
humanae sapientiae sermonibus, sed in demonstratione Spiritus et
potentiae: **5** Ut fides vestra non sit in sapientia hominum, sed in potentia
Dei. **6** Porro sapientiam loquimur inter perfectos: sapientiam quidem non
seculi huius, neque principum seculi huius, qui abolentur: **7** Sed loquimur
sapientiam Dei in ysterio, quae est recondita: quam praesinivit Deus ante
secula in gloriam nostram, **8** Quamnemo principum seculi huius cognovit:
si enim cognovissent, nequaquam Dominum gloriae crucifixissent. **9** Sed
quem admodum scriptum est, Quae oculus non vidit, nec auris audivit,
nec in cor hominis ascenderunt, quae praeparavit Deus iis qui ipsum
diligunt. **10** Nobis autem Deus revelavit per Spiritum suum: Spiritus enim
omnia scrutatur, etiam profunditates Dei. **11** Quis enim hominum novit
quae ad eum pertinent, nisi spiritus hominis qui est in ipso? Ita et quae
Dei sunt, nemo novit, nisi Spiritus Dei. **12** Nos autem non spiritum mundi
accepimus, sed Spiritum qui est ex Deo: ut sciamus quae a Christo donata
sunt nobis: **13** Quae et loquimur, non in eruditis humanae sapientiae
sermonibus, sed Spiritus sancti: spiritualibus spiritualia coaptantes. **14**
Animalis autem homo non comprehendit quae sunt Spiritus Dei. sunt
enim illi stultitia: nec potest intelligere, quia spiritualiter diiudicantur. **15**
Spiritualis autem diiudicat omnia, ipse vero a nemine diiudicatur. **16** Quis
enim cognovit mentem Domini, qui adiuvet ipsum? nos autem mentem
Christi habemus.

3 *Ann. 1 Cor. 2*, ad loc.: Ambrosius legit: *praedicans vobis mysterium Dei,*
   nec ita legit solum, verum etiam interpretatur. Unde diverso videtur
   usus exemplari Graeco. Siquidem apud illos inter *martyrion* et *mysterion*
   nonnulla vocum affinitas est. Cf. also CWE 43:43, n.2.

4 *Paraphrase* 1 Cor. 2:1–3; Froben, 1532, fol. 89: [N]on veni admirandae
  cuiuspiam eloquentiae viribus instructus, aut eximia quadam philosophiae
  cognitione suscipiendus, quod hominum genus sciebam apud vos plurimi
  fieri.

5 *Paraphrase* 1 Cor. 2:4, CWE 43:44; Froben, 1532: Quemadmodum illa
  nullis hominum praesidiis, sed solius dei protectu munita erat adersus
  improborum violentiam, ita sermo meus nequaquam instructus erat
  rhetorum ornamentis, aut philosophorum argumentis, qui declararet
  quantum ipse pollerem, vel eloquentia, vel eruditione, sed tamen efficax
  fuit ad transfigurandos vos, non ostentatione doctrinae, sed spiritu ac
  virtute dei, qui afflatu miraculisque, nostro, licet incondito sermoni vim
  addebat.

6 *Paraphrase* 1 Cor. 2:4–6; CWE 43:44; Froben, 1532: quod a superioris vitae
  tenebris ad Evangelii lucem estis translati, re tam incredibili penitus
  persuasa, existimet vos humanae doctrinae aut eloquentiae debere,
  quam nobis non vindicamus, sed potentiae divinae, per quam sermo
  noster efficacior fuit, quam philosophorum oratio, quamlibet arguta aut
  composita.

7 *Ann.* 1 Cor. 2:6, ad loc.

8 *Paraphrase* 1 Cor. 2:6; CWE 43:45; Froben, 1532: Porro qui stultitiam docere
  videmur apud incredulos, Christi crucem praedicantes, iidem apud eos,
  qui plene credunt, eximiam quandam sapientiam praedicare videmur,
  sed hanc longe diversam ab ea, quae mundi huius causas humanis
  rationibus frustra scrutatus: nec humanam qua se iactant ac venditant, qui
  vulgo summates habentur: quorum autoritas una cum ipsa sapientia per
  Christum abrogatur et antiquatur, prodita illorum stultitia.

9 *Ann.* 1 Cor. 2:7, ad loc.: 'Sed loquimur', inquit, 'non propalam aut passim,
  ne simus offendiculo, sed secreto, nec inter quoslibet, ne rosas obiiciamus
  porcis, sed inter perfectos, neque quam libet sapientiam, quam alii
  philosophi publice profitentur, sed arcandam illam et reconditam atque,
  ut ita loquar, retrusam.' It is a Dutch proverb, obviously a modification of
  Matt. 7:6, although it isn't included in Erasmus' *Adagia*. Roses cast before
  swine are depicted in a 1559 oil painting by the Dutch painter Pieter
  Bruegel the Elder, *Netherlandish Proverbs* (probably not coincidentally
  originally entitled *The Folly of the World*).

10 Froben, 1532, fol. 90: Quamlibet eruditos in cognitione rerum visibilium,
   quamlibet turgidos scientia legis, tamen hoc arcanum illos fefellit, solis
   iis communicandum, quos animi modestia deo conciliasset. Id enim
   fore praedixerat Esaias, declarans hanc, de qua loquimur, sapientiam
   secreto mentibus inspirari: Quae, inquit, nec conspecta sunt unquam

humanis oculis, nec humanis auribus audita, nec unquam cuiusquam hominis cogitatione concepta sunt, ea paravit deus iis, a quibus syncere diligitur, qui fide philosophantur, non rationibus. Non meruerunt hoc elati principes, nec tumidi philosophi. Nobis velut amicis arcanum hoc patefecit deus, non per humanam doctrinam, sed per afflatum occultum sui spiritus.

11 *Ann.* 1 Cor. 2:13, ad loc.: At mihi magis probatur, hic intelligamus sermonem apostolorum non constare doctrina humana, sed afflatu divino.

12 *Ann.* 1 Cor. 2:13, "Spiritalia comparantes," ad loc. Appositiora sunt quae scribit Chrysostomus, ad confirmandum Evangelium non esse opus humana philosophia, sed sufficere sibi scripturam, velut ad probandum, quod Christus natus sit de virgine aut mortuus revixerit, non adhibendae sunt philosophorum rationes, sed vel oracula typique Veteris Instrumenti vel miracula. Qui in Paradiso creavit arbores absque semine, qui Adam creavit ex argilla, Evam e costa viri, terram e nihilo, ei facile fuit e virginis substantia creare corpus humanum aut mortuum redder vitae. Cf. Chrysostom, *In 1 Cor. hom. 7, 4,* Migne *PG* 61, 59.

13 CWE 43:48; Froben, 1532: Atque haec est philosophia, quam ut a spiritu Christi hausimus, ita vicissim tradimus piis ac simplicibus, non verbis arte compositis, quemadmodum tradunt philosophiae professores, id quod profitentur, sed verbis inconditis quidem illis, verum spiritualem doctrinam tradentibus.

14 Hoffmann, *Rhetoric and Theology*; O'Rourke Boyle writes, "The implications for theological method [of translating *logos* as *sermo* instead of *verbum*] are substantial, for Erasmus held the *Logos* as the paradigm of human language, whose most eloquent expression was true theological discourse" (*Erasmus on Language and Method in Theology*, 30).

15 *Ann. 1 Cor. 2* (1535): At mihi probatur, ut hic intelligamus sermonem apostolorum non constare doctrina humana, sed afflatu divino ... Quid hic dicent theologi quidam ut sibi videntur qui tradendo sacras literas, nihil crepant, nisi philosophiam Aristotelicam?

16 Response to Bouwsma, "Calvinism as Theologia Rhetorica?" 22. Also, "Rhetoric was not only pious but also pastoral, not merely appropriate toward God but very persuasive toward men. This distinguished it from the dialectic which the scholastics adopted as their method: rhetoric had an efficacy not only to convince but also to convert" (23).

17 Froben, 1532: diversum est sapientiae genus, diversa sit et tradendi ratio.

18 *Paraphrase* 1 Cor. 2:13–14; CWE 43:49; Froben, 1532: Auditor enim spiritualis, spirituali philosophiae congruit, purgato per fidem intellectu,

et castigato per charitatem affectu. Nam crassus et animalis homo, qui rerum visibilium scientia tumet, et humanis affectibus ducitur, non recipit ea quae sunt spiritus divini, pro stultitia ducens ac deridens, quicquid ab iis quae sapit, diversum est. Non enim credit nisi quod vel experimento compertum habet, vel humanis rationibus approbatum.

19 Froben, 1516, fol. 12: Hoc philosophiae genus in affectibus situm verius, quam in syllogismis, vita magis est quam disputatio, afllatus potius quam eruditio, transformatio magis quam ratio.

20 In *Ann. 1 Cor.*, on the phrase *animalis autem homo* of 1 Cor. 2:14, Erasmus provides the following note: Velut animum, hoc est, affectus sequens humanos. Etenim quum Paulus hominem dividat in treis partis, carnem, animam, et spiritum: hic animae vocabulo, pro carne videtur abusus.

21 See Mitchell, *Paul, the Corinthians and the Birth of Early Christian Hermeneutics*, esp. 45–57.

22 See CWE 43:49: "And he does not observe that this philosophy, which teaches that Christ was born of a virgin; that he was true God and true man equally; that by dying he conquered death, and from death rose to life again; that what he has fulfilled in himself he will also fulfill in his members; that the path to true happiness lies through tribulations; that the attainment of immortality comes through death – this is not grasped by human reasoning, but by the Spirit's inspiration" (Froben, 1532: nec animadvertit, quod haec philosophiae, quae docet Christum e virgine natus, verum deum fuisse pariter et verum hominem, moriendo devicisse mortem, a morte revixisse, idem praestaturum in membris suis, quod in se praestitit, per afflictiones iter esse ad veram felicitatem, per mortes perveniri ad immortalitatem. Hoc non comprehenditur humana ratiocinatione, sed afflatu spiritus).

23 For a recent, if brief, look at Erasmus' understanding of the Spirit as teacher considered within the context of the problem of certainty in the early modern period, see Schreiner, *Are You Alone Wise?*, esp. 213ff.

24 CWE 43:50, modified and my emphasis; Froben, 1532: Nam quae traduntur, ex intimis divinae mentis arcanis deprompta sunt, non ex humanis ratiocinationibus ... Nova ratione divina mens voluit afferre suos, quae falleret omnem hominis curiositatem.

25 *Comm. 1 Cor.* 2:3 (Zurich: Froschauer, 1534): Opponit autem spiritum et virtutem Persuasioni. Haec post rhetorum ornamenta nihil habet, at sermo veritatis vegetus est, vivax, potens, adeoque hominum pectora transformans. Rhetorum persuasio brevissimo tempore aures demulcet auditorum, at verbum veritatis aculeum figit, tenet et transmutat.

26 *Comm. 1 Cor.* 2:3 (Zurich: Froschauer, 1534): Vera fides potentiae dei innititur, non praesidio humano.

27 *Comm. 1 Cor.* 2:6 (Zurich: Froschauer, 1534), ad loc.: Sapientiam autem non saeculi huius, id est eam quam miratur et excolit mundus eloquentia et naturalibus nitens ratiocinationibus observansque circa inutilium et superstitiosarum rerum quaestiones.

28 *Comm. 1 Cor.* 2:6 (Zurich: Froschauer, 1534), ad loc.: Philosophia aboletur. Et qui deum secundum traditiones hominum colunt, frustra colunt.

29 Zurich: Froschauer, 1534: Iam ut istud a solo spiritu citra mundanae philosophiae fastum edocti sumus, ita vicissim citra fucum mundanae sapientiae philosophiam Christi simpliciter et plane, iis exponumus, qui spiritualium rerum capaces sunt.

30 *Comm. 1 Cor.* 2:13 (Zurich: Froschauer, 1534), ad loc.: Pugnat hic locus vehementer adversus eos, qui in rebus divinis nihil nisi Aristotelicum sit crepant.

31 Zurich: Froschauer, 1539, fol. 186; he quotes from *Paraphrase* 1 Cor. 2:1–3; Froben, 1532, fol. 89: Etenim primum venirem ad vos, arcanam et reconditam evangelii sapientiae vobis traditurus, non veni admirandae cuiuspiam eloquentiae viribus instructus, aut eximia quadam philosophiae cognitione suscipiendus, quod hominum genus sciebam apud vos plurimi fieri.

32 Zurich: Froschauer, 1539, fol. 187; from *Paraphrase* 1 Cor. 2:4, CWE 43:44; Froben, 1532: Quemadmodum illa nullis hominum praesidiis, sed solius dei protectu munita erat adersus improborum violentiam, ita sermo meus nequaquam instructus erat rhetorum ornamentis, aut philosophorum argumentis, qui declararet quantum ipse pollerem, vel eloquentia, vel eruditione, sed tamen efficax fuit ad transfigurandos vos, non ostentatione doctrinae, sed spiritu ac virtute dei, qui afflatu miraculisque, nostro, licet incondito sermoni vim addebat.

33 Zurich: Froschauer, 1539, fol. 187: ... philosophorum oratio, quamlibet arguta aut composita. Cf. *Paraphrase* 1 Cor. 2:4, and above. Also, from fol. 189: His autem verbis Paulus occulte semper perstringit pseudapostolos, qui se verborum lenocinio et curiosis quaestionibus apud Corinthios venditabant [etc.]. This is from Zwingli, *Annotatiunculae per Leonem Iudae* (Zurich: Froschauer, 1528), fol. 21.

34 Zurich: Froschauer, 1539, fol. 190.

35 Zurich: Froschauer, 1539, fol. 189. Cf. *Paraphrase*, ad loc. (and CWE 43:39): Humana quae sunt, humano more traduntur. Quae coelestia ac spiritualia, novo modo tradenda erat.

36 *1 Corinthians* (trans. Fraser), 48; Estienne, 1556: *Logon apo tes sophias* nunc distinguit: unde quod prius admonui, confirmatur, non de inani tantum garrulitate eum hactenus loquutum: sed totum humanae doctrinae cultum comprehendisse.

37 Or "Christ simply," which retains the ambiguity. *Comm. 1 Cor.* 2:2–3 (trans. Fraser), 49; Estienne, 1556: Quod mihi defuerunt ornamenta sermonis, quod etiam disserendi elegantior subtilitas defuit, inde factum est, quia non affectavi, imo magis adspernatus sum: quia unum illud mihi in pretio erat, ut Christum simpliciter annuntiarem.

38 *Comm. 1 Cor.* 2:2–3 (trans. Fraser), 48; Estienne, 1556: ... quod Paulus affirmet se nihil pro scientia, vel scientiae loco duxisse praeter unum Christum.

39 *1 Corinthians* (trans. Fraser), 49; Estienne, 1556: Ac si diceret, non faciet ignominia crucis ut non suspiciam eum a quo est salus, vel ut me pudeat totam in eo sapientiam meam includere: illum, inquam, quem propter crucis probrum superbi homines fastidiunt ac repudiant ... nulla mihi scientia tanti fuit, ut aliud cognoscere appeterem quam Christum, licet crucifixum.

40 Still very helpful is Alister McGrath's *Luther's Theology of the Cross.* The most recent monograph on Calvin's christology is Stephen Edmondson, *Calvin's Christology.*

41 On the hiddenness of God in Luther and Calvin, see B.A. Gerrish, "'To the Unknown God': Luther and Calvin on the Hiddenness of God," *The Journal of Religion* 53:3 (1973), 263–92.

42 *1 Corinthians* (trans. Fraser), 49; Estienne, 1556: Pulcher locus, unde intelligimus et quid docere debeant fideles ministri, et quid nobis discendum sit tota vita, et prae quo nihil non pro stercore habendum.

43 *1 Corinthians* (trans. Fraser), 53; Estienne, 1556: Rationem assignat cur non magni fiat a mundi principibus evangelii doctrina: quia mysteriis involuta sit, et ideo abscondita. Ita enim supereminet humani ingenii perspicaciam evangelium, ut quamlibet sursum oculos attolant qui prae aliis ingeniosi putantur, ad eius altitudinem nunquam perveniant: interim tamen quasi ad pedes abiectum foret, eius humilitatem despiciunt. Ita fit ut quo superbius ipsum contemnunt, absint ab eius cognitione.

44 Cf. CWE 43:47, and Chrysostom *In 1 Cor. Hom.* 7.2 (PG 61, 57).

45 *1 Corinthians* (trans. Fraser), 53–4; Estienne, 1556: Nam si Deus nihil frustra statuit, sequitur nos operam non perdituros in audiendo evangelio quod nobis destinavit: se enim modulo nostro attemperat, quum nobis loquitur.

46 See ibid., 56, and Erasmus, *Ann.* 1 Cor. 2:9, "Sicut scriptum est," ad loc.

47 *1 Corinthians* (trans. Fraser), 56.

48 *1 Corinthians* (trans. Fraser), 57; Estienne, 1556: Postquam conclusit universos homines sub caecitate, et humanae menti hoc ademit ne possit ad Deum proprio marte conscendere: nunc ostendit qualiter ab hac caecitate eximantur fideles: nempe quia Dominus peculiari spiritus illuminatione ipsos dignatur. Itaque quo est humana mens hebetior ad

intelligenda Dei mysteria, quo maior est eius incertitudo, eo certior est fides nostra, quae spiritus Dei revelatione suffulta est.

49 For a treatment of Calvin on certainty, see Schreiner, "Calvin and the Exegetical Debates about Certainty." Schreiner argues for the importance of certainty, and its relationship to the Spirit, in the sixteenth century in *Are You Alone Wise?* See also Pitkin, *What Pure Eyes Could See*, 138ff., and, on Luther and Calvin, Zachman, *The Assurance of Faith*. On the importance of the Spirit as a teacher and guide, see also Zachman, *John Calvin as Teacher, Pastor, and Theologian*, e.g., 128ff. and 158ff.

50 *Comm. 1 Cor.* 2:10 (trans. Fraser), 58; Estienne, 1556: Non aliter posse comprehendi evangelii doctrinam quam spiritus sancti testimonio: rursus eorum, qui a spiritu sancto tale testimonium habent, non minus firmam ac solidam esse certitudinem quam si manibus palparent quod credunt: quia spiritus fidus est ac indubius testis.

51 My translation; Estienne, 1556: Quis enim hominum novit quae ad eum pertinent, nisi spiritus hominis qui est in ipso? Ita et quae Dei sunt, nemo novit, nisi Spiritus Dei.

52 *1 Corinthians* (trans. Fraser), 57; Estienne, 1556: Quisque enim suarum cogitationum conscius est. Quid autem in corde cuiusque lateat, alter nescit.

53 *1 Corinthians* (trans. Fraser), 58; Estienne, 1556: Nam quum lingua sit character mentis, communicant inter se homines suos affectus: ut alii alios suarum cogitationum habeant conscios. Cur non ergo ex Dei verbo comprehendamus, quae sit eius voluntas? ... Interior hominis cogitatio, quam alii ignorant, illi uni est perspecta. Eam postea si aliis patefacit, id non facit quominus solus eius spiritus noverit quid in ipso sit.

54 See this book's conclusion for examples and the link between this notion and Christ as *Sermo* in John 1:1.

55 See Erasmus' *Paraphrase* (CWE 43:48): "But no mortal observes what lies hidden in the innermost retreats of the soul."

56 *1 Corinthians* (trans. Fraser), 58–9; Estienne, 1556: Hoc autem discriminis inter Dei et hominum cogitationes interest ... sermo autem Dei arcana quaedam est sapientia, ad cuius sublimitatem non pertingit humanae mentis imbecillitas.

57 Schreiner, *Are You Alone Wise?* 79–131.

58 *1 Corinthians* (trans. Fraser), 59; Estienne, 1556: Ita lux in tenebris lucet, donec caecorum oculos aperiat spiritus.

59 Zachman, *John Calvin as Teacher, Pastor, and Theologian*, 128.

60 *1 Corinthians* (trans. Fraser), 59; Estienne, 1556: Locus plus satis perspicuus ad refellendum illud diabolicum sophistarum dogma de perpetua fidelium haesitatione ... nec aliam salutis fiduciam admittunt quam quae pendeat a coniectura morali vel probabili.

61 *1 Corinthians* (trans. Fraser), 59; Estienne, 1556: Electos spiritu donatos esse,
quo testificante certo sciant se adoptatos esse ad spem aeternae salutis.

62 *1 Corinthians* (trans. Fraser), 59; Estienne, 1556: alioqui enim trepida semper
erit ac nutabit: uia videmus quam audacter se efferat humanum acumen,
cuius fastum contrario heroicae magnanimitatis fastu calcari necesse est a
filiis Dei.

63 *1 Corinthians* (trans. Fraser), 59; Estienne, 1556: Scientiae vocabulum ad
exprimendam melius fiduciae securitatem positum est. Notemus tamen
eam non concipi naturali modo, nec mentis captu apprehendi: sed totam
a revelatione spiritus pendere. Cf. Erasmus' *Paraphrase* on this section of
1 Corinthians: "Human matters are taught in a human manner; heavenly
and spiritual matters needed to be taught in a new way, and that not to
every sort of person certainly, but only to those who by imbibing in the
Spirit of Christ are now fit for spiritual teaching, since in fact they are
spiritual themselves"; and the editors' note on this section: "It is clear
throughout this passage, moreover, that Erasmus intends 'in a new way' to
refer primarily to the idea that Christian wisdom is imparted 'spiritually,'
not through human reasoning or eloquence, but through the inbreathing or
imbibing of the Holy Spirit" (CWE 43:49).

64 Pitkin, *What Pure Eyes Could See*, 143.

65 *1 Corinthians* (trans. Fraser), 60; Estienne, 1556: Sermones eruditos
humanae sapientiae vocat qui humanam eruditionem sapiant sintque
expoliti ad rhetorum normam, vel referti philosophicis ampullis, ita ut in
sui admirationem rapiant auditores. Sermones autem doctos spiritus qui
ad sincerum simplicemque stilum et maiestate spiritus dignum magis sint
compositi quam ad vanam ostentationem.

66 For a discussion of the christological knowledge of God from the
perspective of fallen humanity in the *Institutes*, see Pitkin, *What Pure Eyes
Could See*, 144ff.

67 *1 Corinthians* (trans. Fraser), 61; Estienne, 1556: Hominem animalem
vocat, non ut vulgo accipiunt, crassis concupiscentiis, vel (ut loquuntur)
aensualitati suae addictum: sed quemlibet hominem solis naturae
facultatibus praeditum. Quod ex opposito liquet: animalem enim cum
spirituali confert. Quum per hunc intelligatur is, cuius mens illuminatione
spiritus Dei regitur: non dubium quin ille hominem in puris (ut loquuntur)
naturalibus relictum significet. Anima enim naturae propria est, spiritus
vero ex dono est supernaturali. Susan Schreiner points out that Calvin is
reticent, unlike other of his contemporaries, to attribute infallibility to the
"spiritual man," however (*Are You Alone Wise?* 106).

68 *Ann.* 1 Cor. 2:14 (ed., trans. Donnelly, modified), 52–3: Quarto, hoc uno
loco vocavit Animalem hominem eam hominis partem, quam nostri

rationem vocant et optimum naturae, ut sit animalis homo ab anima
vivens, non secundum crassissimi corporis voluptatem, sed secundum
animam, rationis usum qualis vel Socrates, vel Zeno, vel Paulus ante
voncersionem esse potuerunt ... Hic significantiae gratia dicit animalem,
ut emphatice significet se proprie de homine secundum eius potiores
partes loqui.
69 *1 Corinthians* (trans. Fraser), 61; Estienne, 1556: Qualis sapientia, quae
totam hominis intelligentiam tam longo intervallo superat, ut ne eius
quidem gustum possint capere.
70 Tota fere sapientiae nostrae summae, quae vera demum ac solida sapientia
censeri debeat, duabus partibus constat ... (Estienne, Geneva: 1559).
71 It should be noted that often determining what is and isn't a direct
quotation in Calvin's works is a bit more slippery than one might imagine.
Richard Muller has pointed out the problematic nature of, e.g., the
McNeill/Battles English edition of the *Institutes*, which inserts biblical
references in the text in cases where Calvin isn't in fact quoting directly,
but merely alluding, or even simply using biblical language to express
himself. Editions like these have the advantage of illustrating quite clearly
just how infused Calvin's thinking was with biblical language and idiom,
and also the extent to which the *Institutes* is a work of exegetical theology,
but they can also be misleading. (See Muller, *The Unaccommodated Calvin*,
174ff.) Max Engammare has shown this to be the case also in Calvin's
sermons on Genesis (see his "Calvin connaissait-il la Bible?"; also Gilmont,
Calvin and the Printed Book, esp. 143–8 and notes).
72 Quod mirisice imponebat sapientiae titulo, pro extrema stultitia foetebit
(the Latin is from Estienne, 1559; the McNeill/Battles English edition
provides sigla indicating which edition a particular section appeared in
first, and I have simply followed them here).
73 *Inst.* II.vi.1 (McNeill/Battles); Estienne, 1559: Itaque veniendum ad illud
Pauli, Quoniam in sapientia Dei non cognovit mundus per sapientiam
Deum, placuit Deo per stultitiam praedicationis salvos facere credentes.
Sapientiam Dei appellat magnificum hoc theatrum caeli et terrae,
innumeris miraculis refertum, ex cuius intuitu sapienter Deum cognoscere
decebat: sed quia tam male illic profecimus, revocat nos ad fidem Christi,
quae ob stultitiae speciem incredulis fastidio est. Quanquam ergo humano
ingenio non respondet praedicatio crucis, humiliter tamen eam amplecti
oportet, si ad Deum opificem nostrum et fictorem, a quo sumus alienati,
redire cupimus, ut nobis iterum pater esse incipiat. Certe post lapsum
primi hominis nulla ad salutem valuit Dei cognitio absque Mediatore.
74 McNeill/Battles, 581. Atqui si humanae voluntatis (ut Paulus concionatur)
nemo est testis nisi spiritus hominis qui in ipso est, divinae voluntatis qui

certus esset homo? Et si Dei veritas apud nos in iis quoque rebus vacillat quas oculo praesenti intuemur, qui firma stabilisque foret, ubi Dominus ea pollicetur quae nec oculus videt, nec ingenium capit? Adeo autem hic consternatur et deficit humana perspicacia, ut primus in Domini schola proficiendi gradus sit, ab ea deficere.

75 *Inst.* III.ii.34; McNeill/Battles, 582. Ita ubi trahimur, mente et animo evehimur supra nostram ipsorum intelligentiam. Nam ab eo illustrata anima novam quasi aciem sumit, qua coelestia mysteria contempletur, quorum splendore ante in se ipsa perstringebatur. (Estienne, 1559)

76 For the connections between Pauline folly and Platonist ecstasy in Erasmus, see Screech, *Ecstasy and the Praise of Folly*.

77 McNeill/Battles, 583. Ad Corinthios, ubi fidem non pendere ex sapientia hominum dicit, sed fundatam esse in potentia spiritus (Estienne, 1559).

78 McNeill/Battles, 583; Estienne, 1559: Admiratione exclamare possum, non disputatione monstrare.

79 *Inst.* II.2.20; McNeill/Battles, 280. Most of the section is new in the 1539 edition. Restat igitur ut intelligamus, nemini patere in regnum Dei ingressum nisi cui novam mentem spiritus sanctus sua illuminatione fecerit. Omnium vero clarissime Paulus, qui disputationem hanc ex professo ingressus, postquam stultitiae ac vanitatis damnavit universam hominum sapientiam adeoque prorsus exinanivit, ita concludit demum, animalem hominem non posse percipere quae sunt spiritus Dei; stultitiam esse illi, nec posse intelligere, quia spiritualiter diiudicantur. Quid istud significat? Quia humanae perspicaciae penitus abscondita, per solam spiritus revelationem pateiunt; adeo ut pro stultitia ducantur, ubi spiritus Dei non illucet. Ante autem supra oculorum, aurium, mentium capacitatem extulerat quae praeparavit Deus diligentibus se; quin sapientiam humanam quasi velum quoddam esse testatus fuerat, quo mens a cernendo Deo impeditur. Quid volumnus? Proununtiat apostolus infatuatam a Deo sapientiam huius mundi: et nos scilicet acumen illi tribuemus, quo ad Deum et coelestis regni adyta penetrare possit? Facessat a nobis tanta vecordia (Estienne, 1559).

80 See also, e.g., *Inst.* II.13.12.

4. Milk for Babes: A Pauline Eloquence

1 A substantial part of this chapter was published in Essary, "Milk for Babes."

2 Auerbach, "*Sermo Humilis*."

3 Fumaroli, *L'Age de l'éloquence*, 71; and further that "fort différente de celle des orateur païens puisqu'elle est entièrement fondée sur l'interprétation des Ecritures." See, more recently, Paul Kolbet, *Augustine and the Cure of Souls*. See also *The Rhetoric of St. Augustine of Hippo* (ed. Enos and Thompson; Baylor UP, 2008), Bene, *Erasme et Saint Augustin*, 400ff. and, more recently, Kathy Eden, *Hermeneutics and the Rhetorical Tradition*, 41–78.

4 Fumaroli, *L'Age de l'éloquence*, 70, and see 106ff.

5 Shuger, *Sacred Rhetoric*, 63. Shuger has treated this subject in the early modern period well in several places, with a primary focus on the genre of sacred rhetorics; see especially *Sacred Rhetoric* but also "Foundations of Sacred Rhetoric." For a good overview of rhetoric and hermeneutics in the Christian tradition, with attention to Erasmus operating in the classical and Augustinian tradition see Eden, *Hermeneutics and the Rhetorical Tradition*. On early modern preaching, see, recently, Kneidl, "*Ars Praedicandi*: Theories and Practice." On Erasmus, see especially Hoffmann, *Rhetoric and Theology* and "Erasmus: Rhetorical Theologian"; John O'Malley, "Grammar and Rhetoric in the *Pietas* of Erasmus," 81–98; Mack, "Erasmus' Contribution to Rhetoric and Rhetoric in Erasmus' Writing," 27–46; O'Rourke Boyle, *Erasmus on Language and Method in Theology*; Bentley, *Humanists and Holy Writ*, 112–93. For an assessment of Erasmus and rhetoric that maintains that his theology is only a secondary concern, see Chomarat, *Grammaire et rhétorique chez Érasme*.

6 For the *Ciceronianus*, see CWE vol. 28 and ASD I-2.

7 Rummel, *The Humanist-Scholastic Debate*, 123–4. See also her "God and Solecism: Erasmus as a Literary Critic of the Bible," 54–72, for an analysis of the tension involved in Erasmus' attempts to render the Latin New Testament into a more grammatically and stylistically responsible (i.e., a more *eloquent*) translation than the Vulgate, and his claims that the apostles, in their rusticity, embodied a particular kind of efficacious eloquence appropriate to their subject matter.

8 The most extensive treatment of Calvin and rhetoric in theology is Millet, *Calvin et la dynamique de la parole*; see also Bouwsma, "Calvinism as Theologia Rhetorica?"; Jones, *Calvin and the Rhetoric of Piety*; also, *Affect before Spinoza*, the dissertation (with attention particularly to the ideas of *affectus* and *persuasio*, mostly in the *Institutes*) of Russ Leo. Still helpful is E. David Willis, "Rhetoric and Responsibility in Calvin's Theology," 43–64. On Calvin's indebtedness to the Augustinian rhetorical tradition, and his context in Renaissance rhetoric, although with little reference to Erasmus, see Selinger, *Calvin Against Himself*, esp. 152–76. On Melanchthon's

somewhat different perception of *Paulus rhetor*, see Wengert, *Human Freedom*, 50ff. and Weaver, "A More Excellent Way: Philip Melanchthon's Corinthians Lectures of 1521–1522," 31–63. For a study of a pastoral-rhetorical program of Pauline simplicity as well as accommodation in late sixteenth-century England, which recognizes the contributions of Erasmus and Calvin to this important trend in Christian pastoral rhetoric, see Kneidel, "'Mighti Simplenesse': Protestant pastoral rhetoric and Spenser's *Shepheardes Calender*," 275–312.

9 See also Erasmus, *Apologia de "In principio erat sermo"* (LB IX 11B–122F); Jarrott, "Erasmus' 'In Principio Erat Sermo': A Controversial Translation," 35–40; O'Rourke Boyle, "Sermo: Reopening the Conversation on Translating JN 1,1," 161–8; and Christ-von Wedel, *Erasmus of Rotterdam* (2013), 133–44. Christ-von Wedel in fact writes, erroneously, that Zwingli and Beza are the only "non-radicals" to have followed Erasmus in translating *Logos* as *Sermo*.

10 Pitkin touches on some of the related issues in "The Spiritual Gospel? Christ and Human Nature in Calvin's Commentary on John," 187–204. See also this book's conclusion.

11 Torrance, *Hermeneutics*, 147–8.

12 The caricatured dichotomy is as old as Plato's *Protagoras*, and it persists in contemporary thinkers such as Stanley Fish: see, e.g., Shuger, "Foundations of Sacred Rhetoric," 47ff., for an argument, *contra* Fish, that early modern "sacred rhetoric" confounds the neat dichotomy of dialectic v. rhetoric.

13 Muller, *The Unaccommodated Calvin*, 39–40.

14 See, e.g., essays by Schneider and Hoffmann in *Philip Melanchthon (1497–1560) and the Commentary*. On Melanchthon's influence on Calvin in the areas of rhetoric and dialectic, see Millet, *Calvin et la dynamique*, esp. 122–35; on Calvin's debt to a humanist conception of *persuasio* and *fiducia* in his understanding of faith, see 212, although Millet neglects to mention Erasmus here, only citing Valla, Bude, and Bucer.

15 Shuger, "Foundations of Sacred Rhetoric," 50.

16 Shuger, "Foundations of Sacred Rhetoric," 54.

17 Millet, *Calvin et la dynamique de la parole*. It is a massive book, but for the section relevant to our chapter, see esp. 185–257.

18 Moss, *Renaissance Truth and the Latin Language Turn*, 264.

19 Strohm, "Methodology in Discussion of 'Calvin and Calvinism'," 72. See also Millet, *Calvin*, passim, and "*Docere/movere*."

20 *Ann* 1 Cor. 1:17 ad loc.; Froben, 1535: id est, Ut non fiat inanis. Nam inane dicitur quod non est solidum, sed specie blanditur. Illud obiter annotabis

optime lector, quam solicite curarit divus Paulus ut evangelium Christi
purissimum esset ab omnibus humanis adminiculis, ne quid inde sibi
vendicare posset hic mundus, adeo ut nec eloquentiam voluerit adiungere,
aut eruditionem humanam. At his temporibus quum oneremus Christum
opibus, negociis prophanis, honoribus, imperiis, exercitibus, voluptatibus,
et quibus tandem non? solam eloquentiam execramur, Et hac una in parte
vel anteimus apostolos. nam illi simpliciter dixerunt, sed cordate, sine
lenociniis, at rursum sine spurcitia sine portentis; inaffectate loquuti sunt,
sed prudenter; et ut paucis icam, quemadmodum alio modo potentes erant
ac divites, alio modo nobiles et inclyti, ita diuerso modo tum eruditi, tum
eloquentes.

21 For a relatively recent, and excellent, treatment of many of the issues
    involved, see Cummings, *The Literary Culture of the Reformation*.

22 See Auerbach, *"Sermo Humilis,"* e.g., at 51: "Thus the style of the Scriptures
    [which serves as the normative model for Christian teachers and preachers
    according to Augustine] throughout is *humilis*, lowly or humble. Even
    the hidden things (*secreta, recondita*) are set forth in a 'lowly' vein. But
    the subject matter, whether simple or obscure, is sublime. The lowly, or
    humble, style is the only medium in which such sublime mysteries can be
    brought within the reach of men. It constitutes a parallel to the Incarnation,
    which was also a *humilitas* in the same sense, for men could not have
    endured the splendor of Christ's divinity." Fumaroli also points out the
    close relationship in Augustine's thought of Christian rhetoric and the
    Incarnation: "En ce sens, le chapitre XII du L. I est au cœur de la rhétorique
    augustinienne: *Verbum caro factum est*. L'incarnation du Verbe, l'utilisation
    par Dieu d'un corps de chair pour signifier aux hommes son message,
    révèle non seulement qu'il y a communication possible entre Dieu et les
    hommes, mais que cette communication est le mystère central de l'histoire
    chrétienne du salut" (71).

23 *Holy Scripture Speaks*, 31. See also Vessey, "'Lingua Christi Praedicatrix':
    The Tongue and the Book in Erasmus' Paraphrases on the Pastoral and
    Catholic Epistles," *ERSY* 17 (1997), 70–97.

24 See Mack, "Erasmus' Contribution to Rhetoric and Rhetoric in Erasmus'
    Writing," esp 31ff., for the idea that "rhetorical ideas condition Erasmus'
    way of thinking and arguing about editing, bringing out the meaning of
    the Bible, and religious teaching."

25 Auerbach, *"Sermo Humilis,"* 37.

26 Johan Huizinga, in assessing Erasmus' turn against the Ciceronians later
    in life, goes so far as to suggest that, "We here see the aged Erasmus on the

path of reaction, which might eventually have led him far from humanism. In his combat with humanistic purism he foreshadows a Christian puritanism" (*Erasmus and the Age of the Reformation*, 173). Probably Huizinga suggests a bit too strongly that the younger Erasmus operated at the same level of purism as did the new Ciceronians (see 172); translating *Logos* as *Sermo*, far from being an instance of humanist purism, seems to have its roots in a particular sort of theological orientation.

27 *Paraphrase* 1 Cor. 2:1–3; CWE 43:43. Froben, 1532: non veni admirandae cuiuspiam eloquentiae viribus instructus, aut eximia quadam philosophiae cognitione suscipiendus, quod hominum genus sciebam apud vos plurimi fieri. Adeo nihil horum quae mundo praeclara videbantur, professus sum, ut non aliud existimaverim inter vos scire me, quam Iesum Christum, et hunc sane crucifixum. Hominem praedicavi, sed a deo unctum, et a prophetis promissum ad redimendum genus humanum. Quod in illo est humillimum, inde sum Evangelii praedicationem auspicatus.

28 Lefevre d'Etaples had made a similar argument: [Paulus] non venit ad Corinthios in pompa verborum et calamistrata oratione: sed in simplici minime fucato sermone ut decet dei apostolum. Non enim iudicavit se magis quam illos scire philosophiam, geometriam, or oratoriam, sed se magis scire dominum nostrum Ihesum Christum et huc ipsum pro mundi vita fuisse crucifixum et reliqua mysteria admirandae et non modo supermundanae sed et superdivinae conversationis eius (*S. Pauli epistolae XIV ex Vulgata, adiecta intelligentia ex graeco cum commentariis* [Frommann-Holzboog: Faksimilie-Neudruck der Ausgabe Paris 1512], 108 verso).

29 *Paraphrase* 1 Cor. 2:3–6; CWE 43:44. Froben, 1532: Porro qualis erat vitae habitus talis et oratio. Quemadmodum illa nullis hominum praesidiis, sed solius dei protectu munita erat adversus improborum violentiam, ita sermo meus nequaquam instructus erat rhetorum ornamentis, aut philosophorum argumentis, qui declararet quantum ipse pollerem, vel eloquentia, vel eruditione, sed tamen efficax fuit ad transfigurandos vos, non ostentatione doctrinae, sed spiritu ac virtute dei, qui afflatu miraculisque, nostro, licet incondito sermoni vim addebat. (see CWE 43:44 n. 6: Cf. Origen, *CC* 6.2, where he quotes 1 Cor. 2:4 defending the simplicity of the gospel against unprofitable philosophical speech.)

30 *Paraphrase* 1 Cor. 1:17–20; CWE 43:37. Froben, 1532: Neque enim id fieri voluit humanae sapientiae, facundiaeve praesidiis, quibus nihil huiusmodi praestari poterat, sed incomposito simplicisque sermone rem tam arduam geri voluit, ut tota laus facti deo transcribatur, cui placuit per contemptam et ignominiosam Christi crucem innovare mundum universum.

31 *Paraphrase* 1 Cor. 2:3–6; CWE 43:44. Froben, 1532: ... existimet vos humanae doctrinae aut eloquentiae debere, quam nobis non vindicamus,

sed potentiae divinae, per quam sermo noster efficacior fuit, quam
philosophorum oratio, quamlibet arguta aut composita.

32 CWE 66:xxvii.

33 Bateman, "From Soul to Soul: Persuasion in Erasmus' Paraphrases on the
New Testament," 14.

34 Bateman, "From Soul to Soul," 7.

35 Hoffmann, *Rhetoric and Theology*, 84.

36 Bateman, "From Soul to Soul," 14.

37 *Paraphrase* 1 Cor. 3:1–2; CWE 43:50–51; Froben, 1532, fol. 91: apud rudes
rudi sermone sum usus, crassis crassius sum locutus, ac velut apud
infantes balbutii. Habet enim et fides profectus suos. Vos igitur cum adhuc
infantes viderem in philosophia Christi, doctrinae crassioris ceu lacte vos
alui, non solido cibo doctrinae perfectioris.

38 *Paraphrase* 1 Cor. 3:2; Froben, 1532, fol. 92: Ego sum, Aristotelicus, ego
Platonicus, ego Stoicus, ego Epicureus [etc.].

39 From the *Ratio*; qtd. in Rummel, *The Humanist-Scholastic Debate*, 136.

40 See Vessey, "'Lingua Christi Praedicatrix': The Tongue and the Book in
Erasmus' Paraphrases on the Pastoral and Catholic Epistles," *ERSY* 17
(1997), 70–97.

41 See Augustine, *De doct. chr.* IV.25–7 on the idea that Scripture is of
the highest eloquence precisely *because* it is humble and therefore
accommodating. And see the description of Augustine's ideal Christian
style by Fumaroli: "La première qualité, et de loin, du style chrétien est la
clarté (*claritas, perspicuitas*). Il importe en effet avant tout de démêler les
obscurités de l'Ecriture, et de rendre celle-ci transparente à tous, savants et
ignorants" (*L'Age de l'éloquence*, 73).

42 *Paraphrase* 1 Cor. 4:16–21; CWE 43:68. Froben, 1532: Neque enim in
magnificis dictis sita est Evangelii vis, quae cuiuis in promptu sunt, sed
in vi, aut virtute coelesti, quae malorum tolerantia, quae concordia, quae
totius vitae innocentia, quae miraculis declaratur.

43 *Paraphrase* 1 Cor. 3:15–18; CWE 43:58; Froben, 1532: Qui frigidas ceremonii
cum ignea Christi charitate?

44 Hoffmann, *Rhetoric and Theology*, 82–3.

45 *Paraphrase* 1 Cor. 3:4–9; CWE 43:54; Froben, 1532, fol. 92: Siquidem frustra
laboret qui plantat, frustra qui rigat, nisi coelum afflet vim suam occultam,
sed hoc magis efficacem quod occulta est.

46 *Paraphrase* 1 Cor. 3:9–12; CWE 43:55; Froben, 1532: Coeleste ac spirituale
fundamentum est, non convenit huic structura carnalis ac terrenae doctrinae.

47 *Ann.* 1 Cor. 3:10, ad loc.: Hic *sophon* plane posuit pro docto et scito.

48 *Paraphrase* 1 Cor. 3:9–12; Froben, 1532: Ego Christum vobis scopum
proposui.

49 *Paraphrase* 1 Cor. 3:12–13; CWE 43:56; Froben, 1532: ... is structuram
   addit Christo fundamento dignam: sin humanas addit constitutiunculas,
   de cultu, de victu, de frigidis ceremoniis, de que similibus rebus, quas
   homines conminisci solent, non in rem Christi, sed in suam ipsorum
   gloriam, aut etiam in quaestum, ut orsi a tam nobili fundamento
   degenerent in superstitiosos pro piis, iam lignum, foenum ac stipulam
   induxit ... Si doctrina quae acce, reddat vos invictos ad omnes humanos
   affectus, palam est efficacem esse: sin reddit imbecilles ad ferenda
   incommoda, si iritabiles, si morosos, si contentiosos, si obtrectatores, si
   fucatos, hinc satis liquet adulterinam fuisse doctrinam.
50 Faber, "Desiderius Erasmus' Representation of Paul as Paragon of Learned
   Piety," 48–9.
51 See, e.g., O'Rourke Boyle on this, working from the *De ratione studii*:
   "Unlike the dialecticians of Plato's republic, pressing to know reality
   itself without words, the pupil of the Christian commonwealth was to
   apprentice himself to language. Did not the truth proceed from God's
   mouth? Was not Christ himself divine language? Erasmus did not
   commend those who scrambled to learn truths but neglected their artful
   expression ... Those men who pretend to behold reality bare, declaring that
   they ignore its language, are the very ones who quibble most sophistically
   about verbal particles. For Erasmus this claim characterizes the schoolmen,
   who choke on the words they seek to transcend" (*Erasmus on Language and
   Method in Theology*, 38).
52 *Paraphrase* 1 Cor. 3:15–18; CWE 43:58; Froben, 1532: Neminem fallit
   Christus, si quis huic innitatur. At videat quisque ne praesidiis humanis
   male fretus, fallat seipsum.
53 *Paraphrase* 1 Cor. 3:15–18; CWE 43:58–9; Froben, 1532: Nihil est quod
   felicitatem vestram a philosophiae aut legis praesidiis expectetis. Neque
   quisquam hoc sese caeteris anteponat, quod humana doctrina polleat.
   Imo qui sibi videtur esse sapients, iuxta mundanam aestimationem,
   sapienter stultescat, ut vere fiat sapiens. Definat esse stultae sapientiae
   turgidus professor et idoneus erit, qui sit sapientissimae stultitiae
   discipulus.
54 *Paraphrase* 1 Cor. 3:22ff.; CWE 43:60; Froben, 1532: sive occurrunt
   praesentia, neglectim utendum est momentariis, sive futura, ad haec
   magno animo connitendum, quae licet non cernatis oculis corporis, tamen
   oculis fidei cernitis. Bullinger reproduces this section, and then some, in
   his commentary (1 Cor. 3:22ff.), referring to Erasmus only by the term
   "Paraphrastes."
55 Bateman, "From Soul to Soul," 13.

56 *Paraphrase* 1 Cor. 2:11–13; CWE 43:48. Froben, 1532: Ita res conditas
   contemplantur ac investigant complures, caeterum quae sunt abstrusa
   in mente consilioque divino, nemo novit, nisi spiritus aeternus, qui
   deo intimus est, et ob id illi conscius omnium. Homo impartit homini
   cogitationes arcanas tacito susurro. Deus impartis piis suum consilium per
   spiritum, non hominis, qui praeter humanas res nihil adferre potest, sed
   dei. Qualis est spiritus, talia docet. Habet et mundus hic spiritum suum,
   eo qui corripiuntur, mundana tum sapiunt, tum amant. At nobis divini
   spiritus afflatus coelestia suggerit, ut intelligamus, quantum bonorum
   deus nobis largitus sit per Christi crucem.
57 *Paraphrase* 1 Cor. 2:13; CWE 43:48. Froben, 1532: ... diversum est sapientiae
   genus, diversa sit et tradendi ratio.
58 *Paraphrase* 1 Cor. 2:13; CWE 43:48. Froben, 1532: Quae coelestia ac
   spiritualia, novo modo tradenda erant, nec id sane quibuslibet, sed iis
   duntaxat, qui hausto Christi spiritu iam habiles sunt doctrinae spirituali.
59 *Paraphrase* 1 Cor. 2:13; CWE 43:49. Froben, 1532: Auditor enim spiritualis,
   spirituali philosophiae congruit, purgato per fidem intellectu, et castigato
   per charitatem affectu.
60 *Ciceronianus*, CWE 28:383. On accommodation to subject matter generally
   in the *Ciceronianus*, see esp. CWE 28:380ff. See also O'Rourke Boyle,
   Erasmus on Language and Method, 48.
61 O'Rourke Boyle, *Erasmus on Language and Method*, 49.
62 See, e.g., CWE 28:395.
63 *Ciceronianus* (CWE 28:393).
64 *Paraphrase* 1 Cor. 4:8–9; CWE 43:65; Froben, 1532: nos humiles et indignis
   modis afflicti Christum vobis pure praedicavimus.
65 *1 Corinthians* (trans. Fraser), 32.
66 *1 Corinthians* (trans. Fraser), 32; Estienne, 1556: Nempe quum turgerent
   ambitione, quo plebem raperent in admirationem sui, verborum pompa et
   humanae sapientiae larva se venditabant.
67 Wendel suggests the influence of Erasmus' *Paraphrases* as early as Calvin's
   commentary on Seneca's *De clementia*, which includes several instances of
   paraphrase. See *Calvin: Origins and Development of His Religious Thought*,
   esp. 31.
68 See above for Erasmus' use of these same adjectives in his *Paraphrase*.
69 *1 Corinthians* (trans. Fraser), 32; Estienne, 1556: Ac si diceret:
   scio quantopere sibi blandiantur vestri isti delicati doctores sua
   magniloquentia: ego autem praedicationem meam rudi et crasso
   minimeque polito dicendi genere constitisse, non tantum confiteor, sed
   etiam glorior. Sic enim agi oprotuit, atque haec mihi ratio fuit divinitus

praescripta. Interesting is Calvin's use of the mode of paraphrase (he does it fairly regularly in the commentaries) which, of course, is perfectly Erasmian (see note 67 above).

70 *1 Corinthians* (trans. Fraser), 33 (modified); Estienne, 1556: Non est ergo quod hic dicit Paulus, in vontumeliam artium accipiendum, quasi pietati adversentur.

71 *1 Corinthians* (trans. Fraser), 33–4; Estienne, 1556: Prae aliis ergo ad crucis humilitatem revocandi erant, ut discerent nudum Christum et simplex evangelium absque fuco ullo amplecti.

72 Estienne, 1556: Christi crucem exinaniri non tantum mundana sapientia, sed verborum quoque splendore.

73 See Zachman, *John Calvin as Teacher, Pastor, and Theologian* (esp. 29–55), for a discussion of Melanchthon and Calvin as defenders of the responsible use of classical rhetoric in Christian teaching (especially with an eye to clarity), with careful attention to the divergences which arose between them over the course of a complicated friendship.

74 *1 Corinthians* (trans. Fraser), 34.

75 *1 Corinthians* (trans. Fraser), 34; Estienne, 1556: Altera est ut in rudi et impolio sermone magis conspicua appareret veritatis suae maiestas, et sola spiritus efficacia absque externis adminiculis in hominum animos penetraret.

76 At the end of the sixteenth century, writers of sacred rhetorics will make a distinction between *eloquentia* and *elegantia,* as Debora Shuger has shown: "Ludovico Carbo thus defines *elegantia* 'as harmonious and ornate style of speaking, designed to delight, as was once popular among the sophists.' But he immediately proceeds to differentiate this style from that appropriate to rhetoric: 'In *elegantia* is a certain power of delighting, in eloquence the power of persuasion. The former shines and sparkles, occupying the senses with trifles; the latter burns and flames in order to move souls.' The opposite of sophistic prose in most Renaissance discussions is not an unadorned, 'philosophical' style but the conjunction of power and luminosity" (Shuger, "The Philosophical Foundations of Sacred Rhetoric," 117). The distinction is, of course, functionally present in our exegetes as well, if not brought out in the semantic analysis of these two words.

77 *1 Corinthians* (trans. Fraser), 32; Estienne, 1556: Sermonis sapientiam vocat, non *logodaidalian,* quae nihil est quam inanis loquacitas: sed eloquentiam veram, quae constat prudenti rerum inventione, dispositione ingeniosa, et elegantia sermonis. Hanc sibi defuisse testatur, quin etiam suae praedicationi neque aptam, neque utilem fuisse.

78 1 *Corinthians* (trans. Fraser), 34; Estienne, 1556: Altera vero, ut nostram
obedientiam ac docilitatem melius experiretur, et simul ad veram
humilitatem erudiret. Solos enim parvulos in scholam suam admittit
Dominus.

79 1 *Corinthians* (trans. Fraser), 48; Estienne, 1556: Paulus de sua docendi
ratione dicere aggressus, ad generalem praedicationis evangelicae naturam
mox descenderat: iterum nunc ad se ipsum revertitur, ut ostendat nihil in
se contemni, quod non sit ex propria evangelii natura et illi quodammodo
adhaereat. Conceit ergo sibi non adfuisse humanae vel facundiae vel
sapientiae praesidia, quibus instructus aliquid effecerit: sed ex quo se
destitutum istis opibus fuisse fatetur: inde magis elucere in suo ministerio
Dei potentiam subinfert, quae huiusmodi subsidiis non indiguerit.

80 It might be noted that Melanchthon seemed to have been more interested
in rendering Paul's discourse in Ciceronian terms, something Erasmus did
not insist on doing precisely because he wanted to conceive of Christian
eloquence as different from classical eloquence. While Erasmus did indeed
apply classical rhetorical forms in his analysis of Paul (*pace* Wengert,
Human Freedom, 50–1; see the section below on *accommodatio*), he was also
careful – and Calvin followed him here – to insist on the importance of
Paul's own form of lowly eloquence, which was more powerful for its lack
of human supports.

81 Bouwsma, *John Calvin*, 127.

82 1 *Corinthians* (trans. Fraser), 34; Estienne, 1556: Quid autem si quispiam
hodie paulo nitidius disserendo, evangelii doctrinam eloquentia illustret?
an propterea repudiandus erit, quasi vel eam contaminet, vel obscuret
Christi gloriam? Respondeo, primum nihil pugnare cum evangelii
simplicitate eloquentiam, quae sine fastidio illi non tantum cedat et
subiiciat, sed etiam tanquam ancilla dominae serviat.

83 1 *Corinthians* (trans. Fraser), 34–5.

84 Estienne, 1556: Haec ergo eloquentia nec damnanda, nec adspernanda est,
quae non huc spectat ut Christianos in externo verborum colore detineat,
ut eos inebriet vana oblectatione, ut suo tinnitu aures feriat, ut sua pompa
tanquam involucro obruat Christi crucem: sed potius ut ad nativam
evangelii simplicitatem nos revocet, ut ipsa sponte se in ordinem redigens
solam crucis praedicationem extollat, ut denique tanquam praeconis officio
fungatur ad comparandam piscatoribus illis et idiotis audientiam, qui nihil
praeter spiritus energiam gratiae habent.

85 1 *Corinthians* (trans. Fraser), 35; Estienne, 1556: [S]uam quoque esse spiritui
Dei eloquentiam: sed quae nativo magis et proprio, vel potius intrinseco
(ut loquuntur) splendore, quam adscititiis ornamentis luceat.

86 My translation. *Proinde eiusmodi eloquentia spiritui Dei convenit, quae non ostentatione turgeat, nec crepet inanem sonitum: sed quae solida sit et efficax plusque sinceritatis habeat quam elegantiae.* See also Augustine, *De doctr. chr.* IV.59–60, and IV.66: "The teacher will avoid all words which do not communicate" (*On Christian Teaching*).

87 Also at *Comm. 1 Cor.* 2:13. And cf. Bullinger on 1 Cor. 2 on the opposition of the Spirit with the power of rhetoric: *Opponit autem spiritum et virtutem Persuasioni. Haec post rhetorum ornamenta nihil habet, at sermo veritatis vegetus est, vivax, potens, adeoque hominum pectora transformans* (*Comm. 1 Cor.* [Zurich: Froschauer, 1534], fol. 44). Bullinger later associates the negative qualities with the Anabaptists: *In primis autem damnantur qui fiducia linguae freti dulcia quaedam cantillant compositaque et elaborata oratione suaviter de evangelio garriunt: quales nostrum saeculum complures habet Anabaptistas ...* (ibid., fol. 45).

88 *Comm. Gal.* 1:1 (trans. Parker), 47. *Talis repraesentatio, nulla eloquentia, nullis rhetorum coloribus fieri potest, nisi adsit illa spiritus efficacia, de qua dictum fuit in utraque ad Corinthios. Itaque qui rite evangelii ministerio defungi volent, discant non tantum loqui et declaimitare: sed etiam penetrare in conscientias, ut illis Christus crucifixus sentiatur et sanguis eius stillet.* On *hypotyposis*, or vivid imagery and its importance for eliciting emotion in preaching in the sixteenth century, see, e.g., Erasmus, *Ecclesiastes* CWE 68:885.

89 Calvin follows Erasmus against the Vulgate in translating the Greek *proegraphe* as *depictus*, and in his annotation Erasmus notes that Theophylact had read it in this way, and equates *graphein* with *pingere* (to paint). See *Ann. Gal* 1:1, *Ante quorum oculos*. In his *Paraphrase* Erasmus had also drawn the contrast between the portrait of Christ stamped on the minds of the Galatian faithful and seeing Christ crucified in person, complete with a reference to wooden idols (CWE 42:108).

90 *1 Corinthians* (trans. Fraser), 51 (Latin in next note).

91 *1 Corinthians* (trans. Fraser), 51; Estienne, 1556: *Et merito humanae sapientiae tribuit to pithanon. Verbum enim Domini maiestate sua tanquam violento impulsu nos ad obediendum sibi cogit: humana autem sapientia suas habet illecebras, quibus irrepat, et suum quasi lenocinium, quo sibi conciliet auditorum animos.* For Calvin's use of the Greek *to pithanon* here, see Walchenbach, *John Calvin as Biblical Commentator*, ch. 3, where he analyses all the instances of Calvin referring explicitly to John Chrysostom in his *Comm. 1 Cor.*

92 Bouwsma argues further that it is always connected to *eruditio*; see *John Calvin*, 115ff.

93 *1 Corinthians* (trans. Fraser), 51; Estienne, 1556: Huic demonstrationem spiritus et potentiae opponit: quam plerique ad miracula restringunt, ego autem latius accipio, nempe pro manu Dei potenter se modis omnibus per apostolum exserente ... Nam que nostra est in considerandis Dei operibus hebetudo, quum adhibet inferiora organa, quasi velis quibusdam obtecta est eius virtus quominus liquido nobis pateat: in Pauli autem ministerio promovendo, quia nullum carnis aut mundi adminiculum operabatur, quasi nuda Dei manus se proferebat: certe magis conspicua erat eius virtus.

94 Very similar formulations appear in Bullinger's commentary; see, e.g., on 1:17, ad loc.

95 *1 Corinthians* (trans. Fraser), 51; Estienne, 1556: Si fulta fuisset solis eloquentiae viribus apostoli praedicatio, poterat subverti maiore eloquentia: deinde nemo solidam veritatem dixerit quae splendore orationis nitatur: adiuvari quidem potest, sed niti non debet.

96 *Comm. 1 Cor.* 2:13 (*1 Corinthians* (trans. Fraser), 60–1, modified); Estienne, 1556: Dicit ergo sese aptare spiritualia spiritualibus, dum verba rei accommodat: hoc est, coelestem illam spiritus sapientiam temperat oratione simplici, et quae nativam spiritus energiam prae se ferat. Interea perstringit alios, qui affectata verborum elegantia et subtilitatis ostentatione captant plausum hominum: tanquam aut solidae veritatis inanes, aut qui spiritualem Dei doctrinam indecoro fuco corrumpant.

97 Bouwsma, "Calvinism as Theologia Rhetorica?" 10.

98 Bouwsma, *John Calvin*, 116.

99 Torrance, *The Hermeneutics of John Calvin*, 143; citing *Comm. 1 Cor.* 1:17. See also 145–55.

100 *1 Corinthians* (trans. Fraser), 75, modified; Estienne, 1556, ad. loc. Calvin gives an example of such "human fictions": "speculative questions which generally cater more for some ostentation or foolish desire, rather than the salvation of men."

101 Charles Trinkaus made note of this feature in Calvin's thought in an early essay: "Renaissance Problems in Calvin's Theology," 59–80. See the extensive study by Arnold Huijgen, *Divine Accommodation in John Calvin's Theology*. See also Bouwsma, *John Calvin*, 116ff.; Holder, *John Calvin and the Grounding of Interpretation*, 45ff. and n.54 for bibliography; Raymond Blacketer, *Pedagogy and Rhetoric in Calvin's Interpretation of Deuteronomy* (Springer, 2006); Wright, "Calvin's Accommodating God," 3–19. Wright discounts the influence of the Roman rhetorical tradition as having significant influence (and the "fashionable recent tendency to explain too much of Calvin in terms of the rhetorical tradition"), but his comments

are confined to Quintillian, and he says nothing of the rhetorical tradition as it develops in the Renaissance, which obviously had extensive influence on Calvin. For a general overview of the topic in Judaism and Christianity, see Benin, *The Footprints of God.*

102 See Balserak, "'The accommodating act par excellence?' An Inquiry into the Incarnation and Calvin's Understanding of Accommodation," *Scottish Journal of Theology* 55:4 (2002), 408–23 (note 16 also contains a useful history of scholarly treatments of accommodation in Calvin); see also his *Divinity Compromised: A Study of Divine Accommodation in the Thought of John Calvin* (Springer, 2006).

103 Huijgen treats accommodation in the Fathers and in Calvin in *Divine Accommodation* at 57–92 and 113–26. See also Millet, *Calvin et la dynamique,* 160, 170, 174, 197–8, 247; also Wright, who considers Origen, Augustine, Chrysostom, and Erasmus as sources, in "Calvin's 'Accommodation' Revisited," 171–93.

104 Hoffmann, *Rhetoric and Theology,* 106 (see 106–12 for discussion). There has been a tendency in Erasmus scholarship to make a distinction between theological accommodation and rhetorical accommodation. See Bateman's comment in "From Soul to Soul," n55. Regardless of the provenance of Erasmus' use of accommodation, it seems fairly clear to me that for him theological accommodation cannot be separated from rhetorical accommodation. This is the force of his doctrine of revelation in Christ, the *Logos* qua *Sermo,* as it has been aptly and amply interpreted by O'Rourke Boyle. See also Kahn, *Rhetoric, Prudence, and Skepticism,* 102–14 for a discussion of decorum (theological and rhetorical) in the *Praise of Folly.* On accommodation in Erasmus more generally, see also Eden, "Rhetoric in the Hermeneutics of Erasmus' Later Works," and *Hermeneutics and the Rhetorical Tradition,* 64–78; Peter Walter, *Theologie aus dem Geist der Rhetorik,* 33–53; and, recently, if somewhat indirectly and pertaining more to the idea of mimesis in the *Enchiridion,* Cummings, "Erasmus and the Invention of Literature," *ERSY* 33 (2013), 23–54 (esp. 44ff.).

105 Huijgen, *Divine Accommodation,* 126–33.

106 Ibid., 129.

107 Ibid., 130–1.

108 Huijgen (101) actually points out that Erasmus' Christological and Pauline form of accommodation in some texts fits uncomfortably with the quasi-platonist form of accommodation outlined in the *Ratio,* but in his analysis of Calvin's reception of Erasmus' accommodation, he reverts to the portrait of Erasmus the Platonist to argue for difference. However, it is precisely in the Christological/Pauline context of accommodation where Calvin and Erasmus have the most in common.

109 See, e.g., Calvin, *Inst.* I.viii.1; and Erasmus, *Paraphrase on 1 Cor.* 3:1–2: "velut apud infantes balbutii." Paul also conquers all the Mediterranean with "babbling eloquence" (*eloquenti balbutie*), according to Erasmus in his dedicatory letter of the *Paraphrase on 1 Cor.*, and with a *facunda infantia*, literally an ineloquent eloquence. Cf. Augustine, in *De Trinitate*, "Holy Scripture, adapting itself to children, does not shun any sort of discourse, from which our understanding, as though nourished by it, rises gradually to divine and sublime things" (PL xlii, 820: *sancta Scriptura parvulis congruens, nullius generis rerum verba vitavit, ex quibus quasi gradatim ad divina atque sublimia noster intellectus velut nutritus assurgeret*).

110 CWE 66:35. *Enchiridion* (LB I 501A): Balbutit nobis divina sapientia et veluti mater quaepiam officiosa ad nostram infantiam voces accommodat.

111 Eden, *Hermeneutics and the Rhetorical Tradition*, 77.

112 *Paraphrase* 1 Cor. 3:1 (CWE 43:50); Froben, 1532: Ad cuiusque captum accommodandus est sermo.

113 CWE 43:17; Froben, 1532: Cum Paulus noster ubique vafer sit, ac lubricus, in his tamen duabus epistolis sic Polypum ac Chamaeleontem, sic Proteum, ac Vertumnum quendam agit, ut cum Corinthiis plus quam Graecis agens, quodammodo iuxta vetus proverbium *pros kreta kretizein* videatur, in omnia se vertens, quo illos transfiguret in Christum. Adeo ceu per varios labyrinthi flexus, sese voluit ac revoluit, subinde alius atque alius nobis prodiens.

114 CWE 43:18; Froben, 1532: Nusquam enim non agit Christi negocium: nusquam non consulit gregis sui commodis, sidi medici ritu, nullum remediorum genus non admovens, quo perfectam sanitatem suis restituat.

115 CWE 43:20. The editors here note that Chrysostom and Theophylact, too, recognized Paul's tendency to soften his message for the sake of persuasion. Erasmus uses the phrase also in his 1515 letter to Martin Dorp in defense of the *Praise of Folly* in order to justify the use of satire as a mode of theological teaching.

116 *Paraphrase* 1 Cor. 3:2 (CWE 43:51); Froben, 1532: Proinde cum primum vos adirem, non potui vobis summa tradere, tanquam plene spiritualibus, sed deieci sermonem meum ad vestram imbecillitatem, apud rudes rudi sermone sum usus, crasis crassius sum locutus, ac velut apud infantes balbutii.

117 *Paraphrase* 1 Cor. 1:23–5; Froben, 1532: Deiecit se quodammodo deus a sua sublimitate ad nostram humilitatem (my translation); *Ann. 1 Cor. 1* ("quod stultum est Dei"): Nec est quod abominemur hunc sermonem, stultitia

dei: quam non horruit Augustinus epistola centesima secunda, scribens ad hunc modum: Haec stultitia dei, et stultitia praedicationis multos contrahit ad salutem. Si deus demisit se ad nostram imbecillitatem, ut fortes redderet, quid novum si se demisit ad nostram stultitiam, ut ex stultis redderet sapientes? (1535: Reeve and Screech [Brill: 1990]; this section was added in 1519).

118 See the *Paraphrase on Galatians* (CWE 42:117) and Sider, "Historical Imagination and Representation of Paul in Erasmus' Paraphrases on the Pauline Epistles," 99.

119 See *Paraphrase* 1 Cor. 3:1–3.

120 Eden, *Hermeneutics and the Rhetorical Tradition*, 77–8.

121 See also note above on the *Paraphrase* on 1 Cor. 3:22, a large section of which Bullinger reproduces in his commentary.

122 *Comm. 1 Cor.* 3:1–2 (Zurich: Froschauer, 1534), fol. 58: Deiiciendus erat sermo meus ad vestram imbecillitatem. Carnales enim, id est *nepioi* infantes eratis in negotiis Christi et mysteriis coelestibus, proinde vobiscum utcunque balbutiendum erat velut cum infantibus.

123 *Comm. 1 Cor.* 3:1–2 (Zurich: Froschauer, 1539), fol. 191 (cf. *Paraphrase*, Froben 1532, fol. 91): Cum, inquit, primum vos adirem, sermonem meum accommodavi vestro captui ... Deieci autem sermonem meum ad vestram tunc imbecillitatem, apud rudes rudi sermone usus, crassis crassius loquutus sum, et velut apud infantes balbutii ... Cum adhuc vos infantes viderem in philosophia Christi, doctrinae crassioris ceu lacte vos alui, non solido cibo doctrinae perfectioris.

124 *1 Corinthians* (trans. Fraser), 49; Estienne, 1556: Pluribus exponit quod iam ante attigerat, nihil se habuisse in hominum oculis splendidum aut excellens, quo magni fieret ... Minore in pretio habendus videbatur, quod tam abiectus erat ac humilis secundum carnem: ostendit, in eo melius enituisse Dei virtutem, quod nullis humanis adminiculis suffultus tantum potuerit.

125 *1 Corinthians* (trans. Fraser), 50; Estienne, 1556: Quum ergo neglecta eius simplicitate prurirent desiderio nescio cuius sapientiae magis inflatae et politioris, externoque colore, imo adscititio fuco magis quam vivo spiritu caperentur: nonne satis suam ambitionem prodebant?

126 See *Calvin et la dynamique*, 196 and 231–2.

127 We have also seen Erasmus refer to the cross of Christ as a *humilis et abiecta res* (*Paraphrase* 1 Cor. 1:18). It is worth reproducing (in part) Auerbach's extended definition of the Latin *humilis* here: "*Humilis* is related to *humus*, the soil, and literally means low, low-lying, of small

stature. Its figurative meanings developed in various directions. In general it signifies worthless, paltry, trifling, both in an absolute sense and in relation to other objects. In a social and political context it consequently connotes lowly origin, lack of education, poverty, lack of power and prestige; from an ethical point of view it applies to base, unworthy actions or attitudes, slavishness in words and gestures, vileness; it can also mean dejected, pusillanimous, cowardly ... The word can apply to a degraded life and a degrading death; it is frequently synonymous with modest, inelegant, of poor quality, shabby" ("*Sermo Humilis*," 39).

128 Bouwsma, "Calvinism as Theologia Rhetorica?" 11.

129 See, e.g., Muller, *Calvin and the Reformed Tradition* (2013), 58ff.

130 *1 Corinthians* (trans. Fraser), 66; Estienne, 1556: Hic quaeritur num Christum transfiguraverit Paulus pro auditorum varietate. Respondeo, ad docendi modum vel formam id potius quam ad doctrinae substantiam referri. Christus enim idem lac est pueris, et adultis solidus cibus: eadem evangelii veritas utrisque, sed pro suo modo administratur. Prudentis ergo doctoris est, eorum, quos docendos suscipit, captui se attemperare: ut apud infirmos et rudes ab elementis incipiat, nec altius conscendat quam sequi possint.

131 See also the comment on 1 Cor. 2:7, which implies a relationship between God's overarching providential purpose and his accommodation to human capacity, and which precludes the excuse of someone refusing to listen to the gospel on account of their not being prepared to hear: "For if God established everything to some purpose it follows that we will lose nothing in hearing the Gospel, which he intended for us, for when He speaks to us He accommodates Himself to our capacity" (*1 Corinthians* (trans. Fraser), 53–4; Estienne, 1556: Nam si Deus nihil frustra statuit, sequitur nos operam non perdituros in audiendo evangelio quod nobis destinavit: se enim modulo nostro attemperat, quum nobis loquitur).

132 At *Comm. 1 Cor.* 3:3, Calvin writes that until the *carnales* renounce the flesh, they cannot make progress in the *schola Domini*; Estienne, 1556: Quamdiu caro, hoc est, naturalis vitiositas, in homine dominatur, sic occupat ipsius hominis ingenium, ut non sit ingressus sapientiae Dei. Quare si quid proficere volumnus in schola Domini, primum est ut nos proprio sensu et propria voluntate abdicemus.

133 *1 Corinthians* (trans. Fraser), 34; Estienne, 1556: Altera vero, ut nostram obedientiam ac docilitatem melius experiretur, et simul ad veram humilitatem erudiret. Solos enim parvulos in scholam suam admittit Dominus.

134 Furthermore, there seems to be a paradox in Calvin's thought here, where God reveals himself completely in Christ, but at the same time accommodates himself to our (epistemological) capacity; see, e.g., Zachman, *Image and Word*, 260ff.

135 See Screech, *Ecstasy*, 37ff.

136 Screech, *Ecstasy*, 69.

137 *Ann. 1 Cor.* 1:25 ("quod stultum est Dei"): Nec est quod abominemur hunc sermonem, stultitia dei: quam non horruit Augustinus epistola centesima secunda, scribens ad hunc modum: Haec stultitia dei, et stultitia praedicationis multos contrahit ad salutem. Si deus demisit se ad nostram imbecillitatem, ut fortes redderet, quid onvum si se demisit ad nostram stultitiam, ut ex stultis redderet sapientes?

138 CWE 43:40; *Paraphrase* 1 Cor. 1:23–5; 1532 text: Deiecit se quodammmodo deus a sua sublimitate ad nostram humilitatem: descendit a sua sapientia ad nostram stultitiam, et tamen quod in illo stultum est visum, praecellit universam mundi sapientiam: et quod in illo visum est imbecille, validius fuit omnibus humanis viribus.

139 *Paraphrase* 1 Cor. 1:28–30; CWE 43:41–2; Froben, 1532: Per humiles orta est Evangelii gloria: per humiles dilatatur, ut versis rerum vicibus, humilitas expugnet altitudinem, simplicitas coarguat humanam astutiam.

140 CWE 43:22; from the *Argumentum*, Froben, 1532: Proinde a supercilio mundanae philosophiae ad crucis humilitatem revocat, quae licet ostentationem non habeat, vim tamen et energiam habet.

141 *Paraphrase* 1 Cor. 2:1–3; and ASD VI-3, 583.

142 Gordon, *Humanist Play and Belief*, 214–15.

143 Walter Kaiser argues that Erasmus' understanding of nature is important to his critique of Stoicism: "Stultitia rejects the Stoics, as well as the philosophers, the metaphysicians, the scientists, and the Schoolmen, because they employ antinatural means to understand nature" (*Praisers of Folly*, 95). For Erasmus' indebtedness to Valla for Folly's critiques of Stoicism on Christian grounds, see Letizia Panizza, "Valla's *De voluptate ac de vero bono* and Erasmus' *Stultitiae Laus*: Renewing Christian Ethics," *Erasmus of Rotterdam Society Yearbook* 15 (1995), 1–25.

144 Tracy (*Erasmus: The Growth of a Mind*, 50ff.) argues that Erasmus begins to slough off his appreciation of Stoic anthropological ethics around the time of the writing of the *Moria*, and the shift will be necessary for the development of the *philosophia Christi*. Kaiser also argues for an "anti-Stoical Epicureanism" in the *Moria*, but with an image rather of a ludic Christ who enjoins his followers to joy and laughter, *à la* Folly (*Praisers of Folly*, 81–3). Already in his 1499 debate with John Colet, however,

Erasmus' attitude to Stoic *apatheia* is highly critical (see the *De Taedio Iesu,* CWE vol. 70, passim).

145 See Essary, "The Radical Humility of Christ in the 16th Century."

146 *1 Corinthians* (trans. Fraser), 80. *CO* 49:359: Ex opposito igitur in mundo stultus est, qui, propria ratione abdicata, tanquam clausis oculis regi se a Domino patitur: qui, sibi difidens, totus in Dominum recumbit: qui totam suam sapientiam in eo constituit, qui docilem se et obedientem Deo tradit. In hunc modum necesse est nostram prudentiam evanescere, quo Dei voluntas supra nos regnet: nos exinaniri propria ratione, ut Dei sapientia impleamur. Also, "God declares from above that whatever the mind of man conceives and purposes is simply nothingness" (*1 Corinthians* (trans. Fraser), 81; *CO* 49:360: dum ex alto pronuntia Deus vanitatem esse meram quidquid concipit et agitat hominis ingenium).

147 The Vulgate and Erasmus' 1516 *Novum Instrumentum* also read *exinanivit.* Erasmus later changes his NT to read *inanivit,* arguing in the 1519 *Annotations* that *exinanio* could be more ambiguous and not as strong.

148 My translation. *CO* 49:359: vel qui in mundo excellit opinione sapientiae, apud se ultro stultus fiat, se ipsum exinaniens.

5. Blaming Philosophy, Praising Folly

1 CWE 43:286–7; Froben, 1532, fol. 202: Olim credebatur philosophia Christiana, non disputabatur, Et pia simplicitas hominum, sacrorum voluminum oraculis erat contenta. Nec egebat variis praescriptis ultro prompta charitas, omnia credens, nusquam haerens. Mox Theologiae patrocinium capessebant humanis instructi disciplinis, sed serme his, quas hodie Rhetoricas vulgus appelat. Paulatim magis ac magis adhiberi coepit philosophia: primum Platonica, mox Aristotelica. Coeptum quaeri de multis, quae vel ad mores, vel ad coelestium rerum speculationem pertinere videbantur. Quae res primum visa est propemodum necessaria. At sensim eo succrevit, ut plerique neglecta linguatum ac politioris literaturae peritia, imo neglectis divinis voluminibus, in curiosis supervacaneis, et immodicis quaestiunculis, velut ad Sireneos scopulos consenescerent. Iam ars esse coepit Theologia, potius quam sapientia, Theatrica verius, quam ad veram pietatem accommoda. Hanc praeter ambitionem, avaritiamque vitiarunt et aliae pestes, adulatio, contentio, ac superstitio.

2 See, for example, the prefatory letter to John Colet in the *Disputatiuncula de taedio Iesu* of 1503 (ASD V-7, 210; CWE 70:10).

3 CWE 43:286–7; Froben, 1532, fol. 202–3: Quibus rebus ubi tandem eo
   ventum est, ut Christus ille purus, properno dum esset obrutus humanis
   argutationibus, ac limpidissimi, quandam evangelicae doctrinae fontes,
   Philistaeorum scrobe oppleti, divinaeque scripturae certissima regula,
   nunc huc, nunc illuc detorta, nostris seriret affectibus magis quam gloriae
   Christi, quidam pia certe mente conati sunt orbem ad pristinam studiorum
   simplicitatem revocare, atque a lacunis iam fere turbidis, ad vivas illas
   ac purissimas scatebras reducere. Eam ad rem conficiendam, linguarum
   ac bonarum, ut vocant, literarum cognitio visa est in primis conducere,
   quarum neglectu videmur huc prolapsi.
4 Notably Latomus and Lee, who published critical works of Erasmus
   in 1519 in the wake of his publication of the New Testament cum
   annotations; see the Preface in CWE 43; and Rummel, *Erasmus and His
   Catholic Critics.*
5 The term *philosophia Christiana* appears in an Erasmian context in a
   Wittenberg volume at least as early as 1520 in a letter to the *"pio lectori"*
   appended to Erasmus' Latin translation of Paul's letter to the Romans,
   printed by Melchior Lotter (*Epistola Pauli ad Romanos D. Erasmo interprete,
   rerum theologicarum, & summam, & methodum continens* [Wittenberg: 1520]).
   This interesting little book, which appears to be a school edition, also
   contains an *Adhortatio ad Paulinae doctrinae studium* by Melanchthon (where
   he several times uses the phrase *philosophia Pauli*). I thank Barbara Pitkin
   for bringing the edition to my attention.
6 Gilson, *The Spirit of Medieval Philosophy*, 1–2.
7 Gilson, *The Spirit*, 2.
8 The two camps Gilson has in his sights are "pure rationalists" or "Neo-
   Thomists" and "Augustinians," respectively described as follows:
   "Augustinianism would accept a Christian philosophy were it content to
   renounce philosophy and be simply Christian; neo-Thomism would accept
   a Christian philosophy were it content to abandon the claim to Christianity
   and be merely a philosophy. Would it not be simpler to disassociate the
   two notions altogether, to hand philosophy over to reason and restore
   Christianity to religion?" (Gilson, *The Spirit*, 9).
9 For an overview of the problem of Christian philosophy in the
   Renaissance, see Kristeller, "Thomism and Italian Thought in the
   Renaissance." For an overview of the term in general, see Leclerq,
   "Pour l'histoire de l'expression 'philosophie chrétienne'," 221–6. For
   an introduction to the term in Calvin, see Partee, *Calvin and Classical
   Philosophy*, 2–23, and "Revitalization of the Concept of 'Christian

philosophy' in Renaissance Humanism," 360–9. See also Engel, *John Calvin's Perspectival Anthropology*, 88–123, for a consideration of the relationship between earthly and heavenly philosophy in Calvin, although her general formula, that Calvin's "emphasis on the distinction between the two types of philosophy ... is made only from the perspective of God the redeemer," is a bit misleading (see 91). The uselessness of worldly philosophy in doing theology holds not only from a divine, but also from a human perspective. It is true, as Engel claims, that there is some relative merit for worldly philosophy in the sphere of mundane existence, but it does not follow that there is anything "perspectival" about Calvin's claim that worldly philosophy ought not to be mixed with the Christian philosophy – this is not a relative claim: it is true both for God and for humans.

10 Gilson, *The Spirit*, 35, my emphasis.

11 Kristeller, "Thomism and Italian Thought in the Renaissance," 34n7.

12 Deinde Iudaismus et philosophiae superstitionem cum Christi doctrina miscebant, observantes quaedam legis instituta et superstitiose observantes, solem, lunam, ac stellas, et elementa huius mundi, quibus docebant nos esse obnoxios (Froben 1532, ad loc.).

13 Diligenter autem monet, ne psuedapostolorum magniloquentia, confictisque visionibus angelorum sibi imponi paterentur, et vel in Iudaismum, vel in philosophicam superstitionem prolaberentur (Froben 1532, ad loc.).

14 Froben, 1532, fol. 243.

15 In fact, in Calvin's Latin, Paul speaks of *philosophiam et inanem deceptionem*, which follows Erasmus' and accurately reflects the Greek. Calvin also refers to an "empty philosophy" at *Inst.* 4.10.8, in an exposition of Colossians 2.

16 See Jean Calvin, *Commentarii in Pauli epistolas ad Galatas, ad Ephesios, ad Phillipenses, ad Colossenses* (ed. Helmut Feld; Series II. Opera Exegetica; Droz, 1992), 383n.2. Bullinger warns against the *argutias Philosophicas* and the *fabulas Judaicas*, and also writes: Iudaisantibus enim haud impares erant quidam ad Christianismus a Paganismo conversi qui praesidio eloquentiae suffulti multa arguta et Philosophica simplicitati fidei immiscere tentabant, quos non inferiori minusque ardenti spiritus servore atque Nazaraeos persequitur et cavendos suadet, ingeminans subinde in Christo nos esse completos, Christum semel habere omnia (Bullinger, *Argumentum Ep. ad Col* (Zurich: Froschauer, 1535, fol. 230r–v). Pellikan mentions the *dogmata philosophiae* and the *qui ex circuncisione crediderunt* in his argumentum: *Comm. in Ep. ad Col, Argumentum* (Zurich: Froschauer, 1539, fol. 417).

17 *COR* II/2, 383: Quandam simul (meo iudicio) ad argutias, quibus ludebant, in hoc vocabulo respexit, subtiles illas quidem, sed tamen futiles et profanas.

18 *COR* II/2, 383: Aditum enim ad Deum per angelos comminiscebantur et multas eiusmodi speculationes ingerebant, quales in libris Dionysii de caelesti hierarchia continentur, ex schola Platonicorum haustae.

19 *COR* II/2, 383: Hic ergo scopus est praecipuus, ad quem tendit, ut in Christo omnia esse doceat.

20 **Vulgate: 2:1** Volo enim vos scire qualem sollicitudinem habeam pro vobis et pro his, qui sunt Laodiciae, et quicumque non viderunt faciem meam in carne, **2** ut consolentur corda ipsorum instructi in caritate et in omnes divitias plenitudinis intellectus, in agnitionem mysterii Dei, Christi, **3** in quo sunt omnes thesauri sapientiae et scientiae absconditi. **4** Hoc dico, ut nemo vos decipiat in subtilitate sermonum, **5** Nam etsi corpore absens sum, sed spiritu vobiscum sum, gaudens et videns ordinem vestrum et firmamentum eius, quae in Christum est, fidei vestrae. **6** Sicut ergo accepistis Christum Iesum Dominum, in ipso ambulate, **7** radicati et superaedificati in ipso et confirmati fide, sicut didicistis, abundantes in gratiarum actione. **8** Videte, ne quis vos depraedetur per philosophiam et inanem fallaciam secundum traditionem hominum, secundum elementa mundi et non secundum Christum.

    Erasmus (1535): 2:1 Nam volo vos scire, quantam solicitudinem habeam de vobis et his qui sunt Laeodiciae, et quotquot non viderunt faciem meam in carne, **2** ut consolationem accipiant corda illorum, quum fuerint compacti in charitate et in omnem opulentiam certae persuasionis intelligentiae, in agnitionem mysterii dei et patris et Christi, **3** in quo sunt omnes thesauri sapientiae ac scientiae reconditi. **4** Hoc autem dico, ne quis vobis imponat probabilitate sermonis. **5** Etenim quamvis carne sim absens, tamen spiritu vobiscum sum, gaudens ac videns vestrum ordinem et soliditatem vestrae in Christum fidei. **6** Quemadmodum igitur accepistis Christum Iesum dominum, ita in eo ambulate, **7** sic ut radices habetatis in illo fixas, et in illo superstruamini confirmeminique per fidem, sicut edocti estis, exuberantes in ea cum gratiarum actione. **8** Videte ne quis sit qui vos depraedetur per philosophiam et inanem deceptionem, iuxta constitutionem hominum, iuxta elementa mundi, et non iuxta Christum.

    Calvin (1556): 2:1 Volo autem vos scire quantum certamen habeam pro vobis, et iis qui sunt Laodiceae, et quicunque non viderunt faciem meam in carne; **2** Ut consolationem accipiant corda ipsorum, ubi compacti fuerint in charitate, et in omnes divitias certidudinis intelligentiae, in agnitionem mysterii Dei, et Patris, et Christi. **3** In quo sunt omnes thesauri sapientiae et intelligentiae absconditi. **4** Hoc autem dico, ne quis vos decipiat persuasorio sermone. **5** Nam etsi corpore sum absens, spiritu tamen sum vobiscum, gaudens et videns ordinem vestrum, et stabilitatem vestrae in Christum fidei. **6** Quemadmodum igitur suscepistis Christum Iesum Dominum, in ipso ambulate: **7** Radicati in ipso, et aedificati, et confirmati in fide, quemadmodum edocti estis, abundantes in ea cum gratiarum actione. **8** Videte ne quis vos praedetur per philosophiam et inanem deceptionem, secundum traditionem hominum, secundum elementa mundi, et non secundum Christum.

21 Et ideo dicit *plenitudinis intellectus*, id est, in copiam ... *Instructi* ergo in copia divinae sapientiae, quae copia implet intellectum (*Lectura* on Col. 2:2, par. 80, ad loc.).

22 *Ann. Lucam* 1:1 (*quae in nobis completa sunt rerum*), ad loc. (see Reeve, 149). See also ASD VI.3, 601 on Erasmus' tendency in modifying the Vg. *plenitudo* for *certitudo*.

23 See CWE 56:124.

24 Erasmus, *Ann. Col.*, ad loc.: "Divitias plenitudinis") *plerophorias* ... magis sonat certam persuasionem, quoties alicuit plene sit fides, ita ut nihil iam addubitet, quemadmodum admonuimus in initio evangelii secundam Lucam. Optat enim illis certam cognitionem mysterii, ne quid omnino haesitent.

25 *Paraphrase* Col. 2:2 (my translation); Froben, 1532, fol. 246.

26 See Wengert, *Human Freedom, Christian Righteousness*, 105. Aside from Wengert on Melanchthon, Colossians, and philosophy, see Kusukawa, *The Transformation of Natural Philosophy*; on Col. 2, see 65f.

27 *Para. Col.* 2:2f; CWE 43:409 (modified); Froben, 1532, fol. 246: patefacto iam arcano per Iesum Christum, quod hactenus celatum erat, videlicet extra unum hunc, nihil nobis expetendum humanae sapientiae, sive quid promittunt huius mundi philosophi, sive quid pollicentur Mosaicae legis doctores, sive quid alii iactant sese doctos ex angelorum colloquiis, cum in hoc uno reconditi sint et abstrusi omnes thesauri sapientiae, et cognitionis fructiferae. Ex hoc fonte compendio licet haurire, quicquid ad veram salutem pertinet.

28 The full title is *De scripturae sanctae authoritate, certitudine, firmitate et absoluta perfectione, deque Episcoporum qui verbi Dei ministri sunt institutione et functione, contra superstitionis tyrannidisque Romanae antistitis, ad Sereniss* (Zurich: Froschauer, 1538).

29 Bullinger, *Comm. Col.* (Zurich: Froschauer, 1535), ad loc.

30 Et Cicero diserte docet eloquentiam sine sapientia vehementer esse perniciosam (Zurich: Froschauer, 1538), fol. 2v.

31 Millet, *Calvin et la dynamique*, 202–3.

32 See Schreiner, *Are You Alone Wise?* esp. 79–130 on the question of certainty and the authority of the Spirit in sixteenth-century Protestantism. On Calvin, see Bouwsma, *John Calvin*, 100ff., and Zachman, *The Assurance of Faith*.

33 Pellikan, *Comm. Col.* (Zurich: Froschauer, 1539), fol. 424.

34 *Scholia* 1528, 19r; see Wengert, *Human Freedom*, 199n149: Ita enim discent, fidem oportere, quandam certam in mente sententiam non ambiguam opinionem esse.

35 *CR* 15:1247.

36 Wengert, *Human Freedom*, 105.

37 *COR* II/2, 418: ut certe non potest ab ea magis avelli quam a sole calor aut lumen.

38 Millet, *Calvin et la dynamique*, 213: "Elle est désignée dans le Nouveau Testament par un terme technique, '*Plerophoria*,' que Calvin, dans son commentaire de Luc 1, 1, reproche à Erasme d'avoir traduit par 'plénitude'."

39 The full passage is as follows: *Divitias certitudinis intelligentia*: Quia plerique tenui gustu contenti nihil praeter confusam et evanidam notitiam habent, nominatim ponit divitias intelligentiae. Quo nomine significat plenam et luculentam perceptionem. Et simul admonet pro intelligentiae mensura etiam in charitate proficiendum esse. Nomine certitudinis fidem ab opinione discernit. Is enim vere demum cognoscit Deum, qui non vacillat dubitatione aut nutat, sed qui stat in firma constantique persuasione. Hanc constantiam et stabilitatem Paulus saepius *plerophorian* vocat. Quo etiam nomine hic utitur et cum fide perpetuo coniungit, ut certe non potest ab ea magis avelli quam a sole calor aut lumen. Diabolicum igitur scholasticorum dogma, quod sublata certitudine coniecturam moralem (quam appelant) in illius locum substituit (*COR* II/2, 418).

40 *Comm. Col.* 2:2: *COR* II/2, 418–19; (trans. Fraser, *Commentary on Galatians, Ephesians, Philippians, and Colossians*, 325): Nam exponit, quae sit illa scientia, cuius meminit: nempe aliud esse quam Evangelii cognitionem. Venditant enim et pseudoapostoli suas imposturas sapientiae titulo.

41 *Comm. Col.* 2:2: *COR* II/2, 419 (trans. Fraser, ibid., modified, 326): Verum hinc discamus sola fide, non ratione, nec perspicacia humanae mentis Evangelium posse capi, quia alioqui res est a nobis abscondita.

42 *Comm. Col.* 2:3: *COR* II/2, 419 (trans. Fraser, ibid., 326): Quo significat nos perfecte sapere, si Christum vere cognoscimus, adeo ut insania sit praeter ipsum quicquam scire velle.

43 *Comm. Col.* 2:3: *COR* II/2, 419 (trans. Fraser, ibid., modified, 326): Thesauros autem dicit absconditos, quia non eminent magno splendore conspicui, sed potius sub crucis humilitate et simplicitate contemptibili quasi delitescunt. Est enim semper crucis praedicatio (ut habuimus ad Corinthios) mundo stultitia.

44 See *Comm. 1 Cor.* 1:6; 1:30; 3:11.

45 *Comm. Col.* 2:3: *COR* II/2, 419 (trans. Fraser, ibid., 326): Inter sapientiam et intelligentiam hoc loco non pono magnum discrimen, quia tantum duplicatio ad augendum valet, asci dixisset nihil alibi posse inveniri scientiae, eruditionis, doctrinae, sapientiae.

46 Sapientia enim est cognitio divinorum, scientia vero est craturarum cognitio (*Comm. Col.*, par. 81).

47 See *Comm. 1 Cor.* 12:8, ad loc.

48 Wengert, "The Biblical Commentaries," *Philip Melanchthon (1497–1560) and the Commentary*, 143. For the textual and printing history of Melanchthon's works on Colossians, see Wengert, *Human Freedom*, 15ff.

49 Wengert, "The Biblical Commentaries," 144. The *Hyperaspistes* was published in 1526, following Luther's *On the Bondage of the Will* of 1525, and Erasmus published a second part the following year.

50 *Scholia* 1528, 22r (octavo): Quidam inepti intellexerunt hic ornatum orationis, sed longe alia mens est Pauli, cum enim doctrina Christiana dissentiat a ratione, iubet nos cavere, ne decipiamur argumentis a ratione sumptis ... Et vocabulum *pithanologia*, quo hic usus Apostolus, significat non ornatum orationis seu elocutionem, sed callide et verisimiliter cogitata argumenta (trans. Wengert; see *Human Freedom*, 33 and notes).

51 Wengert, *Human Freedom*, 33, also 54.

52 See *MSA* IV.4.35, and Weaver, "A More Excellent Way: Philip Melanchthon's Corinthians Lectures of 1521–1522," 31–63.

53 See Erasmus, *Ann. Col.*, ad loc.

54 CWE 43:409–10; *Para. Col.* 2:6f. (1532): Atque haec quae dicimus eo tendunt, ut etiam atque etiam caveatis, ne quis humanis artibus instructus adversus evangelice doctrinae simplicitatem, fucum vobis faciat, et imponat falso sermone, sed in speciem probabili ac verisimili. Solent enim huius mundi sophistae captiunculis quibusdam, et argutiis rationum humanarum animos simplicium illa queare, Non me clam est, esse quosdam tales apud vos, insidiantes synceritati fidei vestrae.

55 See Wengert, *Human Freedom*, 42.

56 *Paraphrase* Col. 2:3 (my trans.); Froben, 1532, fol. 247: ... evangelicae doctrinae solidum fundamentum, ita quae tali fundamento digna sint superstruatis. Ne vacillantes ad quemvis ventum novae doctrinae, nunc

huc, nunc illuc nutetis, sed firmi et oimmobiles persistatis in eo, quod
semel didicistis.

57 Bullinger, *Comm. Col.* 1535, ad loc. (my translation): Caveamus ergo
a tricis Sophistarum a syllogismis philosophorum a probabilitate et
delectione rhetorum et a nexibus dialecticorum. Non quod probabiliter
et vere dicendi rationem in vero aspernemur, hanc enim necessariam
esse credimus, sed illam damnamus potius Pithanologiam qua verum
corrumpitur et falsum artificiosa et subdola rationum quarundam textura
denique et orationis suavitate animis instillatur simplicium. Huiusmodi
enim orationes post probabilitatem et temporariam delectionem nil
prorsus veri et solidi habent: interim vero animos vulgarium irretiunt
abducunt atque pervertunt.

58 Bullinger, *Comm. Col.* 1535, ad loc.: quae significat probabilitatem et
orationem persuasibilem. Finxerunt autem Graeci deam quandam
persuadendi Pitho, quem deam in Periclis labris scriptis Empolis
sessitavisse, eo quod dicendo aculeum relinqueret in animis auditorum,
et ut Aristophanes dixit fulguraret, tonaret Graeciamque permisceret.
Ennius illam appellavit Suadam, quem et imitatus Marcianus nunc
Suadam nunc vero pitho nuncupat. Horatius Suadelam, Cicero Leporem,
Quintilianus vero quandam persuadendi deam. Proinde intelligimus et nos
per Pithanologiam instructam quandam et ad persuadendum efficacem
dicendi rationem, qua plurimum valuisse quosdam Colossensium sophos
certa coniectura est ...

59 Pellikan, *Comm. Col.* 2:4 (Zurich: Froschauer, 1539), fol. 425: Haec autem
quae dicimus eo contendunt, ut etiam atque etiam caveatis, ne quis
humanis artibus, et philosophia gentilium sola ratione, quae erronea dictat,
docente, qualia Epicurus, Plato, Aristoteles, multa habet contraria pietati
verbi dei instructus, adversus evangelicae doctrinae simplicitatem fucum
vobis faciat, et imponat falso, picto, incerto callidoque sermone, quamlibet
in speciem probabili ac verisimili.

60 *CR* 12:695; cf. Pellikan, *Comm. Col.* 2:4 (Zurich: Froschauer, 1539), fol. 425:
Non hic Paulus ait philosophiam malam esse, abusus vituperatur, res ipsa
non improbatur, ut si quis dicat, Vide ne vinum te decipiat.

61 Pellikan, *Comm. Col.* 2:4; Zurich: Froschauer, 1539, fol. 425: Non est ex
philosophia, de divina ad nos voluntate vel ex ratione iudicandum.
Sicut Epicurus negavit deo res nostras curae esse, animas mortales.
Aristoteles dixit mundum esse aeternum, et similia. Quidam quoque
admiscuerunt doctrinae Christianae philosophiam, rationi quoque
tribuerunt vim efficiendae in nobis fidei erga deum. Discrimen potius est
habendum inter evanglii doctrinam, animarum salvandarum medicinam

necessariam, et inter philosophiam, quae est doctrina vitae corporalis et moralis, cuius usus et donum a deo est, et necessarius reipublicae, et in suo genere bonus, ac investigandus diligenter, et pro eo deo gratiae referendae sunt, quamlibet iustificent hominem coram deo, quod facit fides vera ex sacris edocta.

62 *COR* II/2, 420: Quia hominum figmenta (ut postea videbimus) speciem habent sapientiae, praeoccupators esse oportet piorum animos hac persuasione: satis uperque esse Christi notitiam. Et certe haec clavis est, quae ianuam omnibus pravis erroribus obserare potest. Quid enim in causa fuit, cur tot impiis opinionibus, tot idololatriis, tot stultis speculationibus se homines implicuerint, nisi quia despecta Evangelii simplicitate altius aspirare ause sunt?

63 Trans. Parker, 326 (modified); *COR* II/2, 420: Nulla denique erit pithanologia, quae animos eorum vel minimum digitum flectat, qui suam mentem Christo addixerint.

64 *COR* II/2, 420: Locus certe insigniter efferendus.

65 CWE 43:411; *Para. Col.* 2:8f.; Froben, 1532: Vigilant qui insidiantur synceritati vestrae, vobis contra vigilandum, ne capti magnifica quadam specie philosophiae, seducamini a soliditate fidei ad inanes hominum commentatiunculas, ac praeda fiatis hostibus: id fiet, si aversi a praescripto veritatis evangelicae, duci coeperitis constitutionibus ac praescriptis humanis, quae sita sunt in rebus visibilibus, et in elementis huius mundi crassis, quum Christi doctrina coelestis sit, ac veram tradat pietatem, in animis sitam, non in cibo potuve, non in cultu corporis, non in observatione dierum, aut lotione manuum, quae nihil conducunt ad veram religionem. Ista magis avocant a Christo, distrahuntque a fonte, a quo petenda sunt omnia.

66 For Jerome, see PL 26:397; for Ambrosiaster, see CSEL 81, 43:4–10; and cf. the *Paraphrase* on Gal. 4:3: "When formerly we were not yet able to grasp this gift because it requires completely heavenly minds, we also were confined like children, by laws quite carnal and clearly accommodated to our weakness. For we did not yet understand that heavenly teaching but were only impressed by things which can be discerned with corporeal eyes. These are the kinds of things which consists of the elements of this lower world, as distinctions among days, choices of foods, differences in ritual, animal sacrifices, marks on the body" (CWE 42:115).

67 Froben, 1532: umbras Mosaicae legis, aut humanae philosophiae prestigias ...

68 *Comm. Col.* 2:8 (Zurich: Froschauer, 1535), ad loc.: Philosophia inquit illa est de qua hic loquor quae facit ut a vera fide deflectentes non unice innitamur

Christo domino, proinde nobis cavenda est. Alia enim suggerit quae ad perfectionem et veram sapientiam pertineant, disputans videlicet de viribus hominis, de virtutum effectibus, de finibus bonorum et malorum, quae sane disputationes suam habent probabilitatem. ·

69 *Comm. Col.* 2:8 (Zurich: Froschauer, 1535), ad loc.: Atque tales miscebant quidam Sophi Colossensium prophana eruditione inflati praedicato Christi evangelio: quemadmodum Nazaraei circumcisionem sacrificia et legem quoque una cum Christo pradicabant. Praterea alia quaedam tradebant illi figmenta propria quibus a Christo avocabant auditores.

70 *Comm. Col.* 2:8 (Zurich: Froschauer, 1535), ad loc.: Proinde quod ante aliquot verba appelavit Pithanologiam hoc ipsum nunc Philosophiam nuncupat. Est autem in ea voce Catachresis vel synechdoche. Non enim omnes Philosophiae partes neque ipsam veram philosophiam, quae ad iustam eruditionem parandam necessaria est, cavendam docet, sed quae probabili specie imponit.

71 *Comm. Col.* 2:8 (Zurich: Froschauer, 1535), ad loc.: Additur et aliud quod mentem Pauli·clarius exponat, Per inanem deceptionem. Quicquid ergo decipit aut a vero abducit, quicquid probabilitatis et veri speciem habet revera autem vanum inane, subdolum et mendax est, Philosophia est. Imo subiungitur et aliud quod adhuc planius quid sentiat exponat, iuxta inquit constitutionem hominum, iuxta elementa mundi et non iuxta Christum. Quasi dicat, Philosophia autem de qua loquor nititur constitutionibus ac praescriptis humanis, quae sita sunt in rebus visibilibus, in externis, in elementis huius mundi in iis quoque ad quae stupet mundus, quae omnia a Christo abducunt. Hoc autem philosophiae genus sequebantur Colossenses. pesudoapostoli, partim ad praesidia humanae sapientiae confugientes, partim circumcisionem sacrificia et legalia urgentes, quasi ad iustificationem et veram sapientiam parandam solus Christus inefficax sit.

72 *Comm. Col.* 2:8 (Zurich: Froschauer, 1535), ad loc.: Hodie quoque videre est quanta suppellectile quidam doceant opus esse ad consequendam vitam beatam. Nec sine probabilitatis specie, sine rationibus, adde et sine scripturarum locis, sed detortis, id faciunt. Alius enim vires liberi arbitrii praedicat, alius opera meritoria et satisfactionis iactat, alius monachatus regulas easque varias et severas laudat, alius Divinorum Missarum et indulgentiarum largissimas gratias amplexandas suadet. Perraro sit mentio Christi et expiationis eius. Scriptae sunt de his amplissimae disputationes. Caeterum damnantur hic omnia ista a Paulo. Philosophica enim sunt hoc est inania ex hominum constitutione prolata, quae et circa externa versantur et a Christo abducunt.

73 *Comm. Col.* 2:8 (Zurich: Froschauer, 1535), ad loc.: Abutuntur hoc loco syncerioris eruditionis linguarum disciplinarumque hoc est bonarum literarum osores.

74 *Comm. Col.* (Zurich: Froschauer, 1539), fol. 426; N.B. Modern verses 5, 6, and 7 are all contained in a single verse (5) in this edition, according to the marginal enumeration, resulting in the marginal number "6" next to our verse 8.

75 *1 Corinthians* (trans. Fraser), 304. Estienne, 1556: Adiungit, in omni sapientia: quo significat unicam recte sapiendi regulam esse voluntatem illam Dei, cuius meminerat. Quisquis enim simpliciter ea scire cupit quae placuit Deo revelare, is demum novit quid sit recte sapere: si quid ultra appetamus, id nihil aliud erit quam desipere modum non tenendo. Per vocabulum *suneseos,* quod prudentiam vertimus, intelligo diuudicationem, quae ex intelligentia manat. Utraque spiritualis vocatur Paulo: quia non aliter ad eas pervenitur quam spiritus directione. Animalis enim homo non percipit ea quae Dei sunt. Quamdiu reguntur homines carnis suae sensu, habent ipsi quoque suam sapientiam, sed quae mera est vanitas, utcunque in ea sibi placeant. Videmus qualis sit theologia sub papatu, quid contineant philosophorum libri, quam sapientiam in pretio habeant profani homines. Sed meminerimus, eam quae sola commendatur a Paulo, inclusam esse in Dei voluntate.

76 *Comm. Col.* 2:8 (my translation); *COR* II/2, 423: Meo autem iudicio intelligit, quicquid ex se comminiscuntur homines, dum volunt proprio sensu sapere, idque non absque specioso rationis praetextu, ut sit in speciem probabile.

77 *Comm. Col.* 2:8 (my translation); *COR* II/2, 423–4: Neque enim in reiiciendis hominum commentis, quae nullam habent commendationem, multum est negotii, sed in iis, quae fallaci sapientiae opinione mentes capiunt.

78 *Comm. Col.* 2:8 (my translation); *COR* II/2, 424: Aut si uno verbo quis malit: Philosophia nihil aliud est quam persuasorius sermo, qui pulchris ac plausibilibus argumentis se insinuet in animos hominum.

79 *Comm. Col.* 2:8; *COR* II/2, 424: Tales, fateor, erunt omnes philosophorum argutiae, si quid de suo addere velint ad purum Dei sermonem.

80 *Comm. Col.* 2:8 (my translation); *COR* II/2, 424: Itaque philosophia nihil aliud erit quam spiritualis doctrinae corruptela, si Christo permisceatur.

81 *Comm. Col.* 2:8 (my translation); *COR* II/2, 424: Sed meminerimus Paulum sub philosophiae nomine tantum damnasse omnes adulterinas doctrinas, quae nascuntur ex humano capite, qualemcunque habeant rationis colorem.

82 *Comm. Col.* 2:8 (my translation); *COR* II/2, 424: Nota autem, quod tam mundi elementis quam hominum traditioni Christum opponit. Quo significat, quicquid in hominum cerebro fabricatum est, non esse

Christo consentaneum, qui unicus a Patre Doctor nobis ordinatus est, ut simplicitate Evangelii sui nos retineat.

83 *Comm. Col.* 2:8; *COR* II/2, 424: Alii translationem esse putant: ut elementa sint puerilia rudimenta, quae non perducunt ad solidam doctrinam. Alii accipiunt in proprio significatu pro rebus externis et corruptioni subiectis, quae nihil ad Dei regnum faciunt. Prior expositio magis arridet, sicut et ad Galatas capite 4,3. Cf. CWE 43:411: "... human precepts and regulations, which are based on visible realities and on the gross elements of this world." Feld, in his notes, suggests that Calvin is disagreeing with Erasmus in his choice of interpretation (which he may be) on this verse; but at Gal. 4:3, Erasmus, as we've noted, reads *elementa mundi* as pertaining to Jewish ceremonies adapted for teaching to children. Calvin could also have had Jerome in mind here (see note 66 above).

84 Utitur autem sapientia verbi, qui suppositis verae fidei fundamentis, si qua vera in doctrinis philosophorum inveniat, in obsequium fidei assumit (Thomas Aquinas, *Super Epistolas S. Paul Lectura*, ad loc.).

85 Erasmus does, however, condemn the "400 years of theology" that led up to his own time for severely missing the mark in the dedicatory epistle to his *Paraphrase on John* (see CWE 46:8).

86 Gilson, *The Spirit of Medieval Philosophy*, 22–3.

87 Gilson, *The Spirit*, 23. Gilson is playing on Goethe's 136th Proverb: Wer Wissenschaft und Kunst besitzt / Hat auch Religion; / Wer jene beide nicht besitzt / Der habe Religion! ("The one who has science and art / also has religion; / the one who has neither / let him have religion!")

88 Partee, *Calvin and Classical Philosophy*, 4. Gilson himself, as Partee points out, disallows Erasmus and Calvin entry into the ranks of Christian philosophers, since their understanding of the term entails the privileging of faith over reason.

89 Partee, *Calvin*, 9. Partee excludes Luther from the group on the grounds that he strictly distinguishes between philosophy and theology. This, to my mind, isn't far from Gilson's exclusion of Erasmus and Calvin on account of their insistence on the role of faith over reason. I hope to show in this chapter that neither Gilson, nor Partee in cases like this, mean by "Christian philosophy" what Erasmus and Calvin mean.

90 Partee, "Revitalization of the Concept of 'Christian philosophy' in Renaissance Humanism," 361.

91 *Paraphrase* 1 Cor 2:6; CWE 43:45; Froben, 1532: Porro qui stultitiam docere videmur apud incredulos, Christi crucem praedicantes, iidem apud eos, qui plene credunt, eximiam quandam sapientiam praedicare videmur, sed hanc longe diversam ab ea, quae mundi huius causas humanis rationibus frustra scrutatur.

92 *Paraphrase* 1 Cor. 2:8f.; CWE 43:47; Froben, 1532: Quamlibet eruditos in cognitione rerum visibilium, quamlibet turgidos scientia legis, tamen hoc arcanum illos fefellit, solis iis communicandum, quos animi modestia deo conciliasset.

93 *Paraphrase* 1 Cor. 1:21f.; CWE 43:39; Froben, 1532: neque rursus orbium motus, aut syderum vires, aut fulminum causas praedicamus, quarum rerum cognitio Graecis addit supercilium.

94 *Paraphrase* 1 Cor. 1:20; CWE 43:37; Froben, 1532: Ubi interim sapiens legis scientia tumens? ubi scriba legis interpretatione superbus? ubi philosophus, qui scrutatur arcana naturae, et opificis oblitus, res conditas admiratur?

95 *Paraphrase* 1 Cor. 2:8–11; CWE 43:47; Froben, 1532: sapientiam secreto mentibus inspirari ... non meruerunt hoc elati principes, nec tumidi philosophi.

96 On 1 Cor. 2:6's Sapientiam autem, etc.: Ex hoc loco apparet quid Paulus senserit, quum tribueret deo stultitiam, nimirum ad collationem huius apientiae quam loquebatur inter perfectos (Reeve and Screech [1990]).

97 *Ann. 1 Cor. 1 (in mysterio quae abscondita)*: ne rosas objiciamus porcis.

98 *Paraphrase* 1 Cor. 2:8–11; CWE 43:47; Froben, 1532: Is quoniam divinus est, et a deo profectus, etiam abditissima retrusissimaque dei secreta rimatur, quo non pertingit humana curiositas.

99 *Paraphrase* 1 Cor. 2:11–13; CWE 43:48, Froben, 1532: Ita res conditas contemplantur ac investigant complures, caeterum quae sunt abstrusa in mente consilioque divino, nemo novit, nisi spiritus aeternus, qui deo intimus est, et ob id illi conscius omnium.

100 *Paraphrase* 1 Cor. 2:8–11; CWE 43:47; Froben, 1532: Nobis velut amicis arcanum hoc patefecit deus, non per humanam doctrinam, sed per afflatum occultum sui spiritus.

101 *Paraphrase* 1 Cor. 1:10; Froben, 1532: Christianae philosophiae eadem apud omnes sunt dogmata, neque novit istos sectarum et opinionum humanarum rivulos. Unus est omnium praeceptor et autor.

102 Engel, *John Calvin's Perspectival Anthropology*, 103–4.

103 The *Argument* was used to introduce French editions from 1541 to 1551; the McNeill/Battles English version contains this "Subject Matter of the Present Work" as well, and ascribes it to the "French Edition of 1560," but this must be a mistake, as that edition, printed by Crespin in Geneva, doesn't contain the *Argument*.

104 *Institution de la religion chrestienne* (Geneva: Du Bois, 1541), fol. 10: Pourtant l'office de ceux qui ont receu plus ample lumiere de Dieu que les autres, est, de subvenir aux simples en cest endroict: et quasi leur prester la main, pour les conduire et les ayder a trouver la somme de ce que Dieu

nous a voulu enseigner en sa parole. Or cela ne se peut mieux faire par Escritures, qu'en traictant les matieres principales et de consequence, lesquelles sont comprises en la Philosophie Chrestienne. Car celuy qui en aura l'intelligence, sera prepare a proffiter en l'eschole de Dieu en un iour, plus qu'un autre en trois mois.

105 *Institutes* III.xx.1 (trans. Battles); Estienne, 1559: Haec quidem secreta est abscondita que philosophia, et quae syllogismis erui non potest.

106 *Institutes* III.vii.1 (trans. Battles); Estienne, 1559: Sit hic itaque primus gradus, hominem a seipso discedere, quo totam ingenii vim applicet ad Domini obsequium. Obsequium dico non modo quod in verbi obedientia iacet, sed quo mens hominis, proprio carnis sensu vacua, se ad Spiritus Dei nutum tota convertit. Hanc transformationem (quam renovationem mentis Paulus appellat) quum primus sit ad vitam ingressus, philosophi omnes ignorarunt. Solam enim rationem homini moderatricem praeficiunt, hanc solam putant audiendam, huic denique uni morum imperium deferunt ac permittunt. At Christiana philosophia illam loco cedere, Spiritui sancto subiici ac subiugari iubet: ut homo iam non ipse vivat, sed Christum in se ferat viventem ac regnantem.

107 Bouwsma has argued that Calvin's anti-rational tendencies in his theology slowly develop over his career, and that in his early days in Geneva his theology was heavily determined by his "intellectualist anthropology" (see *John Calvin*, 98–109).

108 *1 Corinthians* (trans. Fraser), 8. *CO* 49:298–9: Praeterea multum alioqui verborum adversus praeposteros illos doctores vel garrulos rhetores disputando, consumit. Perstringit eorum ambitionem: reprehendit quod evangelium in humanam philosophiam transfigurent ... puto eos excogitasse novum docendi modum a Christi simplicitate alienum, quo sui admirationem excitarent. Hoc accidere necesse est omnibus qui se nondum exuerunt, ut ad opus Domini prorsus expediti accedant ... et ut scenae serviant, evangelium fucando deformant, ut sit instar mundanae philosophiae.

109 *1 Corinthians* (trans. Fraser), 9. Estienne, 1556: Siquidem adulteratur quum ita inficitur nativa eius simplicitas, et quasi fucatur, ut nihil a mundana philosophia differat.

110 *1 Corinthians* (trans. Fraser), 10. Estienne, 1556: Ac interim sententiam illam fusius explicat, contineri in evangelio coelestem arcanamque sapientiam: quae nec ingenii acumine aut perspicacia, nec toto carnis sensu apprehendatur, nec persuadeatur rationibus humanis, nec verborum lenocinio aut pictura indigeat.

111 *1 Corinthians* (trans. Fraser), 10. Estienne, 1556: Tandem concludit, non tantum a carnis prudentia remotam esse evangelii praedicationem et in crucis humilitate positam: sed etiam carnis iudicio non posse aestimari qualis sit: idque facit ut a perversa confidentia proprii sensus eos abducat, quo perperam omnia metiebantur.

112 *1 Corinthians* (trans. Fraser), 21. Estienne, 1556: Corinthios abundare scientia, sicut ab initio Deus efficaciam apud eos evangelio suo dederat.

113 Willis, "Rhetoric and Responsibility in Calvin," 49.

114 *1 Corinthians* (trans. Fraser), 40. Estienne, 1556: Et sane alioqui humanae rationi absurdius nihil est quam audire Deum mortalem, vitam morti obnoxiam, iustitiam peccati similitudine obtectam, benedictionem subiectam maledictioni: ut eo modo redimantur homines a morte et beatae immortalitatis participes fiant, ut vitam adipiscantur, ut abolito peccato regnet iustitia, ut mors et maledictio absorbeatur.

115 CWE 43:39; see also CWE 43:49: "And he [i.e., that 'natural person'] does not observe that this philosophy, which teaches that Christ was born of a virgin; that he was true God and true man equally; that by dying he conquered death, and from death rose to life again; that what he has fulfilled in himself he will also fulfill in his members; that the path to true happiness lies through tribulations; that the attainment of immortality comes through death – this is not grasped by human reasoning, but by the Spirit's inspiration" (Froben, 1532: nec animadvertit, quod haec philosophiae, quae docet Christum e virgine natus, verum deum fuisse pariter et verum hominem, moriendo devicisse mortem, a morte revixisse, idem praestaturum in membris suis, quod in se praestitit, per afflictiones iter esse ad veram felicitatem, per mortes perveniri ad immortalitatem. Hoc non comprehenditur humana ratiocinatione, sed afflatu spiritus).

116 Erasmus writes, paraphrasing 1 Cor. 15, that "the pre-eminent part of the gospel's teaching is belief in the resurrection of the dead" (CWE 43:174). The prefatory matter of the *Paraphrase* contains multiple references to the incompatibility of belief in the resurrection with worldly philosophy. In the *Argumentum* he blames the philosophers specifically for casting doubt in the minds of the Corinthians on the matter: "But it was the particular result of philosophy alone that they were calling into doubt the resurrection of the dead, the foundation of our faith" (CWE 43:21). In the dedicatory letter Erasmus calls the resurrection of the dead the "foundation and the crown of our belief," and, criticizing some unknown contemporary Italian philosophizing preachers, notes that the problem of the future resurrection for a reasonable Christianity persists even in

his day: "Against this plague Paul fights with all his might, but even so
I fear that this viper still lives in some men's hearts; for in Italy every
year in sermons before the people they try to defend the resurrection,
thinking that they will be home and dry on this question, once they
can show that Aristotle did not entirely abolish the immortality of the
soul" (CWE 43:13). Doubting the resurrection on the grounds that it
is unreasonable or even, apparently, attempting to demonstrate that it is
compatible with human philosophy, is a *plague* and a *viper* (although he
admits, a bit later, that he wishes Paul himself had been a little clearer on
the details of the matter, to the chagrin of Noel Beda and the Sorbonne
censors) (see CWE 43:14 and n61). We have also seen that Calvin,
while he thought that for the most part Paul was criticizing the *manner*
of teaching rather than specific theological errors when writing to the
Corinthians, one doctrinal error introduced at Corinth was doubt in the
resurrection. In the *Argumentum*, Calvin writes that Paul, in chapter 15,
"shows that the resurrection hope is so necessary that if it is cut out,
then the whole Gospel collapses in utter ruin" (trans. Fraser, 14). Calvin
also writes, beginning to comment on chapter 15, that while he cannot be
sure whether the Corinthians were doubting bodily resurrection only or the
entirety of a future life, he thinks that Paul is defending the resurrection of
the body only. (Erasmus takes up both issues in his *Paraphrase*.)

117 *1 Corinthians* (trans. Fraser), 40. Estienne, 1556: Verum est enim, hunc
mundum theatri instar esse, in quo nobis Dominus conspicuam gloriae
suae figuram exhibet: nos tamen, quum tale spectaculum nobis ante
oculos pateat, caecutimus, non quia obscura sit revelatio, sed quia nos
mente alienati sumus ... Nam utcunque Deus palam appareat, non alio
tamen quam fidei oculo ipsum possumus adspicere.

118 *1 Corinthians* (trans. Fraser), 39; Estienne, 1556: Sic vitio nostro
imputandum est, quod salvificam Dei notitiam non ante consequimur
quam proprio sensu exinaniti.

119 *Comm. 1 Cor.* 2:10 (trans. Fraser, modified), 57. Estienne, 1556: Itaque quo
est humana mens hebetior ad intelligenda Dei mysteria, quo maior est
eius incertitudo, eo certior est fides nostra, quae spiritus Dei revelatione
suffulta est.

120 *Comm. 1 Cor.* 3:11 (my translation). Estienne, 1556: Qui ergo Christum
didicit, in tota coelesti doctrina iam est absolutus.

121 *Comm. 1 Cor.* 3:15; Comm. 1 Cor. (trans. Fraser), 77. Even the saints
have erred in this way, according to Calvin, including Cyprian,
Ambrose, Augustine, Gregory, and Bernard. *CO* 49:357: Nempe qui in

Christo aedificant, sed propter carnis imbecillitatem patiuntur aliquid humanum, aut per ignorantiam nonnihil ab exacta verbi Dei puritate deflectunt. Quales etiam fuerunt multi ex sanctis, Cyprianus, Ambrosius, Augustinus, et similes: adde etiam si libet, ex recentioribus, Gregorium et Bernardum ...

122 *1 Corinthians* (trans. Fraser), 94; cf. also *Comm. 1 Cor.* 3:19 and Erasmus' paraphrase of same.

123 See also Pitkin, *What Pure Eyes Could See*, esp. 160.

6. The Affective Christian Philosophy

1 See, e.g., Jerome, *Commentarius in Matheum* 4.26.37 (PL 26, 197); Augustine, *Enarratio in psalmum 21* (PL 36, 172).

2 See, e.g., Aquinas, *Summa Theologiae* 3a, q.46, art. 6, where Aquinas states that death is naturally horrible to human nature in the context of Christ's psychological suffering in the Passion.

3 For literature, see Tracy, "Humanists among the Scholastics," 30–51; Fokke, "An Aspect of the Christology of Erasmus of Rotterdam," 161–87; Santinello, "Tre meditazioni umanistiche sulla passione," 77–128; Grazia, "Colet et Érasme au sujet de l'exégèse de Mt. 26, 39," 259–72; Michael J. Heath's introduction to the De taedio in CWE 70:2–8; and the introduction by Godin in the recently published Amsterdam (ASD) edition V-7, 192–206.

4 For a detailed analysis of the theological precedents among the ancient and medieval theologians represented in the debate, see especially Tracy, "Humanists among the Scholastics."

5 For the dating of these sermons and the circumstances surrounding their delivery and printing, see the introduction in Wilhelmus Moehn (ed.), *Plusieurs Sermons de Jean Calvin* (Droz, 2011).

6 My translation, with consultation of the 1581 English version by Thomas Stocker. Il n'a pas refuse de soustenir les angoisses qui sont apprestees a tous ceux que leur conscience redargue, et qui se sentent coulpables de mort eternelle et damnation devant Dieu ... Et ne faut point que nous ayons honte, voyans que le Fils de Dieu s'est assuieti a telle infirmite. Ce n'est point sans cause que S. Paul nous exhorte par son exemple de n'avoir point honte de la predication de la croix, combien qu'elle soit folie a d'aucuns, et en scandale a beaucoup. Car d'autant plus que nostre Seigneur Iesus s'est abbaisse, en cela voyons nous que les offenses dont nous estions redevables a Dieu ne se pouvoyent point abolir sinon qu'il

fust mis iusques a l'extremite ... Car s'il n'avoit senti en sa personne les craintes, les doutes et les torments que nous endurons, il ne seroit pas si enclin a nous estre pitoyable comme il est (*CO* 46:834–5).

7 See Shuger, *Sacred Rhetoric*, esp. 58–64.

8 Shuger has demonstrated what can be accomplished with such an approach in *The Renaissance Bible*; Karant-Nunn has examined the significance of emotion in the cultural history of the Reformation in *The Reformation of Feeling*. On religion and emotion more generally, see the excellent collection edited by Corrigan, *Religion and Emotion*.

9 Tilmouth, *Passion's Triumph Over Reason: A History of the Moral Imagination from Spenser to Rochester*.

10 I use "passions," "affections," and the arguably anachronistic "emotions" interchangably here, for, despite some recent arguments in the history of emotions, emotion terms (Latin *passio* and *affectus* and their Romance cognates, e.g.) were used with great imprecision in the sixteenth-century. See further, Essary, "Passions, Emotions, or Affections? On the Ambiguity of Sixteenth-Century Terminology," forthcoming in *Emotion Review*.

11 See, e.g., Erasmus, *Enchiridion* (CWE 45:44): "It is true that the Stoics and the Peripatetics have slightly different views on the passions, but there is universal agreement that we must live according to reason and not according to the passions."

12 On Erasmus especially, see Monfasani, "Erasmus and the Philosophers," 57ff.; on Calvin, see Partee, *Calvin and Classical Philosophy*.

13 Aristotle's descriptive account of the human essence, or the "what it is to be" human, is much more complicated, in the end, than we have space to deal with here. The most obvious place to look for his anthropology is in the *De anima*, but there also you find his account of the active intellect (or *nous poietikos*), which has bred all sorts of controversy in terms of subsequent interpretation. Aside from the problem of the active intellect as a separable (ostensibly non-human) component (see *De anima* III.5) is the difficulty of defining *essence* in Aristotle's metaphysics more generally. At times Aristotle will say that the soul (*psuche*) is the life-giving form (*eidos*) of man (see *De anima* II 415b9–14), and at others that the essence (*to ti en einai*) is equivalent to a thing's form (*eidos*); which might lead us to conclude that the form of man, which is the soul, is also the essence, and that since the *rational* soul is what sets humans apart from brutes, it is the *rational* soul that is *essentially* human. Unfortunately it isn't so simple, but this is certainly outside the purview of our project. For *form* as *cause* as *essence*, see *Metaphysics* 1013a26–7 and 1013b22–3; for *form* as *essence* per se, see 1032b1–2, 1033b5–7, 1035b15ff., 1037a29, 1044a36. In any event,

subsequent Aristotelian tradition smoothed out many of these difficulties in their interpretations, and it is the subsequent Peripatetic strand, especially as it is "baptized" in the medieval period, with which Calvin and Erasmus would have presumably been more intimately familiar.

14 See, e.g., *Inst.* II.ii.17. In addition, Muller writes, "Calvin clearly held to the traditional Aristotelian 'faculty psychology,' according to which the soul (*anima*) could be distinguished into the faculties or parts (*partes*) of intellect (*intellectus*) and will (*voluntas*) and could be viewed as the seat of the affections of the will" (*The Unaccommodated Calvin*, 165; see the accompanying endnote for references to this position in Calvin's corpus). Pitkin notes that in the 1536 *Institutes* Calvin suggests that what sets humans apart from animals is their capacity to worship God, but that later in the same edition he suggests that it is the human "longing for truth or power of perception" that is unique. But she also points out that Calvin "nearly always dismisses the relevance of [the philosophers'] insights when it comes to anthropology" (Pitkin, "The Protestant Zeno," *The Journal of Religion* 84:3, 353n30, and 360). See also Partee, *Calvin and Classical Philosophy*, 51–65; and Kok's dissertation, *The Influence of Martin Bucer on John Calvin's Interpretation of Romans*, 85ff., for a discussion of Calvin's anti-philosophical anthropology as it appears in *Comm. Rom.*

15 *Nicomachean Ethics* 1177a22; trans. Ross. The *Nic. Ethics* and the commentaries on it were, according to Jill Kraye, the most important texts in the Renaissance for understanding Aristotelian ethics (*The Cambridge History of Renaissance Philosophy*, 326); see also *Cambridge History*, 325–48, for an overview of Aristotelian ethics in the Renaissance and its reception in Christian thought.

16 *Nicomachean Ethics* 1128a10; trans. Ross.

17 Attaining *eudaimonia* on earth – which entails "giving an essential role to external and corporeal goods" – is itself incompatible with the concept of Christian beatitude according to many sixteenth-century dissenters, for this is only attainable in the hereafter (*Cambridge History*, 342ff.).

18 See Auerbach, *Literary Language and Its Public*, 67ff., for an outline of the Stoic elevation of the virtue of *impassibilis/apatheia* beyond the neutral Aristotelian position regarding *passio*, and the claim that the Stoic position has had wider influence in the history of Western thought. For a comprehensive overview of ancient Stoicism and its reception into the early medieval period, see Colish, *The Stoic Tradition*.

19 Long, *Hellenistic Philosophy*, 173.

20 Qtd. in Long, *Hellenistic Philosophy*, 175.

21 Long, *Hellenistic Philosophy*, 175.

22 It might be argued that Stoicism in this regard is more thoroughgoing in wedding intellectualism to ethics than the Aristotelian model presented above. While Peripatetic intellectualism is ideally moderate in terms of the passions – seeking, as it does, the golden mean between excessive and insufficient emotion – it defines itself primarily in terms of the contemplative life and the proper use of the intellect in contemplation, whereas the Stoic ideal of *apatheia*, while not anti-contemplative, defines itself most explicitly as reasonableness over and against emotion, as it often seeks to eliminate rather than to moderate emotional impulses. See further, *The Cambridge History of Renaissance Philosophy*, 365–7.

23 On the relationship of soul to body, see, e.g., Erasmus' colloquy "The New Mother" (CWE 39, esp. 596–604).

24 The literature cannot be recounted here, but on Erasmus' indebtedness to various philosophical traditions, see the recent article by Monfasani, "Twenty-fifth Annual Margaret Mann Phillips Lecture: Erasmus and the Philosophers," 47–68; Partee, *Calvin and Classical Philosophy*; for Erasmus' and Calvin's reception of Stoicism, with bibliography, see Pitkin, "Erasmus, Calvin, and the Two Faces of Stoicism."

25 On the *summum bonum* of classical philosophy contrasted with that of Christianity in the Renaissance, see *The Cambridge History of Renaissance Philosophy*, 319–25; for various Renaissance responses to this aspect of Aristotle's ethics (but with no mention of Erasmus or Calvin), see, idem, 335–9. For a note on Valla's anti-Aristotelian rhetorical philosophy, especially regarding the vita contemplativa, and which might usefully be compared with Erasmus and Calvin's, see Grassi, *Renaissance Humanism*, 82–6.

26 Paster et al., *Reading the Early Modern Passions*, 23; see also Strier, *The Unrepentant Renaissance: From Petrarch to Shakespeare to Milton*, ch. 1. And see Pitkin, "Erasmus, Calvin, and the Two Faces of Stoicism."

27 Paster et al., *Reading the Early Modern Passions*, 32.

28 Calvin's relationship to Stoicism has hardly been ignored. His first publication was a commentary on Seneca's *De Clementia*, which guaranteed that his modern interpreters would long look for Stoic influence in his later writings as well. Peter Leithart has examined in detail his reception of Stoicism in his mature work. His position on the ethics of emotion, specifically, vis-à-vis Stoicism, has been adequately outlined by Kyle Fedler ("Calvin's Burning Heart"). For recent treatments, with further bibliography, see Pitkin, "Human Nature in Calvin's Commentary on Seneca's *De Clementia*," *Anthropological Reformations – Anthropology in the Reformation* (forthcoming). See the three-part series of essays, "Stoicism in Calvin's Doctrine of the

Christian Life," *Westminster Theological Journal* 55 (1993) and 56 (1994). Also on the mixed reception of Stoicism in Calvin, see Helm, "Calvin and Stoicism," 169–82, and Pierre-François Moreau, "Calvin: fascination et critique du stoicisme," *Le stoicisme au XVI et au XVII siècle* (edited by Pierre François-Moreau, Albin Michel, 1999), 59–64.

29 Pitkin, "Erasmus, Calvin, and the Two Faces of Stoicism."
30 See *Enchiridion* LB V 13 F / CWE 66:44; criticisms of Stoicism appear, e.g., in the *De taedio Iesu* (passim); the *Moria* (see above); the *Explanatio Symboli* (CWE 70:246); for Calvin, see *Inst.* I.15.6–8, II.2.12 (for the human being as "rational animal"), and below for anti-Stoic rhetoric.
31 CWE 27:104; ASD IV-3, 106: Iam primum illud in confesso est, affectus omnes ad stulticiam pertinere, quandoquidem hac nota a stulto sapientem discernunt, quod illum affectus, hunc ratio temperat; eoque Stoici perturbationes omnes ceu morbos a sapiente semovent. Verum affectus isti non solum paedagogorum vice funguntur ad sapientiae portum properantibus, verumetiam in omni virtutis functione ceu calcaria stimulique quidam adesse solent, velut ad bene agendum exhortatores. Quanquam hic fortiter reclamat bis Stoicus Seneca, qui prorsum omnem affectum adimit sapienti. Verum cum id facit, iam ne hominem quidem relinquit, sed novum potius deum quendam *demiourgei*, qui nusquam nec extitit unquam, nec extabit; imo, ut apertius dicam, marmoreum hominis simulacrum constituit, stupidum et ab omni prorsus humano sensu alienum.
32 See ASD IV-3, 107, lines 628–30.
33 Muller, *The Unaccommodated Calvin*, 164, 167.
34 Hoc philosophiae genus in affectibus situm verius, quam in syllogismis, vita magis est quam disputatio, afllatus potius quam eruditio, transformatio magis quam ratio (*Novum Instrumentum omne*, Froben: 1516).
35 For a recent study with bibliography, see Essary, "Fiery Heart and Fiery Tongue," 5–34.
36 CWE 67:399 and 67:260.
37 CWE 29, 266; and *Paraphrase* Eph. 6:14 (CWE 43, 354); this phrase is Ovidian; see *Metamorphoses* (11.146).
38 See Leo's dissertation, *Affect before Spinoza*, 395–400. It might be that further study of Melanchthon on the emotions will reveal more substantial continuities from both directions (see, recently, Zahl, "On the Affective Salience of Doctrines," 428–44). His 1552 *Liber de anima*, while it would have been too late to influence Calvin's earlier editions of the *Institutes*, has a substantial discussion of the emotions, both virtuous and not. In

that text, however, Melanchthon repeatedly defines the heart as the seat of the affections, and while he also certainly understands the heart as an organ operated on by God, it would seem that he retains a distinction between the function of the heart in that capacity and the function of the brain as the seat of reason. In a subsection criticizing the Stoic account of the passions as judgments, for example (entitled "Qui sunt errores Stoicorum de Adfectibus?"), he writes, "Adfectus non esse opiniones, manifesta demonstratio est. Quae subiectis differunt, diversae res sunt. Opinio est in cerebro, adfectus in corde" (Wittenberg, 1558, fol. R3). Markus Hofner has suggested that Melanchthon's conception of the heart changes from a biblical-theological notion to one grounded more in the scientific discourse of Galen and Aristotle between the 1521 and 1559 *Loci Communes*. See Hofner, "The Affects of the Soul and the Effects of Grace: On Melanchthon's Understanding of Faith and Christian Emotions," in *The Depth of the Human Person: A Multidisciplinary Approach*, ed. Michael Welker (Eerdmans, 2014).

39 See also I.v.9, where Calvin uses similar language.

40 ... quo scilicet et maior est cordis diffidentia quam mentis caecitas, et animum securitate instrui quam mentem cogitatione imbui difficilius est.

41 *Inst.* III.vi.4; McNeill/Battles. Added in 1539. Non enim lingua est doctrina, sed vitae: nec intellectu memoriaque duntaxat apprehenditur, ut reliquae disciplinae, sed tum recipitur demum ubi animam totam possidet, sedemque et receptaculum invenit in intimo cordis affectu ... quanto meliori ratione nugaces istos sophistas detestabimur, qui Evangelium in summis labris volutare contenti sunt, cuius efficacia centuplo magis quam frigidae philosophorum paraeneses, in affectus cordis intimos penetrare, animae insidere, ac totum hominem afficere debuerat?

42 For Calvin's development of this idea in successive editions of the *Institutes*, and its relationship to his criticism of scholastic implicit faith, see Pitkin, *What Pure Eyes Could See*, ch. 5 (esp. 135ff.). Muller also points out that language of *cor* is mostly missing from Calvin's 1536 *Institutes*, but that it enters his theological discourse shortly after (*The Unaccommodated Calvin*, 163–4).

43 *Inst.* III.ii.8; McNeill/Battles, 552. See also I.v.9, and III.ii.33, 36. Also, on the role of "affect" in Calvin's understanding of faith, especially in the 1559 *Institutes*, see Leo, *Affect before Spinoza*, esp. ch. 1.

44 *Inst.* III.vi.4: quanto meliori ratione nugaces istos sophistas detestabimur, qui Evangelium in summis labris volutare contenti sunt, cuius efficacia

centuplo magis quam frigidae philosophorum paraeneses, in affectus cordis intimos penetrare, animae insidere, ac totum hominem afficere debuerat?

45 Bouwsma, "Calvin and the Renaissance Crisis of Knowing," 205.

46 *1 Corinthians* (trans. Fraser), 32.

47 *Sermon II on 1 Timothy*: Pourtant apprenons que Dieu ne veut point qu'il y ait des teples pour gaudir et pour rire, comme si on iouoit ici des farces: mais il faut qu'il y ait une maieste en sa parole, de laquelle nous soyons esmeus et touchez: et puis qu'il y ait instruction profitable a salut (CO 53:24). See also Fraser, *Calvin's Preaching*, 114ff., for several instances of Calvin's insistence that "mere" instruction from the pulpit is not sufficient. For a broader consideration of Calvin's position on rhetoric in this regard, see Millet, *"Docere/movere," Calvinus sincerioris religionis vindex*, 35–51. And see Cummings, *The Literary Culture of the Reformation*, 274–5, for another example of Calvin's endorsement of the Spirit's power "d'emouuoir et enflammer le coeur" in a preface to Marot's and Beza's edition of the metrical Psalms.

48 My translation. Deinde nemo ad docendum erit unquam idoneus, nisi qui evangelii virtutem prius ipse imbiberit, ut non tam ore loquatur quam cordis affectu (*CO* 49:299).

49 *Pace* Thomas Dixon, who suggests, in his influential book *From Passions to Emotions* and elsewhere, that "classical Christian" usage abides a fairly rigid distinction between the unruly and even sinful *passiones* and the less problematic and even virtuous *affectus*. See further, Essary, "Passions, Emotions, or Affections? On the Ambiguity of Sixteenth-Century Terminology," forthcoming in *Emotion Review*.

50 CWE 70:32; ASD V-7, 230.

51 CWE 70:59.

52 CWE 70:34; ASD V-7, 232.

53 CWE 70:23; ASD V-7, 224.

54 Shuger writes, commenting on the *De taedio*, that Erasmus departs from Paul's "binary psyche" to posit his own three-fold anthropology. But Paul describes the "natural (*psuchikos*) man" at 1 Cor. 2:14, and Erasmus understands this (*animalis homo*) to be a morally neutral description – mediate between the spiritual and the carnal – and also explicitly understands his own three-fold division to be Pauline (see CWE 70:61; LB 1287E). In *Ann. 1 Cor.* 2:14 (*animalis autem homo*), Erasmus provides the following note: Velut animum, hoc est, affectus sequens humanos. Etenim quum Paulus hominem dividat in treis partis, carnem, animam, et spiritum: hic animae vocabulo, pro carne videtur abusus. For a recent discussion, see Cummings, "Erasmus and the Invention of Literature," 32ff.

55 CWE 70:60. LB V1287B: Tertium inter hos duos medium, qui neque ad honesta tanquam honesta, neque ad turpia tanquam ad turpia; sed ad ea fertur, quae naturae sunt amica: ab iis resilit, quae laedunt incolumitatem, aut etiam tranquillitatem. Primus ille iudicio constat et gratia, secundus depravatione, tertius naturali affectu.

56 See LB V1287E (CWE 70:61).

57 See esp. CWE 70, 60–2.

58 On "affections" (*affectus*) in Erasmus' anthropology, see, e.g., CWE 43:189 n.64 and *Ann. Rom.* 1:31.

59 CWE 70:56; ASD V-1, 252: Unde non ita nimis me delectat illa Hieronymi interpretatio, qua dicit hanc in Redemptore noesticiam propassionem fuisse, non passionem, quae illum iuxta divi Bernardi distinctionem turbarit modo, non etiam perturbarit. Si passionem appelant eam, quae rationem a statu suo dimoveat, si perturbari vocant a statu mentis dimoveri, non reclamo; at ego non dubitem et passionem nominare, quae mentem Iesu saltem secundum inferiorem partem non turbarit solum, sed vehementissime perturbarit.

60 See *Summa Theologiae* 3a, q. 46, art. 7.

61 CWE 70:31; Incidentally, he continues to quote Ambrose as "exempting Christ from both [i.e., *analgesia* and *apatheia*]" and quotes him thus: "Nor should people be praised for their bravery, if they are more stunned than hurt when they take a wound" (CWE 70:31; Ambrose, *Expositio in Lucam* 10.56). Calvin quotes from the same Ambrose passage commentary on the synoptic gospels (Matt. 26:37 and par.): *neque enim habent fortitudinis laudem, qui stuporem magis vulnerum tulerint quam dolorem*. On Calvin's use of Ambrose here as potentially betraying his debts to Erasmus' treatise, see Essary, "Calvin's Interpretation of Christ's Agony."

62 Erasmus is also involved in a controversy over christological matters with Lefevre d'Etaples, specifically over the interpretation of Hebrews 2:7, which resulted in the publication of his *Apologia ad Fabrum* in 1517 (the text is in CWE 83 and ASD IX-3). This text, too, is important for understanding Erasmus' emphasis on the realism of the humanity of Christ.

63 My translation: nunc testes haberet extremae imbecillitatis humanae (*Tomus primus Paraphraseon Des. Erasmi Roterodami* [Froben, 1535], fol. 164). Bullinger follows Erasmus here, and in the explicit reading of Christ's fearing his own death: Delegit autem hos tres, quibus et transfigurationem exhibuerat, ut quos in monte spectatores adhibuerat suae maiestatis, eosdem et humilitatis suae et imbecillitatis extremae haberet testes. Atque

hic tandem coepit dominum sensim invadere sensus et horror mortis. (*In ... Matthaeum commentariorum* (Zurich: Froschauer, 1542), fol. 239).

64 My translation: simulque doceret, ut quoties ingruit huiusmodi malorum tempestas atrocior quam ut humanae vires ferre possint, prorsus diffisi nobis, totos nos divino praesidio commitamus. Est autem mortis horror, si quando corripuit hominem, vel ipsa morte acerbior. (*Tomus primus Paraphraseon Des. Erasmi Roterodami* [Froben, 1535], fol. 164).

65 Horror certe mortis, si quando corripuit hominem ipsa est morte acerbior (Zurich: Froschauer, 1542, fol. 239–40).

66 See *Paraphrase in Marcam* 14:33ff. in *Tomus primus Paraphraseon Des. Erasmi Roterodami* (Froben, 1535), fol. 127.

67 *Paraphrase on Matthew* 26:39. My translation: Pater mi, si fieri potest, transfer hoc mortis poculum a me, nam sentio corporis affectum vehementer abhorrentem a morte. (*Tomus primus Paraphraseon Des. Erasmi Roterodami* [Froben, 1535], fol. 164).

68 CWE 49:162, modified. Natura corporis horrebat cruciatum ac mortem imminentem. (*Paraphrase in Marcam; Tomus primus Paraphraseon Des. Erasmi Roterodami* [Froben, 1535], fol. 127)

69 My translation: Hic igitur tum coepit invadere Iesum, sensitque mirum animi dolorem ac moerorem. Nec enim animi cruciatum obscurum esse voluit suis amicis selectis, quo plane viderent illum esse vere hominem, corporis pariter atque animi affectionibus obnoxius. (*Tomus primus Paraphraseon Des. Erasmi Roterodami* [Froben, 1535], fol. 164).

70 See, e.g. CWE 70:34, 48.

71 See, e.g., Gail Kern Paster, *Humoring the Body*, and responses by Strier, *The Unrepentant Renaissance*, Cummings and Sierhuis, *Passions and Subjectivity in Early Modern Culture*, and Essary, "Clear as Mud: Metaphor, Emotion, and Meaning in Early Modern England," forthcoming in *English Studies*.

72 See the introduction to CWE, vol. 70, for further details.

73 CWE 70:449, my emphasis; ASD V-1, 392: Nec statim desperandum, si differtur consolatio; iterum atque iterum redeundum est ad clamorem, non oris, sed cordis. Etenim si nos, quod Dominus externe fecit, spiritualiter imitemur, aderit bonus angelus, qui sudorem sanguineum abstersurus est ab animo nostro; et aut eripiet a discrimine aut robur addet spiritui, ut mortem fortiter perferamus.

74 Covington, "The Garden of Anguish," 280–308.

75 CWE 70:408 (modified); ASD V-1, 354: Huius igitur horror superat omnem horrorem, quem tamen clementissimus redemptor, ut nobis mitigaret, in sese recipere dignatus est. Quod in horto expavit et angore extremo sic

correptus est, ut sudaret sanguinem, nostrae naturae erat infirmitas. Quod autem affixus cruci clamat: Deus meus, Deus meus, quur deservisti me? Longe a salute mea verba delictorum meorum videtur gehennae horrorem animo persensisse. Quid enim superest a Deo destitutis nisi extrema desperatio? Nec mirum videri debet, si hanc tristissimam affectionem in se recepit, qui peccata omnium in se receperat, ut utrunque malum, nostris viribus insuperabile, sua misericordia redderet superabile? ... Nos gehennam merveramus, ille innocens expavescit pro nobis; quo si similis affectus invadat animum nostrum ex scelerum conscientia vel ex imbecillitate naturae, non abiiciamus nosmetipsos, sed in Christum intentis oculis etiam desperando speremus.

76 Erasmus' *Pararphrase* of Jesus' weeping in John 11, published in 1523, in fact sets out a similar gloss of Christ's sorrow over human sinfulness, although not with the soteriological component found here. Luther's comments on Psalm 22:2 consider Christ's psychological agony, especially on the cross, but also in Gethsemane. Indeed, the contours of Luther's argument, especially vis-à-vis the question of Christ's emotions related to ours, are quite similar to Erasmus' *Disputatiuncula*, and it's certainly possible that there is two-way influence at work in the long term. The emphasis on Christ's despairing of God's wrath as a sinner would seem to be a peculiarly Lutheran twist.

77 CWE 70:47.

78 Bullinger, in his commentary, also notes that his mental pain was greater than his bodily pain: Et animi mentisque dolores tanto superant cruciatus corporis, quanto mens carne praestantior est. (Zurich: Froschauer, 1542, fol. 239).

79 Calvin typically preached on a book of the Bible from beginning to end, but this sermon did not follow an ordinary sequence of Gospel commentaries – he didn't preach on the harmony of the Gospels until later, in fact – but was part of a series of sermons on the divinity, nativity, and humanity of Christ. It was first published in French in 1558 and reissued in 1563. Thomas Stocker's 1581 English translation of the *Divers sermons* follows the second edition, and my English rendering here often follows Stocker's.

80 Elsewhere I've considered Calvin's debts to Erasmus's *De taedio* in his 1555 *Commentary on the Gospel Harmony*: see Essary, "Calvin's Interpretation of Christ's Agony," 59–70.

81 Christian emotions were also typically defended in Reformed commentaries on Jesus' weeping at the scene of Lazarus' death in John 11, as Craig Farmer has shown, and Calvin was no doubt influenced by these commentaries in his expositions of Christ's emotions elsewhere (see Farmer, *The Gospel of John in the Sixteenth Century*, 163–7).

82 See Karant-Nunn, *The Reformation of Feeling*.

83 On Calvin's tendency to approach the same biblical texts from different
perspectives when preaching and when writing commentaries, see
Engammare, "Le Paradis à Genève," 329–47.

84 For an argument that Calvin imagined the sermon as a "practice of doctrine,"
see Peter Ward, "Coming to Sermon: The Practice of Doctrine in the
Preaching of John Calvin," *Scottish Journal of Theology* 58:3 (2005), 319–32.

85 Mais d'autre coste nous voyons que le pris de nostre redemption a este bien
cher, quand nostre Seigneur Iesus Christ est si angoisse, qu'il soustient les
frayeurs de la mort: voire iusques a suer les gouttes de sang, qu'il est la
comme ravi, demandant s'il est possible qu'il puisse eschapper d'une telle
destresse. Quand donc nous voyons cela, c'est bien pour nouse faire venir
a la cognoissance de nos pechez. Il n'est pas question de nous endormir
yci par flatterie, quand nous voyons que le Fils de Dieu est plonge en telle
extremite, qu'il semble qu'il soit au profond des abysmes (*CO* 46:838).

86 In the *Commentary on the Gospel Harmony*, Calvin argues more forcefully
than in the sermon that Christ's sweating drops of blood is not indicative
of an ordinary fear of death, but rather of a fear of the full wrath of God
that Christ faced in dying.

87 Susan Karant-Nunn picks out this lack of focus on the body as a
distinguishing feature of Calvinist passion narratives when compared with
Catholic and Lutheran ones; see *The Reformation of Feeling*, passim.

88 Or ceste attente de nostre Seigneur Iesus Christ ne peut estre, si non que
nous soyons resolus et persuadez qu'il a tellement combatu contre les
frayeurs de la mort, que toutesfois nous en sommes affranchis, et que la
victoire nous est acquise (*CO* 46:842).

89 *Inst.* II.16.12, 1559: Et sane nisi poenae fuisset particeps anima, corporibus
tantum fuisset redemptor.

90 Erasmus, for example, argues that only the soul descended, while the body
remained in the tomb, but he does seem to believe that the soul did in fact
literally descend into Hell (see his treatment of the Creed in *Explanatio
Symboli*, esp. CWE 70:306–11; and the colloquy *Inquisitio de fide* CWE
39:419–47; also *Ecclesiastes* CWE 68:988).

91 In arguing that the *descensus* of the Apostle's Creed precedes Christ's
death, Calvin is preceded by Cusanus, Pico della Mirandola, and
Lefevre d'Etaples, who (Lefevre) in fact also associates the *descensus* with
Gethsemane. Erasmus' view is mostly traditional, while Luther's view is
complicated: for an overview of the history of interpretation of this part
of the Creed, see the 1974 dissertation by David Truemper, *The "Descensus
ad Inferos" from Luther to the Formula of Concord* (Department of Systematic
Theology of the Joint Project for Theological Education, Lutheran School of
Theology at Chicago). For Erasmus, see note above.

92 *Inst.* II.16.10, 1559: ut sciamus non modo corpus Christi in pretium redemptionis fuisse traditum: sed aliud maius et excellentius pretium fuisse quod diros in anima cruciatus damnati ac perditi hominis pertulerit. Calvin presumably has Sebastian Castellio in mind here, for he defends his position against the charge (which had been leveled by Castellio) that extending the Harrowing of Hell to cover Christ's psychological agony would confound the order of events of the passion, a point Calvin dismisses as trifling and who further argues that the Creed is simply describing (allegorically) the agony he underwent in before the eyes of men.

93 Tilmouth, "Passion and Intersubjectivity in Early Modern Literature," 29ff.

94 Tilmouth, "Passion and Intersubjectivity," 30. Indeed, Erasmus' *De preparatione ad mortem*, translated into English in 1538, also details the active force of Christ's passions and wounds.

95 See Strier, *The Unrepentant Renaissance*, 17; also the introduction by Brian Cummings and Freya Sierhuis for discussion in *Passions and Subjectivity in Early Modern Culture*.

96 Karant-Nunn, *The Reformation of Feeling*, esp. 101–16.

97 Et qu'il ne faut point douter que par son moyen nous ne puissions maintenant surmonter toutes solicitudes, toutes craintes, tous effrois, et que puissions invoquer Dieu estans asseurez que tousiours il ha les bras estendus pour nous recevoir a soy (*CO* 46:842).

98 Au reste, en ce qu'il s'adresse a Dieu son Pere, il nous monstre bien le remede pour nous soulager de toutes nos angoisses, pour addoucir nos tristesses, et mesmes pour nous remettre au dessus, quand nous serions comme abysmez. Car si nous sommes faschez et angoissez, nous scavons que Dieu n'est pas nomme en vain Pere de consolation. Si nous en sommes donc separez, ou est ce que nous trouverons vertu sinon en luy? Nous voyons cependant qu'il ne s'est point voulu espargnez au besoin. Voyla donc le Fils de Dieu qui nous conduit par son exemple au vray refuge quand nous sommes en tristesse et angoisse (*CO* 46:841).

99 See Fedler, "Calvin's Burning Heart," 133–62.

100 Bohatec identifies Calvin's *novi Stoici* with Bude (*Bude und Calvin*, 408–11), and while this may be, Calvin's contemporary Reformed exegetes also accused the Anabaptists of a form of Neostoicism and used the scene of Jesus weeping in the Gospel of John as an opportunity to attack their views (see Farmer, *The Gospel of John in the Sixteenth Century*, 164–7); on Melanchthon, see Jill Kraye, "Stoicism in the Renaissance from Petrarch to Lipsius," *Grotiana* 22 (2001), 34.

101 *Inst.* III.viii.9, my translation. Vides ut patienter ferre crucem, non sit prorsus obstupescere, et omni doloris sensu privari. quemadmodum

Stoici magnanimus hominem stulte olim descripserunt qui exuta humanitate, rebus adversis perinde ac prosperis: tristibus perinde ac laetis afficeretur. imo qui instar lapidis nulla re afficeretur. Et quid ista sublimi sapientia profecerunt? nempe simulacrum sapientiae depinxerunt, quod neque repertum est unquam inter homines, neque extare potest. Quin potius dum nimis exactam ac praecisam patientia habere volunt, eius vim sustule runte vita humana. Nunc quoque sunt inter Christianos novi Stoici, quibus non modo gemere ac flere, sed tristari quoque et solicitum esse vitiosum est. Atque haec quidem paradoxa fere ab otiosis hominibus procedunt, qui speculando magis quam agendo se exercentes, nihil quam talia paradoxa parere nobis queunt. At nihil nobis cum ferrea ista philosophia, quam magister ac dominus noster non verbo tantum, sed exemplo etiam suo damnavit. Nam et suis et aliorum malis in gemuit et illachrymavit: nec aliter discipulos suos instituit. Mundus, inquit, gaudebit: vos autem lugebitis ac flebitis. Ac, ne quis vitio id verteret, proposito edicto beatos pronuntiavit qui lugent. Nec mirum. Nam si improbantur omnes lachrymae, quid de Domino ipso iudicabimus, cuius e corpore sanguineae lachrymae distillarunt? Si quaelibet formido infidelitatis notatur, quo loco habebimus horrorem illum quo non leviter consternatum fuisse legimus? si omnis tristitia displicet, quomodo placebit quod animam suam fatetur esse tristes usque ad mortem? (Estienne, 1559).

102 Latin in previous note.

103 See *Institutes* III.viii.10; cf. *Disputatiuncula* CWE 70:60–2 / ASD V-7, 256–8. I had not noticed these similarities when working on the paper published in 2014.

104 See CWE 70:256–8. Erasmus argues that the possibility of conflicting wills in humans results in virtue not only of the fact that the soul has two parts – rational and sensible, per the Peripatetic tradition – but that even in "the highest part" Christ (and *a fortiori* the rest of us) willed and did not will to suffer and die (see CWE 70:62–3).

105 Et cependant soyons resiouis, voyans que la mort n'ha plus nulle puissance sur nous qui nous soit nuisible. Il est vray que tousiours naturellement nous craindrons la mort, et la fuyrons: mais c'est afin de nous faire penser a ce benefice inestimable qui nous a este acquis par la mort du Fils de Dieu: c'est afin de nous faire tousiours considerer que c'est de la mort en soy, et qu'elle emporte l'ire de Dieu, que c'est comme le gouffre d'enfer.

106 Au reste quand nous avons a batailler contre telle crainte, que nous scachions que nostre Seigneur Iesus Christ a tellement prouveu a toutes

ces craintes la, que nous pouvons au milieu de la mort mesme venir la teste levee devant Dieu. Il est vray que nous avons a nous humilier devant toutes choses, comme desia nous avons dit: qu'il faut bien que pour hayr nos pechez, et pour nous y desplaire nous soyons touchez du iugement de Dieu, pour en estre espouvantez. Mais cependant si faut-il que nous levions la teste, quand Dieu nous appelle a soy (*CO* 46:841–2).

107 Et quand la mort nous voyons les abysmes de malediction, que nous voyons le gouffre de l'ire de Dieu pour nous engloutir, et que ne soyons point saisis d'une seule frayeur, mais d'un million, et que toutes creatures crient vengeance contre nous (*CO* 46:844).

108 Or cependant nous avons tousiours a retenir que le Fils de Dieu ne se propose pas yci seulement pour exemple et miroir, mais qu'il nous veut monstrer combien nostre salut luy a couste cher (*CO* 46:844).

109 Quant a nous, qui sommes environnez de ceste masse de peche, nous sommes tellement eslourdis, que nous sommes bien eslongnez de la volunte de Dieu: car en tous nos appetis il y a quelque exces, il y a mesmes rebellion manifeste souventesfois. Mais si nous considerons l'homme en son integrite, c'est a dire sans ceste corruption de peche, encores il est certain qu'il aura ses affections bien eslongnees de Dieu, et toutesfois pour cela elles ne seront point vicieuses. Comme quand Adam ne se fust point ainsi perverti, et qu'il eust persiste en l'estat en condition ou il avoit este cree, si est-ce qu'il eust eu et chaut et froit, qu'il pouvoit endurer et solicitudes et craintes, et choses semblables (*CO* 46:839).

110 Voyla comme en a este nostre Seigneur Iesus Christ. Nous scavons qu'en toutes ses affections, il n'a eu ni tasche ni macule, que le tout n'ait este regle a l'obeissance de Dieu: mais cependant il n'a pas laisse (a cause qu'il avoit prins nostre nature) d'estre suiet et a crainte et a ceste horreur dont il est maintenant parle, et a solicitudes, et a choses semblables (*CO* 46:839).

111 Pour ce que nouos scavons qu'une passion ravit souventesfois l'esprit d'un homme, en telle sorte qu'il ne pense point ni a ceci ni a cela, mais estant presse du mal present, il se iette la et n'ha point quelque autre regard pour se retenir. Quand donc nous sommes ainsi ravis, ce n'est pas a dire que le reste soit du tout efface de nos coeurs, et que nous n'ayons nulle affection (*CO* 46:839).

112 Nous ne pouvons pas appercevoir cela en nous: comme en eau trouble on ne iuge rien. Voyla donc les affections humaines qui sont pour nous faire flotter et de coste et d'autre, pour nous donner telles esmotions que nous avons besoin d'estre retenus de Dieu: mais celles qu'ont les hommes estans descendus d'Adam sont comme un bourbier ou il y a de l'infection

meslee tant et plus, en sorte que nous ne pouvons pas contempler quelle a est ceste passion de nostre Seigneur Iesus Christ, si nous l'estimons par nos personnes (*CO* 46:839–40).

113 On this work in general, see Albert Rabil, Jr, "Erasmus' Paraphrase of the Gospel of John," 142–55; and the introduction to CWE 46; also Irena Backus, "Jesus and His Family," 151–74.

114 CWE 46:144. Iesus autem videns Mariam totam in luctu esse, Iudaeos item, qui illam comitabantur, una flentes, non philosophantur cum ea, quemadmodum fecerat cum forore Martha, cui semota turba, fuerat colloquutus: neque quicque pollicetur, quum iam locus ac tempus adesset re praestandi quod erat Marthae pollicitus. Primum infremuit spiritu, ac semetipsum turbavit, videlicet humanae naturae veritatem prae se ferens, mox divinae virtutis indicium prolaturus.

115 See CWE 46:144.

116 CWE 46:144. Froben, 1535: Non erant affectus fucati, quod animo inhorruit, quod turbatus est: sed hoc intererat, quod hos affectus in sese recepit, non ex infirmitate naturae, sed ex rationis arbitrio: nec eadem erat caeterorum flentium, ac Iesu turbati ratio. Illi humano quodam affectu mortem corporis deplorabant: Iesus magis indignabatur peccatis hominum, perquae tam multae perirent animae.

117 See, e.g., CWE 46:11. On the portrayal of the human Jesus in the paraphrases on Luke and John, with an argument that Erasmus' human Jesus is meant to serve as an antidote to the *Imitatio Christi* tradition, see Backus, "Jesus and His Family."

118 CWE 46:144. Froben, 1535: Postquem igitur horrore spiritus et animi turbatione, vultu, oculis, totoque corporis habitu manifestum specimen dedisset humanae naturae, simul interim docens, non oportere huiusmodi affectibus succumbere, aut ab his quae virtutis sunt, avocari: cohibita animi turbatione, dixit: Ubi posuistis cum? non quod ignoraret, sed ut a miraculo secluderet omnem suspicionem fuci. Respondent cognati: Domine, veni et vide. Ea vox arguebat monumentum non procul abesse, iamque velut ad sepulchrum commonstratum, renovato dolore lachrymatus est Iesus. Fremitus ac turbatio praecesserat, indicium doloris in animum irrumpentis. Lachrymae iam animi vulnerati victique veluti sanguis est: sed hae lachrymae non ab animo victo proficiscuntur. Non enim Lazaro mortuo impendebantur, sed nobis ut illum crederemus verum hominem fuisse: simulque disceremus, quam miseranda, quam deploranda sit mors animae, quam tamen homines perinde nec horrent, nec deplorant.

119 Phillips cites Chrysostom and Theophylact here as precedents, who provide a similar reading with a didactic emphasis, and also Lyra who,

interestingly, refers to Aristotle's *Nicomachean Ethics* book 4, which contains the *locus classicus* for the Peripatetic position on the emotions.

120 See, e.g., CWE 70:53; Ambrose, *Expositio in Lucam* 57–8 (PL 15 1818).

121 CWE 46:145; Froben, 1535: Iesus autem iam vicinus monumento, quo plane doceret horrendum esse statum hominis, iam in peccatis inveterati: quantaque poenitudine, quot lachrymis sit opus, ut per dei misericordiam resipiscat ad vitam innocentiae, rursus infremuit, ac semetipsum turbavit: in se videlicet exprimens imaginem rei, quam in nobis oportet exhibere, se velimus a malis, quibus diu assuevimus, resipiscere.

122 Farmer, *The Gospel of John in the Sixteenth Century*, 163–7.

123 First published in 1431, and later under the title of *De vero falsoque bono* (1444 and 1449), this work had a demonstrable influence on Erasmus, and especially on the *Praise of Folly*. See, e.g., Peter Bietenholz, *Encounters with a Radical Erasmus*, 125ff. See also Jill Kraye, "Stoicism in the Renaissance from Petrarch to Lipsius," 21–46.

124 Farmer, *The Gospel of John in the Sixteenth Century*, 164.

125 Ibid.

126 Ibid., 165.

127 Ibid., 167.

128 Pitkin, "The Spiritual Gospel?" 187–204.

129 Nisi condoluisset Christus illorum lachrymis, stetisset potius vultu rigido. Quum autem sponte se illis conformat usque ad fletum, *sumpatheian* testatur. Causam enim talis affectus, meo iudicio, exprimit Evangelista, quum dicit vidisse Mariam et reliquos flentes. Quanvis non dubitem altius eum spectasse, nempe ad communem generis humani miseriam. Tenebat enim, quid sibi mandatum esset a Patre, et quorsum in mundum missus esset: nempe ut nos eximeret malis omnibus. Hoc ut opere ipso praestitit, sic ostendere voluit serio animi affectu se praestare. Ergo Lazarum suscitaturus, antequam remedium opemque afferat, fremitu spiritus, arcto doloris sensu et lachrymis testatur malis nostris perinde se affici, acsi ea in se pateretur. *In evangelium secundum Johannem Commentarius pars altera* (ed. Feld, COR II/2; Droz, 1998), 62–3.

130 *Comm. John* (COR II/2), 63. Cf. Augustine, *Tract in Ioannem* 49.18. Erasmus follows Augustine in reading this passage to mean that Christ brought the emotions on himself voluntarily to serve a higher purpose, but doesn't in general think that Christ was otherwise free from human emotion, as we've seen.

131 Regnat enim vulgo hic morbus, ut mariti uxoribus vidui ... dolorem suum ambitiose quibus possunt modis augeant *Comm. John* (COR II/2), 62.

132 Ita saepe accidit, ut parum valeant eorum consolationes, qui suis amicis nimium blande indulgent. *Comm. John* (*COR* II/2), 62.

133 Letter LXIV to Monsieur de Richebourg (*Letters of John Calvin*, ed. Jules Bonnet, 246).

134 Letter LXIV to Monsieur de Richebourg (*Letters of John Calvin*, ed. Jules Bonnet, 247).

135 Leithart, in glossing this passage, concludes that Calvin's position should be understood as a "moderate Christianized Stoicism" ("Stoicism in Calvin's Doctrine of the Christian Life," 53), but there doesn't seem to be any specific reason to choose Stoicism over (moderate Christianized) Platonism or Peripateticism in this regard. Leithart also writes that in interpreting Gethsemane, Calvin has Christ's fear of death as operating "within the bounds of reason" (54), which specific language Calvin doesn't use, and concludes likewise that Calvin is expressing modified Stoic tendencies. This seems forced. Indeed, in his attempt to tease out the influences of Stoicism on Calvin's thought, Leithart seems to go overboard in the end, refusing to take Calvin seriously when he condemns Stoic *apatheia* and argues that emotion ought to be chastened in obedience to God (not reason). Leithart even suggests, in a normative homiletic conclusion, a "more biblical approach" to the emotions, in contrast to Calvin's "Stoic injunctions," wherein Christians "strive not for moderate passions, but for strong God-directed passions" (1994, "Part III," 85). It is a striking conclusion to an article that begins with several pages of examples of Calvin arguing for the permissibility of exhibiting all sorts of emotions in the context of piety.

136 See Backus, *Historical Method and Confessional Identity in the Era of the Reformation (1378–1615)* (Brill, 2003), 63–101. We know Calvin was quite familiar with Aristotle's position on the passions in the *Nicomachean Ethics*, as he cites the text in his early commentary on Seneca's *De Clementia*.

137 Cochran, "The Moral Significance of Religious Affections," 158.

138 My translation; *CO* 45:720: Separari tamen a nostra debet, quae a Christo suscepta fuit carnis infirmitas: sicuti longe distat. Nam in nobis ideo nullus vitio affectus caret, quia omnes modum ac rectum temperamentum excedunt: Christus autem tristitia et metu sic turbatus fuit, ut tamen adversus Deum non insurgeret: sed maneret compositus ad veram temperantiae regulam ... Christum in metu et tristitia infirmum fuisse absque ulla vitii macula: nostros autem omnes affectus, quia in excessum ebulliunt, esse vitiosos.

139 Imo dupliciter vitiosi sunt ac perversi hominum affectus: primum quia turbulento motu feruntur, nec ad veram modestiae regulam ordinati sunt; deinde quia non semper oriuntur ex legitima causa, vel saltem non referuntur ad finem legitimum. Intemperiem esse dico, quia nemo gaudet

vel trustatur, quantum satis est et quantum Deus permittit (*Comm. John* (COR II/2), 63).

140 Iam Christus humanos affectus suscepit, sed citra *ataxian*, qua fit, ut qui passionibus carnis obsequitur, Deo non obtemperet. Turbavit quidem seipsum Christus et vehementer commotus fuit, sed ita, ut se continuerit sub Patris voluntate. In summa, si passiones eius cum nostris conferas, non minus inter se distabunt quam aqua pura et illimis tranquilloque tractu fluens a turbidis lutosisque spumis differt (*Comm. John* (COR II/2), 63–4). For more on Calvin's use of *ataxia*, see Fedler, "Calvin's Burning Heart," 153–4.

141 Pitkin, "Calvin as a Commentator on the Gospel of John," *Calvin and the Bible*, ed. Donald McKim (Cambridge: 2006), 193.

142 Pitkin, "Calvin as a Commentator," 64. Porro ad ferream Stoicorum duritiem respuendam unum Christi exemplum sufficere nobis debet ... Sic Paulus non saxeum a nobis stuporem requirit, sed temperari luctum iubet, ne tristitiae nos dedamus sicut increduli, qui spem non habent (*Comm. John* (COR II/2), 64).

143 *Comm. John* (COR II/2), 63–4.

144 "The Two Faces of Renaissance Humanism: Stoicism and Augustinianism in Renaissance Thought," in *A Usable Past: Essays in European Cultural History* (Berkeley, 1990), 26.

145 See Tilmouth, *Passion's Triumph Over Reason*, introduction and ch. 1. Tilmouth is right to point to Erasmus' *Enchiridion* as representative of Renaissance rejuventation of classical models of psychomachia, but the *Enchiridion* is not exhaustive of Erasmus' much more complex view of the emotions found throughout his works. Richard Strier similarly suggests that Tilmouth places passion's triumph over reason too late in suggesting it takes place at the beginning of the seventeenth century (see *The Unrepentant Renaissance*, 42 n.43), and Strier also incorporates Luther into his analysis of sixteenth-century revaluation of the passions.

Conclusion

1 The clearest outline of this connection is Marjorie O'Rourke Boyle, *Erasmus on Language and Method in Theology*, ch. 1.

2 O'Rourke Boyle, *Erasmus on Language and Method in Theology*, 30.

3 Christ-von Wedel, *Erasmus of Rotterdam*, 136. For fuller discussion of the *Paraphrase*, see ibid., 111–25 and 133–44.

4 For Oecolampadius, see *Annotationes piae ac doctae in Evangelium Ioannis* (Froben, 1533), fols. 4–5.

5 *Comm. John* 1:1 (COR II/2, 13): Nam ut 'sermo' character mentis dicitur
  in hominibus, ita non inepte transfertur hoc quoque ad Deum, ut per
  Sermonem suum dicatur nobis seipsum exprimere. See Erasmus, *Apologia
  'In principio erat sermo'* in LB IX 120B. See also *Paraphrasis in Evangelium
  Ioannis* (Froben, 1542), fol. 502: Nec est alia res quae plenius et evidentius
  exprimat occultam mentis imaginem, quam oratio non mendax. Haec enim
  vere speculum est animi, qui corporeis oculis cerni non potest. Quod si cui
  volumus animi nostri voluntatem esse cognitam, nulla re certius id fit, aut
  celerius, quam oratione, quae ex intimis mentis arcanis deprompta, per
  aures audientis, occulta quadam energia, animum loquentis transfert in
  animum auditoris.

6 *Ann. John* 1:1: Caeterum quod illic quidam interpretantur *In principio*:
  id est, 'in filio', hic certe locum non habet. Erat verbum. *Logos* Graecis
  varia significat, 'verbum', 'orationem', 'sermonem', 'rationem', 'modum',
  'supputationem'; nonnunquam et pro libro usurpatur, a verbo *lego*, quod
  est 'dico' sive 'colligo'.

7 Aliae significationes *tou logou* non ita conveniunt. Est quidem
  Graecis *logos* et definitio et ratio et supputatio. Sed nolo supra fidei
  meae captum argute philosophari. Et videmus Dei Spiritum adeo
  eiusmodi argutias non probare, ut nobiscum balbutiens, quam
  sobrie de tantis arcanis sapiendum sit, tacendo clamet (*Comm. John*
  (COR II/2), 13).

8 *Comm. 1 Cor.* 2:11; Estienne, 1556: Nam quum lingua sit character mentis,
  communicant inter se homines suos affectus. For the significance of this
  notion in Calvin's hermeneutics more generally, see Cummings, *The Literary
  Culture of the Reformation*, 250ff.

9 *Adages* I ii 18; CWE 31:163.

10 See CWE 66:72.

11 CWE 66:72. On the significance of these lines for the role of affective
   mimesis in Erasmus' literary theology, see Cummings, "Erasmus and the
   Invention of Literature," *ERSY* 33 (2013), 37–8.

12 CWE 28:402; ASD I-2, 651.

13 CWE 28:442; ASD I-2, 704: Nec oratio tua cento quispiam videatur aut
   opus Musaicum, sed spirans imago tui pectoris, aut amnis e fonte cordis
   tui promanans.

14 CWE 67:255; ASD V-4, 38. Cf. Augustine *De Trinitate* XV.18.

15 CWE 67:257; ASD V-4, 42. Cf. *Ciceronianus* CWE 28:441.

16 When considered from the perspective of the written and read Speech
   of God (that is, the biblical text), we might just as well call it a "literary
   theology" as well, especially given the analysis of Erasmus' approach

to biblical literature by Cummings in "Erasmus and the Invention of Literature," 23–54.

17 Indeed, one need look no further than here for proof of the fact that Erasmus' *Paraphrases* are often heavily loaded theological commentaries in their own right.

18 Miror, quid Latinos moverit, ut *ton logon* transferrent 'Verbum'. Sic enim vertendum potius fuisset *to rhema*. Verum ut demus aliquid probabile sequutos esse: negari tamen non potest, quid 'Sermo' longe melius conveniat. Unde apparet, quam barbaram tyrannidem exercuerint theologastri, qui Erasmum adeo turbulente vexarunt ob mutatum in melius vocem unam (*Comm. John* 1:1 (COR II/2), 14). Cf. Erasmus, *Apologia 'In principio erat sermo'*: Ac principio quidem negari non potest ab ipso Evangelista, qui haud dubie Graece scripsit, Christum dici *logon*, quae vox cum sit polysemos, nunc sermonem aut verbum, nunc orationem, nunc rationem, nunc sapientiam, nunc computum significans ... Quod nos proprie verbum dicimus, Graeci vel *rhema* vel *lexin*, quorum neutrum opinor reperiemus in literis sacris usurpatur pro filio dei (Froben, 1520, fol. 7 of the introduction, which is in volume 3).

19 For an overview of Servetus' engagement with Erasmus, see Bietenholz, *Encounters with a Radical Erasmus*, 33–9. And see ibid., chapter 4, for the continued unfolding of the conflicted Erasmian tradition with Sebastian Castellio's publication of the *De haereticis* in 1554 as a response to Servetus' execution, which contains several passages on toleration from Erasmus' works.

20 *Inst.* I.iv.3 (trans. Battles).

21 Adage III v 1; CWE 35:65.

22 For details of Calvin's efforts at uniting the Protestant cause, see Gordon, *Calvin*, ch. 10.

23 Amos, *Bucer, Ephesians, and Biblical Humanism*, 90. On Bucer as a "father figure" to Calvin, see Gordon, *Calvin*, 88–91.

24 Coogan, *Erasmus, Lee, and the Vulgate*, 24.

25 Badiou, *Saint Paul: The Foundation of Universalism* (trans. Ray Brassier; Stanford UP, 2003), 42.

Bibliography

Amos, N. Scott. *Bucer, Ephesians and Biblical Humanism*. Springer, 2015.

Auerbach, Erich. *Literary Language and Its Public in Late Latin Antiquity and in the Middle Ages*. Translated by Ralph Manheim, Bollingen Series LXXIV, Pantheon, 1965.

Augustine. *On Christian Teaching*. Translated by R.P.H. Green, Oxford UP, 1997.

Augustijn, Cornelis. *Erasmus: His Life, Works, and Influence*. U of Toronto P, 1986.

Aristotle. *Nicomachean Ethics*. Translated by David Ross, Oxford UP, 1998.

Backus, Irena. "Calvin's Concept of Natural and Roman Law." *Calvin Theological Journal*, vol. 38, 2003, pp. 1–20.

– "The Issue of Reformation and Skepticism Revisited: What Erasmus and Sebastian Castellio Did and Did Not Know." *Renaissance Scepticisms*, edited by Gianni Paganini and Jose Maia Neto, Springer, 2009, pp. 63–89.

– "Jesus and His Family in Erasmus' Paraphrases on Luke and John." *Holy Scripture Speaks*, edited by Hilmar Pabel and Mark Vessey, U of Toronto P, 2004, pp. 151–74.

– "L'influence de l'exégèse d'Erasme sur le milieu calvinien à Genève." *Erasme et les théologiens réformés*, edited by E.M. Braeckmann, Bruxelles, 2005, pp. 141–7.

Baschera, Luca, Bruce Gordon, and Christian Moser. *Following Zwingli: Applying the Past in Reformation Zurich*. Ashgate, 2014.

Bateman, John. "From Soul to Soul: Persuasion in Erasmus' Paraphrases on the New Testament." In *Erasmus in English*, vol. 15, 1987, pp. 7–16.

Bejczy, Istvan Pieter. *Erasmus and the Middle Ages: The Historical Consciousness of a Christian*. Brill, 2001.

Bene, Charles. *Erasme et Saint Augustin*. Geneva: Librarie Droz, 1969.

Benin, Stephen. *The Footprints of God: Divine Accommodation in Jewish and Christian Thought*. SUNY Press, 1993.

Bentley, Jerry. *Humanists and Holy Writ*. Princeton UP, 1983.

Bietenholz, Peter B. *Encounters with a Radical Erasmus: Erasmus' Work as a Source of Radical Thought in Early Modern Europe*. U of Toronto P, 2009.

Bouwsma, William. "Calvin and the Renaissance Crisis of Knowing." *Calvin Theological Journal*, vol. 17, 1982, pp. 190–211.

– "Calvinism as Theologia Rhetorica?" Berkeley: Center for Hermeneutical Studies, 1987, pp. 1–21.

– *John Calvin: A Sixteenth-Century Portrait*. Oxford UP, 1989.

Brashler, James. "From Calvin to Erasmus: Exploring the Roots of Reformed Hermeneutics." *Interpretation*, vol. 63, no. 2, 2009, pp. 154–66.

Breen, Quirinus. *Christianity and Humanism: A Study in the History of Ideas*. Edited by Nelson Peter Ross, Eerdmans, 1968.

Calvin, John. *Calvin's Commentary on Seneca's De Clementia*. Edited by Ford Lewis Battles and André Malan Hugo, Brill, 1969.

– *1 Corinthians*. Translated by John W. Fraser. Edited by David W. Torrance and Thomas Forsyth Torrance, Eerdmans, 1996. Calvin's New Testament Commentaries 9.

– *Institutes of the Christian Religion*. Translated by Henry Beveridge, Peabody, MA: Hendrickson, 2008.

– *Institutes of the Christian Religion*. Edited by John T. McNeill, translated by Ford Lewis Battles, Westminster John Knox, 1960. 2 vols.

– *Scripta Didactica et Polemica*. Edited by Joy Kleinstuber. Geneva: Droz, 2009.

Campi, Emidio. "Probing the Similarities and Differences Between John Calvin and Heinrich Bullinger." *Calvinus Clarissimus Theologus*, edited by Herman Selderhuis, Vandenhoek & Ruprecht, 2012, pp. 57–82.

Carrington, Laurel. "The Boundaries Between Text and Reader: Erasmus' Approach to Reading Scripture." *Archiv fur Reformationgeschichte*, vol. 88, 1997, pp. 5–22.

Chomarat, Jacques. *Grammaire et rhétorique chez Érasme*. Société d'Édition "Les Belles Lettres," 1981.

Christ-von Wedel, Christine. *Erasmus of Rotterdam: Advocate of a New Christianity*. U of Toronto P, 2013.

– "Erasmus und die Zurcher Reformatoren: Huldrich Zwingli, Leo Jud, Konrad Pellikan, Heinrich Bullinger und Theodor Bibliander." *Erasmus in Zurich*, edited by Christ-von Wedel and Leu, Neue Zürcher Zeitung, 2007.

Cochran, Elizabeth Agnew. "The Moral Significance of Religious Affections: A Reformed Perspective on Emotions and Moral Formation." *Society of Christian Ethics*, vol. 28, 2015, pp. 150–62.

Colet, John. *Commentary on First Corinthians*. Edited by Bernard O'Kelly and C.A.L. Jarrot, Medieval and Renaissance Texts and Studies, 1985.

Colish, Marcia. *The Stoic Tradition from Antiquity to the Early Middle Ages*. Brill, 1985. 2 vols.

Compier, Don H. "The Independent Pupil: Calvin's Transformation of Erasmus' Theological Hermeneutics." *Westminster Theological Journal*, vol. 54, 1992, pp. 217–33.

Coogan, R. *Erasmus, Lee, and the Vulgate*. Droz, 2004.

Coppens, J. *Scrinium Erasmianum*. Brill, 1969.

Corrigan, John, editor. *Religion and Emotion: Approaches and Interpretations*. Oxford UP, 2004.

Cottier, Jean-François. "Erasmus's *Paraphrases*: A 'New Kind of Commentary'?" *The Unfolding of Words: Commentary in the Age of Erasmus*, edited by Judith Rice Henderson, U of Toronto P, 2012.

Covington, Sarah. "The Garden of Anguish: Gethsemane in Early Modern England." *Journal of Ecclesiastical History*, vol. 65, no. 2, 2014, pp. 280–308.

Cummings, Brian. "Erasmus and the Invention of Literature." *Erasmus of Rotterdam Society Yearbook*, vol. 33, 2013, pp. 22–54.

– *The Literary Culture of the Reformation: Grammar and Grace*. Oxford UP, 2009.

Cummings, Brian, and Freya Sierhuis, editors. *Passions and Subjectivity in Early Modern Culture*. Ashgate, 2014.

DeLubac, Henri. *Medieval Exegesis: The Four Senses of Scripture*. Eerdmans, 1998. 3 vols.

Dixon, Thomas. "'Emotion': The History of a Keyword in Crisis." *Emotion Review*, vol. 4, 2012, pp. 338–44.

– *From Passions to Emotions: The Creation of a Secular Psychological Category*. Cambridge UP, 2003.

Dodds, Gregory. *Exploiting Erasmus: The Erasmian Legacy and Religious Change in Early Modern England*. U of Toronto P, 2013.

Dowey, Edward A., Jr. *The Knowledge of God in Calvin's Theology*. 1952. Columbia UP, 1994.

Eden, Kathy. "Equity and the Origins of Renaissance Historicism." *Yale Journal of Law and the Humanities*, vol. 5, 1993, pp. 137–45.

– *Hermeneutics and the Rhetorical Tradition*. Yale UP, 1997.

– "Rhetoric in the Hermeneutics of Erasmus' Later Works." *Erasmus of Rotterdam Society Yearbook*, vol. 11, 1991, pp. 88–104.

Edmondson, Stephen. *Calvin's Christology*. Cambridge UP, 2009.

Enenkel, Karl A.E. *The Reception of Erasmus in the Early Modern Period*. Brill, 2013.

Engammare, Max. "Calvin connaissait-il la Bible? Les citations de l'Écriture dans ses sermons sur la Genese." *BSHPF*, vol. 141, 1995, pp. 163–84.

- "Cinquante ans de révision de la traduction biblique d'Olivetan: Les bibles réformées genevoises en français au XVI siècle." *Bibliothèque d'humanisme et renaissance*, vol. 53, 1991: 347–77.
- "Le Paradis à Genève: Comment Calvin prêchait-il la chute aux Genevois?" *Études Théologiques et Religieuses*, vol. 69, 2004, pp. 329–47.

Engel, Mary Potter. *John Calvin's Perspectival Anthropology*. Wipf and Stock, 2002.

Erasmus, Desiderius. *The Collected Works of Erasmus*. Toronto, U of Toronto P, 1974–.
- *Desiderii Erasmi Roterodami opera omnia*. Edited by Jean LeClerc, Leiden, 1703–6. 10 vols.
- *Erasmus' Annotations on the New Testament: Galatians to the Apocalypse: facsimile of the final Latin text with all earlier variants*. Edited by Anne Reeve and M.A. Screech, Brill, 1997.
- *Opera omnia Desiderii Erasmi Roterodami*. Amsterdam: North-Holland, 1969– . 9 vols. in parts.
- *Praise of Folly*. Translated by Clarence Miller, Yale UP, 2003.

Essary, Kirk. "Calvin's Interpretation of Christ's Agony at Gethsemane: An Erasmian Reading?" *Toronto Journal of Theology*, vol. 30, no. 1, 2014, pp. 59–70.
- "Fiery Heart and Fiery Tongue: Emotion in Erasmus' *Ecclesiastes*. In *Erasmus Studies*, vol. 36, no. 1, 2016, pp. 5–34.
- "Milk for Babes: Erasmus and Calvin on the Problem of Christian Eloquence." *Reformation and Renaissance Review*, vol. 16, no. 3, 2014, pp. 246–65.
- "The Radical Humility of Christ in the 16th Century: Erasmus and Calvin on Philippians 2:6-7." *Scottish Journal of Theology*, vol. 68, no. 4, 2015, pp. 398–420.

Evans, G.R. *Problems of Authority in the Reformation Debates*. Cambridge UP, 1992.

Faber, Riemer A. "Desiderius Erasmus' Representation of Paul as Paragon of Learned Piety." *A Companion to Paul in the Reformation*, edited by R. Ward Holder, Brill, 2009, pp. 41–60.
- "The Humanism of Melanchthon and of Calvin." *Melanchthon und der Calvinismus*, edited by Herman J. Selderhuis, Frommann-Holzboog, 2005, pp. 11–28.
- "The Influence of Erasmus' *Annotationes* on Calvin's Galatians Commentary." *Dutch Review of Church History*, vol. 84, 2004, pp. 268–83.

Farmer, Craig. *The Gospel of John in the Sixteenth Century*. Oxford UP, 2004.

Fedler, Kyle. "Calvin's Burning Heart: Calvin and the Stoics on the Emotions." *Journal of the Society of Christian Ethics*, vol. 22, 2002, pp. 133–62.

Fokke, G.J. "An Aspect of the Christology of Erasmus of Rotterdam." *Ephemerides theologicae Lovanienses*, vol. 54, 1978, pp. 161–87.

Foucault, Michel. *History of Madness*. Translated by Jonathan Murphy and Jean Khalfa, Routledge, 2006.

Fumaroli, Marc. *L'Age de l'éloquence*. Droz, 1980.

Gamble, Richard. "Calvin as Theologian and Exegete: Is There Anything New?" *Calvin Theological Journal*, vol. 23, 1988, pp. 178–94.

Ganoczy, Alexander. *The Young Calvin*. T&T Clark, 1988.

Ganoczy, Alexander, and Stefan Scheld. *Die Hermeneutik Calvins*. Frans Steiner, 1983.

Gerrish, B.A. "'To the Unknown God': Luther and Calvin on the Hiddenness of God." *The Journal of Religion*, vol. 53, no. 3, 1973, pp. 263–93.

Gilmont, Jean-Francois. *John Calvin and the Printed Book*. Translated by Karin Maag, Truman State UP, 2005.

Gilson, Étienne. *The Spirit of Medieval Philosophy*. 1936. Notre Dame UP, 2009.

Godin, André. *Érasme, Lecteur d'Origène*. Droz, 1982.

Gordon, Bruce. *Calvin*. 2009. Yale UP, 2011.

– *The Swiss Reformation*. Manchester UP, 2002.

Gordon, Walter. *Humanist Play and Belief: The Seriocomic Art of Desiderius Erasmus*. U of Toronto P, 1990.

Grafton, Anthony. *Defenders of the Text*. Harvard UP, 1994.

Graham, M. Patrick, and Timothy J. Wengert. *Philip Melanchthon (1497–1560) and the Commentary*. Sheffield Academic P, 1997.

Grassi, Ernesto. *Renaissance Humanism*. Binghamton, 1988.

– *Rhetoric as Philosophy: The Humanist Tradition*. Penn State UP, 1980.

Grazia, Mara Maria. "Colet et Érasme au sujet de l'exégèse de Mt. 26, 39." *Théorie et pratique de l'exégèse*, edited by Irena Backus and Francis Higman, Droz, 1990, pp. 259–72.

Hauser, Alan J., and Duane F. Watson, editors. *A History of Biblical Interpretation: Volume 2: The Medieval through the Reformation Periods*. Eerdmans, 2009.

Helm, Paul. "Calvin and Stoicism." *Melanchthon-Schriften der Stadt Bretten*, edited by Günter Frank and Herman Selderhuis, Frommann-Holzboog, 2012, pp. 169–82.

Hoffmann, Manfred. "Erasmus: Rhetorical Theologian." *Rhetorical Invention & Religious Inquiry*, edited by Walter Jost and Wendy Olmsted, Yale UP, 2000, pp. 136–62.

– "Faith and Piety in Erasmus' Thought." *The Sixteenth Century Journal*, vol. 20, no. 2, 1989, pp. 241–58.

– "Rhetoric and Dialectic in Erasmus' and Melanchthon's Interpretation of John's Gospel." *Philip Melanchthon (1497–1560) and the Commentary*, edited by M. Patrick Graham and Timothy Wengert, Sheffield Academic Press, 1997, pp. 48–78.

– *Rhetoric and Theology: The Hermeneutic of Erasmus*. U of Toronto P, 1994.

Holder, R. Ward, editor. *A Companion to Paul in the Reformation*. Brill, 2009.

– *John Calvin and the Grounding of Interpretation: The First Commentaries*. Brill, 2006.

– "Paul as Calvin's (Ambivalent) Pastoral Model." *Dutch Review of Church History*, Brill, 2004, 284–98.

Huijgen, Arnold. *Divine Accommodation in John Calvin's Theology*. Vandenhoeck & Ruprecht, 2011.

Huizinga, Johan. *Erasmus and the Age of the Reformation*. 1924. Harper Torchbook, 1957.

Jarrott, C.A.L. "Erasmus' Biblical Humanism," in *Studies in the Renaissance*, vol. 17, 1970, pp. 119–52.

– "Erasmus' Annotations and Colet's Commentaries on Paul: A Comparison of Some Theological Themes." *Essays on the Works of Erasmus*, edited by R.L. Demolen, Yale UP, 1978, pp. 125–44.

– "Erasmus' 'In Principio Erat Sermo': A Controversial Translation." *Studies in Philology*, vol. 61, no. 1, 1964, pp. 35–40.

Jones, Serene. *Calvin and the Rhetoric of Piety*. Westminster John Knox, 1995.

Kaiser, Walter. *Praisers of Folly*. Harvard UP, 1963.

Kahn, Victoria. *Rhetoric, Prudence, and Skepticism in the Renaissance*. Cornell UP, 1985.

Karant-Nunn, Susan. *The Reformation of Feeling*. Oxford UP, 2010.

Kelsay, John. "Prayer and Ethics: Reflections on Calvin and Barth." *Harvard Theological Review*, vol. 82, no. 2, 1989, pp. 168–84.

Kneidel, Greg. "*Ars Praedicandi*: Theories and Practice." *The Oxford Handbook of the Early Modern Sermon*, edited by Peter McCullough, Hugh Adlington, and Emma Radington, Oxford UP, 2011, pp. 3–20.

– "'Mighti Simplenesse': Protestant pastoral rhetoric and Spenser's *Shepheardes Calender*." *Studies in Philology*, vol. 96, no. 3, 1999, pp. 275–312.

Kok, Joel. *The Influence of Martin Bucer on John Calvin's Interpretation of Romans: A Comparative Case Study*. Dissertation, Duke University, 1993.

Kolbet, Paul. *Augustine and the Cure of Souls*. Notre Dame UP, 2009.

– "Heinrich Bullinger's Exegetical Method: The Model for John Calvin's?" *Biblical Interpretation in the Era of the Reformation*, edited by Richard Muller and John Thompson, Eerdmans, 1996, p. 241–54.

Kraye, Jill. "Moral Philosophy." *The Cambridge History of Renaissance Philosophy*, edited by Schmitt and Skinner. Cambridge UP, 1988, pp. 301–86.

Kristeller, Paul Oscar. *Renaissance Thought: The Classic, Scholastic, and Humanist Strains*. Harper Torchbook, 1961.

– "Thomism and Italian Thought in the Renaissance." *Medieval Aspects of Renaissance Learning*. Columbia UP, 1974.

Kroeker, Greta Grace. *Erasmus in the Footsteps of Paul*. U of Toronto P, 2011.

Kusukawa, Sachiko. *The Transformation of Natural Philosophy: The Case of Philip Melanchthon.* Cambridge UP, 1995.

Lane, Anthony N.S. *John Calvin: Student of the Church Fathers.* T&T Clark, 1999.

Leclerq, Jacques. "Pour l'histoire de l'expression 'philosophie chrétienne'." *Mélanges de sciences religieuses,* vol. 9, 1952, pp. 221–6.

Lee, Sou-Young. "Calvin's Understanding of Pietas." *Calvinus Sincerioris Religionis Vindex,* edited by Wilhelm Neuser and Brian Armstrong, Sixteenth Century Journal Publishers, 1997, pp. 225–40.

Leithart, Peter. "Stoicism in Calvin's Doctrine of the Christian Life." *Westminster Theological Journal,* vols. 55 and 56, 1993–4, pp. 59–85 and 191–208.

Leo, Russ. *Affect before Spinoza: Reformed Faith, Affectus, and Experience in John Calvin, John Donne, John Milton, and Baruch Spinoza.* Dissertation, Duke University, 2009.

Long, A.A. *Hellenistic Philosophy: Stoics, Epicureans, Skeptics.* 1974. Duckworth, 1996.

Mack, Peter. "Erasmus' Contribution to Rhetoric and Rhetoric in Erasmus' Writing. *ERSY,* vol. 32, no. 1, 2012, pp. 27–46.

Mansfield, Bruce. *Erasmus in the Twentieth Century.* U of Toronto P, 2003.

– *Man on His Own.* U of Toronto P, 1992.

– *Phoenix of His Age: Interpretations of Erasmus, c. 1550–1750.* U of Toronto P, 1979.

McConica, James. "Erasmus and the Grammar of Consent." *Scrinium Erasmianum,* vol. 2, edited by Joseph Coppens, Brill, pp. 77–99.

McGrath, Alister. *Luther's Theology of the Cross: Martin Luther's Theological Breakthrough.* Wiley- Blackwell, 1991.

Mellinghoff-Bourgerie, Viviane. "Calvin émule d'Erasme: L'irriducibilitié d'une conscience humaniste." *Calvin et ses contemporains,* edited by Olivier Millet, Droz, 1996, pp. 225–45.

– "De la 'philosophie du Christ' d'Erasme à la doctrine de Calvin." *Erasme et les théologiens réformés,* edited by E.M. Braeckmann, Bruxelles, 2005, pp. 99–126.

Menchi, Seidel. *Erasmo in Italia: 1520–1580.* Torino: Bollati Boringhieri, 1987.

Millet, Olivier. *Calvin et la dynamique de la parole: Étude de rhétorique réformée.* Bibliothèque littéraire de la Renaissance, série 3, 1992.

– "*Docere/movere*: les catégories rhétoriques et leurs sources humanistes dans la doctrine calvinienne de la foi." *Calvinus sincerioris religionis vindex,* edited by Wilhelm Neuser and Brian Armstrong, Sixteenth Century Journal Publishers, 1997, pp. 35–51.

Mitchell, Margaret. *The Heavenly Trumpet: John Chrysostom and the Art of Biblical Interpretation.* Westminster John Knox, 2002.

– *Paul, the Corinthians and the Birth of Christian Hermeneutics.* Cambridge UP, 2010.

– *Paul and the Rhetoric of Reconciliation.* Westminster John Knox, 1993.

Monfasani, John. "Twenty-fifth Annual Margaret Mann Phillips Lecture: Erasmus and the Philosophers." *ERSY*, vol. 32, 2012, pp. 47–68.

Moss, Ann. *Renaissance Truth and the Latin Language Turn.* Oxford UP, 2003.

Muller, Richard A. *The Unaccommodated Calvin.* Oxford UP, 2000.

– *Calvin and the Reformed Tradition.* Baker Academic, 2013.

– "Scholasticism in Calvin: A Question of Relation and Disjunction." *Calvinis Sincerioris Religionis Vindex*, edited by Wilhelm Neuser and Brian Armstrong, Truman State UP, 1997, pp. 247–66.

– "*Scimus enim quod lex spiritualis est:* Melanchthon and Calvin on the Interpretation of Romans 7:14–23." *Philip Melanchthon (1497–1560) and the Commentary*, edited by M. Patrick Graham and Timothy Wengert, Sheffield Academic Press, 1997, pp. 216–37.

Muller, Richard A., and John Thompson, editors. *Biblical Interpretation in the Era of the Reformation.* Eerdmans, 1996.

Nauert, Charles. 1998. "Humanism as Method: Roots of Conflict with the Scholastics. *The Sixteenth Century Journal*, vol. 29, no. 2, 1998, pp. 427–38.

Oberman, Heiko. *The Harvest of Medieval Theology: Gabriel Biel and Late Medieval Nominalism.* Baker Academic, 1963.

– *John Calvin and the Reformation of the Refugees.* Droz, 2009.

O'Malley, John. "Grammar and Rhetoric in the *Pietas* of Erasmus." *Journal of Medieval and Renaissance Studies*, vol. 18, 1988, pp. 91–98.

O'Rourke Boyle, Marjorie. *Erasmus on Language and Method in Theology.* U of Toronto P, 1977.

– "Fools and Schools: Scholastic Dialectic, Humanist Rhetoric; From Anselm to Erasmus." *Medievalia et Humanistica*, vol. 13, 1985, pp. 173–95.

– *Rhetoric and Reform: Erasmus' Civil Dispute with Luther.* Harvard UP, 1983.

– "Sermo: Reopening the Conversation of Translating JN 1,1." *Vigilae Christianae*, vol. 31, no. 3, pp. 161–8.

– "Weavers, farmers, tailors, travellers, masons, prostitutes, pimps, Turks, little women, and Other Theologians." *Erasmus in English*, vol. 3, 1971, pp. 1–7.

Overfield, James. *Humanism and Scholasticism in Late Medieval Germany.* Princeton UP, 1984.

Pabel, Hilmar. "Praise and Blame: Peter Canisius' Ambivalent Reception of Erasmus." *The Reception of Erasmus in the Early Modern Period*, edited by Karl Enenkel, Brill, 2013.

Pabel, Hilmar, and Mark Vessey. *Holy Scripture Speaks: The Production and Reception of Erasmus' Paraphrases on the New Testament.* U of Toronto P, 2002.

Paganini, Gianni, and Jose Maia Neto. *Renaissance Skepticisms.* Springer, 2009.

Panizza, Letizia. "Valla's *De voluptate ac de vero bono* and Erasmus' *Stultitiae Laus*: Renewing Christian Ethics." *Erasmus of Rotterdam Society Yearbook*, vol. 15, 1995, 1–25.

Parker, T.H.L. *Calvin's Doctrine of the Knowledge of God*. Eerdmans, 1959.
– *Calvin's New Testament Commentaries*. 1971. Westminster John Knox, 1993.
Partee, Charles. *Calvin and Classical Philosophy*. Brill, 1977.
– "Revitalization of the Concept of 'Christian philosophy' in Renaissance Humanism." *Christian Scholar's Review*, vol. 3, no. 4, 1974, pp. 360–9.
– "The Soul in Plato, Platonism, and Calvin." *Scottish Journal of Theology*, vol. 22, no. 3, 1969, pp. 278–95.
Paster, Gail Kern. *Humoring the Body: Emotions and the Shakespearean Stage*. Chicago UP, 2004.
Paster, Gail Kern, et al., eds. *Reading the Early Modern Passions: Essays in the Cultural History of Emotion*. U of Pennsylvania P, 2004.
Payne, John. *Erasmus: His Theology of the Sacraments*. Bratcher, 1970.
– "Erasmus and Lefevre d'Etaples as Interpreters of Paul." *Archiv fur Reformationsgeschichte*, vol. 65, 1974, pp. 54–83.
– "Toward the Hermeneutics of Erasmus." *Scrinium Erasmianum*, edited by Joseph Coppens, Brill, 1969, pp. 13–25. 2 vols.
Pitkin, Barbara. "Erasmus, Calvin, and the Two Faces of Stoicism in Renaissance and Reformation Thought." *The Routledge Companion to the Stoic Tradition*, edited by John Sellars, Routledge, 2016, pp. 145–59.
– "The Protestant Zeno: Calvin and the Development of Melanchthon's Anthropology." *The Journal of Religion*, vol. 84, no. 3, p. 345–78.
– "The Spiritual Gospel? Christ and Human Nature in Calvin's Commentary on John." *The Formation of Clerical and Confessional Identities in the Sixteenth Century*, edited by Wim Janse and Barbara Pitkin, Brill, 2006, pp. 187–204.
– *What Pure Eyes Could See*. Oxford UP, 2000.
Popkin, Richard. *The History of Skepticism: From Savonarola to Bayle*. Oxford UP, 2003.
Rabil, Albert, Jr. *Erasmus and the New Testament: The Mind of a Christian Humanist*. 1972. UP of America, 1993.
– "Erasmus' Paraphrase of the Gospel of John." *Church History*, vol. 48, no. 2, 1979, pp. 142–55.
Rice, Eugene. "John Colet and the Annihilation of the Natural." *Harvard Theological Review*, vol. 45, no. 3, 1952, pp. 141–63.
– *The Renaissance Idea of Wisdom*. Harvard UP, 1958.
Rummel, Erika. editor. *Biblical Humanism and Scholasticism in the Age of Erasmus*. Brill, 2008.
– *Erasmus' Annotations on the New Testament: From Philologist to Theologian*. U of Toronto P, 1989.
– *Erasmus and His Catholic Critics*. De Graaf, 1989.
– "God and Solecism: Erasmus as a Literary Critic of the Bible." *Erasmus of Rotterdam Society Yearbook*, vol. 7, 1987, pp. 54–72.

– *The Humanist-Scholastic Debate in the Renaissance and Reformation.* Harvard UP, 1998.
– "St. Paul in Plain Latin: Erasmus' Philological Annotations on 1 Corinthians." *Classical and Modern Literature*, vol. 7:4, 1987, pp. 309–18.
– "Why Noel Beda Did Not Like Erasmus' *Paraphrases.*" *Holy Scripture Speaks*, edited by Hilmar Pabel and Mark Vessey, U of Toronto P, 2000, pp. 265–78.
Santinello, Giovanni. "Tre meditazioni umanistiche sulla passione." *Studi sull'umanesimo europea: Cusano e Petrarca, Lefevre, Erasmo, Colet, Moro*, edited by Giovanni Santinello, Padova, Antenore, 1969, pp. 77–128.
Schreiner, Susan. *Are You Alone Wise?* Oxford UP, 2011.
– "Calvin and the Exegetical Debates about Certainty in the Reformation." *Biblical Interpretation in the Era of the Reformation*, edited by Muller and Thompson, Eerdmans, 1996, pp. 189–215.
– *In the Theatre of His Glory.* Baker Academic, 1995.
Screech, M.A. *Ecstasy and the Praise of Folly.* Duckworth, 1980.
– "Good Madness in Christendom." *The Anatomy of Madness: Essays in the History of Psychiatry*, vol. 1, edited by W.F. Bynum, R. Porter, and M. Shepherd Tavistock, 1985, pp. 25–40.
Seigel, Jerrold. *Rhetoric and Philosophy in Renaissance Humanism.* Princeton UP, 1968.
Selinger, Suzanne. *Calvin Against Himself.* Archon, 1984.
Shuger, Debora Kuller. "The Philosophical Foundations of Sacred Rhetoric." *Rhetorical Invention and Religious Inquiry.* Yale UP, 2000, pp. 47–64.
– *The Renaissance Bible: Scholarship, Sacrifice, and Subjectivity.* Baylor UP, 2010.
– *Sacred Rhetoric: The Christian Grand Style in the English Renaissance.* Princeton UP, 1988.
Sider, Robert. "Historical Imagination and Representation of Paul in Erasmus' Paraphrases on the Pauline Epistles." *Holy Scripture Speaks*, edited by Hilmar Pabel and Mark Vessey, U of Toronto P, 2002, pp. 85–109.
Simpson, James. *Burning to Read.* Harvard UP, 2009.
Smalley, Beryl. *The Gospels in the Schools: 1100–1280.* Hambledon, 1985.
– *The Study of the Bible in the Middle Ages.* 1968. Notre Dame UP, 1974.
Steinmetz, David, editor. *The Bible in the Sixteenth Century.* Duke UP, 1990.
– *Calvin in Context.* Oxford UP, 2010.
Strier, Richard. *The Unrepentant Renaissance: From Petrarch to Shakespeare to Milton.* U of Chicago P, 2011.
Strohm, Christoph. "Methodology in Discussion of 'Calvin and Calvinism'." *Calvinus Praeceptor Ecclesiae*, edited by Herman Selderhuis, Droz, 2004.
Thompson, John. "Erasmus' Influence on Zwingli and Bullinger." *Biblical Interpretation in the Era of the Reformation*, edited by Muller and Thompson, Eerdmans, 1996.

Thompson, Sister Geraldine. 1972. "'Water Wonderfully Clear': Erasmus and Figurative Writing." *Erasmus in English*, vol. 5, 1972, pp. 5–10.

Tilmouth, Christopher. "Passion and Intersubjectivity in Early Modern Literature." *Passions and Subjectivity in Early Modern Culture*, edited by Brian Cummings and Freya Sierhuis. Ashgate, 2013, pp. 13–32.

– *Passion's Triumph Over Reason: A History of the Moral Imagination from Spenser to Rochester*. Oxford UP, 2007.

Torrance, T.F. *Calvin's Doctrine of Man*. Eerdmans, 1957.

– *The Hermeneutics of John Calvin*. Scottish Academic Press, 1988.

Tracy, James D. *Erasmus: The Growth of a Mind*. Droz, 1972.

– "Erasmus and the Arians: Remarks on the 'Consensus Ecclesiae'." *The Catholic Historical Review*, vol. 61, no. 1, 1981, pp. 1–10.

– *Erasmus of the Low Countries*. U of California P, 1966.

– "Humanists among the Scholastics: Erasmus, More, and Lefevre d'Etaples on the Humanity of Christ." *Erasmus of Rotterdam Society Yearbook Five*, 1985, pp. 30–51.

Trinkhaus, Charles. *In Our Image and Likeness: Humanity and Divinity in Italian Humanist Thought*. Notre Dame UP, 1970. 2 vols.

– "Renaissance Problems in Calvin's Theology." *Studies in the Renaissance*, vol. 1, 1954, pp. 59–80.

Walchenbach, John R. *John Calvin as Biblical Commentator: An Investigation into Calvin's Use of John Chrysostom as an Exegetical Tutor*. Wipf and Stock, 2010.

Walter, Peter. *Theologie aus dem Geist der Rhetorik. Zur Schriftauslegung des Erasmus von Rotterdam*. Tubinger Studien zur Theologie und Philosophie, 1. Mainz: Matthias–Grunewald–Verlag, 1991.

Weaver, William. "A More Excellent Way: Philip Melanchthon's Corinthians Lectures of 1521–1522." *Renaissance and Reformation/Renaissance et Réforme*, vol. 37, 2014, pp. 31–63.

Welborn, L.L. *Paul, the Fool of Christ: A Study of 1 Corinthians 1–4 in the Comic-Philosophic Tradition*. T&T Clark, 2005.

Wendel, François. *Calvin: The Origins and Development of His Religious Thought*. Translated by Philip Mairet. William Collins, 1965.

Wengert, Timothy. *Human Freedom, Christian Righteousness: Melanchthon's Exegetical Dispute with Erasmus of Rotterdam*. Oxford UP, 1998.

White, Micheline. "The Perils and Possibilities of Book Dedication: Anne Lock, John Knox, John Calvin, Queen Elizabeth, and the Duchess of Suffolk." *Parergon*, vol. 29, no. 2, 2012, pp. 9–28.

Willis, E. David. *Calvin's Catholic Christology*. Brill, 1966.

– "Rhetoric and Responsibility in Calvin's Theology." *The Context of Contemporary Theology: Essays in Honor of Paul Lehmann*, edited by Alexander McKelway and E. David Willis, 1974, pp. 43–64.

Wright, David F. "Calvin's Accommodating God." *Calvinus sincerioris religionis vindex*, edited by Wilhelm Neuser and Brian Armstrong. Sixteenth Century Journal Publishers, 1997, pp. 3–33.

– "Calvin's 'Accommodation' Revisited." *Calvin as Exegete: Papers and Responses Presented at the Ninth Colloquium on Calvin and Calvin Studies*, edited by Peter De Klerk, 1993, pp. 171–93.

Zachman, Randall. *The Assurance of Faith: Conscience in the Theology of Martin Luther and John Calvin*. Fortress, 1993.

– "Gathering Meaning from Context: Calvin's Exegetical Method." *The Journal of Religion*, vol. 82, no. 1, 2002, pp. 1–26.

– *Image and Word in the Theology of John Calvin*. Notre Dame UP, 2008.

– *John Calvin as Teacher, Pastor, and Theologian*. Baker Academic, 2006.

– *Reconsidering John Calvin*. Cambridge UP, 2012.

Zahl, Simeon. "On the Affective Salience of Doctrines." In *Modern Theology*, vol. 31, no. 3, 2015, pp. 228–44.

Index

accommodation: in Augustine,
215n60; in Calvin and Erasmus,
89–90, 94, 175n17, 219n101,
220nn102, 103, 104, 108, 223n131;
divine linguistic, 60, 62, 70, 77–81,
87–97; Pauline doctrine of, xv, xix,
163; in Paul's teaching, 31, 77, 91–3
Adam, 35, 40, 45, 54, 141, 149, 152,
154, 159, 160
adiaphora, 10, 71, 106
Ambrose, 25, 27, 55, 156, 184n9,
240n121, 248n61
Ambrosiaster, 27, 53, 114, 184n9
Anabaptists, 157–8, 218n87, 252n100
Anselm of Canterbury, 102, 120
anthropology, xvi, xx, 131–45, 168–9;
Aristotelian, 132–8, 242–3n13,
243nn14, 18, 244nn22, 25;
Calvin's 38, 41, 124, 150, 158–61,
238n107, 243n14; Erasmus', 11,
26, 27, 224n144, 247n54, 248n58;
humanist, 71; Paul's, 56; Stoic,
98–9, 152
apatheia, 98–9, 129, 134–6, 140–2,
149–50, 157, 225n144, 243n18,
244n22, 248n61, 257n135
Aquinas, Thomas, 46, 81, 102, 106,
109, 118–21, 142, 165, 241n2

Aristotelianism, 29, 77, 161, 169; and
emotion, 132–8; and eternity of the
world, 113; four causes, 46; Italian,
17; scholastic, 13, 46–8, 54–5, 58,
100; Thomist, 46, 121. *See also*
anthropology
Aristotle, xv, 98, 121, 133–4,
164–5, 192nn79, 80, 239–40n116,
242–3n13, 244n25, 245–6n38,
255–6n119, 257n136. *See also*
Aristotelianism
assurance, 12, 15, 26, 28, 61–3, 106–8,
113, 118, 120, 127, 138, 148, 151
Augustine of Hippo: on Christ's
emotions, 128, 155–6, 158, 256n130;
and the Christian philosophy, 100,
121; and Christian rhetoric, 13,
15, 67–8, 74, 165, 178n47, 184n9,
211n22, 213n41, 218n86, 221n109;
on the foolishness of God, 26–7, 55,
97, 102, 111, 118, 185n20, 240n121
Averroism, 36

Barth, Karl, 40
Beda, Noel, 4, 28, 91, 168, 239–40n116
Bernard of Clairvaux, 142, 240n121
Beza, Theodore, 5, 163–4, 173–4n8,
182–3n4, 210n9, 247n47